UNIX® *Desktop Guide to Emacs*

UNIX® Desktop Guide to Emacs

Ralph Roberts and Mark Boyd

Consulting Editors: Stephen G. Kochan and Patrick H. Wood

PROGRAMMING
S E R I E S

SAMS

A Division of Macmillan Computer Publishing
11711 North College, Carmel, Indiana 46032 USA

Publisher
Richard K. Swadley

Publishing Manager
Joseph Wikert

Managing Editor
Neweleen Trebnik

Senior Editor
Rebecca Whitney

Acquisitions Editor
Linda Sanning

Development Editor
Ella Davis

Production Editor
Cheri Clark

Copy Editor
Kezia Endsley

Technical Reviewer
Phil Beetley

Editorial Assistants
San Dee Phillips
Molly Carmody

Book Design
Scott Cook
Michele Laseau

Art Director
Tim Amrhein

Cover Art
Larry Stuart

Production
Claudia Bell
Brad Chinn
Dennis Clay Hager
Brook Farling
Betty Kish
Phil Kitchel
Bob LaRoche
Laurie Lee
Howard Peirce
Cindy Phipps
Joe Ramon
Tad Ringo
Louise Shinault
Mary Beth Wakefield
Vicki West

Indexer
Johnna VanHoose

Composed in ITC Garamond and MCP Digital by Macmillan Computer Publishing

Printed in the United States of America

Overview

Contents

Part III Reference Section

Part IV Appendixes

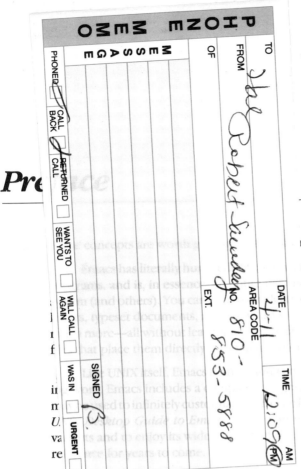

Preface

...concepts are worth ... ut. Emacs is one.

...Emacs has literally hundreds, more than most text editing programs, and is, in essence ... terface for the UNIX operating ... (and others). You can ... nic mail, manipulate files, write ... ... typeset documents, ... from Usenet and Internet, and ... more—all without lea ... , many users have initialization ... that place them directly ... ever they log into the system.

... UNIX itself, Emacs ... productive way of accomplish ... Emacs includes a ... programming language, and it ... ... ed to infinitely cust ... nonprogrammers. This book, ... *Desktop Guide to Em* ... master Emacs in all its many ... ... and to enjoy its ... es. It also will serve as a handy ... ... for years to come.

... ne. It supplies the power to
ma ... ... word processing program can match.

Who Can Use This Book

Those who will find this book useful include:

- General UNIX users (a Usenet poll in 1988 found that half of all UNIX users already use Emacs). These people, often frustrated by Emacs' plethora of commands, need this book. Whether BSD or SysV, whether 386, mini, or mainframe, Emacs is literally everywhere.

- Newcomers to the UNIX world who want to learn Emacs.

- DOS and other operating system users (various versions of Emacs have been ported to other systems).

- College-level computer science instructors who want a book they can recommend to students who must learn this ubiquitous UNIX text editor.

- Programmers (yes, programmers use Emacs extensively to write source code or when writing shell scripts). With Emacs, you can edit shell sessions in progress. You can edit an interactive session just like you can any static file.

- Anyone documenting on a UNIX system.

- Anyone text processing on a UNIX system from a 286, 386, 486, HP, Sun, VAX, and even to the mighty Cray supercomputers and beyond. If it runs UNIX, it runs Emacs, and this book is needed.

Book Overview

We've divided the book into four handy sections for you. The first section covers the basics. It includes an overview of Emacs and its many advantages, the philosophy of Emacs, how to access Emacs on UNIX and other systems, and how to customize your Emacs initialization file and installation considerations. It covers the necessary terminology, conventions, and so forth. This section also explains the organization of the screen.

The second section of the book covers important parts of Emacs such as characters, keys, commands, and entering and exiting Emacs. It also describes basic editing operations, including inserting text, changing the location of the point, erasing text, and saving and opening new files. Buffers, a bedrock concept of Emacs, are described in this section as well. The second section also teaches you to undo changes, kill and move text, search and replace text, open multiple windows, and perform many other actions. Practical examples are included.

The third section, approximately half of the book, is a reference section. Commands are grouped first by editor, then alphabetically by key binding, and also alphabetically by command name. The book defines commands as they appear and supplies usage examples as well to clarify the command meaning.

The fourth section includes four appendixes with additional useful information.

Features of this book include:

- Complete coverage of the various types of Emacs, including GNU, Freemacs, MicroEmacs, and others, including several commercial variants.

- A large command reference section. This section makes the book a "must have" reference guide long after the tutorial material is mastered.

- Information for programmers about using Emacs as their ultimate program editor.

- Information on using Emacs as your everyday shell.

- Information on maximizing the performance of Emacs—both for the individual user and for the system administrator.

Conventions Used in This Book

Key words and phrases conventions:

- `Monospace` typeface for what the reader types.

- *Italic* for new terms being introduced.

- `Monospace` typeface for regular expressions.

- `Monospace italic` typeface for placeholders in regular expressions (as in `RE?`) and for other placeholders (as in type `META-x command`).

- **Bold** typeface for command names (as in **isearch-backwards**).

- *Italic* for the names of variables (as in *case-fold-search*).

Key combination conventions:

- Key names are in all-caps (as in CONTROL or ESC) within regular text. CONTROL-h (a simultaneous press) means to press the CONTROL key and the h key at the same time. CONTROL h (a successive press) means to press the CONTROL key, release, and press the h key. CONTROL-h h means to press the CONTROL and h keys simultaneously, release, and press the h key again.

- In tables, a capital C is used to indicate the CONTROL key, and a capital M indicates the META key. C-x z would mean pressing CONTROL-x, releasing, and pressing z.

Other conventions:

- Buffer names are preceded and followed by * as in *help buffer*.

> **Note:** The ESCAPE key is usually an alternative for the META key. Either may be used in almost every case. Use ESCAPE on keyboards without the META key. For example, ESC v or ESC-v would have the same effect as META-v (**scroll-down**).

So journey with us into the world of Emacs. We promise you an easy and exciting book about this most wonderful and useful of programs. We hope that you, like us, will come to love Emacs.

Acknowledgments

The authors would like to acknowledge here, with grateful thanks, the many people who helped in the preparation of this book. Our heartfelt gratitude goes to everyone, and especially to:

Richard M. Stallman, the creator of Emacs and of the Free Software Foundation, and a strong voice for the League for Programming Freedom.

Also to:

Russell Nelson, who does such a great job with Freemacs.

Daniel Lawrence, who maintains MicroEmacs and has improved it so much.

Joe Wells, who put together the Emacs Frequently Asked Questions list and helped us out with a chapter in this book. You're a gentleman and a scholar, Joe, that's for sure!

Craig Finseth, who keeps track of all the versions of Emacs.

The University of North Carolina at Asheville, with profuse thanks for providing access to the Internet. A fine school with a beautiful mountain campus.

Linda Sanning, a great editor with a great publisher! Doing books for her is truly a joy.

Sandy Burns, Marketing Director of UniPress. Thanks for your invaluable assistance, Sandy! UniPress Emacs is everything you said it was. Very nice.

Todd Doucet, President of Ligaru Softway, for providing a copy of Epsilon. It's a neat, compact, powerful version of Emacs. We liked it.

Don Davis and Vernon Silvers at New Era Computers, who performed an emergency repair when deadlines were pressing us.

And to all the thousands of people who have contributed to improving Emacs over the decades.

Trademark Acknowledgments

All terms mentioned in this book that are known to be trademarks or service marks are listed below. In addition, terms suspected of being trademarks or service marks have been appropriately capitalized. SAMS cannot attest to the accuracy of this information. Use of a term in this book should not be regarded as affecting the validity of any trademark or service mark.

PostScript is a trademark of Adobe Systems, Inc.

UNIX is a trademark of AT&T.

DEC, DECstation, VAX, VMS, and VT are trademarks of Digital Equipment Corporation.

Hercules Graphics Card is a trademark of Hercules Technology, Inc.

IBM, IBM PC DOS, and IBM Color/Graphics Adaptor are registered trademarks and AT is a trademark of International Business Machines Corporation.

Liguru, EEL, and Epsilon are trademarks of Lugaru Software, Ltd.

X Window System and X11 are trademarks of MIT.

WordStar and WordStar 2000 are registered trademarks of MicroPro International Corporation.

MS-DOS, Microsoft, and XENIX are registered trademarks of Microsoft Corporation.

WordPerfect is a registered trademark of the WordPerfect Corporation.

Part

I

The Basics of Emacs

Introduction to Emacs

Finding Emacs

In the Beginning

Chapter 1

Introduction to Emacs

Why would I want to have hundreds of files open at once?"

"But isn't it nice to know that you can."

Emacs is a way of life.

That statement may be an unusual way to start a computer book, but it's true. Emacs is as much a philosophy as it is a text editing program of unsurpassed power. In fact, the power exists *because* of the philosophy. Being familiar with this philosophy will help you see why Emacs is so prevalent today and why it will continue to be so in the future.

In this chapter, we want to get you excited about Emacs and show you why it is worth the effort necessary to learn and use this powerful text editor. We think you'll be glad you did.

The name Emacs is a contraction of Editor MACroS. Macros are simply a group of computer instructions identified by a keyword. When that keyword is summoned, the computer executes all the commands in the macro as if they were entered individually. In the beginning, Emacs was a collection of macros used to perform text editing functions.

Emacs was created in 1975 by Richard M. Stallman. The program very much reflects his personal beliefs, which have grown into the present Free Software Foundation (FSF) and the GNU (Gnu is Not UNIX) project. The Free Software Foundation is an organization founded by Richard Stallman that is opposed to copyrights and patents on software. Emacs was designed to have wide-open architecture and a built-in programming language that would enable infinite user customization. From the beginning, people were encouraged to continue improving Emacs.

1

From the first, Stallman has given away Emacs. He has required only that users "give back all the extensions they made, so as to help Emacs improve," as he wrote in the GNU manual. "I called this arrangement the 'Emacs Commune.' As I shared, it was their duty to share; to work with each other rather than against."

Because of this still-active policy, hundreds of variants of Emacs exist today, all sharing the common principles of organization Stallman first established. Most of these also are free, but there are many commercial implementations as well. The most popular free version is still Stallman's own GNU Emacs—currently in version 18.57, with version 19 soon to be released.

Originally written in a computer language called TECO, Emacs quickly gained popularity. It had become a de facto standard text processor on college computers by 1980.

Last of the True Hackers

The history of computing is beyond the scope of this book, but a quick synopsis is necessary to help you understand the philosophy of Emacs and how it benefits you. From the early sixties to the early seventies, the Artificial Intelligence Laboratory of the Massachusetts Institute of Technology (MIT) in Cambridge, Massachusetts, was *the* cradle of advances in computer technology.

Long-haired young people, who lived on soft drinks and candy bars and existed only to sit in front of a keyboard, laid the foundation for today's computer industry. These "hackers," as they proudly called themselves, sneered at restrictive concepts such as copyrights and software patents. They felt that a well-crafted piece of code in a program was meant to be shared and elaborated on by the other geniuses who loved computers as much as they did.

"Hacker," at that time, was a term of respect and admiration. The tenets of program and idea sharing that they lived by were called the "Hacker Ethics." Alas, events such as the Vietnam War and the tightening of security and legal restrictions on software all but eliminated the hacker subculture at MIT by 1975. Today, you no longer can take someone's code and elaborate on it—you'll find yourself in court very quickly.

The exception, of course, is Richard Stallman's Emacs. In the late seventies Stallman fought a long battle against the institution of passwords on the MIT system, something that was an anathema to real hackers. For a while, Stallman convinced many professors and students to use the "empty string" password in protest (hitting a carriage return only instead of entering a password). The Department of Defense, which funded the AI Lab at MIT in large part, eventually won that fight. The department threatened to cut off all research grants unless the users at MIT bowed to their concept of computer security.

Richard Stallman (or RMS, as he is known on the computer networks) was already a recognized leader in the creation of operating systems and text processing programs (the reason MIT had hired him in the first place). He wanted to write a major text processing program that would embody the Hacker Ethic of sharing and ease of modification.

Stallman's thoughts on software sharing are ably stated in his document *GNU Manifesto*, available on various computer networks. His Free Software Foundation continues to grow. Many people now support his efforts, which include the long-running project of providing a complete, free UNIX-like operating system, of which GNU Emacs is part. His "open" philosophy created the style of Emacs and is still the driving force of the system today.

The "Openness" of Emacs

Richard Stallman's insistence on Emacs being an open product has paid off for all users from the beginning. Because the program not only was the most powerful text editor available but also was free, people began adapting it for all kinds of systems.

When UNIX was developed out of Bell Labs in the late seventies, Emacs was one of the first programs rewritten for its use. James Gosling of Carnegie Melon University received credit for the initial *port* when he rewrote Emacs in the C language and compiled it for execution under UNIX. Both UNIX and Emacs spread like proverbial wildfire, and both continue to do so today.

Although Emacs is used mainly on UNIX systems, it also has been ported to (implemented on) most computers and operating systems now in existence. Many of these implementations are *public domain*, which means you can copy and use them free.

This open policy continues, exemplified by the COPYING file that comes with GNU Emacs:

The license agreements of most software companies keep you at the mercy of those companies. By contrast, our general public license is intended to give everyone the right to share GNU Emacs. To make

1

sure that you get the rights we want you to have, we need to make restrictions that forbid anyone to deny you these rights or to ask you to surrender the rights. Hence this license agreement.

Specifically, we want to make sure that you have the right to give away copies of Emacs, that you receive source code or else can get it if you want it, that you can change Emacs or use pieces of it in new free programs, and that you know you can do these things.

To make sure that everyone has such rights, we have to forbid you to deprive anyone else of these rights. For example, if you distribute copies of Emacs, you must give the recipients all the rights that you have. You must make sure that they, too, receive or can get the source code. And you must tell them their rights.

In other words, you can do just about anything you like with GNU Emacs as long as you share the fruits of your labor free of charge. This idea is one of the bedrock concepts Stallman advocates.

Naturally, there are disadvantages to free software. One of these is lack of any formal documentation (in the form of manuals, guides, and so on). This deficiency makes some people nervous enough to pay several hundred dollars for a commercial version of Emacs. There are many of these, all written to avoid infringing on Richard Stallman and the FSF's basic "copylefts." Of course, these versions still use the same commands and operate the same way as the free Emacs versions do.

The Epsilon Text Editor from Lugaru Software, Ltd., is one of these commercial editors. It is one of the example Emacs used throughout this book, as is UniPress Emacs.

One Hundred Files and More!

The open philosophy of Emacs extends to more than just its wide availability, and Emacs' very operating characteristics reflect this fact. You can enter a directory having one hundred or more files in it and type emacs * to invoke Emacs with a wild-card specifier, and those hundred or more files will all open. Simply use the buffer menu to decide which file you want to edit at the moment. You even can have several editing sessions on the screen at once in different windows, as you will see in Chapter 5.

"What's the use of all that power?" This question is commonly asked by people who are first looking into one of the many versions of Emacs. We don't know the answer, and neither do you—until you need the power. That's the advantage of the openness of Emacs—whatever you need to do usually can be done. There is essentially no limit to serviceability. In contrast, other commercial text editing packages, Word Perfect for example, restrict you to having two files open at once and are very limited in their capability to customize.

Emacs, which contains an integral programming language, also enables almost infinite customization, much of which nonprogrammers can do. Out of the many hundreds of Emacs implementations available, you almost always can find one close to your own needs. Of course, the version can be customized further to more precisely meet your needs. Because Emacs allows for customization, it can increase personal productivity tenfold.

Emacs also protects you by backing up text as you work. If you make a horrendous mistake, perhaps a massive global change that messes up thousands of words in the file, that's no problem. You just call in the backup copy and continue from the point before the mistake.

These features, along with other reasons to use and love Emacs, are discussed throughout this book.

What Emacs Is

According to Stallman, Emacs is an "advanced, self-documenting, customizable, extensible, real-time display editor." In other words, it's a *text editor*. An Associated Press report in March 1991 related that 63 percent of all home and office computer users use their machines primarily for word processing. Because Emacs is available in several versions for home computers also, it is undeniably the most powerful text editor available in home or office. (There's a distinction here between "text editing" and "word processing," which we will get to in just a moment.)

The following paragraphs are explanations of concepts basic to text editors in general. The last explanation—*extensible*—is one of the major capabilities that makes Emacs unique and gives it more power than conventional text editors.

The *Display editor* feature shows the text being edited on the screen and automatically updates text as you enter commands or insert additional text. Because these updates happen usually every two or three characters, the display editor is a *real-time* editor. It cuts down on the amount of information you have to remember—the program remembers for you.

1

The *Self-documenting* feature enables appropriate on-line help messages to pop up. These messages detail your options, list various available commands, and in general make your life a lot easier. In GNU Emacs, typing CONTROL-h elicits the help feature. In both Freemacs and Epsilon, typing a question mark (?) on the command line gives you the help facility.

As discussed previously, *Customizable* enables you to, at any time, change key definitions, rearrange the command set, and change many other minor features. The customizable feature can help tailor Emacs to your working habits and desires.

Extensible enables you to go beyond simple customization (although this feature does call for some knowledge of programming) and write entirely new functions and commands. Because Emacs is made up of many smaller parts, you can easily redefine old functions and add new ones without ever leaving your editing session. Even nonprogrammers can benefit from the extensible feature. Thousands of simpler enhancing programs are available for Emacs, especially for GNU Emacs, on such computer networks as Internet and Usenet. They are easy to download via modem and add to your own Emacs. The possibilities are endless.

We elaborate on these and other features in the following chapters.

What Emacs Is Not

We've been careful in this chapter to call Emacs a text editor rather than a word processor. The recent trend on "personal" computers, such as IBM compatibles and Apple's Macintoshes, has been toward the WYSIWYG ("what you see is what you get") word processing software. These programs print out a page exactly as you see it on the screen. They are complete word processing packages, controlling everything from the initial character entered to the printing of the final version of the document.

Unfortunately, WYSIWYG software is not all that fast or easy in the long run. Because your computer screen must depict hundreds of thousands of points rather than a few hundred characters, the process can be sluggish. WYSIWYG is certainly not real-time editing as is Emacs.

Emacs is not WYSIWYG, nor is it a *text processor* (the portion of word processing software that does the actual printing). Emacs is designed to use a variety of text processors, allowing for an infinite variety of formats for everything from simple line printers to sophisticated typesetting devices.

Again, Emacs' strength lies in its openness. You have far greater flexibility and can do many more formats than any of the WYSIWYG programs, which lock you into one programmer's vision of what you might need, or what the software publisher thinks might sell the best.

What Systems Emacs Does Run On

We could fill the rest of this book with lists of operating systems and hardware that Emacs can run on (but we promise not to). It has been ported to almost everything. There are even several versions available for IBM-compatible MS-DOS machines. We prefer Freemacs, a close yet limited translation of GNU Emacs. As you probably guessed from the name, it too is free!

Borland's Sprint is a commercial word processing package for MS-DOS machines (IBM-compatibles) that evolved from Emacs. In fact, it comes with an Emacs user interface. Included with Sprint is a text processing package with extensive PostScript laser support. Like Emacs, Sprint has an integral programming language, can have several files open at once, has automatic backup, and is almost infinitely customizable.

The fast-expanding UNIX world has many more choices. There are many versions of the UNIX operating system. Versions of Emacs are available for all versions of Berkeley UNIX (4.1-4.3); AT&T's System V (in various releases through the current 4.0, and various brands including AT&T, Interactive, Esix, Intel, SCO, and others); Ultrix (Digital Equipment Corporation's version of Berkeley UNIX); Uniplus; VMS (which is not UNIX but DEC's proprietary operating system); and SCO's XENIX.

The machines Emacs supports range from the original IBM PC (using the 8086), to supercomputers like the Cray. Included are versions specifically for computers such as those made by Alliant, Altos, Amdahl, AT&T, Bull (which took over Honeywell's computer division), CCI, DEC, Gould, Hewlett-Packard, IBM (from personal computers to mainframes), MIPS, Motorola, Nixdorf, Sequent, Sony, Sun, Tandem, Vax (DEC), Wicat, and many, many more.

Apple systems purposely are not mentioned in the previous list because Richard Stallman has boycotted Apple. He objects to Apple's infamous "look and feel" lawsuits against other computer manufacturers. Because the company's broad interpretation of copyrighting discourages the openness Stallman advocates, he discourages porting Emacs to Apple machines.

1

Certainly there is no other text editing software that comes close to being as widespread as Emacs. (The possible exception is vi, the UNIX editing utility. Vi is widespread, but it is simple compared to Emacs. In fact, Emacs has several vi emulation modes.) If you learn Emacs, you can run any of the computers previously mentioned plus hundreds more.

The Future of Emacs

Although Emacs runs under many different operating systems, the future of Emacs coincides with the future of UNIX. Both companies and individual users seem to be turning away from MS-DOS to the more open and powerful UNIX operating systems, especially now that these systems can run on small computers, such as those using Intel's 80386 and 80486 chips.

Because Emacs itself is based on openness, it is much more powerful on an open system like UNIX. The future of Emacs, then, is essentially that of UNIX, and both look extremely bright. New versions of Emacs will be coming out that incorporate advances in hardware and in the UNIX operating systems, such as AT&T's System V, Release 4.0.

Emacs 19, the newest version, will support two styles of multiple windows. One of these styles has a separate screen for the minibuffer, and another has a minibuffer attached to each screen. Other new features include buffer allocation, which uses a new mechanism capable of returning storage to the system when a buffer is killed, and a new input system—all input now arrives in the form of Lisp objects.

You don't have to understand what these features mean just yet, but the information does give more than a hint of how powerful Emacs is.

The Reason for This Book

Emacs' very openness also causes one of its greatest weaknesses: lack of documentation. More and more computer users are gaining access to large, multiuser UNIX systems, either at work, at school, or through the many computer networks now as close as your telephone. Most of these systems have at least one version, and many times several versions, of Emacs running. Your text editing problems are over!

1

Except . . .

"Manual? We only have the one and I can't let you take it home."

Yes, there may be hundreds of users on the system but only one manual. That's why a book like this one is needed.

Although Emacs is "self-documenting" with on-line help, this help is sometimes minimal, often cryptic, and it rarely gives you practical examples that apply to your specific purpose.

Thus, we come to the purpose of this book. It is written in a simple form for real people. Now that you have been enlightened, we hope, with the power and philosophy of Emacs, it's time to start using Emacs and enjoying its productivity.

Next, we will explain how to find out whether you already have a version of Emacs and how to get one if you don't.

2

Finding Emacs

"I t's got to be on here somewhere!"

You may already have Emacs, even if you don't know it.

Two of the major purposes of this book are to be a learning tool and to be a reference guide for Emacs on UNIX systems. Versions of Emacs can run under almost any operating system known (even MS-DOS). Because of the popularity of Emacs in the UNIX world, most medium-to-large UNIX installations already have some version of Emacs on them. All you have to do is find the program and start using it. If you cannot find Emacs on any UNIX installation or you know you don't have the program on your system, you can consult this chapter for tips on getting and installing an Emacs appropriate to your needs.

Finding Emacs on a "Big" System

If Emacs is already on your UNIX system, you should be able to ask the system administrator how to find and install it. Unfortunately, you do not always have someone to ask. Whether you are using a large university system, accessing your company's mainframe computer with a modem, or just working late, you may find yourself on your own.

You probably will have no manual to follow either. Typically, only a few manuals are available, and usually system administration personnel hoard these. Locked away in a file cabinet somewhere, the manuals do you little good. That's an important reason for this book.

Luckily, if Emacs is on the system, it most likely is in the command *path* available for your use. In other words, when you type a command, the system knows to look in certain directories to find it. Emacs, for example, might be in /usr/bin or /usr/local/bin, but its location is not your concern—just type the command to invoke Emacs and see whether it's there.

"What command?" you ask.

Try typing emacs first. Quite often on large systems, GNU Emacs or some reasonably close variant is present under this name. Freemacs is sometimes also present as emacs. Entering ue frequently invokes MicroEmacs, another of the free text editors in the vast Emacs family. Commercial versions of Emacs often use the name they are marketed under, such as epsilon for Lugaru's Epsilon.

Possibly, none of these will work; after all, there are hundreds of versions of Emacs. Or the system administrators may have renamed Emacs. You can try the UNIX **find** command by typing find / -name emacs* -print. This command line searches for files on the system starting with the letters *emacs* and informs you of their location. You may be able to deduce the name of the program from the information the computer gives you.

If all these techniques fail, track down the system administrator either by E-mail or in person. If you determine there is no variant of Emacs on the system, it's time to get and install one.

And by the way, even if you do find a version of Emacs on your system, it might not be the one you want. You might decide that GNU Emacs is too complicated and MicroEmacs is sufficient, or that you would like the support a commercial Emacs vendor offers. The following section will help those wanting to add another type of Emacs as well.

Getting Emacs

The advantage to Emacs—thanks to the philosophy of its creator—is that there are so many free versions. The prime example is Stallman's Free Software Foundation's ultimate Emacs, GNU Emacs, which is available on hundreds, if not thousands, of publicly accessible computer systems and through many other sources.

Because GNU Emacs is the most popular Emacs, we'll discuss it first. GNU Emacs, as discussed in Chapter 1, runs on an incredibly wide range of computers—from desktop personal machines, such as IBM PC-compatibles, up to mighty supercomputers like the Cray.

Obviously, a supercomputer is different from a personal computer. Binary programs—programs a computer can execute to do a job such as text editing—differ depending on the sophistication of the computer. A binary program that runs on a Cray will not run on a personal computer or on any of the many levels of machines in between because their binary languages differ. Therefore, GNU Emacs and most of the other Emacs are distributed as *source code*.

This means that the source files are copied onto a computer, then compiled by that computer into binary files it can understand and run. Thus, to take advantage of free programs like GNU Emacs, your UNIX system must have a C compiler—C being the language that most *portable* UNIX programs are written in. A portable program is one that compiles and runs on the wide range of machines described previously.

In the spirit of the open philosophy of Stallman, the Free Software Foundation's GNU Project offers many other free programs, including a C compiler called gcc (GNU C compiler). It too runs on a wide range of systems. You most likely can get it from the same source as GNU Emacs, but you may need someone to compile a compatible version for your system. Because you will have access to a wealth of free UNIX software, getting gcc on your system is worth the trouble you might encounter.

Commercial Emacs

If you do not want to be bothered with finding and compiling a free version of Emacs, you can contact one of many companies that supply Emacs-flavored text editors already compiled and ready to install on your system.

Lugaru Software Ltd. in Pittsburgh is one such company. The company's Epsilon programmer's editor is one of the examples we use throughout this book. When you order the program, you specify your operating system—DOS, OS/2, SCO UNIX, SCO Xenix, or Interactive 386/ix—and the dealer sends you the proper disks with the *binaries* (compiled programs) for your computer. Using the binaries makes installation much simpler.

Another company—Unipress Software in Edison, New Jersey—offers UniPress Emacs. This commercial version of Emacs runs on larger machines than Epsilon runs on, such as Convergent Technologies, HP 9000/300 and 9000/800, IBM RT and RS/6000, Interactive, Opus 88000, Silicon Graphics 4D series, Solbourne, Sequent, Sun, Tektronic, DECstation 2100 and 3100, and Ultrix systems. UniPress also works on personal computers running SCO UNIX. UniPress Emacs supports the X Window graphical user interface

2

as well. Prices range from around $400 for a single workstation to $1,000 and up for larger systems. UniPress Emacs is closer to Gosling Emacs, the first Emacs ported to UNIX, than to GNU.

Borland's Sprint word processing system is a descendant of Emacs as well, and versions of it are available for both MS-DOS and various types of UNIX. Unlike many Emacs programs, Sprint includes a text processor with extensive PostScript printer support. It also includes an Emacs user interface that enables Sprint to use the same general Emacs commands we cover in these pages.

When you buy a commercial program, you are paying for a text editor tailored to your machine, a text editor that requires less effort to install and begin using. You also are paying for knowledge and feedback from the company regarding problems during both the customization and the learning processes.

UniPress offers registered owners a toll-free number and access to information through the Internet computer network. For an additional yearly fee, UniPress supplies updates to the program.

Commercial versions of Emacs can be purchased through computer dealers, through ads in such publications as *UNIX Today* and *UNIX World*, or directly from the software's publisher, such as Lugaru. See the appendixes of this book for a list of addresses.

Free Emacs

If you are interested in UNIX software and are used to MS-DOS prices, you may experience a case of sticker-price shock. UNIX software prices generally are much higher than comparable DOS or Macintosh programs—hence the efforts of the FSF to make free programs available. You well might decide that the extra effort is worth the savings.

The disadvantage of free software, as stated earlier, is the limited amount of support you have access to. This excerpt from the GNU Emacs "nonwarranty" expresses this disadvantage perfectly:

> Because GNU Emacs is licensed free of charge, we provide absolutely
> no warranty, to the extent permitted by applicable state law. Except
> when otherwise stated in writing, Free Software Foundation, INC,
> Richard M. Stallman and/or other parties provide GNU Emacs "as is"
> without warranty of any kind, either expressed or implied, including,
> but not limited to, the implied warranties of merchantability and
> fitness for a particular purpose. The entire risk as to the quality
> and performance of the program is with you. Should the GNU Emacs

program prove defective, you assume the cost of all necessary servicing, repair or correction.

Sounds like you're on your own, right? Luckily, this is not the case. Certain organizations that support the FSF provide services including installation, training, customization to your system, and problem solving for a fee. FSF regulations require that the actual program and all sources be available to you at no charge, but they do enable companies to charge a fee for Emacs-related services. This book is an example of such an agreement. We cannot sell you GNU Emacs, but we can charge a fee (what you paid for the book) to explain it to you.

In harmony with the philosophy of free software, there is also plenty of free help. People who use Emacs—especially GNU Emacs—tend to become imbued with the philosophy of Emacs. They like to help others.

Free Emacs Support

Many UNIX systems, especially those belonging to academic institutions, are connected through the phone line to the worldwide computer networks of Internet or Usenet or both.

The U.S. government started a system called the ARPANET years ago. It was a wide area experimental network to connect hosts and terminal servers. Internet evolved from ARPANET. As local area networks became more common, many hosts became gateways to local networks. As the Internet document "The Hitchhikers Guide to the Internet" says:

> A network layer to allow the interoperation of these networks was developed and called Internet Protocol (IP). Over time other groups created long haul IP based networks.... These nets, too, interoperate because of IP. The collection of all these interoperating networks is the Internet.

Internet has grown into a global intercom, with thousands of computers tied together. If your UNIX system is part of Internet and you have access permission, you can use computers all over the world in seconds. Internet, which truly deserves a book of its own, is used by many of the same people who use Emacs. Ideally, then, you have thousands of experts available 24 hours a day when using GNU Emacs.

Newsgroups, a type of electronic bulletin board, is the primary method of modular information exchange. There are hundreds of newsgroups, which send posted messages almost instantly around the world. To take advantage of such newsgroups, your computer system must be on Internet and you must subscribe to that particular newsgroup (there is no charge).

2

Those who do not have Internet access need not despair, because another system exists, called Usenet. Usenet also includes thousands of intercommunicating computers and also publishes the same newsgroups as Internet. The only difference is that Usenet is not "real time." Instead, UNIX's integral *uucp* (UNIX to UNIX copy protocol) software is used, and packets of messages are sent automatically over telephone lines, usually late at night for cheaper rates.

You can obtain access to Usenet rather easily, either by connecting your computer to Usenet and acting as a relay, or by getting permission to call a local computer already hooked up and reading the newsgroups as they come in. Connecting with Usenet will enable you to have access to a world of information, including information about other computer systems.

Currently, 13 newsgroups are devoted totally to Emacs:

comp.emacs
gnu.emacs.announce
gnu.emacs.bug!
gnu.emacs.gnews!
gnu.emacs.help
gnu.emacs.lisp.manual
gnu.emacs.sources
gnu.emacs.vm.bug!
gnu.emacs.vm.info!
gnu.emacs.vms!
gnu.epoch.misc

A beginner in Emacs would find comp.emacs and gnu.emacs.help to be of most interest and help.

Hundreds of messages are sent about Emacs, especially GNU Emacs, each week. You can post your own questions and expect a flurry of answers. Good manners require that you first check for the same query so you won't use network resources for duplicate messages.

In addition to participating in the newsgroups, you can exchange private electronic mail with people who are willing to help you solve a problem. All posted messages include the electronic address of the person posting them, so finding people is easy.

The constant flow of free advice and Emacs enhancements follows the philosophy of the FSF and Richard Stallman. By using Internet and Usenet, you can be part of this constant free and beneficial interchange.

Getting GNU Emacs

The best way to get GNU, or any of the other free Emacs, is with a modem. If you have access to the Internet, you can access hundreds of sources. Using the FTP (file transfer protocol) utility, you can transfer the files to your computer and put together whatever version of Emacs you want. The prime source of free Emacs, or the "official" one, is the computer identified as prep.ai.mit.edu at the Massachusetts Institute of Technology, located in Cambridge, Massachusetts. This newsgroup offers all the GNU programs, not just Emacs. If you have access to the Internet, type

```
ftp prep ai.mit.edu!
```

and log in as

```
anonymous
```

Type your user name as the password. Next, make the following sequence of entries:

```
cd gnu
cd emacs
binary
get name-of-file
```

In the last entry, substitute the name of the file you want transferred to your system for `name-of-file`.

For the majority of users who do not have Internet access, GNU Emacs (as well as MicroEmacs, Freemacs, and other free Emacs) is still relatively easy to get with a modem. If you do not have a system connected to the phone lines and you want to get GNU Emacs and the other GNU project programs, you can contact the Free Software Foundation at 675 Massachusetts Avenue, Cambridge, Massachusetts 02139 USA. Although charging for software is against FSF's philosophy, the foundation does charge for the media (tape) on which it is supplied. The tape usually starts at $150, depending on your system.

As you can see, downloading Emacs over the phone, even paying a long-distance charge, is the cheapest way to go. As a service to the UNIX public, Ohio State University offers GNU Emacs (and other GNU programs) by uucp. Bob Sutterfield and Karl Kleinpaste are the authors of a document available on the Internet and Usenet called "GNU-how-to-get." The document describes the service and supplies the necessary phone numbers and other instructions (check for the most recent version).

GNU Emacs uses several megabytes of source code due to the immense number of features it offers. Copying the complete set of files takes about five hours at 2400 baud. "GNU-how-to-get" gave an example cost for a transfer to Portland, Oregon, of $42 at weekend rates—a large phone bill, but nothing compared to hundreds or thousands of dollars for a commercial version of Emacs with considerably fewer features.

Because GNU Emacs is so large, it is broken up into several parts. You can download these all at once or break them up however you want. You don't need to be a programmer to download GNU Emacs, but be prepared to do some research and to learn a little. Don't worry—it's fun and you'll have a tremendous sense of accomplishment when you are done.

Compiling Emacs

Most programs for UNIX are written in the computer language C. They run on anything from micros to huge mainframes after they have been compiled for the system on which they are installed. Only the source code is portable; program binaries are not. You normally receive the source code, so compiling and installing the Emacs onto your system is your responsibility.

Because instructions are included, this process should be easy. A Makefile that leads your system's compiler through the program building process also is included. The Makefile is a "road map" that tells the compiler how to put together the parts of a program. You might have to edit a few parameters to fit your system, but you should encounter nothing of major difficulty.

These instructions apply to most of the free Emacs you can get, but we'll use GNU Emacs as an example. As mentioned, due to length you get the program in several parts. These parts must be assembled before they again can be broken down into the component files needed to build Emacs. One command accomplishes these tasks. If you had the version of GNU Emacs that was current at the time this book was being written, you would enter:

```
cat emacs-18.57-?? ¦ zcat ¦ tar xvf -
```

You would substitute ?? with the release numbers on the file you got.

This command would create one large file and then take it apart into the many component files of GNU Emacs. Then you would be able to read the building and installation instructions included in the distribution. Usually, a script automates the process almost entirely.

Other Free Emacs

GNU Emacs is the largest and best-supported free Emacs in the world. However, you might decide you don't need anything quite that elaborate. Many smaller versions of Emacs are available that are free as well. Two of these versions—Freemacs and MicroEmacs—also are used as examples in this book. Both are subsets of GNU Emacs.

Freemacs, by Russell Nelson, is compact and easy to use, and it is available for MS-DOS as well as UNIX machines. Like GNU, but unlike MicroEmacs, Freemacs includes a programming language that enables infinite modification. Freemacs also is the only MS-DOS version of Emacs that tries to emulate GNU Emacs (which is not easy to do on DOS). You can get Freemacs on the Internet by FTP from the system grape.ecs.clarkson.edu. Or you can call the WFM BBS: 315-265-8207, 1200/2400 8N1, 24 hours. Freemacs is in File Area 4; registration is not required to download it.

MicroEmacs originally was written by Dave Conroy. It is a popular Emacs, found on many systems under the name ue (the *u* is an approximation for the micro symbol). It is available from several sources on Internet, including durer.cme.nist.gov.

Again, the three Emacs mentioned, plus the commercial version called Epsilon, serve as our examples in this book. They cover the gamut of Emacs versions sufficiently for this reference to apply to many other Emacs as well. Two of the other free Emacs are Mg (formerly Micrognu Emacs) and JOVE (for Jonathan's Own Version of Emacs). If you cannot decide which Emacs version to use, remember that you can upgrade your version anytime at no charge. You even can have several versions active at once as long as you give them different names.

Installation and Configuration

Whether you get a free Emacs or buy a commercial version, it has to be installed on your system and configured for your personal use. On a large system, give the Emacs to the administrator to install. This way your new Emacs system is available for other users also.

If you have a personal UNIX system, as so many of us now do, then you'll need to log in as "root" and install the system yourself. Logging in as "root" means you have the authority to log in as the system administrator or with an equivalent level of privileges. As stated earlier, the compiling is usually an automated process after you've done the necessary configuration for your specific system. Instructions for your type of system should be in the documentation files accompanying the source files in the distribution.

When installation is complete and the Emacs of your choice is available for your use, you will move to step two. This step includes configuring the start-up or initialization file and changing the *key bindings* (the keys assigned to carrying out an action) to match your needs and preferences. These processes are covered at length later in the book. You'll find that you can infinitely customize almost any flavor of Emacs.

Calling All Editors

This chapter, by necessity, has been vague. There are hundreds of versions of Emacs and many ways to get them. Other names, addresses, and computer network sources are included in the appendixes. Now, you will learn about the component parts of Emacs.

In the Beginning

T his chapter covers the component parts of Emacs and how they are used. GNU Emacs is the default "standard" in both the UNIX world and this book. We often use GNU in our examples, but we also report significant departures from the norm that exist in other flavors of Emacs.

The GNU Emacs approach to using Emacs demonstrates the difference between Emacs and almost all other text editors. GNU Emacs (the G in GNU is pronounced, by the way) is designed to start when you log onto the computer. Then, when you want to edit a file, you simply command Emacs to load the file into a new buffer. This is called *visiting the file*. Files that you have visited normally are left in their buffers for future use. When your computer session is finished, you exit Emacs and log off the system.

Not only is GNU Emacs an editor, but it also is a working environment that you rarely need to leave. You can read your mail and news, edit text, program and compile source code, and link and test programs—all within the Emacs environment. This flexibility is possible because of Emacs' ability to create other processes, called *inferior shell processes*. The **compile** command, for example, creates an inferior process that runs the make utility. Make tells the system how to compile large programs that are made up of many source files. Make creates further processes to run the compiler and the linker. The output from all these processes is redirected to an Emacs buffer. Any error messages are saved for you in that buffer, so if the compile fails, you have the information you need to fix the problem.

More limited versions of Emacs, such as MicroEmacs and Freemacs, are designed to run in a personal computer environment. They can't offer the same flexibility as GNU Emacs, and their use is limited accordingly.

In a personal computer environment, you usually edit specific files, and when the editing is done, you exit Emacs. MicroEmacs, which has more editing features than Freemacs and can edit larger files, is well suited to use in this manner. Freemacs can be used much like GNU Emacs, within the limits of an MS-DOS environment, or it can be used solely for editing, like MicroEmacs.

As with any program—or any kind of complicated endeavor—you learn fastest by doing. We encourage you to follow along on your computer and to experiment with your Emacs as you read this book. Try the examples and see how they work for you. It's fun to do so, and you should pick up Emacs very quickly.

Entering and Leaving Emacs

The version and your purpose for using Emacs determine the way that you start it running. The UNIX Emacs and Freemacs are designed to be started when you start the computer and to be used as a general-purpose user interface. If you use your Emacs in this general way, enter .emacs, or the appropriate name on your system, to start it running. If you are using an Emacs as a text editor only, you probably want to start it with the name of the particular files as command-line parameters. You also can supply options on the command line. These options are usually a single character, possibly followed by a parameter. The command-line options for each version of Emacs covered in this book are listed in their appropriate reference section. For now, you will learn to start GNU Emacs and MicroEmacs at a particular line in a file.

The *point* is one of the bedrock concepts of text editing. This is the cursor's location, and thus the point at which you insert or delete text. In an Emacs editor, the point is considered to be between two characters, not on one character or the other.

Starting Emacs by typing emacs joe.txt would create a buffer for joe.txt. Typing the GNU Emacs command line emacs joe.txt +300 sam.lis would create two buffers, one for joe.txt and the other for sam.lis. The point in the second buffer would be located at the beginning of line number 300. The MicroEmacs command line emacs joe.txt sam.lis -g300 would create a buffer for joe.txt and put the point at the beginning of line number 300. It also would create a buffer for sam.lis, but it would not load the file until you moved a window to that buffer. In GNU Emacs, every file is visited, and you can specify a different point location in each file. MicroEmacs, on the other hand, loads only the first file, and you can specify a starting position only in that file.

Buffers are the basic editing unit of Emacs. We cover them at length in the next chapter. A buffer is a piece of text being edited. Buffers do not have to correspond to a particular file, but when they do correspond, they are usually a mirror copy of a file. With buffers, you can open, or visit, dozens or hundreds of files. These files are available simultaneously to copy text back and forth, or whatever else you need to do.

When you start an Emacs program, it reads an *initialization file*. This file arranges the Emacs to act the way you program it to. We will cover Emacs initialization files in Chapter 7. For now you just need to know that such things exist and that they affect your Emacs program. In GNU Emacs and Freemacs, initialization files actually are written in the same language as the editors. For GNU Emacs, the initialization file .emacs in your home directory is loaded on start-up. For MicroEmacs, the file emacs.rc is loaded. For Freemacs, the files keys.ed and user.ed are loaded. These files can set Emacs variables to non-default values, change the key bindings, and create new functions.

Figures 3.1 through 3.3 show the opening screens for three Emacs: GNU, UniPress Emacs, and Freemacs.

3

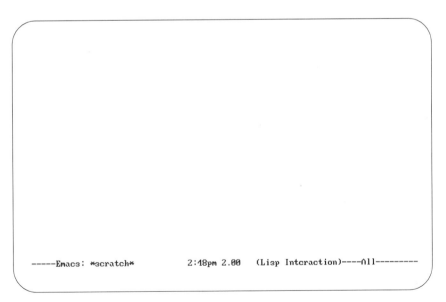

```
-----Emacs: *scratch*          2:48pm 2.00   (Lisp Interaction)----All---------
```

Fig. 3.1. When GNU Emacs is activated without specifying a file name on the command line, you are presented with a blank "scratch" buffer.

```
Unix Emacs V2.20d (11-Sep-89)[24-Sep-90]


Type the help character (^_) for help
Type ^_n to see the release notes for this version
--Type space to start emacs-- (type ? for help)














Buffer: Main    (Normal) [None] Top
```

Fig. 3.2. The initial screen for UniPress Emacs, when opened without any command line specifications, tells you how to find help if needed.

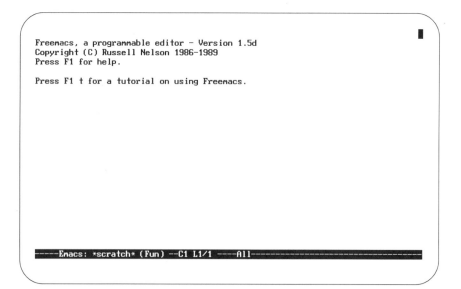

```
Freemacs, a programmable editor - Version 1.5d
Copyright (C) Russell Nelson 1986-1989
Press F1 for help.

Press F1 t for a tutorial on using Freemacs.
```

```
------Emacs: *scratch* (Fun) --C1 L1/1 -----All-------------------------
```

Fig. 3.3. Freemacs, designed to work in an MS-DOS environment, opens with this screen.

There are two ways to leave an Emacs program. The first way is to *suspend* Emacs. Suspending Emacs enables you to return to Emacs later with everything exactly as you left it. The GNU Emacs and Freemacs command to do this is **suspend-Emacs** (CONTROL-z). You also can exit Emacs completely. To exit GNU Emacs or Freemacs completely, use the **save-buffers-kill-Emacs** (CONTROL-x CONTROL-c) command. Emacs asks you whether you want to save each buffer that has been modified. If you choose not to save a modified buffer, Emacs asks you whether you are sure you want to exit. The MicroEmacs commands are **exit-Emacs** (CONTROL-x CONTROL-c) to exit and **i-shell** (CONTROL-x c) to suspend MicroEmacs. (To implement the CONTROL-x c command, you would press CONTROL and x simultaneously, release, and then press c.)

The Screen

When you are in Emacs, the screen on your personal computer or terminal is divided into at least three areas. These areas are the *window*, the *mode line*, and the *echo area*. In the window, you can view and modify the contents of a buffer. The mode line displays information about the buffer. The echo area, also used for the minibuffer in GNU Emacs, receives your entered commands and displays information about the editing process.

The window displays as much of the buffer as it can fit. The buffer usually contains a copy of a file, which is stored on a disk drive. Although you may think you are editing the true file, you actually are editing a copy of the file stored in a buffer. When you save the buffer to the file, you will have actually edited the file.

Figure 3.4 shows an example file, part of *The Price Guide to Autographs* by George Sanders, Helen Sanders, and Ralph Roberts. This file lists the prices for president's signatures, signed letters or documents, letters autographed in the handwriting of the celebrity, and signed photographs.

The window comprises all but the bottom two lines of your screen. It can be divided into several windows that show several buffers at once or that show parts of the same buffer. Figure 3.5 shows a screen in MicroEmacs with information on navigating in buffers.

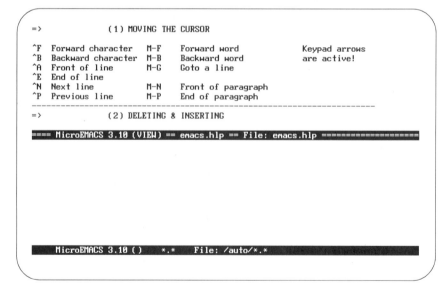

```
        As a historical note, David B. Atchison was Acting President for one
day because Zachary Taylor did not want to assume office on a Sunday. Hence,
Atchison's inclusion within this section. He was a senator from Missouri
and President Pro Tem of the Senate at the time of being Acting President.
        The prices given in this book are retail prices--i.e. the amount you
would pay to a dealer or at an auction. If you sell to a dealer, a
legitimate offer to you would be about half of the retail price. Since the
dealer may have to hold the piece for years before selling it, this is a fair
markup.

NAME                        SIG      LS/DS      ALS        SP

Adams, John               1075.00   1795.00   6645.00
Adams, John Quincy         225.00    675.00   1930.00    1500.00
Arthur, Chester A.         250.00    830.00   1100.00     625.00
Atchison, David R.         200.00    350.00    975.00
Buchanan, James            280.00    500.00    995.00
Bush, George               130.00    330.00    950.00     275.00
Carter, Jimmy              145.00    248.00   1125.00     180.00
Cleveland, Grover          250.00    350.00    542.00     388.00
Coolidge, Calvin           185.00    434.00   1400.00     395.00
Eisenhower,Dwight D.       263.00    475.00   4100.00     425.00
Fillmore, Millard          200.00    783.00    800.00    6000.00
--**-Emacs: pres. (Fun) --C8 L18/65 ----27------------------------------------
```

Fig. 3.4. Using Freemacs, modifying the file when the prices change is easy.

```
=>                (1) MOVING THE CURSOR

^F   Forward character    M-F   Forward word              Keypad arrows
^B   Backward character   M-B   Backward word             are active!
^A   Front of line        M-G   Goto a line
^E   End of line
^N   Next line            M-N   Front of paragraph
^P   Previous line        M-P   End of paragraph
-------------------------------------------------------------------------------
=>                (2) DELETING & INSERTING
==== MicroEMACS 3.10 (VIEW) == emacs.hlp == File: emacs.hlp =================




        MicroEMACS 3.10 ()      *.*    File: /auto/*.*
```

Fig. 3.5. This help file, part of MicroEmacs, shows some of the many ways Emacs lets you move the cursor around in buffers.

The mode line, such as the one shown in Figure 3.6, is at the bottom of the buffer. It shows the buffer name, the mode, whether the buffer has been saved, and other useful information. Several mode lines can appear on the screen at once, one for each open window.

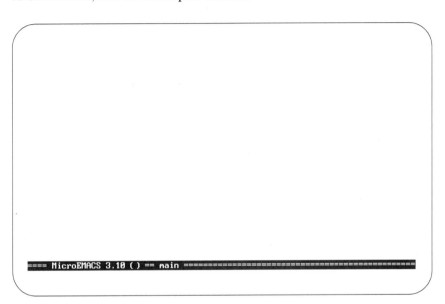

```
==== MicroEMACS 3.10 () == main ================================================
```

Fig. 3.6. A MicroEmacs mode line.

Remember the warning about the special shift key in Emacs, the META key, which we introduced in the previous chapter. This key enables Emacs (in conjunction with other keys) to generate a special extended code for various functions. Some terminals have an actual META key on their keyboard. Personal computers and some other terminals use the ALT or ALTERNATE key. The ESC or ESCAPE key works as the META key on almost every terminal, even when you are calling into a computer over the phone for Emacs.

Our convention for this book (and generally in the Emacs world) is to use M- or ESC as a prefix to indicate the use of the META key (the ESC key always works if you don't have a specific META key on your keyboard). CONTROL (or C in tables) indicates pressing the CONTROL key. All key names, such as CONTROL and META, are in capital letters. Again (this is important), if your keyboard doesn't have a META key, use ESCAPE followed by the other keys instead. For example, M-x becomes ESC x. Thus, although most of the example commands in this chapter are given as ESC key sequences simply for the sake of consistency, you can use the META key in place of the ESC key. This flexibility is what enables Emacs to be used on such a wide range of platforms. You also can enter the actual name of the command rather than the keys it is bound to, such as **go-to-beginning** rather than ESC < or M-<, all of which would take you to the top of the current buffer.

Moving Around the Screen

The process of editing in Emacs is based on the idea of a point in the window (and therefore in the buffer) at which all editing occurs. This point represents the position to the immediate left of the cursor. This is where the action occurs. When you type characters on your keyboard, they are inserted into the buffer at the point. When you use the cursor keys or the control keys CONTROL-p, CONTROL-n, CONTROL-f, and CONTROL-b, the point moves in the window and the cursor moves with the point. If you try to move the point outside of the window, the window moves to keep the point inside.

To edit a file, you need to be able to control the location of the point. There are many Emacs commands for moving the point. Table 3.1 separates these commands by function.

Table 3.1. Emacs Commands for Point Movement

Keystroke	Function
Character-Oriented Movement	
C-p	Move up one line—stay in the same column (p for previous)
C-n	Move down one line—stay in the same column (n for next)
C-f	Move right one character (f for forward)
C-b	Move left one character (b for back)
Word-Oriented Movement	
ESC f	Move right one word (f for forward)
ESC b	Move left one word (b for back)
Line-Oriented Movement	
C-a	Move to the beginning of the line (a is the beginning of the alphabet)
C-e	Move to the end of the line (e for end)

Keystroke	Function
Buffer-Oriented Movement	
ESC <	Move to the beginning of the buffer
ESC >	Move to the end of the buffer

Notice how easy it is to remember these commands. The key bindings are used to help you remember the command's function. Like all Emacs commands, these commands can be changed to suit your taste. Moreover, any command can be bound to multiple key sequences. The single-character cursor-movement commands, for example, often are bound to the arrow keys on your terminal as well as to the CONTROL-p, CONTROL-n, CONTROL-f, and CONTROL-b keys.

Using the Mode Line

The mode line, located at the bottom of your screen directly above the echo area, displays information about the buffer. The most important information it displays is the current *mode* of the buffer. This mode has two parts: a *major mode* and *minor mode*. The major mode determines how Emacs responds to commands. It determines the nature of the editor. The minor mode, which may have several components, modifies the way the major mode behaves.

The default major mode, *Fundamental mode*, is the standard Emacs editing mode. Chapter 8 examines a number of specialized major modes, like C mode for editing C programs and Dired mode for "editing" directories. For now, however, you should stick to Fundamental mode. All the other modes for editing text files are based on Fundamental mode.

One of the most useful minor modes for text editing is Auto-Fill mode. This mode wraps lines of text within the right margin by breaking the lines automatically. It is a typical minor mode in that it modifies the behavior of a major mode. The following line shows a mode line in Freemacs:

```
--**-Emacs: emacsbk.ch4 (Fun Fill)--C37 L76/100 ----79--------------
```

The two asterisks (**) indicate that the buffer has been modified. The name of the buffer is emacsbk.ch4. The major mode is Fundamental (Fun), and a minor mode, auto-fill (Fill), is turned on. The mode line that is displayed depends on the major mode and the type of Emacs program. This mode line also informs you of the location of the point, C37 L76/100----79, which means column 37 in the 76th line out of 100 lines and 79 percent of the way through the buffer.

In GNU Emacs, it's slightly different:

```
--**-Emacs: emacsbk.ch4        (Fundamental Fill)----Bot----------
```

The MicroEmacs mode line for the same file is as follows:

```
=*== MicroEmacs 3.10 (WRAP) == emacsbk.ch4 == File: emacsbk.ch4 ======
```

The following line shows the Epsilon Emacs mode line:

```
Epsilon 5.03 [Fundamental] emacsbk.ch4 25% *
```

Any asterisks in the mode line indicate that changes have been made to the buffer since it was last saved to the file.

Note that these mode lines are similar, but not identical. Also note that Freemacs is more like GNU Emacs than MicroEmacs. These comparisons are mentioned many times in the book because although all versions of Emacs have a similar feel, the minor details are different.

Describing the Echo Area

The echo area, directly under the mode line, contains error and informational messages, command completion, and command parameter entry. For example, if you enter a key sequence that isn't bound to an Emacs command, like CONTROL-x CONTROL-j, your display beeps or flashes, indicating an error. A message also appears in the echo area for many commands. If you enter a command that has output, like CONTROL-x =, which provides information about the point, that information appears in the echo area.

Finally, when you enter a command that requires a non-numerical parameter (such as a file name), Emacs prompts you for the parameters in the echo area. One of the best features of Emacs is automatic completion of many different types of parameters entered in this area. For example, the command CONTROL-x CONTROL-f, **find-file**, prompts you to enter a file name. You need to enter only enough of the file name to uniquely determine the file and, optionally, the path to its directory. If you then press the TAB key or the SPACEBAR, Emacs completes the file name for you. If you haven't entered enough letters to uniquely determine the file name, most versions of Emacs display the names of all the files that match what you have entered. MicroEmacs completes the file name as far as it can, or it beeps if there are no possible completions. Similar features are available for Emacs command names. For those of us who can't type very well, or don't have a perfect memory, these features are worth their weight in gold!

Help!

The first thing a new GNU Emacs user should do after starting Emacs is type CONTROL-h t. This simple help command activates an interactive tutorial file that explains the basic Emacs commands. The help command is beneficial for those who need to learn basic commands. Emacs also has a help command for the user who knows the basics but needs help with the advanced commands.

The most frustrating aspect of a complicated tool like Emacs is that you never can remember all the commands! If you can't remember what the commands are, how can you use them? Or maybe you can't quite remember the syntax of the command. Wouldn't it be nice to know all the commands that relate to the certain aspect of editing you are using? Some of those commands might make sense in the middle of an edit, but most of the time you can remember only that some such command does exist. Oh, the frustration of almost remembering!

Emacs has several kinds of built-in help, each designed to provide a different level of assistance. The simplest kind of help provides the name of the command bound to a particular key, or the key bound to a particular command. Keys in Emacs are not solely single key presses, but include up to four key-press sequences. Commands in Emacs are functions that can be executed while you are editing. For example, to get help on help, you enter the key CONTROL-h CONTROL-h. The key is two presses of the h key while holding down the CONTROL key. That key is bound to, or runs, the command **help-for-help**.

The more advanced levels of help provide a full on-line manual with hypertext links to help you find the information you need. Figure 3.7 shows part of the online documentation for Freemacs.

This book covers all levels of help. But first, you'll learn how to use the simple ones. Help in GNU Emacs is bound to CONTROL-h. You must use the F1 key instead of CONTROL-h with Freemacs and Epsilon. The MicroEmacs help system has many of these same features, but they are not accessed in this manner. See Chapter 14, covering MicroEmacs, for a description of the keys bound to these features. CONTROL-h is a *command prefix* like CONTROL-x or CONTROL-c. Command prefixes must be followed by another key to finish the key sequence. For the help features described in the previous paragraph, use CONTROL-h c, CONTROL-h k, CONTROL-h a, CONTROL-h b, CONTROL-h f, and CONTROL-h w. If you aren't able to remember these commands, you can enter CONTROL-h CONTROL-h, which displays help regarding all the possible help commands.

```
Copyright (c) 1985 Richard M. Stallman.  See end for copying conditions.
Portions Copyright (c) 1986 Russell N. Nelson

You are looking at the Freemacs tutorial.

Freemacs commands generally involve the CONTROL key (sometimes labelled
CTRL or CTL) or the META key (sometimes labelled ALT).  Rather than
write out META or CONTROL each time we want you to prefix a character,
we'll use the following abbreviations:

 C-<chr>  means hold the CONTROL key while typing the character <chr>
          Thus, C-f would be: hold the CONTROL key and type f.
 M-<chr>  means hold the META or ALT key down while typing <chr>.
          If there is no META or ALT key, type <ESC>, release it,
          then type the character <chr>.  "<ESC>" stands for the
          key labelled ESC.

Important note: if you must exit at some point, type C-X C-C.
The characters ">>" at the left margin indicate directions for you to
try using a command.  For instance:
>>  Now type C-v (View next screen) to move to the next screen.
          (go ahead, do it by depressing the control key and v together).
          From now on, you'll be expected to do this whenever you finish
-----Emacs: tutorial.doc (Text Fill) --C1 L1/706 ----Top----------------
```

Fig. 3.7. Part of the tutorial that comes with Freemacs.

Help with Keys

We'll start with two keys that name and describe the commands to which a key is bound. They are **describe-key-briefly** (CONTROL-h c) and **describe-key** (CONTROL-h k). CONTROL-h c, which you execute by pressing CONTROL-h, releasing, and pressing a lowercase letter c, prompts you to enter a key and then displays the name of the command bound to that key in the *echo area* (at the bottom of your screen). CONTROL-h k gives the name of the command and a few lines of information, displayed in a window, about the command. The command **where-is** (CONTROL-h w) is the inverse function. Given the command, CONTROL-h w displays the key, if any, bound to that command.

If you want to know all the keys that are bound to commands, use CONTROL-h b. This command builds a *binding list* of all the key sequences and the commands, if any, bound to them. The binding list is saved in the *help* buffer. Emacs even can sort the list to make the search easier. Many commands, including the ones to sort a region, and all other functions (commands are functions that you can call interactively) are not bound to keys and therefore aren't listed in this buffer. A different type of help is used for those features.

CONTROL-h a (for **apropos**) prompts you for a string and displays all functions that contain the indicated string. This information also is written to the *help* buffer. If you have a list of function names, you can use **describe-function** (CONTROL-h f) for brief descriptions of the functions. By using CONTROL-h a and the binding list, you can uncover many handy features in Emacs. The best way to learn how to use the simpler features is simply to try them. The commands and functions that Emacs has deemed too complex for trial and error are described and explained fully in help.

The Info Mode

In addition to the help regarding keys, functions, and commands, GNU Emacs offers an ultimate help system. Called *info* mode, it accesses a complete set of on-line manuals for Emacs and related programs. The Emacs paper manual is about 300 pages long, and related material, such as the E-Lisp programming language manual, is twice as big. Because it is difficult to find what you need in manuals this size, assuming you have a manual, Emacs contains the info program to offer you the manuals on-line. The on-line manuals are identical to the printed manuals except for the *tree* structure, which was added to make your search easier.

Like the tree structures used in most computer programs, the info trees are upside down, meaning they have the root, or main, *node* at the top of the tree. The info tree is composed of one or more files. A node (topic) in the info tree displays information about the particular topic. All nodes except the root node are linked to a higher node, and most nodes are linked to previous and next nodes on the same level in the tree. These links form a linear structure, or chain. You can move through this chain by entering n, for the next, or p, for the previous, node on the chain. Because all the commands in info are single characters, moving from node to node is fairly easy.

The Info modes of UniPress Emacs (shown in Figure 3.8) and GNU offer a very powerful method of reading documentation using nodes. Nodes can be thought of as places where the branches of trees join, or like file structures on computers. You start at the root and follow the branch topic of interest down to its conclusion, or back up to where it joins (at a node) another topic, which you can then follow down.

```
Node: Top,                                This is the top of the tree

This is the Emacs Info structured documentation reader.  Type h for a
tutorial introduction to Info; type ? for a list of Info commands.  Visit node
Info to learn how to add documentation to this tree.

Time now:  Mon Aug  5 14:59:04 1991    Dir:  /usr/fiction
You: Fiction Writer!

* Menu:




INFO*    Browsing                   (dir)Top              3%  --More--
```

Fig. 3.8. The Info mode of UniPress Emacs.

The chains formed by next and previous links aren't enough to create a tree structure; links also are needed to connect Info nodes. These links are created by menus in nodes. A *menu* is simply a list of subtopics for the current node. If a node has a menu, the menu shows up as text in the current node. Here is an example:

```
* Menu:

* First::   Short description of First, but descriptions may be more than one line of text
* Second:: Short description of Second
* Last::    Short description of Last
```

To retrieve the node named First, type the letter m. Emacs displays the prompt Menu Item: in the echo area. Type First and terminate your entry with ENTER. You also can type the number of the menu item—for example, 2 ENTER to go to the second item in the menu of the current node. This function works for only the first five items in the menu.

Now we'll discuss a real example, the Info node for Emacs Screen Organization. This Info node has three topics: Point, Mode Line, and Echo Area. By selecting one of these topics, you move to one of these three nodes. These nodes are one level below the Info node in the Emacs info tree. Here is what that menu looks like:

```
* Menu:

* Point::      The place in the text where editing commands operate
* Echo Area::  Short messages appear at the bottom of the screen
* Mode Line::  Interpreting the mode line
```

You get to this menu by entering info mode (META-x info). Enter m (for menu) and e (for .emacs) to get to the top level of the Emacs info tree; then enter m and screen to go to the Info node (Emacs) screen. From this node you can go to the (Emacs) mode line Info node by entering m mode ENTER.

The GNU Emacs manual is written in many small chapters with up to 12 sections per chapter. Some of the sections have subsections. Because the info tree must have the same structure as the printed manual, it is three levels deep.

Figure 3.9 portrays a small part of the Emacs info tree structure. It shows part of the tree, including the Characters node and its immediate neighbors. The vertical links (menu going down, up going up) are not shown, but are implied by positioning. The next and previous links are shown, as are the hypertext links (shown in parentheses under each node). Next, you will learn how to move around in an info tree and look at examples using each of these types of links.

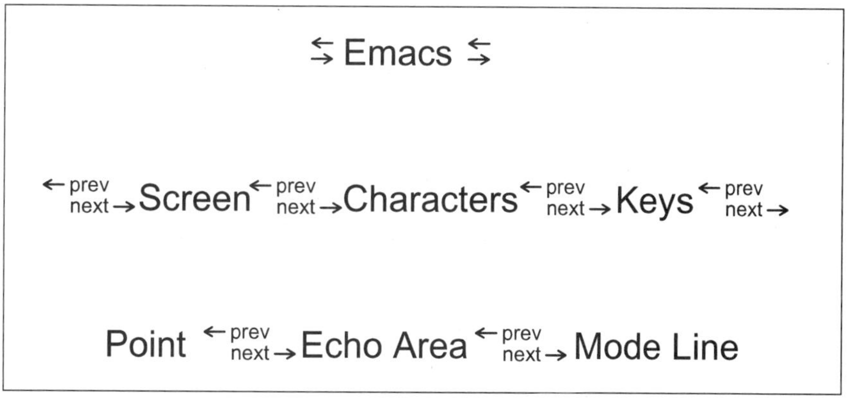

Fig. 3.9. Part of the Emacs info tree structure.

The following list demonstrates the use of the info tree. In this example, we are searching for help on how to do a **query-replace** in Emacs.

1. Start info.

2. Select the Emacs node from a menu in the root node.

3. Select the Searching and Replacing node from a menu in the Emacs node.

4. Select the Replace node from a menu in the Searching and Replacing node.

5. Select the Query option from a menu in the Replace node.

6. Read about the **query-replace** command.

Using the info tree is actually much easier to do than it is to describe.

To start info, you enter META-x info. All entries are followed by the ENTER key. Emacs then opens an info window that displays the root node. To select an item from any menu, you enter m for menu. Emacs then prompts you, in the echo area, for the item name. If you don't enter enough of the item name to distinguish it from other similar names, Emacs will display a list of all possible item names. The actual keystrokes necessary to find the Query-Replace Info node are:

```
META-x info ENTER
me ENTER
msearch ENTER
mrep ENTER
mq ENTER
```

About 30 keystrokes are required to get to one of info's most deeply nested areas, which is a much faster method than using the index in a paper copy of the same manual. You can move back up the tree with the **u**, for **up**, command. Not only can you move quickly up and down the nodes, but you also can follow three other types of links within the tree.

Two of these types of links, the next and previous links, exist throughout the tree structure. They connect nodes of the same level. The Query-Replace node's previous node, for example, is linked to the Replace Commands and Case node. The **n** and **p** commands enable you to move horizontally through the tree. The Query-Replace node has no next node because it is the last subsection of the Replacement Commands subsection. The Replace Commands and Case node has both a next node (Query-Replace) and a previous node (RegExp Replacement). Both of these nodes are linked to the Replacement Commands node with up links.

Even with vertical (menu and up) links and horizontal (next and previous) links, your movement within the tree is still restricted. Info provides a number of other ways to move through the tree, the simplest of which is the **d**, for **directory**, command, which moves you immediately to the root node of the tree. A more complicated command is **g**, for **goto**, which moves you to any node in the tree that you name. **Goto** will move you to a node in another tree as long as you know the node name. There is the **l**, for **last**, command, which moves you back to the last node you viewed. Don't confuse this with the **previous** command, which moves you to the previous node in the current chain. The previous node is on the same level in the tree as the current node. The **last** command moves you to the last node you viewed, no matter where that node is.

There is one remaining type of link, the *cross-reference* link. This link acts like a special case of the **go** command with the destination given in the current node. The syntax for a cross-reference link is similar to the menu entries:

```
*Note reference-name : new-node
```

If you enter f, info prompts you for the reference-name. If your reference-name is found in the current node, info goes to the corresponding new node. To get back from that node, use the **l** command. If you type f? and press the ENTER key, Emacs lists the reference-names in the current node. If you enter a partial name, info lists all similar reference-names.

The **s** command enables you to search through the current info file for matches to a regular expression. Info is actually a special mode for editing files. There is even an **e**, for **edit**, command to enable you to edit Info nodes.

> **Caution!** Info files are not simple text files; they have extra control characters that give them their node structure. See the info tree on info for more info on creating your own info files!

The **g** (**goto**) command can specify a new info file as well as a node in that file. The format for this is *(filename) node-name*; for example, (emacs)screen commands. The previous, next, and up node-names, which are built into each info file, also can specify a file or node, so the tree may be made up of many files. The info tree on Emacs is composed of about 15 files. The info tree on E-Lisp is composed of 25 files!

If these commands seem like a bit much to remember, don't worry. If you enter ? while in the info mode, a complete list of commands, with brief descriptions, is displayed. If you still are confused, enter h and a tutorial on info is displayed.

Learning Emacs

In this chapter we've introduced you to the structure of Emacs, the ways to enter and leave Emacs, the ways Emacs uses the keys on your keyboard, and the method of receiving on-line help. In Chapter 4, you will put your theoretical knowledge to use and start learning how to use Emacs for everyday tasks.

Part

Using Emacs

The Basics of Editing

Intermediate Editing

Formatting

Customization and Programming

Advanced Topics

The Basics of Editing

I t's time to do some practical editing. Again, we encourage you to follow along on your computer.

Characters and Keys in Emacs

Before using Emacs, you should understand some of the things that go on inside it. Your understanding of this section will be necessary for your understanding many of the concepts covered later in the book. In the previous chapter, you looked at the Emacs screen. Now you need to look at the keyboard and understand how characters and keys have different meanings in Emacs.

Characters

Because Emacs is a text editor, it must use a collating sequence, an order in which a computer system arranges data, to represent the text being edited. On most systems, Emacs uses ASCII, which is a standard seven-bit sequence with 95 printing and 32 control (nonprinting) characters. Because ASCII stands for the American Standard Code for Information Interchange, other countries, even English speaking ones, use slightly different codes. Many non-English speaking countries use characters in their alphabet that are not represented by ASCII characters. Usually these characters are defined by adding an eighth bit to the seven-bit ASCII code. These special characters are called *Meta* characters.

In Emacs there are three types of character codes:

- *Printable codes* are generated by pressing ordinary keys like the alphabet and the numbers.

- *Control codes* are generated by holding down the CONTROL-SHIFT key while pressing an ordinary key simultaneously.

- *Meta codes* are generated by special keys or key sequences.

The printable codes and control codes are those defined by ASCII. The Meta codes are extensions beyond seven bits. Emacs uses all three types of codes for increased specialization.

Some of the ASCII control codes already have special meaning in text. For example, the CONTROL-m code is used for ENTER, and the CONTROL-i code is used for TAB. The control codes are executed by holding down the CONTROL key on your keyboard and pressing the given letter (for example, the CONTROL key and the c key give you CONTROL-c).

These control codes and the ESCAPE key (CONTROL-]) have special keys on most keyboards. Of course, the control codes can be generated also by using the CONTROL-SHIFT key and a regular key. There are actually 31 usable control codes (CONTROL-a through CONTROL-z, CONTROL-[, CONTROL-\, CONTROL-], CONTROL-^, and CONTROL-_).

Because Meta codes are not defined by any standard, the representation of Meta characters depends on the particular kind of Emacs. We treat them as special character codes that are extensions to the standard ASCII. Unfortunately, the term Meta also is used in GNU Emacs to refer to a special shift key. Although some terminals actually have a META key, most do not. Don't confuse the META key with Meta codes. Many desktop computer implementations of Emacs use the ALT or ALTERNATE key as the META key.

Actually, you don't need to use a META key to generate a Meta code! Emacs enables all terminals simply to use the ESCAPE key (CONTROL-]) followed by another key to generate the Meta codes. We use M- as a prefix to indicate the use of the META key. If your keyboard doesn't have a META key, you can use ESCAPE followed by the other key instead. For example, META-x (M-x) becomes ESCAPE x. Note that when you're using the ESCAPE key in place of a META key, M-x means press and release ESCAPE, then type x. (We use M- and ESCAPE interchangeably throughout this book but tend to favor ESCAPE because it works on most terminals.) However, you need to realize also that most Meta codes are generated by multiple key sequences that don't involve the META key, as the following keys demonstrate.

Keys

Remember that any special key sequence recognized by an Emacs generates a Meta code internal to that Emacs. These sequences include all the GNU Emacs key sequences starting with the ESCAPE key and key sequences starting with some other keys (usually CONTROL-x or CONTROL-c). Other special key sequences include those generated by the function keys on many keyboards and, of course, the use of an actual META (or ALT) key with a regular key. In GNU Emacs these codes are referred to as keys. Note that a key can be the result of a single key press, as in the key a, or a shifted key press, as in the key CONTROL-y, or a sequence of key presses, as in CONTROL-x 4 CONTROL-f.

The most frequently used commands normally are bound, by default, to a single- or two-character sequence key. Note that any key can be bound to any Emacs command. Remember that the keys and the commands are entirely separate, except for their bindings. You decide which keys are bound to which commands. Figure 4.1 shows some standard key bindings in MicroEmacs.

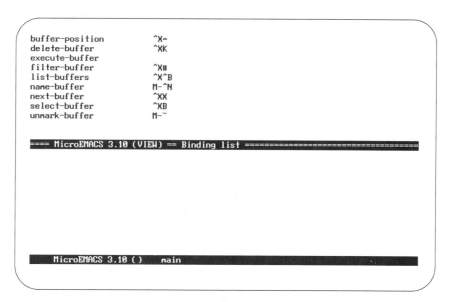

```
buffer-position        ^X=
delete-buffer          ^XK
execute-buffer
filter-buffer          ^X#
list-buffers           ^X^B
name-buffer            M-^N
next-buffer            ^XX
select-buffer          ^XB
unmark-buffer          M-~


==== MicroEMACS 3.10 (VIEW) == Binding list ===============================



      MicroEMACS 3.10 ()     main
```

Fig. 4.1. Some of the default key bindings in MicroEmacs.

Emacs commands are actually programs that you can run in either of two ways. You can enter the key to which the command is bound or else enter the name of the program as a parameter for an **execute-extended-command**

(META-x) key. Programs range from simple ones that move the point (and the cursor) one character forward in the buffer to complex ones that compile other programs.

The program that moves the point forward one character is called **forward-character**, normally bound to the key CONTROL-f. The compile command, naturally enough, is called **compile**; it is not bound to any key by default. MicroEmacs doesn't have the **compile** command. All Emacs versions do have a common set of commands like **forward-character**, but each version also has its own set of extended commands. In this book we always note when a command is uncommon or does not have standard default bindings. We also list the commands and bindings for common Emacs variants in our reference section.

4   Mistakes

Emacs offers many commands to change the text in a buffer. Some of them are used as you enter text to fix typos, but they also can be used to make bigger changes in a buffer. The most commonly used commands are the delete commands. For those of us who can't type very well, the DELETE key may be the most used key on our keyboards.

Emacs has two delete commands: **delete-backward-character** (DELETE) and **delete-character** (CONTROL-d). These commands remove a single character from the buffer: DELETE removes the character to the left of the point, and CONTROL-d removes the character to the right. Note that when you delete the terminating newline, the two lines are joined (that is, CONTROL-e CONTROL-d joins the current line to the next line, and CONTROL-a DELETE joins the current line to the previous one). When you use the delete commands, the deleted characters are not saved; the only way to recover them is by repeating the **undo** command (CONTROL-x u). Because the simpler Emacs variants like Freemacs and MicroEmacs don't have the **undo** command, when you delete a character it is gone.

Emacs has another kind of command used to delete text when you want to delete more than a few characters. In Emacs these are called kill commands. The text they remove from your buffer is saved to the kill buffer and kill ring. Kill commands that you can use when entering or correcting text include those shown in Table 4.1.

Table 4.1. Kill Commands

Command Name	Key
kill-line	C-k
kill-sentence	ESC k
kill-word	ESC d
backward-kill-sentence	C-x DEL
backward-kill-word	ESC DEL
append-next-kill	ESC C-w
kill-region	C-w

Killing Lines

Next to DELETE, the most common command to delete unwanted text is **kill-line**. This command, like the other kill commands, kills from the point to the end of a particular structure. In this case that structure is a line, but it also can be words, sentences, paragraphs, and regions. When you are using special modes, like C mode, you also can kill to the end of comments and expressions. We cover those commands in Chapter 6.

The **kill-line** command is special because you also can use it on blank lines. Blank words, sentences and paragraphs don't make much sense, but blank lines are useful. If you use **kill-line** on a blank line, it removes the line. Big deal—but what if you use it on a line that isn't blank? If you use **kill-line** on a line that isn't blank, it removes the characters between the point and the end of the line. It doesn't remove the newline unless the point is at the end of the line. If the point is at the end of the line, **kill-line** removes only the newline.

The characters removed, including the newline, are saved in the kill buffer. When you do successive kills without any intervening commands, each kill is appended to the *kill buffer*. This is useful for moving blocks of text. If you want to append kills separated by other commands, you can use **append-next-kill** (ESC CONTROL-w). Using CONTROL-k, or other kill commands, and ESC CONTROL-w, you can bring together text from different parts of the buffer. See Chapter 5 for more information on this technique.

If all you want to do is remove the current line, you must position the point at the start of the line with the **beginning-of-line** command (CONTROL-a), then kill the characters on the line with CONTROL-k, then kill the newline with CONTROL-k. That is CONTROL-a, CONTROL-k, CONTROL-k to get rid of the current line. To kill the line directly following the one you just killed, another CONTROL-k, CONTROL-k is needed. Both lines end up in the kill buffer, so you can retrieve them with a single **yank** command (CONTROL-y).

Entering three control characters to kill a line is the price you pay for the flexibility of the CONTROL-k command. You can use it to trim unwanted words off the end of a line or to join successive lines together or to delete entire lines.

Killing Characters and Words

The remaining kill commands are simpler than **kill-line**. They remove characters until they get to the end of the structure. For example, **kill-word** removes everything from the point until the end of the next word. If the point is in the middle of a word, only the remainder of the word is killed. If the point is on white space, Emacs kills forward until the end of the next word. The end of a word is found when going from a character included in a set of characters, called words, to a character that isn't in that set. A set of characters that are called words is defined in one of the Emacs syntax tables. See Chapter 7 for more information. The kill can extend over multiple lines.

Killing Sentences and Paragraphs

The **kill-sentence** and **kill-paragraph** commands act like the **kill-word** command, but with different criteria for detecting the end of the area they want to kill. The end of a sentence is defined by certain punctuation following letters. The end of a paragraph is defined by a blank line or white space at the start of a line. Changing to a new mode can change the definitions of paragraph and sentence. See Chapter 5 for more information on modes.

The **kill-word**, **kill-sentence**, and **kill-paragraph** commands all have "backward kill" versions, but there is no "kill to the beginning of line" command. We note this as one more difference between lines and other structures in Emacs. Also note that Freemacs doesn't kill paragraphs and MicroEmacs doesn't kill sentences.

Killing Regions

Regions also can be killed using the **kill-region** command (CONTROL-w). Because the region extends from the point to the mark, this is very similar to the **kill-line** and **kill-paragraph** commands. It is very easy to define a region in Emacs, so this method is often the best way to kill small pieces of text. Of course, you can kill most of the buffer using this command, and it is easy to forget that the point has been reset to the beginning or end of a buffer! Fortunately, the kill buffer, the kill ring, and even the **undo** command can help you recover lost text.

Correcting Typos

Emacs is written to be used with maximum convenience, and that means being able to correct as you type. Typos can be eliminated without deleting and retyping. If you were to type *probelm* rather than *problem*, for example, you would place the point between the *e* and the *l* and use the **transpose-character** command (CONTROL-t) to fix it.

The **transpose-character** command exchanges the characters on either side of the point. The point moves with the character that was before it. Therefore, repeated application of CONTROL-t, or use of a numeric argument (CONTROL-u *number*) before CONTROL-t, moves the point along the line and carries that character along with it. When the point reaches the end of the line, CONTROL-t transposes the two characters at the end of the line. It won't transpose the newline and it can't move any farther. In MicroEmacs, the **transpose-character** command never moves the point.

MicroEmacs does not have the **transpose-word** and **transpose-line** commands that are present in Freemacs and GNU Emacs. Only GNU Emacs has a **transpose-expressions** command, covered in Chapter 6.

Transpose-word (ESC-t) works just like **transpose-character**. It exchanges the word in front of the point with the word before or under the point and leaves the point after the second word. If you use it repeatedly or with a numeric argument, it moves a word through the buffer. Unlike **transpose-character**, it doesn't stop at newlines. **Transpose-word** treats newlines and tabs like spaces. It also transposes words even if a large amount of white space (spaces, tabs, and newlines) is between them.

The **transpose-line** (CONTROL-x CONTROL-t) command exchanges the line the cursor is on with the line before the cursor. Notice that this is the opposite behavior of **transpose-character** and **transpose-word**. **Transpose-line** also moves the cursor with the line so that the cursor and the line move toward the beginning of the buffer.

Changing Case

In addition to typing characters and words in the wrong order, you often can type words in the wrong case. Emacs, of course, has provided an easy way to fix this mistake. The three commands to change the case of a word are shown in Table 4.2.

Table 4.2. Emacs Commands to Change the Case of a Word

Command Name	Key
downcase-word	ESC l
upcase-word	ESC u
capitalize-word	ESC c

Each of these commands works on the word in front of the point, but you can make these commands work on the word behind the point by preceding them with ESC-– (that is, ESCAPE plus the minus sign). ESC-– gives many commands a –1 numeric argument. Commands also can take a positive numeric argument, and they can take negative numeric arguments other than –1. For example, CONTROL-u 10 ESC-u makes the next 10 words uppercase, and ESC-–4 ESC-c capitalizes the last four words.

Correcting Spelling

Finally you come to the spelling checker, which is something everyone needs, but which is not one of Emacs' strong areas. The appropriate command for quick checks of spelling is **spell-word** (ESC-$). The **spell-word** command creates an inferior process and runs *spell* in it. Spell checks the word before the point and tells you, in the echo area, if it is spelled incorrectly. Then it asks you to correct the spelling! You probably would not have spelled the word incorrectly if you knew how to spell it in the first place. Anyway, creating a new process to check the spelling of one word is silly. You also can check the spelling of the buffer (**spell-buffer**) or a region (**spell-region**), but you still have to provide the correct spelling. If you can, install ispell, a great improvement over spell. In Chapter 7 we show you how to set up GNU Emacs to use ispell.

Marks and Regions

Emacs has commands for familiar textual objects like characters, words, lines, paragraphs, and pages. Emacs also has commands for textual objects that you may not be familiar with like regions, sexp (short for s-expression, the basic syntactic unit of Lisp), and lists. The *region* is the most useful of these concepts.

Sometimes you want to edit a section of text that can't be defined as a character, word, line, or paragraph. This section can be as small as a few characters or as large as the entire buffer, perhaps hundreds of lines. The mechanism called region in Emacs enables you to define this indescribable text. You can delete a region, move a region, copy a region, change case in a region, and much more. Now we'll look at how Emacs defines region.

Describing the Region

As stated earlier, the point is where the editing takes place. It also is used as one of the ends of the region. Because a region needs two ends, the *mark* is introduced. The mark identifies the other end of the region. Thus, the region is the text between the point and the mark.

Setting the Mark

Because Emacs has no concept of the front or end of a region, the idea is to establish a fixed place in the buffer, the mark, that determines one end of the region and let the variable location point determine the other end. Each buffer has its own mark. When set by a command, the mark remains in that fixed position until another command executed in that buffer moves it. The mark is fixed relative to the character that precedes it in the buffer.

The command **set-mark-command**, usually bound to CONTROL-@, is used to explicitly set the mark. There are other commands that also set the mark. For example, the commands that insert a block of text from a buffer or from another file leave the point at the end of the block and the mark at the beginning of the block. This implicit setting of the mark makes it easier for you to work with the newly inserted text. The command **swap-point-and-mark**, usually bound to CONTROL-x CONTROL-x, lets you move the point to the beginning of the block.

The mark also is set at the location of the point when you use the commands **go-to-beginning** (ESC <) or **go-to-end** (ESC >). These commands move you to the beginning or the end of the buffer. The mark is set by these commands so you easily can get back to your previous location in the buffer. This is a different use for the **swap-point-and-mark** (CONTROL-x CONTROL-x) command. Like many commands in Emacs, this command is used for several different purposes.

Using the Mark Ring

The mark has two major functions: marking one end of the region and saving locations in the buffer. Because you can have only one mark active at a time, the last 16 marks used are saved in a *mark ring*. Each time you set a mark, the previous mark is placed on the ring and the oldest mark is lost. Each buffer has its own mark ring.

The command **set-mark-command** takes on a modified meaning when given a *numeric argument*. You give a command a numeric argument by entering CONTROL‑u, the numeric prefix, before you enter the command. If you enter just CONTROL-u and the command, the numeric prefix is four, but you can follow the CONTROL-u with a number. CONTROL-u CONTROL-n moves the cursor up four lines, but CONTROL-u 10 CONTROL-n moves it up ten lines.

Emacs often uses a numeric prefix to modify commands, and sometimes the modification has nothing to do with the actual numeric argument. In this case, there is no point in entering a number after the CONTROL-u.

The numeric argument prefix is CONTROL-u, and **set-mark-command** is usually bound to CONTROL-@; thus, the command to go to the previous mark is CONTROL-u CONTROL-@. This command moves the point to where the mark was and sets the mark to the last value stored on the mark ring. Repeating the command moves the point back to successive marks. Each time you use the command, it sets the current location as the mark and stores the previous mark on the mark ring. If you repeat the command enough times, you go through all the stored marks and end up back where you started.

Using Commands on Regions

To view the different commands for a region, use the command **apropos** to list all commands that have the string "region" in them. A list similar to the following one can be generated in GNU Emacs 18.57 using META-x apropos region:

```
call-process-region
capitalize-region
center-region
copy-region-as-kill          ESC w
count-lines-region           ESC =
delete-region
downcase-region              C-x C-l
eval-region
expand-region-abbrevs
fill-region                  ESC g
```

```
fill-region-as-paragraph
indent-region                      ESC C-\
kill-region                        C-w
lpr-region
narrow-to-region                   C-x n
print-region
shell-command-on-region            ESC ¦
spell-region
texinfo-format-region
underline-region
ununderline-region
upcase-region                      C-x C-u
write-region
```

Freemacs 1.6 generates a more modest list:

```
count-lines-region                 ESC =
downcase-region                    C-x C-l
kill-region                        C-w
shell-command-on-region            ESC-¦
upcase-region                      C-x C-u
write-region
```

Because some of the GNU Emacs commands are rather esoteric, we cover only the commands that are in both GNU Emacs and Freemacs. Some of the other region commands are discussed in later chapters or in the reference section of this book.

write-region, count-lines-region

These are simple commands that can be executed on text appearing in a region. The **write-region** command prompts you for a file name and then writes the region to that file. In **count-lines-command**, Emacs reads through the region and counts end-line markers. The result is displayed in the echo area. Neither of these commands modifies the region.

downcase-region, upcase-region

Both of these commands act as *filters*. A filter is a function that modifies its input some way to produce its output. These commands take their input from the region and replace the region with their output. They filter all text in the region by replacing all uppercase letters with lowercase letters, for example.

Filters are a very important concept in the UNIX world because hundreds of utility programs are designed to act as filters. Emacs provides a simple mechanism for using these programs to process the text in a region.

shell-command-on-region

The **shell-command-on-region** command enables you to use any program on the system as a filter. The text in the region is fed to that program in the same manner as if you had typed the text from the keyboard.

If the **shell-command-on-region** (ESC-¦) command is given a numeric argument (now the command is CONTROL-u ESC-¦), the output from the filter replaces the region. Otherwise, the output goes to the *shell-output* buffer. This is another example in which the use of a numeric prefix modifies the action of the command.

As an example, mark this sentence as the region. Now run the shell command **tr a A**. This uses **tr** as the filter command, which replaces characters with other characters—in this case, *a* with *A*. The output that goes to *shell buffer* is: *As An exAmple, mArk this sentence As the region.* This simple use of the filter program should just give you an idea of how a filter works. If you are a DOS user, many of these same filters are available for DOS and you can use them with Freemacs (ESC-¦) or MicroEmacs (CONTROL-x-#) **shell-command-on-region** commands.

Using kill-region and the Kill Ring

The most common thing to do with a region is to *kill* it. To kill text means to delete it from the current buffer. You can kill characters (using CONTROL-d), spaces (ESC \), words (ESC d), lines (CONTROL-k), sentences (ESC k), paragraphs, and regions (CONTROL-w). Not only can you kill almost any form of text, you also can reverse almost any kill. The GNU Emacs manual says, "Thus we join television in leading people to kill thoughtlessly." Perhaps that quotation overstates the case for television, perhaps not, but Emacs does encourage thoughtless killing by making it possible to easily recover a mistaken kill.

When you kill anything the size of a word or larger, it is removed from the current buffer and saved in a *kill-buffer*. If you kill a region (CONTROL-w) and then enter the **yank** command (CONTROL-y) without moving the point, your current buffer is restored, but the region you cut is still in the *kill-buffer*. You can insert the last region deleted by moving the point and pressing CONTROL-y at the new point. This is a good way to copy part of a buffer. If you kill a region (CONTROL-w) and then move the point and yank from the kill buffer (CONTROL-y), you have moved a block of text from one place to another in the buffer.

Multiple kill commands with no intervening commands append their kills to the kill buffer, but when you kill another region, the contents of the kill buffer are replaced by the newly killed text. But just as Emacs has a mark ring to hold marks that have been replaced, it has a *kill ring* to hold old kills, and the **yank-pop** command (ESC y) to retrieve copy from the kill ring. The **yank-pop** command works very much like the mark ring. However, you must first press CONTROL-y, which inserts the last kill at the point; then, with no intervening commands, you press ESC y repeatedly. Each ESC y replaces the new region with one further back on the kill ring. Because it is a ring, if you continue to press ESC y you will eventually get back to the region that was inserted when you hit CONTROL-y.

With GNU Emacs, a long editing session is needed to cycle through the kill ring. The kill ring uses a lot of memory, one reason that Emacs requires a lot of memory. Fortunately, you don't have to cycle through the ring to get back to the original region. The information you want is still in the kill buffer, as are all the other kills on the kill ring. As a side note, GNU Emacs also maintains an 8,000-character buffer used to hold smaller kills such as characters you deleted individually. The **undo** command, CONTROL-x-u, restores these smaller kills. The **yank** and **yank-pop** commands restore bigger pieces of text.

Registers

Emacs offers many ways of moving text between buffers. You have seen the use of both the kill buffer and the kill ring for this purpose, but you also can use buffers, files, or *registers*. You should be familiar with buffers and files by now, but you probably haven't used registers. We'll go through the commands to move text to and from buffers and files and then talk about using registers to move text.

Moving Text to and from Buffers and Files

GNU Emacs has many commands for moving and building blocks of text. Some of these commands use buffers and files to do their jobs, and others use registers. Table 4.3 lists the commands that use a buffer or a file to collect the block as you build it.

Table 4.3. Commands That Move Text to and from Buffers and Files

Command Name	Key Binding	Meaning
append-to-buffer	C-x a	Insert region at point, leaving point at end of region
copy-to-buffer		Replace buffer with region
insert-buffer		Insert buffer at point
prepend-to-buffer		Insert region at point, leaving point at front of region
append-to-file		Insert region at end of file
insert-file	C-x i	Insert file at point

All these commands prompt the user for a buffer or file name and then create the buffer or file if it is not in existence. The **copy-to-buffer** command replaces the contents of the buffer with the contents of the region. The **insert-file** and **insert-buffer** commands insert the contents of the file or buffer at the point. The **append-to-buffer** and **prepend-to-buffer** commands both copy the region to the buffer at the location of the point. The prepend command leaves the point in front of the new text; the append command places the point after the new text. Successive append commands insert the text blocks in the same order that you append them; successive prepend commands insert the blocks in the reverse order. These commands enable you to build text in the buffer many different ways. Appending text to a file always places the text at the end of the file.

> **Caution!** If you append text to a file you are currently visiting, the buffer containing the file is not updated; the file is written over. Therefore, you might lose any appended text if you save the file from the buffer. For this reason, **append-to-file** should not be used on files that are currently being visited!

Using Registers

Registers in Emacs are similar to registers in a computer: they are places you can store text for quick and easy retrieval. An Emacs register can store a block of text or a position in a buffer, but not both. Emacs has one set of registers that all buffers share. Going to a position stored in a register switches the current window to the buffer that was current when that position was stored and moves the point to its stored position. All the commands that use registers prompt you for the register name, always a single character. Table 4.4 lists the commands that use registers for text transportation.

Table 4.4. Commands That Move Text with Registers

Command Name	Key Binding
GNU Emacs 18.57	
append-to-register	
copy-rectangle-to-register	C-x r
copy-to-register	C-x x
insert-register	C-x g
point-to-register	C-x /
prepend-to-register	
register-to-point	C-x j
view-register	
Freemacs 1.6	
copy-to-register	C-x x
insert-register	C-x g
point-to-register	C-x /
register-to-point	C-x j
view-register	

The chapter on editing covers other, more complicated GNU Emacs functions on copying and restoring rectangular regions. Most of the other copying functions, which are covered here, are common to both GNU Emacs and Freemacs. Even when a command function is common to both versions, the Freemacs command may not do as much.

The **view-register** command is a good example of this disparity. In GNU Emacs, this command displays the string stored in the register or the name of the buffer and the position in the buffer. The Freemacs command informs you whether the register stores information about a string or a position.

The **append-to-region** and **prepend-to-region** commands, which are not bound to keys by default, are similar to the append and prepend commands for a buffer. The region, in this case, must hold a string of characters (another way to describe a block of text). The **append-to-register** command copies the current region to the end of the string stored in the selected register. The **prepend-to-register** command copies the current region to the beginning of the string stored in the register. These commands enable you to build up a string in the register by combining strings from any of the buffers. The new string then can be inserted into a buffer using the **insert-register** (CONTROL-x g) command.

The **copy-to-register** (CONTROL-x x) command stores the current region in the register you select; it remains there until you replace it with another **copy-to-register** or **point-to-register** (CONTROL-x /) command. The **point-to-register** command stores the location of the point, including the buffer name, in the register. The **register-to-point** (CONTROL-x j) command loads the stored position and buffer into the current window. With text or a position stored in a register, it is easy to insert that text or go to that position whenever you need to. Retrieving text and positions is easier than having to shuffle through the kill ring or the mark ring.

The **insert-register** command copies the contents of the selected register to the current buffer at the point. If you try to insert text from a register with a position, Emacs cautions you that the register is not valid in this context. Emacs does not remind you which registers are already in use, nor does it prevent you from overwriting the value in a register. Registers are like scratch pad variables. Just as it is easy to forget where you put the grocery list or the directions to Ralph Roberts' house, it is easy to misplace your registers. They are easy and fast to use, but they are also easy to lose.

Registers are like scratch pads; you can use them for saving and recalling the same way you would use small pieces of paper on your desk. They are computerized Post-it notes. Emacs has many different kinds of registers available; the way you use them depends on your own style of editing.

Suppose you were looking at the files that make up this book. If you wanted to check on another part of the book, you would enter CONTROL-x /r (mnemonic for register) to save your position in a register. Then you could look at other parts of the book. When you wanted to get back to this paragraph, you would enter CONTROL-x j r. Your point would be in the same place as when you entered the **point-to-register** command. Many text-editor programs call this function a bookmark, an appropriate name for this example.

Bookmarks aren't the only things you can use registers for. In keeping with the Post-it notes theme (yes, I use Post-it notes for bookmarks too), registers are a good place to keep frequently referenced bits of text. Registers are easier than buffers to recall because of their one-letter names. Again, think of buffers as documents and registers as pieces of scratch paper. The buffers are usually permanent because you can save them to a file. Registers are temporary; you lose the information when you exit the editor.

You also can use a register as a temporary place to collect pieces of information before you insert them into a buffer. If you have text scattered in many files and you want to put together some kind of summary, a register may be just the thing to use. Mark each piece of information as a region and use the **append-to-register** command to add it to a register. This way you can accumulate the desired summary information in a register and insert that register (CONTROL-x g) at the desired position. You might still need to do some editing, but at least you will have accumulated the information in one location.

Searches

Searching for strings of characters in a buffer is a common use of a text editor. Despite this fact, many text editors and word processors have only rudimentary searching commands. Emacs, on the other hand, has several types of searching commands, from limited to powerful commands. Table 4.5 lists the search commands available in GNU Emacs 18.57.

Table 4.5. GNU Emacs Search Commands

Command Name	*Key Binding*
isearch-backward	C-r
isearch-backward-regexp	
isearch-forward	C-s, ESC O R
isearch-forward-regexp	ESC C-s
re-search-backward	
re-search-forward	
search-backward	
search-forward	
word-search-backward	
word-search-forward	

Searching with Incremental Search Commands

The basic search commands are **isearch-forward** and **isearch-backward**. You probably know what the forward and backward parts mean, but the "i" may not be so obvious. The "i" stands for *incremental*, meaning that the search takes place as you enter the string. In other words, the point jumps forward to the next match as you add letters. This way, you usually find a search string before you've entered the full string, a handy timesaving feature.

The behavior of Emacs during an incremental search can be disconcerting when you first encounter it. As you enter the string to be searched for, the point jumps around in the buffer and the window changes rapidly on your screen. As each character is entered, Emacs searches for a match to the string as it is currently spelled. A search for "joe" first involves a search for "j," then a search for "jo," and finally a search for "joe." Each search continues until a match is found or the end of the buffer is reached. Then the next search is started. The search is not case-sensitive by default. If you want a case-sensitive search, you set the variable *case-fold-search* to nil. Enter ESC x set-variable, press the carriage return or ENTER key, type case-fold-search, hit ENTER, and type nil. You also can set this variable in the initialization file.

When Emacs finds a match, the point moves to the match and that area of the buffer is displayed. If no match is found, Emacs beeps at you. In a large buffer, searching takes a long time, but you can type ahead of the search string. Emacs searches for each successive substring until it matches the entire string or a search fails. With a big buffer, you might want to cancel a failing isearch rather than wait for the entire buffer to be searched. Use CONTROL-g to cancel the search.

If a search fails, Emacs displays the part of the string that was matched and moves the point to the match. The search string remains as you have entered it, and you can use CONTROL-g to delete the part that wasn't matched. If you enter CONTROL-g again, the search is aborted. If you use DELETE to delete the part that Emacs has matched, the point moves back to the first match found on the current substring. You then can enter new characters, and Emacs searches for the new strings as each character is entered.

You can search for the next instance of the same string by simply repeating the search command (CONTROL-s to search forward, CONTROL-r to search backward). A forward search can be repeated as a backward search and vice versa. When you are finished searching, enter ESC or CONTROL-g to cancel the search. Hitting RETURN, as many people do by habit, will just enter a carriage return. You must use ESC or CONTROL-g. If you press the ESC key, the point remains at its last position. If you enter CONTROL-g, the point returns to its position when you started the search. Entering any Emacs command that isn't used to control the search or to change the search string escapes you from the search and executes that command at the current point.

The commands that change the search string are the DELETE key and the printing characters, CONTROL-q, CONTROL-w, and CONTROL-y. The **quoted-insert** command (CONTROL-q) is used to insert nonprinting characters into the search string. You can either use the CONTROL shift key along with another key or enter the character's ASCII code as an octal (base 8) number. The **kill-region** command (CONTROL-w) attaches the word following the point to the search string and advances the point to the space after that word. This function does not always work as it should in Freemacs 1.6. The **yank** command (CONTROL-y) appends the rest of the current line to the search string.

Searching with Regular Search Commands

The **isearch-forward** and **isearch-backward** commands are powerful and easy to use, but many people prefer the more familiar string search commands. These are **search-forward** and **search-backward**. They are not bound by default to keys, but they are easy to invoke. If you enter CONTROL-s or CONTROL-r and then press the ESC key, the isearch prompt changes to a search prompt. You enter a string terminated by RETURN, and Emacs searches for the first occurrence of that string. To repeat the search you must repeat the **search-forward** command.

Searching with Word Search Commands

Emacs also has word search commands. These commands are used to search for groups of words in a buffer. Words are simply strings of characters separated by a space or carriage return. When you enter words separated by single blanks, GNU Emacs matches the words in the string without regard to the kind or amount of white space (that is, blanks, tabs, and even newlines, which Freemacs can't handle) between the words in the buffer. You invoke word searches by entering the name (`ESC x word-search-forward` and `ESC x word-search-backward`) or by entering `ESC-CONTROL-w` at the isearch prompt. This works for both **isearch-forward** (CONTROL-s) and **isearch-backward** (CONTROL-r).

Now, with incremental searching, string searching, and word searching, it might seem that all the bases have been covered. Emacs has been developed in a UNIX environment. One of the features of that environment is the use of *regular expressions* (REs). Regular expressions are *grammars* that specify strings of characters for search purposes. A grammar is a tool used for specifying a set of strings. You might find regular expressions difficult to understand until you take some time to experiment, but you will see that they are very effective. There are both incremental and regular searches based on regular expressions. The incremental regular expression search makes it easier for you to learn how regular expressions work. First we'll discuss how regular expressions are written.

Searching with Regular Expressions

Using regular expressions is the most powerful way to search for text because you can specify a set of strings rather than a single string. Regular expressions are a simple kind of grammar. As stated before, a grammar is a way of specifying a set of strings. Grammars deal not with the meaning of a string but with the types and the ordering of characters in the string. Unless you have studied computer science or linguistics, you probably haven't used many types of grammars. Regular expressions are much simpler to understand than grammars found in natural or programming languages. In fact, they are the easiest kind of grammar to learn.

You probably have used wild-card specifications in which ? and * are replaced by one or more characters. Regular expressions are like wild-card expressions with more capability. With a regular wild card, you might search for all strings beginning with *a* and ending with *c*, for example. With a regular expression, you can search for all strings starting with *A*, *B*, or *Q*, containing not more than four vowels, and ending with a consonant that rests at the end of a line. Whew! By the time you understand how to express that kind of regular expression, you should understand how useful regular expressions are.

Grammars specify a set of character strings. Emacs uses an RE to determine the matching strings in an RE search. Each string that matches must be on a single line of text, but many matches are possible in a single line. If there are many matches on a line, Emacs always chooses the longest possible match. REs can't be used to match strings that extend over a line end. The RE must be expressed as a string using the same character set that will be matched, so some characters must have special meaning in the RE. These special characters are $, ^, [,], ., *, +, ?, and \. First, we'll look at how each of these is used to specify a regular expression.

In our complicated example search, an RE was required to match only strings at the end of a line. The ^ and $ characters are used to select strings starting and ending a line. If ^ is the first character of an RE, that RE matches only strings starting at the beginning of a line. The ^ character does not have a special meaning unless it occurs at the beginning of the RE or, as you shall see shortly, right after a [. For example, ^A is an RE that matches only the string "A" or "a" at the start of lines.

Similarly, if $ is the last character of an RE, that RE matches only strings ending at the end of a line. The $ character does not have a special meaning unless it occurs at the end of the RE. As an example, the RE e$ matches only the string "e" or "E" at the end of a line. Both ^ and $ are like regular expressions that match empty strings at special locations! Later you will see another RE that matches any empty string. You'll have to read on to find out why it is useful to have an RE that matches an empty string.

It's best to test these REs on an Emacs program if you can. The command **ESC x isearch-forward-regexp** prompts you to enter an RE. Emacs searches for strings that match the RE as you enter it. When you are finished, press ESC to leave the point (and cursor) where it is or CONTROL-g CONTROL-g to move the point to its previous location. If possible, try each regular expression as you read.

Complex REs are created by placing simpler REs side by side. The RE ^AE$ is the combination of our two simpler examples. This RE matches strings that start at the beginning of a line, contain the letter *a* followed by an *e* at the end of a line. It won't match lines with anything between the *a* and the *e*. Therefore, it matches lines of the form *ae, Ae, aE,* and *AE*.

From simple string searches, you have learned how to require that the strings you search for start at the beginning of a line or end at the end of a line. Now you'll learn fancier ways of specifying the characters in those strings. For example, you need to be able to specify a group of characters, any one of which could be at a certain position in the match string.

The special characters [and] create REs that select from a group of characters. The RE [cq^$a] specifies the set of characters (c, q, ^, $, and a) and matches *any single character* from that set. To match strings starting with A, B, or Q, you would start the RE with [ABQ].

Note that most special characters are not special when they are inside a character set. If ^ follows the [, however, the RE selects all the characters that *aren't* listed, meaning [^aeiou] would select the consonants, punctuation marks, and digits.

There is also one character that isn't special if it follows the [or [^. If - follows the [, it is a character in the set, but if it falls between two other characters, it indicates a *range*. Therefore, [r-z] selects all the characters between r and z. The - specifies a range unless it comes right after the opening [or [^. [-abc] matches -, a, b, or c, and [^-q] matches any character other than - or q. []abc-] selects], a, b, c, and all characters after c. The] must be the first character after the [. The character set type of RE does not work in Freemacs 1.6, but it does work in MicroEmacs using the Magic mode.

As an example of character set REs, consider the RE ^th[aeiou][^aeiou]. This RE matches strings at the beginning of lines starting with *th*, followed by a vowel, followed by a nonvowel. For example, the strings "this" and "those" are matched if they start at the beginning of the line.

Using Wild-Card Regular Expressions

You've learned how to specify a single character, how to require that the string be at the start or end of a line, and how to let Emacs select from a set of characters. You also have built REs from simpler REs by placing them side by side. Now you will learn how to specify wild-card-like behavior. The character that serves as a wild card in REs is the period (.). This special character matches any character in a string. For example, the RE . always matches the next character in the buffer (or the last character in a reverse search).

Now, how can . be the wild card if it matches only a single character? You need something that matches any group of characters, like * does on the UNIX shell command line. REs have a slightly different way of matching multiple characters. The character * is used to indicate that the single character that RE follows may be repeated zero or more times. All the simple REs you've seen match single characters except for $ and ^, which match empty strings. You can follow any single character with *.

A simple use of the wild-card character . is in the RE h.t, which matches the strings hot, hat, and hit, as well as what, that, and any other string with *h* and *t* separated by a single character. If the RE is h.*t, it matches any string containing an *h* followed by a *t*. For example, it matches hoot, heat, character, right, or match test. Remember, .* means any number of characters including zero, and each character can be any of the ASCII characters, including white-space characters.

Consider the RE .*SPACEBAR (period, asterisk, space). It matches a string containing any number of any characters, because of the .*, as long as the string ends with a space. If you try this one, you'll find it always matches the string starting at the beginning of the line and ending with the last space on a line. If there is no space on a line, there is no match for that line. If the only space is at the start of the line, this RE matches that single space. Remember that .* matches any string of characters, including strings with no characters!

The RE SPACEBAR.*SPACEBAR matches strings starting and ending with spaces, but it always matches the string starting at the first space on the line and extending to the last space on the line. If the line doesn't have two spaces, this RE can't match anything on that line.

These two REs demonstrate something very important about searching: the search always matches the longest string on a line that satisfies the RE. This matching is done before the next character in the RE is processed. The RE .*SPACEBAR SPACEBAR (a period and an asterisk followed by two spaces) illustrates this action. In Emacs, move the point to the end of a line. Now do an RE search by entering ESC x isearch-forward-regexp ENTER SPACEBAR.SPACEBAR SPACEBAR*.

When the period is entered, the point moves to the first character on the next line. This makes sense because this RE (.) matches any single character. Now enter the *. RE. The point jumps back to where it started! You just created an RE that matches the empty string, so the search backtracks to the empty string at the end of the line. The search moves to a new line only if no match can be found on the current line. If there is more than one match on a line, Emacs finds the longest possible match on that line.

Now enter the first space. The point moves forward to the last space on the next line. The RE now specifies any string that ends in a space. There aren't any of these after the point on the first line, only the empty string; thus, the search moves to the first line that has a space. It matches the longest string ending in a space on that line. Now enter the second space. If two spaces occur together on the line that had the match, the point moves to the end of the longest string that ends in two spaces. It may backtrack to do this. If not, the point will move forward to the first line that does have two adjacent spaces. If Emacs can't find two adjacent spaces, the search has failed. In either case, you can get back to where you started by entering CONTROL-g CONTROL-g.

Because *RE** matches zero or more instances of *RE*, and *RE* can be any single-character regular expression, * is very useful. Sometimes though, you want a little more control over the number of repetitions. The + and ? characters also are used after single-character regular expressions. *RE*+ is like *RERE**; it requires at least one instance of *RE*. *RE*? matches zero or one instance of *RE*. The obvious use for + is when you want at least one instance of the single-character *RE*. The ? is used when you are looking for only one instance of the single-character *RE*.

You now have enough knowledge of REs to understand the example shown in the beginning of this section. You need to find all strings starting with

A, B, or *Q,* containing not more than four vowels, and ending with a consonant that is also the last character on a line. OK, create the RE one step at a time:

1. [ABQ]—starting with *A, B,* or *Q*

2. [aeiou]?[aeiou]?[aeiou]?[aeiou]?—not more than four vowels

3. [^aeiou]$—ending with a consonant at the end of the line

So one RE that would select a string meeting those requirements is [ABQ][aeiou]?[aeiou]?[aeiou]?[aeiou]?[^aeiou]$. "Queued" is the longest string it matched when I tried it on the manuscript for this chapter, but it also matched strings like "at", "an", and "by" at the ends of lines. Try it on one of your own files to see what it matches.

Table 4.6 summarizes the special characters discussed so far.

Table 4.6. Special characters used in REs

Character	Meaning	Example Lines Matched
$	match empty string at the end of a line	A$—any line ending in A
^	match empty string at the beginning of a line	^$—a blank line
[,]	delimit a set of characters to be matched	[A-Z]—any line containing a capital letter
.	match any single character	^.$—any line containing only one character
*	repeat the previous RE any number of times	ba*t—any line containing bt, bat, baat, baaat, and so on
+	repeat the previous RE one or more times	ba+t—any line containing bat, baat, baaat, and so on
?	repeat the previous RE zero or one times	ba?t—any line containing bt or bat

Using Advanced Regular Expressions

You have seen ^, $, [,], ., *, +, and ? as special characters in REs. Another special character enables you to search for strings containing these characters. This character is \ (backslash); it is used to *quote* the other special characters. Quote means to treat the following character literally rather than as a special character. The RE \^\$\[\]\. would match the string ^$[]., and only that string. The \ character, when immediately preceding any of these special characters, nullifies that special character's behavior.

The \ character also is used with many other normal characters to create two-character sequences called \constructs. These are the \constructs: \¦, \(...\), \Digit, \`, \', \b, \B, \<, \>, \w, \W, \sCODE, and \SCODE.

The \¦ construct is an OR operator for REs. b*\¦dd means any number of b's or two d's. The \¦ construct gives you the ability to specify alternative REs. It often is used with the construct \(...\), which groups REs together. The \¦ construct applies to the largest possible REs on each side, but the \(...\) enables you to control which REs form the alternatives.

\Digit is the RE equivalent of an **insert-register** command. This construct is used with \(...\). When a substring is matched by an RE enclosed in quoted parentheses, the actual string is recorded. A \ followed by a decimal (1–9) digit *n* means match the same substring as was matched by the *n*th one of those subexpressions in the current RE. Note that \2 doesn't try to match the second RE enclosed in parentheses, but rather tries to match the string matched by that RE.

The RE \([a-z]+\)[a-z]?\1 matches only two- or three-character *palindromes* (strings that read the same forward and backward). This works by matching any string in the enclosed expression, then any single character or the null string, then the string matched by the enclosed expression. Presto, palindromes like magic!

The \ constructs are like ^ and $. They match empty strings at certain positions in the buffer. These are the positions:

beginning of the buffer	\`
end of the buffer	\'
beginning or end of a word	\b
not at beginning or end of a word	\B
beginning of a word	\<
end of a word	\>
matches any word-constituent character	\w
matches any non-word-constituent character	\W

Note that Emacs has syntax tables that determine which characters are word-constituents. There are two final backslash constructs that match single characters based on those syntax tables. They are \sCODE and \SCODE. The CODE part is a single character that represents a class of characters. The obvious example is SPACEBAR, which represents all white space characters (spaces and tabs). Another is w, which represents all the word-constituent characters. There are 13 of these classes, which are documented in the syntax section of the Emacs manual.

As an example of the use of these backslash constructs, the palindrome recognizer can be changed to accept only palindromes that are words. The RE is now `\<\([a-z]+\)[a-z]?\1\>`. The `\<` and `\>` restrict the match strings to words.

Here is another example of an RE similar to one in the GNU Emacs manual:

```
[.?!][]\"')]*\\($\\|\    \)
```

This RE illustrates more uses for the features covered earlier. It starts with a character set that matches ., ?, or !. (Remember that special characters are not special inside a character set.) Then this RE has a character set that matches closed square braces, quotes, or parentheses. The second RE may be repeated zero or more times. The RE ends with an alternative in quoted parentheses, an end of a line, or a tab character.

Replace Functions

The replace functions are as diverse and flexible as the search functions. Table 4.7 lists the commands available with GNU Emacs.

Table 4.7. The Replace Functions of GNU Emacs

Command Name	Key Binding
query-replace	ESC %
query-replace-regexp	
replace-regexp	
replace-string	

There are two kinds of searches, regular expressions and string searches. There are also two kinds of replacement commands, query replacement and simple replacement. All of these commands operate on the currently selected buffer.

The **replace-string** command is the simplest one. If you enter ESC x `replace-string` and press ENTER, you are prompted for the string to replace. After you enter that string, you are prompted for the string to replace it with. After you enter the second string, all instances of the first string that come after the point in the current buffer are replaced with the second string. If you want to replace the string throughout the buffer, you must move the point to the beginning of the buffer first.

The point moves through the buffer as the replacements are done and stops at the end of the last string replaced. Your starting location is saved on the mark ring if you want to return there. The **set-mark** command, with a numeric argument (CONTROL-u CONTROL-@), returns you to that spot.

There are several possible pitfalls in a global **replace-string** operation, but Emacs can protect you from the most common one. When you decide to replace every instance of "red" with "blue" you probably don't want to change "considered" to "consideblue" and "redisplay" to "blueisplay"! That is what **replace-string** will do, unless you give it a numeric argument. Then it restricts replacement to whole words.

Because Emacs searches usually are done without regard to case (the variable *case-fold-search* is not equal to nil), Emacs can use the case of your entered strings to control the replacement case. Emacs is one clever editor! This technique avoids the potential problem of replacing uppercase words with lowercase words. If you use lowercase for both the search and the replacement strings, Emacs preserves the case (lower, upper, or capitalized) when it does the replacements. If you use uppercase letters in the replacement string, they will always be uppercase in the replacement string. If you use uppercase letters in the search string, then no case conversions are done on the replacement string.

You also can control the case by setting the variable *case-replace* to nil; then the replacement string always is inserted as you entered it. If a case-sensitive search is enabled, setting *case-fold-search* to nil causes searches and replacements to be done without changing case.

Replacing with Regular Expressions

Regular expression replacements are also possible. In this case, the string that is replaced is one that satisfies the RE given as the first argument. It is also possible to select and replace only the part of the match string specified by one of the parenthesized REs within the search RE. This feature uses the \Digit selection of strings saved as they are matched by REs surrounded by \(and \).

In the RE search, the strings matched by REs surrounded by \(and \) can be reused for exact matches later in the RE. This enables you to match more complex patterns. In RE replacement, these same substrings can be replaced instead of the entire string matched by the RE. This gives you the power to select substrings for replacement based on the context in which the substring appears. You can mix constant strings and parts, or all, of the matched string to form the replacement string.

Replacement of all strings (or substrings) matching a particular string or RE usually is not what you want to do. Even when Emacs gives you the power to specify the context in which a string should appear, it is better to look at the context yourself and decide whether to do the replacement. Besides, it is much easier to look at the context than it is to figure out an RE that would properly specify it!

Replacing with Query Commands

The commands **query-replace** (ESC %) and **query-replace-regexp** are used when you want to view the text before it is replaced. As you have seen, the **replace-string** and **replace-regexp** commands give you much of the control. By using **query-replace** and **query-replace-regexp**, you are increasing the degree of control you have over replacement. You don't lose any of the features of the nonquery replace commands; query simply is added on. A numeric argument (CONTROL-u before the command) still restricts the search to words. The case of the search string and replace string still can be used to control case.

Query brings its own set of commands that enable you to specify exactly when you want to do the replacement. For each match of the string or RE, Emacs displays the point at the match string and prompts you to enter a single character. The possible responses to this query are shown in Table 4.8.

Table 4.8. Responses to the Query Options

Response	Meaning
C-h	Display the options you have, then query again.
SPACEBAR	Do the current replacement, just like replace would. Then go on to the next query.
DEL	Skip the current replacement.
.	Do the current replacement, just like replace would, then exit the query replace.

Response	Meaning
ESC	Exit the query replace without doing the current replacement.
!	Do all remaining replacements without querying.
^	Oops—go back to the last replacement location. If you decide you want to correct it, you can enter a recursive edit (CONTROL-r).
C-r	Enter a new level of editing. This is like creating a new edit session on the same buffer. It enables you to edit it in any way you like and then return to the query replace by exit-recursive-edit (ESC CONTROL-c).
C-w	Like CONTROL-r, but delete the match string before entering recursive edit.
,	Do the current replacement, display the result, and wait for further input. That further input can be anything that would be input at the query, and the DELETE key or SPACEBAR moves you to the next replacement. This is another place to go into a recursive edit, or undo the change using undo (CONTROL-x-u). If you do do undo (that does sound like a silly thing to do), it exits query-replace and you'll need to do CONTROL-s-ESC (repeat-complex-command) to restart it.

Selecting Lines

In addition to the use of regular expressions in search and replace commands, GNU Emacs (but not Freemacs or MicroEmacs) has some line-oriented commands that use regular expressions to select lines. Because a regular expression is matched by a set of strings and those strings can occur only within a line of text, a regular expression can be used to select lines from within a buffer.

For example, the RE ^$ selects all the blank lines. Perhaps you want all the lines that start with three spaces; try ^SPACEBAR SPACEBAR SPACEBAR (^ followed by three spaces). Maybe you would like all lines containing arithmetic expressions; try [0-9]+[ ]?[-+*/][ ]?[0-9]+ for simple integer expressions. As you can see, it is easy to specify a set of lines by requiring that each contains a string that matches a certain regular expression.

The following GNU Emacs commands use lines selected by regular expressions:

occur or **list-matching-lines**

count-matches

delete-matching-lines

delete-non-matching-lines

None of these commands is bound to a key by default in GNU Emacs, so all the commands normally are executed by using the **execute-command** command (ESC x). The **list-matching-lines** command also is known as **occur**. You can use either name for this command. The **list-matching-lines** or **occur** command prompts you for an RE and then creates a new buffer called *occur*, which contains copies of all the lines selected by that RE. It also gives you a count of how many lines matched. The command **delete-matching-lines** will get rid of all the lines that match an RE. The command **delete-non-matching-lines** will get rid of all the lines that don't match an RE.

The flexibility of these commands comes from the use of regular expressions to select the lines. If you take the time to learn how to use regular expressions, you will learn that they are unique to Emacs and are very helpful. If you don't spend the time now to learn how to create and use REs, you will spend much more time in the future doing things manually that Emacs could have done for you.

The Next Step

In the next chapter, we move from beginning editing to procedures involving whole files, buffers, and windows. You'll learn how to save files and edit text rectangles. You'll also learn about modes (major and minor) and many other goodies. And you'll learn how Emacs protects us with automatic backups. So to paraphrase the classic song, let the good lines scroll!

Chapter 5

Intermediate Editing

A lthough you may understand some of the Emacs text editing processes from the previous chapters, you have much more to learn. As the old Vaudeville announcers used to say, "You ain't seen nothin' yet!"

This chapter introduces the various *modes* of Emacs. It shows you how to control the display and take advantage of the freedom you now have to manipulate buffers and files (the concept that makes Emacs so undeniably superior to all other philosophies of word processing). It also covers auto saving and the joy of using multiple windows.

In this book we give you a lot of examples and keystrokes. Most of these work perfectly in GNU Emacs. When other Emacs— such as MicroEmacs, Freemacs, Epsilon, and UniPress—differ significantly, we give you the alternate keystrokes.

Now, it's Emacs a la mode!

Modes

This statement sounds contradictory: Emacs is a *modeless* editor with a large number of *modes*. Emacs is modeless because unlike *vi*, which is the default major mode for text processing applications including nroff and TeX, it doesn't have a separate command mode. When using vi, you have to go to a special mode to enter commands and then use simple single-letter commands. To return to the text, you enter another command.

Emacs has two kinds of modes: *major modes* and *minor modes*. A major mode is a set of options that configure Emacs to edit a particular type of text. This text can be program code, a letter to Aunt Molly, a company report, or any other kind of text. Hence, there are specific modes for C, Ada, FORTRAN, Text, and dozens of others. A minor mode modifies a major mode. For example, auto fill mode modifies Text mode so the lines of text wrap automatically and do not run off the screen.

Emacs commands are part of the normal input to the editor. Emacs simply recognizes certain sequences, or keys, as special and acts on them in special ways. The remaining keys are acted on simply by inserting the characters into the buffer. These are called *self-inserting keys*. The fact that most keys run the **self-insert** command is basic to the way a modeless editor works.

Although Emacs doesn't have a command mode, it does have other modes. It even has major modes and minor modes. Emacs' major modes are overall settings of the editor that determine the special sequences and how the editor acts on them. In a sense, each Emacs mode is a different editor. Some of these modes are highly specialized, like the *Info* mode or the *Dired* mode. The Info mode is used to read info files that are not text files. The Dired mode is used to handle and edit directories, which are different from text files. Other kinds of modes, like *C* mode and *Text* mode, are simply different extensions of the same basic mode.

```
      Directory of  /usr/menu
   drwxr-x---    2      144 Aug  4 12:14 ./
   drwxr-xr-x   43      688 May 24 10:29 ../
   -rw-r--r--    1      603 Mar 22  1990 menu1
   -rwxr-----    1      512 May  8 10:07 .profile*
   -rw-r--r--    1        0 Nov 27  1990 #%*scratch*#
   -rw-r--r--    1     3819 May 16 15:18 wallchart
   -rw-r--r--    1    13691 May 19 21:39 epfun
   -rw-r--r--    1        0 May 19 20:28 efun
   -rw-r--r--    1     2025 Aug  4 12:14 temp




   Epsilon 5.03 [Dired] /usr/menu:   15%
```

Fig. 5.1. In Epsilon's Dired mode, you can visit files, delete files, view files, and perform other related operations without having to exit your editor.

Modes are like having a lot of very specialized text editors all in one package. The Dired mode (shown in Figure 5.1 in Epsilon), for example, lets you manipulate the current file directory from within Emacs.

Using Major Modes

Emacs has three groups of major modes. There are major modes for different programming languages, sometimes more than one per language. There are also major modes for text processing applications including nroff and TeX. Finally, there are highly specialized modes that edit special file structures.

The basic Emacs mode, *Fundamental mode*, is designed to edit the many different kinds of text files. C mode and Text mode are specialized for editing a particular kind of file. C programs do not have the same structure that a letter to your mother has. No, Emacs doesn't have a Letter To Your Mother mode, but I would be surprised if someone hasn't developed one of his or her own!

Text mode edits sentences, pages, paragraphs, and similar structures. C mode edits blocks and indentations in the C language. Each major mode has its own commands in addition to or in place of the Fundamental mode commands. Each major mode has its own key bindings, but usually only a few keys are rebound.

Using Minor Modes

Minor modes act as modifications to major modes. They change Emacs in some useful way without changing the purpose of the major mode. Examples of minor modes are: *auto save mode*, *auto fill mode*, and *overwrite mode*. The mode line on a window always shows a major mode, and it may show one or more minor modes. In writing this chapter, we are using the major mode text mode and the minor mode auto fill mode. You could go into overwrite mode while still keeping auto fill mode, and you also could add auto-save mode. The only problem is that the mode line gets cluttered!

Major and minor modes can be selected by executing a command consisting of the mode's name with the spaces replaced by a hyphen (-). To switch a buffer to C mode, go to a window in that buffer and enter `ESC-x-c-mode`. To switch the buffer back to Text mode, enter `ESC-x-text-mode`. To add auto fill mode, type `ESC-x-auto-fill-mode`. To delete a minor mode, enter the same mode command again. The minor mode commands *toggle* the modes on if they are off and off if they are on. Major modes can be changed only by replacing them with other major modes.

Emacs automatically chooses the right major mode for a file, based on the last part of the file name. For example, files ending in .c are edited in C mode. There also is more information on modes in Chapter 8, Advanced Topics.

The Display

Your screen is like a movable window. Regardless of whether it is part of a terminal communicating with a large computer somewhere, or just attached to your desktop personal computer, it enables you to look into documents or other types of files such as program sources. You actually are looking at a buffer, an exact copy of the file being edited. More about files later in this chapter.

In Chapter 3, you learned the concept of the point, the place where the cursor is located on the screen, and where text insertion and deletion takes place. You also saw the many ways of moving the point or cursor so that you can edit text at any place on the screen. But what if the point is moved to a spot in the buffer that currently is not being shown on the screen?

If the point goes off the screen in any of the four cardinal directions—up, down, left, or right—Emacs moves the window looking into the buffer. This process is called *scrolling*. Just as you would unroll one end of a paper scroll and the other end would roll up, a new area is displayed when you scroll.

Emacs can have more than one window on the screen. Figure 5.2 shows a GNU screen, divided vertically to view two different buffers. The dollar signs ($) at the edge of each buffer indicate that the lines are longer than shown. You can use horizontal scrolling to see the rest of the lines in the current buffer. Typing ESC x o switches you to the other window.

Scrolling is necessary because your screen is not large enough to display most documents. Most computer terminals or PCs have a window 80 characters wide by 23 lines high. Emacs uses two more lines on the bottom of the screen—the echo area (bottommost line) and the mode line. These lines are not available to display editable text. More advanced displays, such as EGA or VGA, increase this window size to more than 40 lines of text up to 132 characters wide. Even so, you cannot view most files of any size at a single glance.

Scrolling

As you enter text and fill the screen, Emacs automatically scrolls so that you always can see what you're typing. Scrolling is a necessary fact of editing. There are several methods for moving around in your text, program sources, or lists. The text area on your screen can be further divided into windows (covered later in this chapter). You can look at several buffers on the screen at once. The scrolling of each window is independent of the others, and any command given affects only the window that the point is currently in. Table 5.1 lists some of the most useful commands affecting the display.

```
     Emacs really has three groups of $!what he or she thinks you need, not wha$
modes for different programming langua$!Programmers are very nice folk, but the$
language. There are major modes for te$!processing, other than program code. Th$
including 'nroff' and 'TeX.' And there$!have are often missing or so convoluted$
specialized modes that edit very speci$!Emacs, being an open system, is far mor$
very flexible editor!                  !you to create new features at will, whe$
     The basic Emacs mode, Fundamental$!programs you are locked into whatever w$
files, but there are many different ki$!    With an Emacs-style editor, you ha$
Text mode are specialization that make$!formatters, both text and otherwise. Th$
particular kind of file. 'C' programs $!don't [[I]have[I]] to use the formatter t$
that a letter to your mother has. No, $!true of most word processing programs s$
Your Mother mode but I would be surpri$!limitation of conventional word process$
one of their own!                      !several that cannot be overemphasized w$
     Text mode knows about sentences a$!Emacs-style editors.
sort of thing. C mode knows about bloc$!    We will cover some of your text fo$
language. Each major mode has its own $!chapter. These include integral Unix ut$
of the Fundamental mode commands. Each$!'troff,' enhancements like 'ditroff,' a$
bindings, but usually only a few keys $!the public domain but very powerful T[S$
                                       !Emacs, as we will see below, provides [$
[2] Minor Modes                        !set up your text files to be formatted $
                                       !Major text modes included in the GNU ba$
     Minor modes act as modifications $!Nroff, Outline, and T[S]E[S]X. UniPress$
in some useful way, but not changing t$!course, in the open nature of Emacs, th$
--**-Emacs: e.5          3:01pm  --**-Emacs: e.6            3:01pm 2
```

Fig. 5.2. A screen in GNU showing two different buffers.

Table 5.1. Commands Affecting the Display

Command Name	Key Binding	Meaning
recenter	C-l	Clears the screen and redisplays everything while scrolling the current window so that the current point is centered within it.
	arg C-l	With a numeric argument in front of the clear screen command, redisplays the screen with the point on that line rather than the

continues

Table 5.1. Continued

Command Name	Key Binding	Meaning
		center line. Use the META key to enter the argument. For example, ESC 2 C-l redraws the screen and scrolls it so that the point is on line 2 of the current window.
scroll-up	C-v	Scrolls forward through the buffer (actually "down" through the buffer but called scroll-up in GNU Emacs because the text moves up the screen).
scroll-down	ESC-v	(or M-v, M being the META key) Scrolls back or "up" through the text. Command name is scroll-down because text moves down the screen.
scroll-left	C-x <	Scrolls the text in the current window left. You have to press the SHIFT key on most terminals to get the < (less than) character. The sequence of keys would be to press the CONTROL and x keys at the same time, let up, then press the SHIFT and < keys simultaneously. This moves your window into the text to the right.
scroll-right	C-x >	Scrolls the text in the current window to the right, which moves your window into the text to the left.
set-selective-display	C-x $	Makes lines that are deeply indented invisible. Handy when working on outlines and various types of program source code.
beginning-of-buffer	ESC <	The ultimate scroll command, takes you to the top of the current buffer.
end-of-buffer	ESC >	Zips you to the bottom of the current buffer, even if it's thousands of lines long.

You find these scrolling functions in every version of Emacs, although the *key bindings* might be slightly different. For example, Epsilon uses the curly brackets ({ and }) rather than the greater-than and less-than characters (> and <). Other key bindings are changed also, so that typing ESC { scrolls left and ESC } scrolls right (rather than GNU's CONTROL-x < and CONTROL-x >). The other scrolling commands are the same. Epsilon, however, is friendlier to the personal computer than GNU Emacs is; the ALT key works as the META key in the default setting, but ESC works also.

Scrolling Horizontally

Moving up and down in a buffer or file is an easy concept for you to grasp, but *horizontal scrolling*, side-to-side movement, is a more difficult concept to grasp. The window into a particular buffer, as you've already seen, is 80 characters wide by 23 lines high on most screens. The height is smaller if you've divided the screen into one or more windows, but width usually remains constant because you are splitting the screen horizontally (although GNU Emacs gives you the option of vertical splitting also). Even on more sophisticated displays, the standard line width is seldom more than 132 characters.

A width of 80 characters is usually sufficient for standard documents because the common line width for printed documents is 65 characters at 10 pitch or 12 points (printer's terms for 10 characters per inch horizontally). Thus, setting your margins at 65 characters wide means the line is 6½ inches long, which leaves 1 inch apiece for the left and right margins on an 8½- by 11-inch piece of typing paper. All of this is logical when you consider that word processors were at first an electronic mimicry of typewriters.

A single line of program code easily can exceed 80 or even 132 characters in width. Long lists of data in several columns also can be wider than conventional displays. This problem is solved by enabling you to scroll left or right. Emacs also informs you when you need to perform horizontal scrolling, and in which direction.

The default setting of Emacs is *continue* lines. Lines wider than your display are broken, and the overrun is continued on the next line from left to right, as many times as needed. Emacs uses a backspace character (\) to show that a line has been broken. Normally, this is acceptable, but in the case of a list of columns or structured program source code, the format is destroyed and you end up with a jumbled, confusing screen.

In GNU Emacs you can switch from continuing to *truncating* lines on the display by setting the *truncate-lines* variable. This is accomplished by typing ESC x set-variable. When Emacs responds with "set variable" in the echo area, type truncate-lines. You then are asked for a value. Enter any number greater than zero. The backslashes (\) at the end of broken lines change to dollar signs ($), and you no longer see the part of the line past the break. In other words, the part of the file you can see (80 characters wide on a standard display) is formatted correctly. (To restore line continuation, set the *truncate-lines* variable to nil by typing nil, not 0).

With the line truncation feature now on, type the **scroll-left** command (CONTROL-x <), and the text on the screen is scrolled horizontally to the left one screen width, usually 80 characters (or 132 if that's what your monitor shows). This moves the window showing the document, the buffer, to the right. There are now dollar signs at the beginning of all lines, indicating that the left margin is not in view. Any lines that are still wider than this 80-character sliding window also have a dollar sign on the end, indicating that you need to type CONTROL-x < again to slide farther to the right to view these lines.

Returning toward the left margin, you type CONTROL-x >. This scrolls text horizontally to the right, effectively moving your window one screen's width to the left.

You can control the amount of horizontal scroll by giving the **scroll-left** or **scroll-right** commands a numeric argument. Typing ESC-4 CONTROL-x < moves the left edge of your screen to the right four characters. With the numeric argument, you have more precise control over the scrolling process.

Using Selective Display

Many features in Emacs soon will become old friends of yours because of their usefulness. One of these features is the **selective display**—*arg* CONTROL-x $ or **set-selective-display** in GNU Emacs, where *arg* is a number representing the indent of lines you would like to hide. Selective display means that you can choose which lines are shown and which ones are hidden. This is achieved by using line indentation. For example, typing the numeric argument ESC 5 (be sure to include the ESC key) will hide all lines having an indentation of five spaces or more.

Selective display is handy for outlines and program listings. Imagine an outline with the major headings against the left margin, the first subheadings indented 5 characters, and the next level headings indented 10 spaces. If you typed ESC 10 CONTROL-x $, all the lowest-level subheadings would be hidden, and the outline would collapse, showing the major headings and one level of subheadings. Type ESC 5 C-x $, and only the major headings are shown. This enables you to copy an outline or a program source easily. You first remove the clutter and copy the major points; then, by entering CONTROL-x $ without a numerical argument, the outline is restored to full detail.

Figure 5.3 shows a full outline in GNU Emacs, and Figure 5.4 shows the same outline collapsed one level. The outline also can be collapsed one more level to show just the major headings. This facility is very useful in reducing the complexity of outlines so that you can better grasp the big picture.

```
                        How to Pick Apples
  Find the Apples

          Apples Grow on Trees

          Trees are found Outside

                  Trees Are Tall and Green

                  Apple Trees have Apples on Them

  Equipment Needed

      A Ladder to Reach the Apples

              Choose a Ladder Tall Enough to Reach the Apples

              Place the Ladder Vertically, not Horizonally, for
              Greater Height

      A Bag to Put Picked Apples Into

-----Emacs: apple.pic          1:51pm 1.09    (Text Fill)----All--------------
```

Fig. 5.3. A full outline in GNU Emacs.

```
                        How to Pick Apples
  Find the Apples

          Apples Grow on Trees

          Trees are found Outside
  ...
  ...

  Equipment Needed

          A Ladder to Reach the Apples
  ...
  ...

          A Bag to Put Picked Apples Into




-----Emacs: apple.pic          1:53pm 1.09    (Text Fill)----All--------------
```

Fig. 5.4. The same outline, collapsed.

When lines are hidden, three periods mark their previous location. Most text editing commands still work on the hidden text, so exercise some caution. If you do a global search and change, for instance, words on the hidden line are changed also.

Files

Files are saved and edited in a *two-tier* system. Instead of editing the actual file, you are working on a copy of it stored in an Emacs buffer, the basic editing unit. You can have almost any number of buffers going at once—hundreds or even thousands of files (try that in WordPerfect or vi).

The buffer on the screen is not necessarily identical to the file on your floppy or hard disk, even though it has the same name. If an asterisk (*) appears after the file name on the mode line, for example, the file in the buffer has been changed but not saved to disk. When *reverting* (replacing the buffer contents with the contents of the file) or *saving* (replacing the file contents with the contents of the buffer), the file and the buffer must correspond exactly, which means there is no asterisk on the mode line.

Reverting to the file means that any editing changes you have made since last saving are lost. Use this option only when the edited text has been damaged enough that starting over is easier than correcting it. The save option also works in the other direction, saving the text on the screen to a separate disk file. This process enables you to keep both the original and the edited version. The **write-file** command (CONTROL-x CONTROL-w) enables you to write the current buffer to another file (you are asked for the new file's name in the echo area). This command exists in GNU Emacs, MicroEmacs, Epsilon, Freemacs, and UniPress Emacs, among others.

Thus, the name of the file that appears on the mode line actually refers to two separate files. The first file is a regular UNIX (or other operating system) file that may or may not exist. If you create and type in a document—even though you gave it a file name when creating the buffer—it is not recorded on the disk until the first time you save it (CONTROL-x CONTROL-s). The other file (of the same name) is the one that exists within Emacs' word processing environment; that is, in a buffer you see on the screen. To revert to a previously saved file, you type ESC x revert in GNU Emacs, ESC x revert-file in UniPress Emacs, or the **find-alternate-file** command (CONTROL-x CONTROL-v) in GNU, Freemacs, or Epsilon. The **find-alternate-file** command, used when visiting files, gives you the option of replacing the buffer with the file's contents.

This barrage of commands might seem a bit confusing at first, but it's not. One of Emacs' strengths is its ability to manipulate files via buffers. A buffer, as defined in the dictionary, is a cushion. Because you can operate on only a copy of the file, rather than the file itself, you are cushioned from losing files or making mistakes (whether your own mistakes or those caused by a computer glitch). Emacs also cushions you with its multiple levels of undo and automatic saving to a "save" file. No other type of word processing program has adopted this protective philosophy of the Emacs family of editors.

Using File Names and Paths

The manipulation of files, of course, is basic to any type of text editing program. In Emacs, you are able to copy, rename, delete, and append new material to files. You also can see and do various operations to file directories, all within Emacs.

If you save a buffer back into a file, Emacs usually stores the name and path of the file, so you just have to type CONTROL-x CONTROL-s to save. If you've typed text into a scratch buffer (a buffer not associated with a file), you have to supply a file name. The same is true of reverting, or replacing the buffer's contents with the associated file.

Otherwise, in performing file-related operations, you are asked to supply the file's name or at least part of the name. GNU Emacs, for example, has a *completion* feature. If you can remember only part of a command, type those first few characters and hit the TAB key. A list of the possible completions is displayed in a window that pops up on the screen. The same display is shown with file names. If you can't remember the file's name but you know it begins with the letter *a*, type ESC x find-file. When you are asked for the file name, type a TAB (the letter *a* followed by the TAB key). A completion list of all files in the current directory beginning with the letter *a* should be shown. If there is only one file, it is loaded onto the buffer you now see on the screen.

When a file is associated with a buffer, its name is the *default* file name of that buffer, and the current directory becomes the default directory for the buffer (path). This can be handy, indeed. You can have one hundred files open, and every one of those files has a default directory. The name of that directory in GNU Emacs is recorded in a variable called *default-directory*. If a hundred buffers are open, there will be a hundred *default-directory* variables, one for each buffer.

If you open a new buffer and do not specify a path name of an existing file, Emacs first looks in the current directory (the one in the *default-directory* variable). If the file is not found in the current directory, Emacs creates the file the first time you save the buffer. Typing a slash (/) when specifying a new buffer name overrides this feature. You then are expected to provide the full path name, even for a file in the current directory.

Changing the directory does not change the default-directory. The old path remains attached to that buffer, and any new buffers opened from it use the old directory as the current directory. This makes organization during editing sessions a breeze.

For example, say you have created a directory for correspondence. After you have opened one letter from any directory you want, you can open another letter file in any directory in the program by typing the path name of the old letter buffer (opening the file sets the *default-directory* variable to that directory's path). When you get the hang of it, you always will have several buffers open at once. It's the only efficient way to work.

The **dired** (directory edit) command lists all the files in the directory associated with the current buffer (this is true in GNU, Freemacs, Epsilon, and UniPress, but not in MicroEmacs). Figure 5.5 shows the result of using the **dired** command in GNU Emacs. The list appears in a temporary buffer window. To open a file, move the cursor to the file name and press the f key (for **Find-File**) in GNU, Freemacs, and Epsilon. In UniPress, hit the RETURN key instead.

```
-rw-r--r--   1 ralph     root        8079 May 19 12:16 emacs.ol
-rw-r--r--   1 ralph     root       17647 May 25 01:41 emacs.pro
-rw-r--r--   1 ralph     group      17325 Mar 17 20:51 emacs.pub
-rw-r--r--   1 ralph     root       30326 Jan 26  1989 emacs.tut
-rw-r--r--   1 ralph     root      245061 Mar 19  1989 emacs.txt
-rw-r--r--   1 ralph     root      116996 Mar 17 20:52 emacs2
-rw-r--r--   1 ralph     root       16511 Apr 25  1990 emacs2.pro
-rw-r--r--   1 ralph     root      108875 Mar 17 20:52 emacs3
-rw-r--r--   1 ralph     root       16361 May 31  1990 emacs3.pro
-rw-r--r--   1 ralph     root      105255 Mar 17 21:31 emacs4
-rw-r--r--   1 ralph     root        1743 Jun  8 15:09 emacsak.new
-rw-r--r--   1 ralph     root       21245 May 19 12:16 emacsbk.1
-rw-r--r--   1 ralph     root      124228 May 24 12:21 emacsbk.10
-rw-r--r--   1 ralph     root        6887 May 24 13:14 emacsbk.11
-rw-r--r--   1 ralph     root       16293 May 24 11:39 emacsbk.12
-rw-r--r--   1 ralph     root       18429 May 24 11:39 emacsbk.13
-rw-r--r--   1 ralph     root       28390 May 24 12:19 emacsbk.14
-rw-r--r--   1 ralph     root       23348 May 19 12:16 emacsbk.2
-rw-r--r--   1 ralph     root       25200 May 19 12:16 emacsbk.3
-rw-r--r--   1 ralph     root       67291 May 19 12:16 emacsbk.4
-rw-r--r--   1 ralph     root       68649 May 19 12:16 emacsbk.5
-rw-r--r--   1 ralph     root       57331 May 19 12:16 emacsbk.6
-rw-r--r--   1 ralph     root       51519 May 19 12:16 emacsbk.7
--%%-Dired: emacs              2:51pm 2.07   (Dired)----37%--------------------
```

Fig. 5.5. A listing of the current file directory using the dired command in GNU Emacs.

In GNU and UniPress, you always can determine the current directory by typing ESC x pwd. The full path appears at the bottom of the screen in the echo area. You can change the default directory for any buffer by typing ESC cd, then editing the path that appears in the echo area. Hit RETURN when you are finished. In Epsilon, use the F7 function key to change the default directory.

Visiting Files

Visiting files means copying them into a buffer where you can edit them. One way to open an existing file (especially if you don't know the name) is by using **dired**, as you saw. Emacs provides several faster ways to open files, however. The basic commands to visit files (in almost every Emacs version) are shown in Table 5.2.

Table 5.2. Commands for Visiting Files

Command	*Key Binding*	*Meaning*
find-file	C-x C-f	Visit a file.
find-alternate-file	C-x C-v	Visit an alternate file.
find-file-other-window	C-x 4 C-f	In GNU this lets you open a buffer in another window while retaining the current one on the screen also.

The name of the buffer always appears on the mode line so you'll always know which buffer you're editing. Again, if you see an asterisk (*) on the mode line, the buffer has been changed since it was last saved to a file. This unsaved buffer is called, in Emacs parlance, a *modified* buffer.

The **find-file** command is the one you will use most often. Typing CONTROL-x CONTROL-f either opens a file in the current directory or creates a new one if none by that name exists. At any time in the opening or creation process, you can abort the procedure by typing the **keyboard-quit** command (CONTROL-g). The panic stop, as it is called, aborts almost every operation in Emacs.

Should you incorrectly type the name of a file that you want to open, use the **find-alternate file** command (CONTROL-x CONTROL-v). This command enables you to retype the file's name (correctly this time, eh?) and copy it into the current buffer without opening a new one. The buffer's name automatically is corrected also.

The **find-alternate-file** command also has another use. If you have made changes to the buffer that you want to discard—such as a global search and change that went awry—you also can use this function to revert to the previous version of the file on disk. Note that this process works only if an asterisk is still on the mode line, meaning the file has not been saved. When you do this and Emacs asks whether you want to save the buffer, answer no; otherwise, the whole exercise is for naught. You also can use **find-alternate-file** to open another file and look at it or use it in some way while you are in the current file.

As an aside, if the changes to the buffer that you want to get rid of are not too catastrophic, you can type CONTROL-x u (**undo** command) instead of reverting. This "undoes" your last change. Typing the command again undoes the change before that, and so on. As ever, Emacs offers you a number of ways out of any problem. We said it before (and we'll say it again): Emacs *protects* you.

Listing Files

UNIX divides disks up into *directories* for easy tracking of files. When you list files, you normally are listing the ones in the current directory. Being able to get such a list of files makes choosing the files far easier than remembering the names on your own.

Viewing a directory listing is simple in most versions of Emacs. When you type CONTROL-x CONTROL-f, you are presented with some kind of "Find file:" prompt in the echo area. Depending on the flavor of Emacs, the name of the current directory might be listed.

Hitting RETURN usually prompts the directory for viewing so that you can pick a file name to visit. In many Emacs, the RETURN key prompts the dired (directory edit) buffer to the screen, along with a number of file-handling options. Earlier versions of GNU Emacs behave a little differently. Instead of hitting the RETURN key after CONTROL-x CONTROL-f, hit the SPACE key once and you'll see a "completion" list consisting of all the files you can open in the current directory. The latest GNU Emacs, version 18.57, now prompts dired if you hit the RETURN key.

At the "Find file:" prompt, you usually can edit the path and thus change to a new directory. Then you can hit the RETURN or SPACE keys (depending on which Emacs you are using) and view the new directory's listing.

GNU Emacs also offers two more sophisticated ways of looking at a directory. The **list-directory** command (CONTROL-x CONTROL-d) yields a "brief" listing of files, similar to the UNIX "ls" command. Entering CONTROL-u CONTROL-x CONTROL-d is equivalent to the "ls -l" command. These commands yield a verbose listing, showing not just the name of the files but also the sizes, dates, and owners. You also can specify new directories or use wild cards with both of these commands, such as `CONTROL-u CONTROL-x CONTROL-d /usr/ralph/*.txt`, which would show all files ending with the .txt extension in the directory /usr/ralph.

Using Dired

In Emacs, there is a dired mode, command, and buffer. The Dired, or Directory Edit, mode enables you to manipulate the files in a directory. Typing `ESC x dired` in GNU, Epsilon, or UniPress produces a special buffer containing a list of the files in the current directory. You can find dired in Freemacs by typing `CONTROL-x CONTROL-f` and hitting the RETURN key.

When the dired buffer is in a window on the screen, you can use the regular Emacs point movement commands to navigate it. Several special dired commands (usable only in a dired buffer) enable you to manipulate files. The dired commands in different versions of Emacs vary slightly, but generally follow GNU Emacs' lead, as shown in Table 5.3.

Table 5.3. Commands Used in Dired (Directory Edit) Mode

Command	Meaning
d	Delete. Mark a file for deletion.
u	Undelete a file; that is, remove the deletion mark, which is a *D* in the leftmost margin.
x	Execute marks, such as delete all files selected for deletion.
f	Find a file by visiting it and loading the contents into a buffer for editing.
o	Other window. Find a file and load it into a buffer but make a window for it and leave the present buffer on the screen also.
r	Rename a file.
c	Copy a file.
v	View a file. Enables you to visit it and easily move around, but you cannot edit it.

GNU Emacs offers a few additional features in dired. Additional commands unique to GNU's dired are shown in Table 5.4.

Table 5.4. GNU Emacs Commands Used in Dired Mode

Command	Meaning
#	The pound sign (#) key marks all auto-save files for deletion.
~	The tilde (~) marks all backup files for deletion.
.	The period (.) marks some of the numbered backup files for deletion (just the ones in the middle—this is fully explained in the Backup section later in this chapter).

Although all the files in these categories are globally marked, you can *unmark* any file by moving to that file and typing the letter *u* (for undelete).

Saving Files

Occasionally during the process of editing buffers and certainly when you are finished, you need to *save* the file. Saving is the process of replacing the file's present contents (if any) with the contents of the buffer. The buffer remains intact until you kill it.

Saving is important, and Emacs makes it easy for you to save. Table 5.5 lists the commands most often used in saving files.

Table 5.5. Commands Used for Saving Files

Command	Key Binding	Meaning
save-buffer	C-x C-s	Save the current buffer into the file associated with it.
save-some-buffers	C-x s	Save all unsaved buffers, whether one or one thousand.
not-modified	ESC ~	Ignore changes (remove the asterisk from the mode line—clear the modification flag). (Note: This command does not actually save the file.)

Command	Key Binding	Meaning
write-file	C-x C-w	Save the current buffer into a new file and change the buffer's name (associate it with the new file).

Leaving Emacs closes all buffers. If you still have modified buffers, you are asked whether you want to exit. Your answer, most of the time, should be no, because you want to make sure that your work is saved to the disk. If you have a grasp of how many buffers you have open and what's going on in all of them, it is probably a good habit to use the **save-some-buffers** (CONTROL-x s) command rather than the **save-buffer** (CONTROL-x CONTROL-s) command. If you have several files open and you know you don't want to indiscriminately save all buffers, use the latter command. Just make sure you have examined every unmodified buffer before leaving Emacs and saved those you wanted saved.

If you do not want to save a buffer, you can either kill it (use CONTROL-x k) or mark it as unmodified (ESC ~). The latter command is preferred if you want to keep the buffer around to copy information from.

One useful technique in word processing is the use of *templates*. A template is simply a guide to follow. In the next chapter you are going to see how to format documents for printing. If you had to print many similar letters, for example, it would be silly to retype the formatting commands every time you write a letter. With Emacs, you can visit the proper letter template (that is, open it into a buffer). You might want to have templates for business letters, letters to friends, thank-you notes, various holiday greetings, and so forth. When the template file is in a buffer, use CONTROL-x w to write it to another buffer (so the template remains unchanged), and simply type your letter and print it. This command saves you lots of time.

Emacs, of course, is most often used on multiuser systems such as those employing the UNIX operating systems. That means if you are editing a file common to several other users, there could be a conflict—someone else could have made a change to the file and saved it since you visited the file and loaded it into a buffer. Emacs (you guessed it) protects you here also. It checks the date and time of the file before saving your buffer to the file. If the date and time when you last saved the file does not match the date and time the file now has, Emacs informs you so you can take corrective action. This example falls under a series of problems called "simultaneous editing," covered a little later in this chapter.

The rule of thumb for saving files is "Save early, save often, and save a lot!" You can't save too frequently, and again, it's a habit that saves you extra work. Of course, Emacs always protects you from both your own mistakes and those of the computer. These methods of protection are covered later in the chapter.

Buffers

A buffer is an object that Emacs creates to hold text or other data. Opening (visiting) a file copies the contents of that file into a buffer. Thus, part of the power of the Emacs philosophy of word processing is that you are never working on the actual file, only a copy.

Edited text files are just one type of buffer. Mail buffers are used for creating, reading, and answering your electronic mail. Help buffers provide on-line help, including key bindings and the various functions of the Emacs you are using. The scratch buffer is one that is not yet associated with a file or function. Info buffers provide information, and the dired buffer lists the files in the current directory or in a directory of your choice. Figure 5.6 shows some of the many UniPress Emacs commands relating to buffers.

```
buffer-is-visible
buffer-name-arg
buffer-size
buffer-to-resource
buffer-to-string
buffer-to-temp-file
comm-buffers
copy-current-buffer
copy-region-to-buffer
copy-region-to-killbuffer          which can be invoked by ESC-w
count-chars-buffer
--More--(14%) (type ? for help)




Buffer: Main      (Normal) [None] Top
```

Fig. 5.6. The buffer concept is one of the things that give all versions of Emacs so much advantage over conventional editors.

You can have thousands of buffers open at the same time in Emacs, but only one of these (even if five or six are shown on your display) is the *current buffer*. The current buffer is the one that your cursor is in, and the one on which almost all commands operate. Functions like CONTROL-x CONTROL-s, which saves all unsaved buffers (even the hundreds you might not see), are the exception rather than the rule. Normally, a command affects only the current buffer.

Creating Buffer Names

All buffers have names. Usually you can create a buffer with any length of name you like, but because most buffer names are tied to actual files on disk, the limits on names that the operating system imposes apply to the buffer name when it's written to disk the first time. For example, using SCO Xenix—and being tied to its file name length limitations, you could create a buffer named BufferWithLongName. However, when you save this buffer to a disk file, Xenix truncates the name to BufferWithLong.

You lose nothing if a name is truncated, except perhaps some of the descriptive information the longer name imparts. To take full advantage of descriptive names, you'll have to know the file name limitations that the underlying operating system imposes on the flavor of Emacs you are running.

When you first open Emacs (assuming no file name is specified on the command line), an empty buffer is presented on the screen. In GNU Emacs this empty or starting buffer is named *scratch*. Epsilon and MicroEmacs both call it the "Main" buffer. There is no associated file name on the mode line. UniPress Emacs also calls the empty buffer "Main" but adds "[none]" on the mode line to show that the buffer is not yet tied to a file on disk.

Figure 5.7 displays information from MicroEmacs' online documentation regarding buffers.

Upper- and lowercase make a difference in buffer names. Thus, names such as filename, FileName, and FILENAME are three separate buffers. In a UNIX system, buffers are saved to disk with the same name (that is, retaining the mixture of case), assuming name length requirements are not exceeded.

GNU Emacs' *scratch* buffer, by the way, gives you the additional feature of enabling Lisp expressions to be evaluated within it.

5

```
=>                    (13) MULTIPLE BUFFERS
A BUFFER is a named area containing a document being edited.  Many buffers
may be activated at once.
^XB     Switch to another buffer.  <CR> = use just-previous buffer
^XX     Switch to next buffer in buffer list
M-^N    Change name of current buffer
^XK     Delete a non-displayed buffer.
^X^B    Display buffer directory in a window
-------------------------------------------------------------------------
=>                    (14) READING FROM DISK

^X^F    Find file; read into a new buffer created from filename.
        (This is the usual way to begin editing a new file.)
^X^R    Read file into current buffer, erasing its previous contents.
        No new buffer will be created.
^X^I    Insert file into current buffer at cursor's location.
^X^V    Find a file to make current in VIEW mode
-------------------------------------------------------------------------
=>                    (15) SAVING BUFFERS AND REGIONS TO DISK

^X^S    Save current buffer to disk
^X^W    Write current buffer to disk
^XN     Change file name of current buffer
==== MicroEMACS 3.10 (VIEW) == emacs.hlp == File: emacs.hlp ================
```

Fig. 5.7. MicroEmacs, as all the Emacs do, gives you a lot of power in working with buffers.

5

Manipulating Buffers

The three main commands that ease the manipulation of buffers in every flavor of Emacs are listed in Table 5.6.

Table 5.6. Commands That Manipulate Buffers

Command Name	Key Binding	Meaning
switch-to-buffer	C-x b	Select another buffer (that is, change buffers).
list-buffers	C-x C-b	Show all buffers (a window with a list of all the buffers currently open appears).
kill-buffer	C-x k	Kill a buffer (you are prompted to save if the buffer has been modified).

Using the **switch-to-buffer** command, you can select any open buffer, or you can create a new one by typing ESC x b, entering the buffer name, and hitting the RETURN key. Remember, in GNU Emacs, if you cannot remember the entire name or its correct spelling, the completion function finishes the command for you.

Epsilon, GNU, and Freemacs have a more sophisticated method of finding, deleting, and saving buffers. In Epsilon, the function is called the bufed function. It is invoked by typing ESC x bufed. A window similar to the dired window appears, and you can move or scroll to view the buffer names. GNU Emacs and Freemacs have the same function under a different name. Type ESC x buffer-menu if you have one of these Emacs.

If you create a new buffer with CONTROL-x b and a buffer name, that buffer is not associated to a file until you actually save the buffer using CONTROL-x CONTROL-s or another method of saving. However, visiting a file using CONTROL-x CONTROL-f immediately opens a buffer that *is* associated with that file, unless the file already exists in another buffer. In this case, you are moved to that buffer and it becomes the current one.

In GNU Emacs, typing CONTROL-x CONTROL-q toggles the status of the buffer to *read only*. This status means that no editing commands will have any effect on the text in the buffer. Entering the same key combination again toggles the buffer back to one you can edit.

GNU also offers four other functions of interest in manipulating buffers. Entering ESC x rename-buffer changes the name of the current buffer (you are protected from choosing the name of another active buffer). ESC x view-buffer calls up a buffer, but doesn't enable editing (a safe way to review one). This command acts the same as ESC x view-file, which enables you to look at a file on disk without danger of inadvertent modification.

Typing CONTROL-x a in GNU appends one buffer to another, and ESC x insert-buffer lets you copy text from one buffer to another.

Of course, in all versions of Emacs, you can mark a region, copy or kill it, and then insert the copied or killed text into a new buffer of your choice. The following list describes this process for Epsilon Emacs.

1. Place your cursor at the beginning of the text you want to copy. Hold down the CONTROL key and press the @ key once. This sets the mark.

2. Move to the end of the region you want to move. Type ALT-w. This copies the region into the kill buffer.

3. Go to the appropriate buffer (using the commands discussed), move the cursor to the proper place, and type CONTROL-y. The text, regardless of size, is "yanked" into place.

This process is similar for GNU Emacs:

1. Use the **set-mark** command (which is CONTROL-@) to mark the start of the region. Use any of the movement commands to move to the end of the text.

2. Type CONTROL-x x. Emacs asks you for a register name. Register names are single characters that copy the text into a register.

3. Go to the buffer you want to insert the text in, move to the proper point, and type CONTROL-x g. Emacs asks you for a register name. Enter the register name; the text, regardless of length, is inserted.

Backup

5

While editing a file, you already have two copies of that file—the file on disk and the contents of the buffer. Saving the buffer means that the contents of the buffer and the contents of the file are now the same. But what if you decide something is wrong in the recent editing you did, and you want to revert to the version of the file before you made the changes? At least one operating system, DEC's VMS, enables you to do this easily. It stores versions of the edited file (as file;1, file;2, and file;3, with file;3 being the most recently edited). However, neither UNIX nor MS-DOS has that feature, so you must rely on Emacs to do it for you. And you can.

Emacs protects you in many ways. One of them, as shown in Figure 5.8 in UniPress Emacs, is the intelligent closing down in the event of a system crash. GNU offers this same type of protection.

Backing Up Files

GNU Emacs is especially complete in protecting you by backing up files. Other flavors of Emacs protect you also, but to a lesser degree. When you first visit a file, Emacs copies the old version of the file into a backup file. You have the option of keeping just one backup or a whole series of numbered backups.

```
 * menu:

 ; \014Emacs

 LastUpdateBegin
 fiction@author, Wed Aug  7 10:14:28 1991          681574468
 LastUpdateEnd




   INFO*    Editing text                (fiction)Top               9%
 Emacs has been terminated by a Terminate signal.  All of the files
 that you were editing and have changed have been checkpointed.
 /usr/bin/unipress: 291 Terminated
 $ fiction: /usr/fiction >
```

Fig. 5.8. UniPress Emacs closes down when the system crashes.

The default condition creates only one backup file. Thus, when you first open the file, Emacs makes a copy of it on the disk and appends a tilde (~) to the file name to indicate that it's a backup file. No matter how many times you now save the buffer, the backup file remains the same as the original file that you visited. Only when you close the buffer and reopen the file is the backup overwritten with the new "original" file. This process also occurs during a new editing session. Other Emacs use somewhat different methods. Epsilon, for instance, adds the extension .bak rather than the tilde.

In GNU Emacs this backup feature can be turned off (although we recommend leaving it on) by typing ESC x set-variable. When prompted for the variable name, type make-backup-files, wait until Emacs asks for the value, and then type nil. Better to leave that feature on or to type 1 for the value so that you are sure the feature is turned on. You can tell that backup is on when you see files in your editing directories with the tilde. Think of the extra files as insurance, because they sure are!

In a UNIX system, Emacs might sometimes be prevented from making a backup file in the current directory (because of group or user *permissions*). GNU Emacs creates a file in your home directory named %backup%~. Be aware, however, that only one file is made, and it is reserved for the last file you visited in a directory where you did not have write permission.

So without changing the default, you will have one backup file with the same name as the original file with an added tilde. Now, what about numbered backups? Numbered backup files are made every time a file is changed during a session and the session is ended. That is, one backup per session is made. The backup files are called Test, Test.~1~, Test.~2~, and so on. This feature, again in GNU, is turned on with the *version-control* variable. To set it up, you type ESC x set-variable, wait for it to ask you what variable to set, and then enter version-control. You then are queried as to the value. There are three possible answers, shown in Table 5.7.

Table 5.7. Possible Values for the version-control Variable

Value	Meaning
t	Make numbered backup files.
nil	If backup files are already numbered, keep on doing it for that file only, but make only a single backup for new files visited.
never	Forget about numbered backups and make only a single backup.

You can set the numbered backups to work on every buffer or set them as a local variable that acts only on the current buffer. Chapter 6 discusses local variables in greater depth.

Removing Backups Automatically

As you probably guessed, numbered backups eat into available disk space dramatically. Although keeping numbered backups is definitely something you should do on certain types of files, it is not necessary to keep numbered backups for every file. GNU Emacs gives you the option of retaining the first few backups and several of the most recent ones. It deletes most of those in between and liberates precious disk space.

In fact, using variables, you have total control over removal of backup files. There are three variables that can be set for each file. If you have one hundred files open at once, you can have one hundred different ways of removing backup files, one for each buffer/file combination.

You even can open one hundred files (or more) automatically each time you start an editing session, and the cursor will be at the same place you left off work in all one hundred files. To do this, you need a macro by Bob Weiner. The macro is available at no charge from the elisp archives at Ohio State University. We'll explain how to get enhancements to Emacs like this in Chapter 9.

As stated earlier, there are three variables used for removal of backup files. Typing `ESC x set-variable` in GNU Emacs and, when asked for the variable name in the echo area, typing `kept-old-versions` enables you to specify how many old versions to keep. The default value is two. The *kept-new-versions* variable enables you to change this default value.

If you set the *trim-versions-without-asking* variable to any value other than nil, the extra versions that fall between the old and the new ones are deleted automatically. Setting the value to nil means you are asked to confirm each deletion. Using the **period** (.) command in dired also enables you to delete middle versions.

Total protection and total control—all part of the Emacs philosophy.

Copying and Renaming

Backing up files on multiuser systems, such as those running the UNIX operating environment, requires a bit more care. In UNIX, the same file can have many names—that is, it can be linked to other names. There are two ways of making a backup file. Emacs can rename the file (from the edited name to the backup name) and write the contents of the buffer as a new file, albeit under the old name. It also can copy the old file to the backup file, then overwrite the original file. There is a subtle but important difference between these methods.

When a linked file is renamed to a backup file (the fastest way of saving), all the other names that file might have are now attached to the backup file. So another user calling up sales.report is going to get the old version of sales.report, not the one you just spent three hours updating. However, copying a file into a backup file leaves all links on the original file, which is desirable on a multiuser system.

Renaming the file can create another problem, that of ownership. In UNIX, if you create a file (and renaming is like creating a new file), you "own" that file and the system cannot let another user edit the file. This is good for your private files, but unnecessary for files such as sales reports that several people in your group might need to work on.

Naturally, whether to copy or rename is under your control. Once more, you will find GNU's treatment of this problem the most convenient. Like with automatic removal of backups, you have three variables. If the variable *backup-by-copying* is set to any value other than nil, copying is always used. If the variable *backup-by-copying-when-linked* is not nil, all files not linked to other names are renamed (the fastest method), and any multiuser files (those linked to other names) are backed up by copying. If everyone uses the same name (that is, sales.report), the first variable, *backup-by-copying*, is the one that should be used. The third variable, *backup-by-copying-when-mismatch* (if set to non-nil), backs up a file by copying only if backing it up by renaming it would cause a change in the ownership or group permissions. The last option, which places most of the decision making on Emacs' sturdy shoulders, is probably the best option for group work situations.

Editing Simultaneously

When a file regularly is edited by two or more people, there are probably times when two or more of them are editing the file simultaneously. If Emacs did not protect users against this situation, only the changes made by the last user would be in the file, because his or her version would overwrite all others, and the loss of work also would be evident in the backup files.

Loss of work—that's the most unforgivable problem any word processing program can confront you with. Every flavor of Emacs is much too advanced to cause you to lose work. You may be interested in Emacs for many reasons, but the massive array of protective features will make you fall in love with Emacs. Life is too short for tedious retyping or re-creation of work lost by lesser word processors.

Emacs protects you from simultaneous editing by *locking* files. That is, when you have a file loaded into a buffer and you change it (an asterisk on the mode line indicates that the buffer has been modified but not yet saved), Emacs tells the system (by creating the locking file) that the open file is pending a modification. On some systems, Emacs may not be configured to lock files; in such cases, Emacs has a way to protect you as well.

If another user already has opened the file and has modified but not saved his or her buffer before you open yours, Emacs notes, when you make a change, that a conflict exists. In GNU Emacs, the Lisp command **ask-user-about-lock** appears (unless you have customized it) and provides you with three choices. These choices are shown in Table 5.8.

Table 5.8. Possible Values for the ask-user-about-lock Variable

Value	Meaning
s	Steal. You "steal" the lock. In other words, the user who was changing the file loses the lock, and you now have control of the file. Your changes are the ones now saved.
p	Proceed. Enables you to edit the file in spite of the lock.
q	Quit. This causes an error (file-locked), and the changes you were trying to make do not take place. You can come back later and edit the file when the other person is finished, thus not losing his or her changes.

Of these three options, the last is the best in a group work situation.

Epsilon is a stripped-down version of its huge cousin. There are versions of Epsilon for DOS and OS/2. GNU is far too big to run under MS-DOS, and no one has ported GNU over to OS/2 yet (although there is also a version of MicroEmacs 3.10 that runs under OS/2). Despite its size, Epsilon, like all flavors of Emacs, is protecting your work. Should you attempt to edit an Epsilon file that another user is editing, Epsilon informs you of that fact and shows you the date of the buffer file's last save as opposed to the date of the file on the disk. You then are given three choices, shown in Table 5.9.

5

Table 5.9. Possible Values for Epsilon's ask-user-about-lock Command

Value	Meaning
C	Compare the two versions by reading the disk version into its own buffer. You can then use compare-windows or diff to see the changes.
R	Read in the new version now, replacing the version now in your buffer.
S	Save your changes, replacing the version on disk (not always the selfless method to take in a work group).

Ah, but what if the other user is not using Epsilon? What if he or she is editing the same file on UniPress Emacs? Several versions of Emacs can coexist easily and peacefully on the same system, and in the case of UNIX, they all can run at once. UniPress Emacs views the file when you attempt to save it and notes that another user has made a change. It then gives you the message "*filename has been modified, do you want to overwrite it?*" The polite answer, of course, is no until you can make sure that you won't cause someone to lose work.

GNU Emacs protects you in the same way, except the wording is slightly different. It says, "Disk file has changed since visited or saved. Save anyway? (yes or no)." Again, the correct answer is no. Wait and work your changes in with the other person's version.

Most flavors of Emacs provide the same type of protection. So even if other users mix and match versions of Emacs between GNU, MicroEmacs, Epsilon, and UniPress, you still are protected against simultaneous editing.

"I see," you say, "but what if someone uses vi?"

No problem; Emacs still protects you and the other user against simultaneous editing, regardless of the text processing program in use. Unfortunately, the vi user has little protection otherwise and easily can lose his or her work.

Reverting

Auto-saving is yet another way to protect your work. Every so often (you can set the interval), Emacs makes an automatic backup copy of the file. If the power goes off or the system goes down for some other reason, your work won't be lost. A backup file is the previously saved version, the one that was saved *before* your last save of the file. An automatic backup file, on the other hand, is a copy of the current buffer. Auto-saving is covered in the next section of this chapter. First, here's how auto-saving affects reverting.

Reverting a buffer means you are discarding the changes you've made and reloading the original contents of the file. If you've made a series of changes that were OK and it was only the last one that was damaging, it is probably better to try the **undo** command (CONTROL-x u) first. If you killed the text (Emacs considers deletion of anything larger than a single character or a block of white space as a kill), you can **yank-pop** things back from the kill ring. If you have to revert the buffer, you can revert to the original file or, if auto-save has occurred since the last saving of the file, revert to the auto-save file instead. This means that you discard some of your changes, but not all of them. Again, Emacs has protected you from losing work.

Even if you have exited Emacs and returned later, this protection is still in force. If you open the file again and your auto-save file is still more recent than the last time the file was saved, GNU Emacs tells you, "Auto-save file is newer, consider M-x recover-file." M-x is the META key plus the x key or, as we've been using mostly in this book, the same thing as typing ESC x recover-file.

Auto-Saving

Auto-saving brings to mind the dramatic example of having a hundred files open simultaneously. You might have been zipping around in all of these files all morning, making dozens of changes and forgetting to save those changes (although a simple CONTROL-x CONTROL-s saves all buffers in one swoop). Who is looking out for you? Emacs, that's who, or at least GNU.

To protect you from disasters, both manmade and computermade, GNU Emacs periodically backs up all open files automatically, even if you do not have them on the screen. The number of keystrokes since the last save is the determining factor (and you can customize that number). The message "Auto-saving..." flashes in the echo area to let you know what's happening. This soon will become a comforting sight to you.

Understanding Auto-Save Files

Special files are used for auto-save so that the original files are not changed until you specifically request it, usually by typing the command CONTROL-x CONTROL-s for individual files or CONTROL-x s to save all buffers to files. Although you should save often, the auto-save function will protect you if you forget.

Auto-save files created by GNU Emacs are easy to recognize—they use the pound sign (#) to precede and end the regular file's name. For example, if you visited (opened) a file called letter.mom and started editing it, GNU Emacs would create an auto-save file for it named #letter.mom# and would record your changes periodically.

Special buffers, such as the *mail* buffer, which enables you to compose and send electronic mail to other users around the world, also have an auto-save file even if they have no regular file. GNU uses a percent sign (%) to indicate that the auto-save file is of this type, such as #%*mail*# for the mail buffer and #%scratch# for the scratch buffer. The scratch buffer is used when you invoke a buffer without specifying files to edit. The first time you save it, you are asked for a file name, but until then, the #%scratch# auto-save file is used to auto-save anything you've typed into the buffer to disk. In a sense, your files are auto-saved even before you've gotten around to creating them.

Controlling Auto-Save

GNU Emacs, by default, turns on auto-saving for each file you visit if the variable *auto-save-default* is not set to nil. If the value is nil, you can turn the feature on by setting the variable to t. Additionally, you can toggle auto-save for individual buffers on and off by typing ESC x auto-save-mode. GNU states that auto-save is on by reporting in the echo area, "Auto-save on (in this buffer)."

Our recommendation is to always leave auto-save on globally and to turn it off for a particular buffer only if you have an overwhelming, logical reason. Just because a protective feature can be turned off doesn't mean it should be.

One reason for turning auto-save off is because the file you are editing is too large and disk space is at a premium. By the time you have a backup file or files, an auto-save file, and the original file itself, you are starting to use a large amount of disk space. Even in a case such as this, it might not be a good idea to turn off both the backup and the auto-save features. Safety nets, after all, are never needed until you are falling, but they are comforting in that event. In other words, even if disk space is limited, don't throw away all your protection; at least try to keep auto-save turned on.

The variable *auto-save-interval* in GNU Emacs determines how often auto-saving takes place. The default is 300, meaning that the auto-save does its job every time you type 300 characters. If a fatal error happens on the system, Emacs invokes an immediate auto-save to try to save the current state. Even in system crashes, the most that you will lose is 300 characters.

As with everything else about Emacs, you can customize the *auto-save-interval* variable. Your selection depends on the speed of the system and your work habits. Auto-save is fast, so you may want to experiment with a smaller number of characters.

In the MS-DOS world, both Freemacs and MicroEmacs have auto-save, although MicroEmacs saves to the files being edited rather than to special auto-save files. The commercial word processing package Sprint (from Borland International) also has auto-save, and its files are saved to a special auto-save file called the *swap file*. Because Sprint descends from Emacs and still essentially retains the philosophy, it contains all the protective measures, such as auto-save, with a default set for every three seconds.

Using Auto-Save Files

Auto-save files are normally just for insurance—you never need them unless you've lost some data. Auto-save files should not be confused with backup files. Backup files are copies of older versions of the file on disk made when you saved the current version. Auto-save files are changes you've made after the last time you saved the buffer to disk.

In GNU, you type `ESC x recover-file`, hit RETURN, type the name of the file, and hit RETURN again to recover an auto-save file. Emacs prompts you through the process. After the auto-save file is in the buffer, you can use CONTROL-x s to save it into the regular file.

When you replace the buffer with the contents of the auto-save file, auto-saving is turned off for that buffer because that auto-save file now is considered valuable until you make a disposition of the recovered text or data. When you start editing again, be sure to turn auto-save back on by typing `ESC x auto-save-mode`. Killing the buffer (after it has been saved) and visiting the file again automatically restores auto-save.

Windows

You already know what a screen is—it's that glass box right in front of you—but did you know that it has windows in it? The word *windows* has become cliché in the computer world. Essentially, it means that the display screen is divided into two or more areas that act independently. Text scrolling in one area, for example, does not affect other text displayed in another area.

Figure 5.9 shows two buffers on the screen. MicroEmacs, in this case, is being run under a DOS-emulator on a Xenix system. The DOS **dir** command was issued from within Emacs, and its results were put into the top buffer.

You can divide your screen into windows by splitting the available area either horizontally or vertically. Each window created in this manner has a buffer assigned to it, and that buffer, at least in part, is shown in the window.

Unlike buffers and files, which have a direct one-on-one relationship, multiple windows can show different parts of the same buffer. For long buffers or files, this is a distinct advantage because you can look at four or five different parts of the same file all at once on the screen. Or, of course, you can view several different files at once, or any combination of different files and multiple views into the same file.

Each window has its own mode line, and when the window is current, commands usually operate only within that window. Global commands like CONTROL-s s, which saves all modified buffers, and window manipulation commands like ESC-CONTROL-v, which scrolls the text in the other window if two windows are open, are the exception. In GNU Emacs this function is **scroll-other-window**, so you might want to bind it to a more convenient key combination.

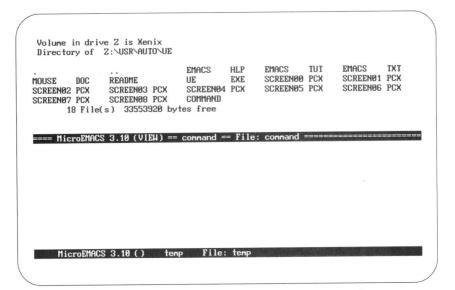

```
      Volume in drive Z is Xenix
      Directory of  Z:\USR\AUTO\UE

      .             ..            EMACS   HLP   EMACS   TUT   EMACS   TXT
      MOUSE   DOC   README        UE      EXE   SCREEN00 PCX  SCREEN01 PCX
      SCREEN02 PCX  SCREEN03 PCX  SCREEN04 PCX  SCREEN05 PCX  SCREEN06 PCX
      SCREEN07 PCX  SCREEN08 PCX  COMMAND
             18 File(s)  33553920 bytes free

===== MicroEMACS 3.10 (VIEW) == command == File: command ========================




      MicroEMACS 3.10 ()    temp    File: temp
```

Fig. 5.9. A screen divided into two windows, showing two buffers open in MicroEmacs.

Manipulating Windows

Some basic actions you might perform with windows include cutting and pasting text from one file to another; comparing different versions of a document; and preparing a report by collating data from other files, such as individual sales reports.

Table 5.10 shows some window manipulation commands that work in most versions of Emacs.

Table 5.10. Commands to Manipulate Windows

Command Name	Key Binding	Meaning
split-window-vertically	C-x 2	Split the current window in two vertically (one above the other). Freemacs supports only two windows.

Command Name	Key Binding	Meaning
split-window-horizontally	C-x 5	Split the current window in two horizontally (one beside the other); text is truncated automatically as needed. Horizontal windows are not available in Freemacs or MicroEmacs.
other-window	C-x o	Switch to the other window. (If more than two are open, this command lets you rotate through them.)
scroll-other-window	M-C-v	Hold down the META key, the CONTROL key, and the v key simultaneously, or tap the ESC key, let up, and press the CONTROL and v keys at the same time (ESC C-v). The text in the other window scrolls.
delete-window	C-x 0	Kill the current window.
delete-other-window	C-x 1	Kill all other windows, leaving the current window as the only one displayed on the screen.
enlarge-window	C-x ^	Make the current window grow taller (and shorten the others). Press CONTROL-x and then the caret (^) key.
enlarge-window-horizontally	C-x }	Cause a horizontal window to grow wider. Press CONTROL-x and then the right curly bracket (}).

GNU Emacs adds some commands that do not necessarily work in other versions of Emacs. Freemacs, which tries to be a DOS clone of GNU Emacs, has these commands also. They are shown in Table 5.11.

Table 5.11. Some GNU Emacs and Freemacs Commands to Manipulate Buffers

Command Name	Key Binding	Meaning
switch-to buffer-other-window	C-x 4 b *bufname*	Select the named buffer in another window, creating the window if needed.
find-file-other-window	C-x 4 f *filename*	Visit the file named and open a buffer for it in another window, creating if needed.
dired-other-window	C-x 4 d *directory*	Open a dired buffer for the named directory, creating the directory if needed.
mail-other-window	C-x 4 m	Open a mail buffer in another window and start composing an electronic mail message.
find-tag-other-window	C-x 4	Find a tag in the current tag table (more about tags in Chapter 8).

In general, windows enable you to take advantage of having many buffers, and thus files, open at once. You can show several files on the screen at once, compare them, move text or program code back and forth, and do other things that conventional word processing programs cannot.

Chapter 6 explains how the window, file, buffer, and text manipulation can be used to format your work into beautiful results.

Formatting

Being able to insert and delete text, check spelling, move paragraphs around, search and replace, and use all the other features that give text editing its magic is only part of the procedure. Eventually you'll want to output the result. The word *format*, as applied to Emacs, refers to two kinds of formatting. There is the immediate formatting or rearranging of text, which you see in a buffer (and which is saved to files on disk), and there is also the format that is printed on paper or passed to another program for additional processing. This latter type of formatting is determined in part by various control codes embedded in the text.

Control codes are an important concept. Emacs is a *display editor*, as opposed to a word processing program. Word processors give you the complete package, including printer drivers. You can create, edit, and print a document all using that one piece of software. WordPerfect and WordStar are examples of word processors. Borland's Sprint, although a version of Emacs, qualifies as a word processor because a *text formatting* program is included. The text formatting program is a separate program that sends Sprint text files to a printer while implementing the embedded formatting commands within the text that are specific to that formatter.

Although the idea of "all in one" might sound great, it can be limiting compared to the Emacs philosophy of openness and freedom. You are limited to some programmer's often myopic vision of what he or she thinks you need, not what you specifically need. Programmers are nice folk, but they usually don't do word processing, other than processing program code. The features a user must have often are missing or so convoluted that they slow production. Emacs, being an open system, is far more versatile because it enables you to create new features at will, whereas with word processing programs, you are locked into whatever was originally programmed.

With an Emacs-type editor, you have a wide choice of external formatters, both text and otherwise. You don't have to use the formatter that comes with Sprint, either. Conventional word processors' limitation in formatting is one of the several limitations that cannot be overemphasized when comparing them to Emacs-type editors.

Some of the text formatting programs are covered in this chapter. These include integral UNIX utilities such as nroff and troff, enhancements like ditroff, and application packages like TeX typesetting software. Emacs, as you will see later, provides major modes to help you set your text files to be formatted by these independent programs. Major text modes included in the GNU basic distribution include Text, Nroff, Outline, and TeX. UniPress Emacs adds Screenplay mode. Of course, in the open nature of Emacs, hundreds of other modes are available on Internet and Usenet. You also can create your own by modifying existing modes to match your own applications.

In addition to being a text editor, Emacs also is a sophisticated program editor. Using the various flavors of Emacs and available major modes, you easily can edit source code in the many formats required by compilers for computer languages including C, Ada, FORTRAN, Pascal, PROLOG, Lisp, and many others. GNU, UniPress, and Epsilon come with several major modes, and others can be added to fit your needs. As is true with Emacs in general, modes can be infinitely customized.

The next section takes a closer look at modes and how they control formatting.

6

Major Text Formatting Modes

As you saw in the previous chapter, Emacs has major modes and minor modes. Major modes are those that change the overall settings of the editor—in essence, they are like several different editors in one. Minor modes modify major ones. There are three groups of major modes: those for text formatting applications, the ones for the different programming languages, and highly specialized modes that edit special file structures, such as Dired and Mail modes.

Major modes are mutually exclusive, meaning you can have only one active per buffer. It is not possible to have a buffer that is both Text mode and C mode, for example. However, you can have any number of buffers open, and each buffer can have its own major mode, independent of any other buffer's mode. The type of mode in effect is shown on the mode line within parentheses (Epsilon uses brackets).

Modes are invoked in two ways. First, you can invoke them manually, by typing ESC x text-mode to enter Text mode in GNU and UniPress, or by typing ESC x lisp-mode to enter Lisp mode. The second way is to have Emacs invoke modes automatically. If you create a buffer named myprogram.c, GNU, UniPress, Epsilon, and Freemacs all politely switch to C mode. Figure 6.1 shows an example of Text mode in GNU.

```
This is an example of text formatting using the auto fill feature of Emacs. Whe\
n you don't have auto-fill-mode turned on, the lines wrap by screen width. Like\
this!

When auto-fill-mode is on (or you use 'Esc q' to format the
paragraph), then the lines will break within the set margins (the
default being a line width of 65 characters), and it will look like
this.

If you want text even neater,  you can cause  it to be JUSTIFIED (left
and right margins both even) by typing 'Esc  1 Esc q'  and Emacs will
automatically insert spaces between words to even up the  margins, and
it will look like this.




-----Emacs: temp            3:41pm 1.11   (Text)----All---------------------
```

Fig. 6.1. Text mode in GNU gives you a flexible and powerful way to create and format documents.

If you create a buffer named moviescript.sp in UniPress, the Screenplay mode automatically is invoked. Screenplay mode does require a little advance configuration in your .emacs_pro file. (More on UniPress initialization file in the next chapter.) Just add these two lines:

```
(load "screenplay.ml")
(auto-major-mode "screenplay-mode" "*.sp")
```

Which major modes are available for your use depends on the flavor of Emacs on your system and the customizations that have been added or purchased. Epsilon comes with only two major modes—Fundamental and C. The basic UniPress package gives you several, including Screenplay mode, but others are add-ons, such as Cmacs for a C mode and Adamacs for the programming language Ada (the Ada language was named after the lovely Lady Ada, who was the world's first programmer).

Sprint also has major modes, although they are called *user interfaces* instead. These change key bindings and command structures so that Sprint mimics other programs. Some of these modes are Emacs, WordPerfect, WordStar, Multimate, and Word. Other types of Emacs can be configured to do this chameleon mimicking also. GNU, for example, can be made to act like vi, and there is at least one WordStar mode for it. So major modes can be used to change not just the way Emacs formats text, but how it interacts with the user.

Figure 6.2 demonstrates how Freemacs can work transparently, allowing the user's creativity to flourish.

```
                    LORD RIFKIN AT PROMETHEUS
                               by
                          Ralph Roberts

      Grand Admiral Lord Rifkin amused himself perusing astronomy
   memory disks while Redoubtable transferred to normal space. He
   ignored disgusted sounds from Princess Namara as the star Prometheus
   slid into view. A pitiful remnant of Main Fleet also emerged,
   forming protectively around their flagmauler.
      "You dally in your hobby," said Namara. "You allow us to be
   hounded. You watch idly as we are decimated by attrition."
      The elderly Grand Admiral shrugged. "The study of celestial lore
   is informative and soothing," he said. "Besides, we are outnumbered
   ten to one. An uneven battle at best."
      Redoubtable's captain interupted. "All ships linked, Milord,"
   he said. "Navcomputer to activate automatically."
      Namara continued. "Why stop here? You prepare not for battle.
   Worse, we are periously near Prometheus. Closer and retreat to
   null- Quant is impossible."
      Redoubtable's captain again spoke. "The rebel fleet materializes
   behind us."
      Namara fearfully watched the screens. "They take an inner orbit.
   Battle is unavoidable. We are lost!"
   --**-Emacs: rifkin. (Fun) --C1 L6/36 ----16------------------------
```

Fig. 6.2. Like a good text editor should, Freemacs can be transparent to the user.

Major modes make editing easy. Because they redefine keys and functions, they make Emacs easier to use with the particular class of text you are editing. Following are some examples of how various major modes work.

Using Fundamental Mode

The basic major mode for most versions of Emacs is called the *Fundamental mode* (the UniPress equivalent is called the *Normal* mode). As the name implies, this is the simplest major mode. No keys are redefined, no variables are changed, and the command functions work in their most general ways. This is the default or starting mode for Freemacs, Epsilon, and UniPress.

To enter the Fundamental mode in GNU and Epsilon, type `ESC  x fundamental-mode`. You should see the word *Fundamental* on the mode line, confirming that Emacs is now in that mode. Creating a buffer or opening a file with a .txt extension automatically switches GNU and Epsilon to Fundamental mode, and UniPress to its equivalent Normal mode.

Basically, Fundamental mode (or Normal mode) is the default major mode for Emacs. When it is used without any minor modes, there is no special treatment of inserted characters. In other words, no formatting occurs. All other major modes are described by their differences from Fundamental mode.

In the spirit of openness, you can change such things as the default mode. In GNU, the default mode is in a variable named *default-major mode*. You can change this during an editing session by entering

```
ESC x set-variable ENTER default-major-mode ENTER 'text-mode
```

(in which ENTER means to press the carriage return or ENTER key). Be sure that you include the apostrophe in front of "text-mode" so that you are entering a string rather than a numerical value. Implementing this variable change means that any buffer you create or any file you visit that does not have a recognized extension, such as .c for a C, is now opened in Text mode. The Text mode has become, for this session, your default mode. So myprogram.c still would be created in C mode, but myprogram without an extension would be created in Text mode. Naturally, you can change the major mode at any time by entering the META key (`ESC x` or `M-x`) and typing the name of the mode, such as `text-mode` or `c-mode` or `lisp-mode`.

You also can customize Emacs to always open new buffers or files that do not have a recognized extension (such as .c) in the major mode you use most often. For GNU, this is done by adding a line in the .emacs initialization file in your home directory (you can create the file if one does not exist). Writers, for example, use the Text mode more than any other, so they would type this line:

```
(setq default-major-mode 'text-mode)
```

All buffers (except for recognized C, Lisp, and other program source code file extensions) now are always opened in Text major mode. Of course, it's a pain not to have *word wrap* in any text editor. Word wrap breaks the line between words when it approaches the right margin and wraps it back around to the next line below. In other words, it's like automatic carriage return. You hit the ENTER key only at the ends of paragraphs. This also is called *automatic filling*. In Emacs, the default line width is 65 characters if filling is on, which is equivalent to one-inch margins at the standard 10 pitch or pica type. You easily can change margins, line width, type size, and so forth if you need to. Automatic filling is a minor mode that modifies the Text major mode. If you want it to always be on with a Text mode buffer, add this line to your .emacs file for GNU (type it below the line that sets the default major mode):

```
(setq text-mode-hook 'turn-on-auto-file)
```

You have to type this only once; Emacs always remembers to turn on the automatic filling. Similar customization files exist for UniPress, Freemacs, MicroEmacs, and Epsilon. These all are covered in the next chapter.

Understanding Text Mode

Speaking of Text mode, how does it differ from Fundamental or Normal mode? The differences help handle the stylistic and syntactic conventions of normal text. These include commands for creating and manipulating sentences and paragraphs, moving over and killing words, filling paragraphs, and much more. Any file editing meant to be read by humans (as opposed to compilers, typesetting programs, and so forth) usually should be done using Text mode.

Epsilon does not come with a Text mode because it is sold as a program editor. Either you have to make do with editing text under Fundamental mode, or you can customize a Text mode for the system. In GNU and UniPress, type ESC x text-mode to enter Text mode, or create a buffer with a .txt extension. Freemacs enters Text mode with the .txt extension as well. In all three of these Emacs, the word *Text* appears on the mode line, confirming that the major mode is in effect. If automatic filling is turned on, it reads *Text Fill* instead.

The two most important features of Text mode are word wrap and paragraph justification. Word wrap, as you've already seen, breaks lines between words so they fall within the right margin. Paragraph justification is affected by the type of *fill* used. Fill, justification, and other on-screen formatting topics such as indentation, tabs, and case conversion are covered later in this chapter.

Using Nroff Mode

The nroff text formatting utility is one of the basic goodies included in most UNIX and UNIX-like operating systems. It is designed to format text for typewriter-style line printers. Its close cousin, troff, formats text for typesetting devices. Some of the same commands are recognized by both, and because there is no separate Troff mode, use Nroff mode for both applications. The Nroff mode in GNU is a modified Text mode that understands nroff (and troff) commands in the text being edited.

Nroff mode differs from Text mode only slightly. Because Nroff mode recognizes nroff commands, any line beginning with such a command is considered to be a paragraph separator and is not filled. Because the nroff commands must be at the start of a line for that utility to see and act on them, any filling that would garble them is not desirable—hence the need for a separate Nroff mode. If you put nroff commands in a plain Text mode buffer, they are treated as normal text. You enter this mode in GNU by typing `ESC x nroff-mode`. In UniPress you load Troff mode first so it acts on nroff commands.

Nroff commands begin with a period at the start of the line. For example, .bp is used to separate pages, .ul N underlines the next *N* lines, and so forth. There are scores of these commands, and the separate UNIX text formatting utilities easily could fill another book. Explaining them is beyond our scope here, but we do want to emphasize that they are well worth learning.

GNU Emacs has three special commands in Nroff mode that are not in Text mode. These are shown in Table 6.1.

Table 6.1. GNU Emacs Commands Specific to Nroff Mode

Command Name	Key Binding	Meaning
forward-text-line	ESC n	Moves to the next line that is not an nroff command.
backward-text-line	ESC p	Like ESC n but moves in reverse; that is, moves back up the buffer.
count-text-lines	ESC ?	Counts the number of lines that are not nroff (or troff) commands and prints the total in the echo area below the mode line.

Using TeX LaTeX Modes

The TeX program is a powerful text formatter written by Donald Knuth. Like GNU Emacs, Freemacs, and MicroEmacs, it is also a free program, and it is widely available on Internet and Usenet. LaTeX, supplied with the program, is a simplified input format used with TeX, although they are two separate versions.

GNU provides two modes for use with TeX. These are the TeX mode and the LaTeX mode (invoked for a buffer by typing ESC x tex-mode or ESC x latex-mode). Remember that because these two modes are extensions of the basic Text mode, you can have all the minor mode modifications that apply to Text mode, or you can create your own if you like.

TeX mode and LaTeX mode differ only slightly but are still two separate modes designed to edit the two different TeX input formats. If TeX text is already in the buffer when TeX mode is called for, GNU decides whether TeX mode or LaTeX mode is appropriate and implements the correct one automatically. If the buffer is empty, the contents of the *TeX-default-mode* variable control which mode is selected.

Editing TeX Buffers

GNU Emacs makes editing a TeX (or LaTeX) buffer easier with several special commands. The way the quotation mark (") is handled is a good example. In typesetting, quotation marks are changed to double apostrophes to enhance readability ("like this"). GNU's TeX modes automatically convert quotation marks depending on context. If a character follows the quotation mark, you get open quotations ("). If a character precedes the marks, closed quotations are inserted ("). This process takes effect immediately in the buffer. The name of this GNU command is **TeX-insert-quote**. To get an actual quotation mark into the buffer (the "normal" kind), you type CONTROL-q ".

Other TeX mode commands are shown in Table 6.2.

Table 6.2. Additional TeX Mode Commands

Command Name	Key Binding	Meaning
TeX-terminate-paragraph	LFD	LFD is the linefeed key found on terminals. If you have a PC or newer keyboard, use C-j (CONTROL-j) because the ENTER key does not work in all cases. Insert a paragraph break (two newlines) and check the previous paragraph to see whether there are any unbalanced braces or dollar signs (explained in the TeX documentation).
validate-TeX-Buffer	ESC x validate-TeX-Buffer	Check every paragraph in the buffer to see whether there are any unbalanced braces or dollar signs.

Command Name	Key Binding	Meaning
TeX-insert-braces	ESC {	Insert braces ({}) and position the point between them.
up-list	ESC }	Move forward past the next unmatched close brace.
TeX-close-LaTeX block	C-c C-f	Close a block in LaTeX mode.

In the LaTeX style of input, the "\begin" and "\end" commands need to balance (a beginning always must be ended somewhere). So the command CONTROL-c CONTROL-f automatically inserts a matching "\end" and moves your cursor between the two so that you can enter text.

Printing TeX

It is not necessary to leave Emacs in order to print a TeX file, or to process it into a .dvi (device independent file) for later output. You even can specify small chunks (regions) of the file for printing, thus enabling you to fine-tune the formatting without having to commit the whole file to paper. The commands to print while in GNU's TeX modes are listed in Table 6.3.

Table 6.3. GNU Emacs' Print Commands

Command Name	Key Binding	Meaning
TeX-buffer	C-c C-b	Call TeX and send it the complete buffer.
TeX-region	C-c C-r	Call TeX and send it only the region marked.
TeX-recenter-output-buffer	C-c C-l	Center the window and show the output from the shell process running TeX so that the last line is showing.
TeX-kill-job	C-c C-k	Kill the shell process running TeX.
TeX-print	C-c C-p	Print the output that you've sent to TeX.
TeX-show-printer-queue	C-c C-q	Show printer queue.

TeX packs incredible versatility into your computer system; we highly recommend it. You can find out more about TeX by reading *The TeXbook*, by

Donald E. Knuth (published by Addison-Wesley). Although commercial versions of TEX are available, remember that there are also several free versions.

Using Outline Mode

Everyone learned something about outlines in elementary and high school. You might be surprised to discover that old Mrs. Wotsherface was not so dumb after all. Outlines can serve useful purposes in our everyday lives. Projects, articles, books, and manuals can be planned with an outline.

GNU Emacs comes with an Outline mode, which you turn on by typing `ESC x outline-mode`. The major difference between Outline mode and the more basic Text mode is that Outline mode divides lines into two types, *heading lines* and *body lines*.

Heading lines are topics in the outline. They begin with stars or asterisks (*) on the line—one star for the first level, two for the second, three for the third, and so on. A convenient feature of the Outline mode is that you can make various levels invisible, meaning you can "collapse" outlines inward so that only major topics are visible. Ellipses (dots) indicate a collapsed outline.

Body lines are lines that don't begin with an asterisk. They belong to the heading line that precedes them. The following example should make body lines clearer:

```
* Fruit

This line is a body line that says something about fruit.

** Apples

Apples is a second-level heading, and this is body text about
apples.

*** Granny Smith Apples

A third-level heading; this is body text.

*** Macintosh Apples

A type of apple often confused with computers. Both can have worms.

** Oranges

Back up a level; not to be mixed with apples.

* Veggies

Back to the top level now; a different topic.
```

A heading and the body lines that follow it are called an *entry*. The lower-level heading and body lines, such as those for Fruit in the previous example, collectively are called a *subtree*.

Of course, you've probably already noticed that the example outline does not have numbered headings, chapter numbers, or any other method of differentiating between headings other than the number of asterisks. Numbered headings aren't added until a text formatter prints the outline. This fact allows for extreme flexibility because you can rearrange the outline without changing the numbering. The true secret of word processing, or computing in general, is to let the software do the work. Emacs certainly is no sluggard and does much more for you than most text editors or word processing programs.

Because which text formatter (or formatters) you use is up to you, you must do some minor customization on the *outline-regexp* variable to number the outlines the way you want. The Scribe text formatter, for example, uses commands such as **@chapter**, **@section**, and **@subsection** to show divisions in documents. These are automatically numbered.

There is a trick (shown in the GNU Emacs manual) to setting the Outline mode to work with Scribe. Type `ESC xset-variable ENTER outline-regexp ENTER`, and then enter `"@chap\\¦@\\(sub\\)*section"` in the echo area. The trick is to make the chapter part (@chap) shorter so that GNU understands the difference between chapters and sections. GNU's basic distribution of Emacs, by the way, includes a major mode for Scribe.

A little experimentation may be required for other types of text formatters, but the results are worth the one-time effort if you use outlines.

Moving Around Outlines

Several commands make moving the cursor while in GNU's Outline mode easier. Note that some key combinations, such as CONTROL-c CONTROL-p, invoke different commands in Outline mode than they do in other modes. Remember that each major mode is like its own text editor. You are customizing Emacs for a specific purpose. Again, hundreds of major modes are available from a wide array of sources (some of which are included in the appendixes of this book). The motion commands in Outline mode are shown in Table 6.4.

Now You See It, Now You Don't

Invisible lines create collapsed outlines. This process is used to remove visual clutter. GNU provides the commands shown in Table 6.5 for collapsing and expanding outlines.

Table 6.4. Commands to Move the Point in Outline Mode

Command Name	Key	Meaning
outline-next-visible	C-c C-n	Move the point (cursor) to the next visible heading line.
outline-previous-visible	C-c C-p	Move the cursor to the previous visible heading line.
outline-forward-same-level	C-c C-f	Move the cursor to the next visible heading line that is at the same level as the one the cursor is currently on.
outline-backward-same-level	C-c C-b	Move the cursor to the previous visible heading that is on the same level as the current one.
outline-up-heading	C-c C-u	Move the cursor to a lower level if visible.

**Table 6.5. Commands to Collapse and Expand Outlines
in Outline Mode**

Command Name	Key Binding	Meaning
hide-body	ESC x hide-body	Make all body lines in the outline buffer invisible.
show-all	ESC x show-all	Make all lines visible.
hide-subtree	C-c C-h	Make everything under the heading invisible, but leave the heading.
show-subtree	C-s C-s	Make everything under a heading visible.
hide-leaves	ESC x hide-leaves	Make the body of the current heading and all subheadings invisible.
show-branches	ESC x show-branches	Make all subheadings of the current heading visible at all levels.
show-children	C-c C-i	Make headings one level down only visible.
hide-entry	ESC x hide-entry	Make the body line of the current heading invisible.
show-entry	ESC x show-entry	Make the body line of the current heading visible.

Using Screenplay Mode

It may come as a shock to you, but Humphrey Bogart did not say "Play it again, Sam" in the classic film *Casablanca*. What he actually said was, "You played it for her and you can play it for me."

Many people have a fascination with movies and perhaps have considered trying their hand at script-writing. UniPress Emacs includes the major mode called Screenplay mode that helps you properly format a movie or television script.

Operation of the Screenplay mode is simple. You can invoke it by typing ESC x screenplay-mode. On the mode line, you see what screenplay *context* you are in, such as "Scene title," "Scene description," "Speaker name," and "Speech." When you type the appropriate material, the formatting is done automatically. Here's an example:

```
1 WRITER'S OFFICE - INT - LATE NIGHT

    Joe Writer is hunched over the keyboard, pounding out his
    deathless prose. A coffeepot bubbles on a side table.
    The only other sound is a rapid click of keys.

                        JOE
                    (PAUSING IN HIS TYPING)
            Should I include a screenplay example
            here? It is a pretty neat application
            of Emacs.

    There is a moment of silence.

                        JOE
                    (ANSWERING HIMSELF)
            Yeah, sure. Why not?

    We hear again the rapid clicking of keys.
```

There are probably Screenplay modes around for other types of Emacs. Enjoy, and remember to thank us when you are accepting your Oscar for Best Screenplay.

Major Program Formatting Modes

Now, moving away from text briefly, we'll discuss Emacs' many different ways to handle program source code.

The various implementations of Emacs were designed primarily as programming editors, although they have been extended to support many other kinds of text editing. GNU Emacs offers several major modes for editing Lisp programs, a mode for C, and a mode for FORTRAN. Freemacs offers a C mode, a Lisp/Scheme mode, a Mint mode, and an assembler mode. UniPress Emacs offers modes for most programming languages. UniPress language modes have features that handle the syntactic structures of the language. Epsilon and MicroEmacs have C mode; Epsilon also has Lisp mode.

In GNU Emacs, the programming language modes, as well as the other modes, use syntax tables to determine much of what they do. The syntax of a character determines its use in the various language modes. A character's syntax usually is different in different modes. For example, the open curly brace character, {, is used to mark the beginning of a block in C source code, but it has no special meaning in FORTRAN or Lisp. The character $ has special meaning in the TEX mode, but not in C mode. Even Control characters and Meta characters can have special meanings. Because each mode may require special meaning for any of the 256 characters used in Emacs, Emacs keeps a table for each buffer that contains information about the syntax of characters in that buffer.

Because Emacs knows about all characters used in special ways in each mode, Emacs can do some fancy things. In the programming language modes, it can take you to the start of the next function or expression. It also can take you to the previous label, or copy or delete the entire function that the cursor is currently in. C mode also is discussed, but the same basic set of features is available in any language mode, and similar features are available in the text-oriented modes.

Using C Mode

The names of the commands discussed are based on the names of Lisp objects because the commands originally were written to support Lisp mode. However, by changing the syntax table, the commands are translated so that they work in C or most other programming languages. This is why Emacs uses syntax tables.

Do you remember all the standard keys for moving around in a buffer, like CONTROL-f, CONTROL-b, CONTROL-n, and CONTROL-p? What about the keys to move to the end of a line, CONTROL-a and CONTROL-e? Or the key to set the mark, CONTROL-@, and the key to transpose characters, CONTROL-t? All of these keys take on new, but similar, actions when preceded by an ESC (or when used with a META key). These are the keys you use when dealing with S-expressions and lists in Lisp or expressions and functions in C.

The definition of an expression (or a *sexps*, as it is called in GNU Emacs), is language dependent. It usually includes symbols, numbers, string constants, and anything contained in parentheses or braces. The definition of a *defun* in Lisp, or function in C, is a simple subset of this definition for expressions.

Functions are defined as anything starting with a open curly brace in column zero and extending to the corresponding closed curly brace. The set of braces that delimit a function may not be nested in any other braces. In C, function definitions cannot be nested. They must be top-level expressions, but they may have other blocks defined with them.

C Mode Commands

Some Emacs C mode commands that deal with expressions and functions are listed in Table 6.6.

Table 6.6. C Mode Commands for Expressions and Functions

Command Name	Key Binding	Meaning
	Expressions	
forward-sexp	ESC C-f	Move forward over an expression.
backward-sexp	ESC C-b	Move backward over an expression.
transpose-sexps	ESC C-t	Transpose expressions.
mark-sexp	ESC C-@	Put mark after the following expression.
kill-sexp	ESC C-k	Kill the next expression.
	Functions	
beginning-of-defun	ESC C-a	Move to beginning of function.
end-of-defun	ESC C-e	Move to end of function.
man	ESC C-h	Make function, enclosing or following the point, for the region.

In most cases these commands are bound to keys that use the ESC prefix followed by a CONTROL character normally used for moving in a buffer. The exception is ESC CONTROL-h. Because functions are one kind of expression, you can use the first set (ESC CONTROL-f, ESC CONTROL-b, ESC CONTROL-t, ESC CONTROL-@, and ESC CONTROL-k) on functions as well as other kinds of expressions. The second set (ESC CONTROL-a, ESC

CONTROL-e, and ESC CONTROL-h) works only on functions. These commands speed your movement in a C program. To see how they work, load some C code (perhaps from the Emacs distribution) into a buffer and try the commands. You will be impressed when you see the cursor hop to the top or bottom of the current function or expression.

Grinding C

Now lets look at commands that *grind* C programs. Grinding is the GNU Emacs term for keeping a program properly indented. Despite the strange name, this is an important topic because a properly indented program is much easier to read and to debug. Grinding can be accomplished as the program is entered by entering TAB (CONTROL-i) at the beginning of a new line. This indents the line properly. Properness, in this case, is dependent on the major mode and defined by a number of Emacs variables. We will cover these variables after covering another way of getting proper indentation.

If you are at the end of line and you enter a linefeed (CONTROL-j) rather than a carriage return (CONTROL-m), Emacs creates a new line and indents it properly. If you enter a TAB anywhere on the line in a programming language mode, the line is properly indented. These commands work in all major modes, but they run different indentation commands in each mode. Commands for indenting expressions are shown in Table 6.7.

Table 6.7. Commands to Indent Expressions in C Mode

Command Name	Key Binding	Meaning
indent-sexp	ESC C-q	Redo the indentation of all the lines within one expression.
indent-rigidly	C-x TAB	Shift an entire expression rigidly sideways so that its first line is properly indented.
indent-region	ESC C-\	Reindent all lines in a region.
indent-for-TAB	TAB or C-i	Redo the indentation of the current line.
newline-and-indent	C-j	Create a properly indented new line after the current line.

If you place the point in front of a function and enter ESC CONTROL-q, the entire function is properly indented. Remember, a function always must start in column zero. If you use the command with an already-indented expression, the current indentation of the first line is maintained and all the other lines in the expression are indented relative to that indentation.

If you enter CONTROL-x TAB rather than ESC CONTROL-q, the relative indentation of all the lines in the expression is maintained, and the entire block is moved sideways to make the indentation of its first line correct. This is useful after you have inserted a block of code into an existing function. This command does not move lines that start inside strings, nor does it move C preprocessor lines when in C mode.

Finally, you can reindent a region with the command ESC CONTROL-\. This produces the same indentation that would be produced if you entered a TAB at the start of every region.

Proper Indentation

Now you need to learn what proper indentation is and how to control it. Ann Landers can't help you here, but you need someone like her to settle the issue of proper indentation. Because GNU Emacs is the topic, it seems fair to start with Richard Stallman's definitions of proper code. After all, he is not only the creator of Emacs but also one of the best C programmers around.

Here is a function, from etags.c in the GNU distribution, after application of **indent-region**. The "code" is in lower case; the comments about a line's indentation are in upper case below the line. The ^ characters highlight the amount of indentation present.

```
int string_numeric_p (str)
     char *str;
^^^^^--FIVE-SPACE INDENTATION BECAUSE c-argdecl-indent IS 5
{
--IN COLUMN ZERO BECAUSE IT IS A FUNCTION
  while (*str)
^^--TWO-SPACE INDENT BECAUSE c-indent-level IS 2
    {
  ^^--TWO-SPACE INDENT BECAUSE c-continued-statement-offset IS 2
      if (*str < '0' || *str > '9')
    ^^--TWO-SPACE INDENT BECAUSE c-indent-level IS 2
        return 0;
      ^^--TWO-SPACE INDENT BECAUSE c-continued-statement-offset IS 2
    }
  ^^--BACK TO c-indent-level PLUS c-continued-statement-offset
  return 1;
^^--BACK TO c-indent-level
}
```

This style is the one that Richard Stallman recommends. Of course, there are many other styles, and Emacs provides for most of them with seven variables that control indentation in C mode. They are listed here, along with their default values. These values produce Stallman-style indentation.

c-argdecl-indent—The default value is 5. This is the indentation level for the declarations of C function arguments.

c-brace-imaginary-offset—The default value is 0. This is imagined indentation of a C open brace that actually follows a statement.

c-brace-offset—The default value is 0. This is the extra indentation for braces, compared with other text in the same context.

c-continued-brace-offset—The default value is 0. This is the extra indent for substatements that start with open braces. This is added to the *c-continued-statement-offset*.

c-continued-statement-offset—The default value is 2. This gives extra indentation for lines that do not start new statements.

c-indent-level—The default value is 2. This is the indentation of C statements in a block relative to the containing block.

c-label-offset—The default value is 2. This is the offset of labels and case statements relative to the other lines. It is normally negative.

c-tab-always-indent—The default value is t. This means that TAB in C mode always reindents the current line, regardless of where in the line the point is located.

c-auto-newline—The default value is nil. This means do not automatically add a newline before and after braces, or after colons and semicolons.

Many people prefer to put the opening brace at the end of the line starting the control structure. This is the style used in the original book on C by the creators of the language. Here is the same function using this style:

```
int string_numeric_p (str)
char *str;
{
while (*str) {
 if (*str < '0' || *str > '9')
     return 0;
}
return 1;
}
```

This kind of indentation is achieved by setting the four variables *c-argdecl-indent*, *c-continued-brace-offset*, *c-continued-statement-offset*, and *c-indent-level* to 4. The variable *c-brace-imaginary-offset* is set to 0.

If *c-brace-imaginary-offset* is set to 8, you get another popular style. Here is the same function using this style:

```
int string_numeric_p (str)
char *str;
{
while (*str) {
      if (*str < '0' || *str > '9')
          return 0;
      }
return 1;
}
```

Style is always difficult to judge. What is most important is that you be able to read the code you produce. Any reasonable style you are comfortable with is acceptable. What is a reasonable style? If you can't figure out a way to set up GNU Emacs to produce a style, then maybe it isn't reasonable!

If Emacs can indent source code for you, you can use Emacs as a valuable debugging tool. Sometimes you don't get the structure you intend to, and our manual indentation of the code shows the structure you think you have, not the real structure. Allow GNU to indent it for you, and the real structure is revealed.

Using Other Programming Modes

Emacs has the capacity for many more major modes designed for a specific programming language. C, Ada, FORTRAN, Pascal, PROLOG, Lisp—the list goes on and on. In some cases, there are actually several major modes for a single language so that various aspects of editing, testing, compiling, and debugging code are easier.

In fact, if you are a programmer, you will find it easy to modify or create your own major modes to make specific jobs less tedious. Emacs, unlike other program editors, allows for unlimited expansion. The next chapter gives you a good introduction to customizing Emacs.

General Formatting

You've been looking primarily at the major modes that impose specialized formatting on text in the current buffer. These modes format on-screen and set up the text for input into a text processor, program compiler, database manager, or other application that outputs the text.

In addition to the effects on text format exercised through major and minor modes in Emacs, there are also many general formatting features. These features normally work in all editing situations. However, the major mode currently invoked might modify their effect.

Figure 6.3 shows an example text formatting. In this figure, Freemacs is shown editing files from *The Price Guide to Autographs* by George Sanders, Helen Sanders, and Ralph Roberts.

```
*scratch* [No File]
* [No File]
emacsbk.1 z:\usr\ralph\emacs\emacsbk.1
auto z:\usr\auto
autograp z:\usr\auto\autograp
football. z:\usr\auto\autograp\football.
footcol. z:\usr\auto\autograp\footcol.
pres. z:\usr\auto\autograp\pres.
.   duo. z:\usr\auto\autograp\duo.
-----[Hit any key; only space is ignored]-----
        It is, can be the argument, not as exciting to have Sonny and not Cher;
Laurel and not Hardy; Donny and not Marie; Farrah without Jaclyn and Kate. So
here's a look at some combination signatures that could prove fun to add to
your collection (with prices):

LUCY AND DESI: The death of Lucille Ball last year followed
    that of Desi Arnaz in 1987, but does not end the five-decade long
    association of these television pioneers. The "I Love Lucy"
    series stands up today as funny as when it hit the airwaves in
    1951, and shows no sign of aging. Anything signed complete name
    by either one is rare. Most items are simply signed "Lucy and
    Desi," and that has not detracted from the value or demand. A
    card signed by both, first name only, would bring in the area
-----Emacs: duo. (Fun) --C1 L22/214 ----10----------------------------------
```

Fig. 6.3. The window on top shows open buffers; the bottom window has one of the text files copied into it.

Using Indentation

Indentation, or blank space at the beginning of a line before the text starts, is something you will use often. Regular text, for example, indents at the start of a paragraph, or indents both the left and right margins for instances of long quoted material. Program code, as you saw in the section on the C mode, uses many levels of indentation to make reading it easier.

All Emacs use the TAB key to indent a line appropriately. TAB indentation is mode-dependent, meaning that the TAB key may act somewhat differently for various major modes. Table 6.8 shows the general indentation commands for Epsilon, and Table 6.9 shows the indenting commands for GNU Emacs.

Table 6.8. General Indentation Commands for Epsilon

Command Name	Key Binding	Meaning
to-indentation	ALT-m	Move to next indentation.
indent-previous	TAB	Indent previous line.
indent-rigidly	C-x TAB	Indent rigidly.
indent-region	C-ALT-\	Indent the marked region.
center-line	ALT-s	Center the current line.
tabify-region	C-x ALT-TAB	Tabify region (convert all spaces into a combination of tabs and spaces).
untabify-region	C-x ALT-i	Untabify region (convert all tabs to spaces).
indent-under	ALT-TAB	Indent under words on previous lines. Each time you invoke it, the cursor moves to under the next word on the previous line.

Table 6.9. General Indentation Commands for GNU Emacs

Command Name	Key Binding	Meaning
indent-for-tab-command	TAB	Indent current line (as specified by the major mode).
newline-and-indent	LFD	Press ENTER followed by a TAB. For terminals that do not have a linefeed key, use C-j (linefeed), because often the ENTER key only gives you a C-m (carriage return).
delete-indentation	ESC ^	Merge two lines, which cancels an LFD.
split-line	ESC C-o	Split a line at the current point. The line to the right is dropped one line and indented to its current position.
back-to-indentation	ESC m	Move forward (or backward) to the first character that is not blank on the current line.
indent-region	ESC C-\	Indent all lines in a marked region to the column your cursor is on.

continues

Table 6.9. Continued

Command Name	Key Binding	Meaning
indent-rigidly	C-x TAB	Shift a block of lines left or right.
tab-to-tab-stop	ESC i	Indent from the current point to the next preset tab stop.
indent-relative	ESC x indent-relative	Indent from the cursor to under an indentation point on the previous line.

With some minor differences in key bindings and features, Freemacs, MicroEmacs, UniPress, and Sprint all enable you to control indentation as well.

Using Tabs and Spaces

It's not true that all programmers drink Tab. Some of us like Diet Coke. The tabs you are learning about here, of course, are those control characters (CONTROL-i) that the TAB key inserts to give varying amounts of white space. In GNU, with Text mode invoked, the TAB key (using the **tab-to-tab-stop** command) makes converting to tables (text consisting of information in columns) a breeze. Even in other modes you can use ESC i to invoke the same features.

The various flavors of Emacs enable you to modify tab stops (the distance between tabs). In GNU you do this by typing ESC x set-variable ENTER tab-stop-list ENTER and editing the list of column numbers that appear in increasing order.

An even more convenient method is to type ESC x edit-tab-stops (this also works in UniPress). This command creates and selects a buffer showing tab settings. A ruler is shown at the top of this buffer with current tab stops depicted by colons (:) above it. The buffer is in overwrite mode, so hitting the SPACEBAR once when the cursor is on a colon erases that tab stop. Typing a colon inserts a tab stop. When you have edited the ruler to your satisfaction, type CONTROL-c CONTROL-c to return to the previous buffer with the new tab stops inserted.

The default indent setting in GNU Emacs uses a combination of tabs and spaces to implement indentation. However, tabs can be a pain, especially if you are providing material that others will use in some word processing system besides Emacs. Our recommendation is to ditch the tabs completely. As you saw in the section on Indentation, you can mark regions and "untabify" (convert the tabs to spaces) with such commands as CONTROL-x ALT-i in

Epsilon and ESC x untabify in GNU. To use only spaces to indent in GNU, set the *indent-tabs-mode* variable to nil by typing ESC X set-variable ENTER indent-tabs-mode ENTER nil.

Formatting can extend beyond text to actual art, as shown in UniPress Emacs in Figure 6.4.

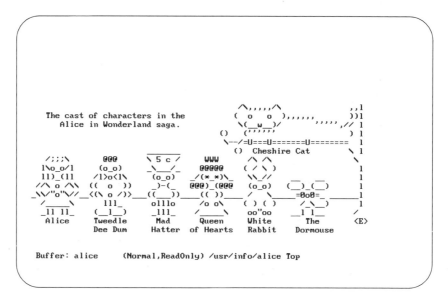

Fig. 6.4. You can use formatting to create art. Yes, Emacs is definitely a wonderland, eh, Alice?

Paginating

One of the basic concepts of formatting is *pagination*. Pagination is the process of dividing a file into pages corresponding with the pages that will be printed with a printer. When you are printing documents such as manuals, manuscripts, and letters, it is better to leave the pagination to your text processor. However, there are times when you would like to force a page break, and you easily can do so by inserting the page separator character, a *formfeed* (^L) by typing CONTROL-q CONTROL-1.

The ^L character is used as the page separator in GNU, UniPress, MicroEmacs, Freemacs, Sprint, and many other text editors. In fact, it is more common than using tabs, and you are probably safe to leave it in documents you export to other users. GNU offers several commands relating to pages, as shown in Table 6.10.

Table 6.10. Commands to Manipulate Pages

Command Name	Key Binding	Meaning
backward-page	C-x [	Move point to the previous page boundary.
forward-page	C-x]	Move to the next page boundary.
mark-page	C-x C-p	Put point and mark around this page.
count-lines-page	C-x l	Count the lines on this page.

Proper page manipulation does require a little planning and a visualization of how the text will be printed. The number of lines in a buffer that make up a page depends on the font and point size of the output device, the size of the paper, and so forth. There are only a few parameters to keep track of, however. People routinely use various flavors of Emacs to format books and manuals because it has so many advantages over other text editing and word processing programs.

Filling

A huge ice-cream sundae with hot chocolate syrup and plenty of chopped nuts as topping can be filling and satisfying. Seeing your text magically format itself on the screen is just as satisfying and darn less fattening.

Filling is the process by which Emacs breaks lines between words so that they all fit as closely as possible within the specified margins. In conventional text files, automatic filling is desired. It makes text more readable, and it saves typing time by freeing you from having to hit the carriage return (ENTER). Filling is one of the key elements of computerized word processing.

Automatic fill is activated in Freemacs, GNU Emacs, Epsilon, and UniPress by the command ESC x `automatic-fill-mode`. The automatic fill mode is a minor mode that modifies the current major mode. With it enabled, the only time you should hit the ENTER or carriage return key is at the end of a paragraph or when inserting blank lines.

There are limits to automatic filling. Should you break a paragraph somewhere in the middle, or merge two paragraphs by deleting anything between them, you may have to reformat the resulting paragraph. Emacs offers several explicit fill commands. The ones for GNU (some of them work in other Emacs as well) are listed in Table 6.11.

Table 6.11. Explicit Fill Commands

Command Name	Key Binding	Meaning
fill-paragraph	ESC q	Fill the current paragraph.
fill-region	ESC g	Fill all paragraphs in the currently marked region.
fill-column	C-x f	Set the fill-column; that is, the right margin.
fill-region-as-paragraph	ESC x fill-region-as-paragraph	Fill the current marked region, considering it to be only one paragraph.
center-line	ESC s	Center a line.

Adding a numerical argument to the fill commands for paragraphs and regions (such as ESC 1 ESC q and ESC 1 ESC g) *justifies* the text by inserting an occasional extra space between words to make the right margin even.

Converting Case

Case as it refers to the alphabet simply means capitalized (uppercase) or not capitalized (lowercase). You can change case quickly and easily. Table 6.12 shows the commands to use.

Table 6.12. Case Commands

Command Name	Key Binding	Meaning
downcase-word	ESC l	Convert the following word to lowercase.
upcase-word	ESC u	Convert the word that follows to uppercase.
capitalize-word	ESC c	Capitalize the next word.
downcase-region	C-x C-l	Convert the currently marked region to lowercase.
upcase-region	C-x C-u	Convert the currently marked region to uppercase.

6

Conclusion

This chapter is only an introduction to formatting. Emacs is extremely rich in format types because it is a text editor and it can be mated with many text processors. Because of its infinite capacity for customization, you can set Emacs to work with the formatting program or programs you need.

And speaking of customization, it's time to see how that's done.

6

Customization and

Programming

E macs is extensible and customizable—otherwise, it wouldn't be Emacs! In this chapter, you will learn some of the ways to program your Emacs to behave the way you want it to.

To be able to customize an Emacs, you have to know a bit about the internals of the version you are using. This chapter begins by covering GNU Emacs, but the concepts you learn here will help you understand how to customize any Emacs. UniPress Emacs, which is similar to GNU Emacs, is covered second. Finally, customizing Freemacs, Epsilon, and MicroEmacs is covered.

GNU Customization

GNU Emacs is written in E-Lisp, a variant of Lisp, which is one of the oldest computer programming languages. Lisp was invented at the same place where Richard Stallman began, at the Artificial Intelligence Lab at MIT. Lisp is an Extensive, general purpose, interpreted language, well suited to develop a display editor.

The GNU Emacs program is a collection of functions written in E-Lisp that collectively comprise the Emacs editor. These functions are programs and most of them call other Emacs functions to do the many things that a display editor needs to do. If you learn to program in E-Lisp and spend some time learning how GNU Emacs works " under the hood." you could actually go in and modify these programs in order to make Emacs work the way you want it to. But you probably don't want to go to that much trouble, and that is why GNU Emacs was designed to be modified easily.

You can modify your GNU Emacs by creating a file called .emacs in your home directory. That file contains an E-Lisp program that is executed every time you start Emacs. The .emacs program can modify Emacs' default key bindings, add new functions based on key sequences (macros), add programs written in E-Lisp, and modify variables that control many of the Emacs functions.

Not all Emacs use a start up or initialization file for customization. In particular, Freemacs and Epsilon enable you to directly modify the functions and variables in the editor. Epsilon also enables you to use an initialization file, but only for simple modifications.

Using E-Lisp

The simple .emacs file that follows in this section shows you how to redefine keys, create your own functions using keyboard macros, change Emacs variables, and add other functions written in E-Lisp. Chapter 9 explains how to find E-Lisp programs that other people have written. Looking at E-Lisp programs written by a variety of people helps you to understand what you can do in your own .emacs file. Thus, this section ends with a sample .emacs file. Before you look at it, however, you need to know a bit about the E-Lisp language.

Lisp is a *list* processing language. Lists are a type of data structure similar to a grocery list or laundry list. They are a linear, ordered grouping of terms. Lisp is a functional language. That means you write programs in Lisp by creating functions from other, simpler functions.

Executing those functions can change the environment of the Lisp program, which, in the Emacs case, includes the buffer you are trying to edit. A function can be simple, like "go to the end of the current line," or complex, like a regular expression search. Complex functions, however, are always built from simpler functions.

In E-Lisp, each program is made up of functions and variables. A function returns a value when processed by the E-Lisp interpreter. Functions also can modify the buffer that is being edited, when it's evaluated. Variables also are evaluated by the E-Lisp interpreter.

To execute an E-Lisp function, the E-Lisp Interpreter evaluates an E-Lisp object associated with the name of the function. In an E-Lisp program, you use the name of the function as a way to ask the E-Lisp interpreter to evaluate the object. If the function is an Emacs command, you also can execute it from within Emacs. To see how all this fits together, look at the use of the function that moves the point to the end of the current line.

Functions

The function that moves the point to the end of line is named **end-of-line** (what else?). The **end-of-line** function, like all E-Lisp functions that are Emacs commands, can be run in several different ways. The simplest way is for you to enter CONTROL-e, which is the key bound to **end-of-line**. If **end-of-line** weren't bound to a key, you could still run it using evaluate-extended-command (ESC x).

Finally, even if the **end-of-line** function weren't an Emacs command, you could evaluate it by making it into an S-expression, putting the S-expression into an E-Lisp program, and running the E-Lisp program.

To change an E-Lisp function into an S-expression, you simply enclose it in parentheses, so **end-of-line** becomes (**end-of-line**).

You also can evaluate S-expressions while editing with Emacs by entering ESC ESC (this is the default key for the command **eval-expression**) followed by an S-expression. So ESC ESC (end-of-line) moves the cursor to the end of the current line. Any E-Lisp function can be evaluated this way. You might try ESC ESC (+ 1 2 3 4). The result, 10, is displayed in the echo area. The + is an E-Lisp function that takes a variable number of numeric arguments and returns the sum of its arguments. (+ 1 2 3 4) is an S-expression.

The **end-of-line** function is also what Emacs calls a *command*, meaning it can be evaluated interactively. Interactive evaluation means that the symbol is read as text and converted to a Lisp object, which is evaluated. Because **end-of-line** is an Emacs command, you also can execute it by using ESC x, the key bound to the GNU Emacs command **evaluate-extended-command**, followed by the command **end-of-line**. That won't work for (+ 1 2 3 4)!

Instead, you can enter the key bound to the **end-of-line** command, CONTROL-e. When you enter a key sequence, GNU Emacs looks it up in the current keymap and, if it finds the key, evaluates the Emacs command bound to it. In each case, the Lisp interpreter evaluates the same function, and the point is moved to the end of the current line in the current buffer.

In the first and second cases, (end-of-line) is an expression. When the E-Lisp interpreter evaluates this expression, the point in the current buffer is moved to the end of the line. In the third case, end-of-line is a symbol that, when evaluated, returns end-of-line object. In the fourth case, the key CONTROL-e is mapped to the end-of-line symbol. The symbol is evaluated to move the point to the end of the line.

Arguments

If a function has arguments, those arguments become part of the E-Lisp interpreter list. The function **next-line**, like many Emacs commands, takes a single numeric argument. In an E-Lisp program the S-expression (next-line 4) moves the cursor down four lines. ESC ESC (next-line 4) also moves the cursor down four lines during your editing session. ESC 4 ESC X next-line, which passes the numerical argument 4 to the command **next-line**, performs the same action also.

If a function requires a non-numerical argument or more than one argument, the list is simply extended to include those arguments. If you invoke a command that requires more than a single numeric argument using ESC x, Emacs prompts you for the arguments. Few Emacs commands require you to enter more than one parameter.

E-Lisp Code

For this to make sense, you need to look at some E-Lisp code. The following examples are from the GNU Emacs help.el file. The help file is the E-Lisp program CONTROL-h invokes. You've probably used it many times if you have been working in GNU Emacs as you read this book, so you should be familiar with its actions. The following code, when executed by E-Lisp, creates a variable.

```
(defvar help-map (make-sparse-keymap)
  "Keymap for characters following the Help key.")
```

The function **defvar** is used to create the variable *help-map* with a value of an empty keymap, returned by the function **make-sparse-keymap**. The string enclosed in double quotation marks is an optional comment. You probably won't be creating many Emacs variables, unless you program on E-Lisp, but it's helpful to know how to change the values of existing variables. Before turning to variable changing, you will read about getting a keymap so that help.el can have its own key bindings.

Notice that the E-Lisp functions discussed, **make-sparse-keymap** and **defvar**, return E-Lisp objects. These objects can be all sorts of different things. The **defvar** function returns the symbol or name of the Emacs variable it created, but that name is not used in this example. The creation of a variable is the important point to grasp. The **make-sparse-keymap** function creates and returns a keymap object. That keymap would be useless if **make-sparse-keymap** were not an argument for the **defvar** function. That function links the keymap object to a symbol, creating a variable. Emacs functions always return something. Most of the commands you use with Emacs as an editor do their work and return a value that is not used.

Defining Keys

Now that you have a keymap, you can see how a key is defined in help.el:

```
(define-key global-map "\C-h" 'help-command)
```

Use the variable *global-map* when defining keys used in all major-modes. This S-expression, when evaluated, adds the key CONTROL-h to the keymap named global-map and associates it with the function **help-command**.

Now here are some keys for the new help-map keymap:

```
(define-key help-map "\C-h" 'help-for-help)
(define-key help-map "?" 'help-for-help)
```

Notice that both keys are associated with the same function. A key can be mapped to only one function, but any number of keys can be mapped to the same function. This eases customization because you can add the key definitions you desire. You also can see how to describe the CONTROL-h key, "\C-h". With this example and the one preceding for ESC-$, "\e$", you should be able to write any Emacs key. Just use \e for ESC and \C- for control.

Defining Functions

The function **define-key** takes three arguments. The first is a keymap, the second is a string that describes a key, and the third is a quoted function that the key should invoke. Notice the "'"! That single quotation mark is an important part of Lisp syntax. It treats the symbol or name associated with the key as an object but doesn't evaluate it when it is assigned. It is evaluated after the key is searched for in the table.

The following is a simple E-Lisp function:

```
(defun view-emacs-news ()
    "Display info on recent changes to Emacs."
    (interactive)
  (find-file-read-only (expand-file-name "NEWS" exec-directory)))
```

The **defun** function defines a function and returns its symbol. It has four parameters; the function name, the function's formal arguments enclosed in parenthesis, an optional descriptive string enclosed in double quotation marks, and the body of the function. All Emacs functions are defined this way, although most of them are more complicated than this one. There are no examples of control structures here, although E-Lisp has lots of them. They won't be covered here because this is a brief introduction to a complex language!

Creating a Function

Look at the example function closely, studying the way it is put together. Understanding the basic way that E-Lisp functions are constructed makes using GNU easier. Even if you never create a function yourself, you will use functions that other people have created and it helps a great deal if you can read some E-Lisp. To help you with this, each part of the example is explained. You can find additional examples in Chapter 9.

The new function's name is **view-emacs-news**. It has no arguments, which is why there is nothing between the parentheses (). Its description is "Display info on recent changes to Emacs." It is an interactive function (**interactive**), which means that it can be called from ESC x or bound to a key. The (find-file-read-only (expand-file-name "NEWS" exec-directory)) part is the body of the function, defining the action taken by the function.

First, consider the **find-file-read-only** function. It creates a read-only buffer and reads a file into it. Because the function needs a file name, the **expand-file-name** function is searched for a file named "NEWS" in the directory with a value found in the variable *exec-directory*. This is typical of an E-Lisp structure. It uses a function (**defun**) to define another function (**view-emacs-news**) in terms of other functions (**interactive**, **find-file-read-only**, and **expand-file-name**). This function's definition also uses a constant, "NEWS," and a variable, *exec-directory*. The *exec-directory* variable is one of many that you can change in your .emacs file.

Although not strictly a part of functional programming, variables are an important part of Emacs and, along with a few simple functions, the key to customization. It takes an E-Lisp programmer to create a new E-Lisp function, but any Emacs user can change the Emacs variables that control many functions. Next, you'll learn how a function gets to be a part of Emacs.

The help.el file is one of the files that comprises Emacs. The actual code interpreted by the E-Lisp interpreter when you type CONTROL-h is the file help.elc. The c stands for compiled, which doesn't make a lot of sense in an interpreted language. It means that the code has been converted to a smaller form that loads and executes faster.

7

Adding Functions

What if you want to add functions to your version of GNU Emacs? The process is similar to the way you cook a chicken according to the book *The Joy of Cooking*. You begin with getting and killing the chicken. Getting the E-Lisp file is like getting the chicken. You could kill it yourself and you could write your own E-Lisp file. Most folks get the chicken from the supermarket and the E-Lisp file from an archive. See chapter 9 for information on how to find your nearest E-Lisp "supermarket."

After you get the E-Lisp file, you should compile it. If it is named something.el, you can generate something.elc by using the command ESC-x byte-compile-file something.el. If something.el is not a correct E-Lisp file, you get error messages, and something.elc is not created. GNU Emacs has good debugging capabilities, but there is not enough room to go into debugging E-Lisp in this book. After you have a compiled file, you need to instruct Emacs to load the file when and if any of the functions in the file is invoked.

Then you add an entry to your .emacs file for each function in the file. The entries look like:

```
(autoload 'function-in-something
         "something"
         "A description of what function-in-something does"
         t)
```

Autoload is another E-Lisp function (there are many E-Lisp functions!) that creates an E-Lisp object which, when executed, loads a file and executes it. In the .emacs given at the end of this section, the **ispell-buffer** command loads ispell.elc, which contains the byte compiled code for several functions. The next argument is the documentation string, and the final argument (t) tells Emacs that this is an interactive function.

The program searches for the file ispell.elc on the path given by the UNIX environment variable *EMACSLOADPATH*. You can set this via the shell. If you run csh (the C-shell), type a line like this in your .cshrc file:

```
setenv EMACSLOADPATH .:/user/local/emacs/lisp
```

If you use the Bourne shell, sh, type two lines like these in your .login file:

```
export EMACSLOADPATH
EMACSLOADPATH= .:/user/local/emacs/lisp
```

If you don't set this variable, Emacs uses the path set in its paths.h file when it was built. You can use your .emacs file to add directories to the front of the default path. If you put this S-expression in your .emacs file, the current directory and the directory /usr/local/emacs/lisp are added to the front of the load-path variable.

```
(setq load-path
      (append
       (list nil
             "."
             "/usr/local/emacs/lisp")
       load-path))
```

Internally, Emacs keeps the load path as a list. **Setq** changes the value of that list by appending the words "." and "/usr/local/emacs/lisp" to the front of the list. The **append** function takes the load-path list, evaluates it, and creates a list containing "." , "/usr/local/emacs/lisp", and the strings that were in load-path. With the **setq** function, you can change the value of an E-Lisp variable.

Converting Keyboard Macros

One feature all Emacs versions have common is the ability to store and recall sequences of key presses. These sequences are called keyboard macros because they enable you to use the keyboard as a simple programming language. GNU Emacs keyboard macros can be bound to a key and given a name just like a regular E-Lisp function.

Simpler commands and functions are easier to add with keyboard macros, rather than with E-Lisp programs. GNU Emacs makes it easy for you to convert keyboard macros into S-expressions that you can include in your .emacs. The command **start-kbd-macro** or CONTROL-x- (starts the recording of keystrokes. The command **end-kbd-macro** or CONTROL-x-) stops recording. The command **name-last-kbd-macro** makes the set of keystrokes act just like a command. Finally, **insert-kbd-macro**, inserts an S-expression, using **fset**. This command generates the same keystrokes as a named keyboard macro into the current buffer. Then you copy the new S-expression into your .emacs file. This process was used to generate the **kbol** function in our sample .emacs file. That file is at the end of the next section.

Finding Functions and Variables

Emacs has many functions and even more variables that control those functions. You can use the **setq** function in your .emacs file to modify these variables. For example:

```
(setq fill-column 50)
```

changes the default column for wrapping lines to 50, and

```
(setq auto-save-default nil)
```

turns off auto-save. Of course, you also can use the **set-variable** command within Emacs. Typing the command ESC-x set-variable ENTER fill-column ENTER 69 (in which ENTER is a carriage return) changes the fill column to 69 in the current buffer. Table 7.1 shows some of the variables in GNU Emacs 18.57. Most of them either have a numeric value or are true/false (t or nil). You can use the **list-options** command to get a complete list.

Table 7.1. GNU Emacs Variables

Variable Name	Description
auto-save-default	The default value, t, auto-saves every file-visiting buffer.
auto-save-intervl	The default value is 300. This is the number of keyboard input characters between auto-saves. Zero means don't auto-save.
case-fold-search	The default value is t, searches ignore case.
case-replace	The default value is t, query-replace preserves case.
completion-auto-help	The default value is t, automatically provides help when asked to complete invalid input.
completion-ignored-extensions	(".o" ".elc" "~" ".bin") Completion ignores any filenames ending in any of these strings.
ctl-arrow	Default value is t, control characters are displayed with the up arrow. If set at nil, control characters are displayed in octal.
default-major-mode	The default value is fundamental-mode, but you can set to any other major mode or make it nil. If default-major-mode is nil, then new buffers use current buffer's major mode.
delete-auto-save-files	The default value is t, so auto-save files are deleted when the corresponding buffer is saved.
echo-keystrokcs	The default value is to echo unfinished commands after 1 second of no input. If you set this to zero, no echoing occurs.

7

continues

Table 7.1. Continued

Variable Name	Description
exec-path	This path is used to search for programs to run in subprocesses. Set from your PATH environment variable.
fill-column	The default value is 70. This is the column for automatic line-wrapping.
kill-ring-max	The default value is 30. This is the maximum number of elements in the kill ring.
left-margin	The default value is zero. This is the column that the indent-line function indents to. Linefeeds invoke this function in fundamental mode.
load-path	A list of directories to search for .el and .elc files. This is set from the EMACSLOADPATH environment variable or taken from paths.h when Emacs was built.
mark-ring-max	The default value is 16. This determines the maximum size of the mark ring.
mode-line-inverse-video	The default value is t. If you don't like a reverse video mode line (setq mode-line inverse-video 'nil).
next-screen-context-lines	The default value is two lines from the previous screen.
shell-file-name	The file name for inferior shells. Set from your SHELL environment variable.
tab-stop-list	The default value is (8 16 24 32 40 48 56 64 72 80 88 96 104 112 120). The list of tab stop positions used by tab-to-tab-stops. Note that this variable is a list and you must enclose it in ( )'s.
tab-width	Default is value 8. This is the distance between tab stops (for display of tab characters) in columns. Not a distinction between the tab-stop-list and tab width. The first is similar to typewriter stops. The second displays a tab character.
visible-bell	The default value is nil, so bell is a beep. If you set this to t, Emacs flashes your screen for bell.
window-min-height	The default minimum height is 4. Any windows shorter than this are deleted.
window-min-width	The default minimum width of a window is 10. Any window narrower is deleted.

7

A Sample GNU Emacs Initialization File

Here is an example .emacs file that redefines several keys using the E-Lisp function **define-key**. It adds one new function using the E-Lisp **fset** function to create a macro consisting of a sequence of keystrokes. The default is set to Text mode, and the functions in the ispell package are set up for use. The ispell package is written in E-Lisp. A semicolon at the start of a line means that everything on the line is a *comment* and will not be executed. You can create a file on your system for GNU Emacs as shown in the following example.

```
; A simple .emacs file for GNU Emacs
; First, redefine ESC-z to be suspend-emacs--it was
; zap-to-char.
(define-key global-map "\ez" 'suspend-emacs)
; Next, define CONTROL-x CONTROL-k to be kbol.
; Note that the kbol function doesn't exist yet.
(define-key global-map "\C-x\C-k" 'kbol)
; Create a function kbol that erases from the point
; to the beginning of the line. The fset function attaches
; the symbol kbol to a keyboard macro. Note that the
; string is ^@ (set-mark-command) followed by ^A
; (beginning-of-line) and then ^W (kill-region), use CONTROL-q
; followed by CONTROL-@ (or CONTROL-a or CONTROL-w) to insert
; the real control characters, don't enter the '^' character
; and then the '@' (or 'a' or 'w') character!
(fset 'kbol "^@^A^W")
; Next, set the Emacs variable default-major-mode to text
; mode.
(setq default-major-mode 'text-mode)
; Now set the file ispell.elc to autoload if you use any
; of the commands i-spell-word, i-spell-complete-word,
; ispell-region, and ispell-buffer. If you don't have
; ispell, don't use the rest of this .emacs file.
(autoload 'ispell-word "ispell" "Check spelling of word at
or before point" t)
(autoload 'ispell-complete-word "ispell" "Complete word at
or before point" t)
(autoload 'ispell-region "ispell" "Check spelling of every
word in region" t)
(autoload 'ispell-buffer "ispell" "Check spelling of every
word in buffer" t)
; And finally, redefine ESC-s to be ispell-word. It was
; spell-word.
(define-key global-map "\e$" 'ispell-word)
; And here is Emacs' way of saying that you can use the
; ESC-ESC command to evaluate lisp expressions.
(put 'eval-expression 'disabled nil)
```

UniPress Emacs

This list of variables is similar to the one that UniPress Supplies with the documentation for UniPress Emacs, a commercial Emacs for UNIX systems (binary license lists for $395). UniPress Emacs is the descendent of the original UNIX port of Emacs by James Gosling. It is similar to GNU Emacs, but it has a different programming language, MLisp; a different set of variable names; and a different set of default key bindings. MLisp is a much simpler language than E-Lisp, and it is easier to program in MLisp. On the other hand, MLisp is not as versatile.

For example, UniPress Emacs does not have the **fset** function, so keyboard macros must be converted to MLisp for storage in the initialization file. On the other hand, UniPress Emacs does have special functions, called **genon** and **genoff**, for keystroke conversion. Here is the sample .emacs, rewritten as a .emacs_pro file for UniPress Emacs. The file .emacs-pro, which does the same things for UniPress Emacs that our Emacs does for GNU Emacs, is given at the end. First, you need to be familiar with MLisp.

A Sample UniPress Emacs Initialization File

```
; A simple .emacs_pro file for UniPress Emacs

; First we redefine ESC-z to be pause-emacs.

(bind-to-key "pause-emacs" "\033z")

; Next we define ^X^K to be kbol - this function doesn't
; exist yet.

(bind-to-key "kbol" "\^X\^K")

; Now we create a function kbol which erases from the point
; to the beginning of the line. This function executes
; three built in Emacs functions. It could have been
; generated from keyboard input using genon and genoff.

(defun
        (kbol
                (set-mark)
                (beginning-of-line)
                (copy-region-to-killbuffer)
        )
)

; Next we set the Emacs variable default-major-mode to text
; mode.
```

```
(setq default-major-mode "text-mode")

; And finally we set up some MLisp functions to autoload.

(auto-load "incr-searc.ml" "incremental-search")
(auto-load "incr-searc.ml" "reverse-incremental-search")

; And we end with the value to return.

(novalue)
```

Understanding MLisp

Unlike GNU Emacs, UniPress Emacs comes with printed documentation on all its variables and functions and examples of MLisp code. It has similar variables to GNU Emacs and many of the same functions, although some have different names. In the area of customization, its major distinction is its variety of editing modes for programming language structures.

UniPress Emacs' default key bindings are often different from GNU Emacs. It's easy to redefine them, however, because GNU Emacs has a special mode with UniPress Emacs key bindings.

MLisp, also known as Mock Lisp, is a functional language. It has only integer and string variables and constants. Integer constants are groups of decimal digits, possibly preceded by a minus sign. String constants, delimited by double quotation marks, can contain control characters expressed as \n, for newline; \t, for tab; \r, for carriage return; and \b, for backspace. In addition, any control character can be expressed in the form \^C, and any ASCII code can be expressed as an octal (base 8) number in the form \010. MLisp has only *if-then-else* and *do-while* control structures.

MLisp functions, like E-Lisp functions, are invoked using the form

```
(function-name argument1 argument2 argument3 ...)
```

MLisp also has interactive functions, which may be called from within Emacs and which may be bound to a key. MLisp also has noninteractive functions. The noninteractive functions are called *primitive functions*. They can be used only in an MLisp program. MLisp functions are defined using the primitive function **defun** with syntax similar to E-Lisp. See the example in the simple .emacs_pro file. Here are some example expressions of MLisp functions:

```
(+ 5 6)
```

Add the two numbers and return the sum.

```
(setq right-margin 69)
```

Set the value of an Emacs variable.

```
(search-forward "\thello \^L")
```

Search for the string hello preceded by a TAB and followed by a formfeed (^L). The TAB could also be written \009 or as \^I.

Freemacs

Many Emacs variants also run under DOS. Freemacs is the MS-DOS version that feels most similar to GNU Emacs. It is based on a different functional language, called *Mint*. Mint is not much like MLisp or E-Lisp. It is powerful, but hard to read and understand. It has no control structures; all programming is done with functions and a clever string processor. A recent comment about Freemacs was that Mint was faithful to the spirit of TECO, the language of the original Emacs, in that it takes weeks of study just to begin to understand it!

Freemacs doesn't have, or need, the kind of customization mechanism you have seen for GNU and UniPress Emacs. The customization process for Freemacs is easy, but like everything about Freemacs, it's different from all other editors and not well documented! To customize Freemacs, you change the behavior of a working copy and save that behavior in the libraries that are loaded when Freemacs is started.

Three libraries are automatically loaded—EMACS.ED, KEYS.ED, and USER.ED—in stock Freemacs. A variable that you can modify enables you to load additional libraries. The first of the three libraries, EMACS.ED, defines the Freemacs editor. It is the fundamental library for Freemacs. The second library, KEYS.ED, defines the key bindings Freemacs uses. The third library, USER.ED, adds new functions.

The customization process involves creating new functions written in Mint, assigning them to the appropriate library, compiling and debugging them within Freemacs, and finally writing modified libraries containing the new functions. Key bindings are simple functions written to the KEYS.ED library. Freemacs has built-in functions that ease this process. Freemacs also enables you to create Mint functions from named keyboard macros, much like GNU Emacs does.

So far, we have treated customization as the process of creating a file that modifies the behavior of the Emacs in some way. The .emacs and .emacs_pro files discussed earlier in this chapter modify the editor each time it is started.

In Freemacs, you modify the editor, debug and test the modification, and save the modified editor.

Of course, you could modify the source of a UNIX Emacs so that your customization was built into it, but that approach doesn't make sense when the editor is shared by many users. Each user has his or her own idea of how Emacs should be customized. The Freemacs approach is sensible for a DOS editor because it is used by a single person.

Customizing Freemacs

In the .emacs and .emacs_pro initialization files, you set variables, for example *default-major-mode* in .emacs, that determine the default behavior of the editor. Every user of an Emacs on a UNIX system can set the preferred default behavior using the initialization file in their home directory. In Freemacs, the default settings are determined by whatever is stored in the libraries that are loaded when Freemacs starts up. To change the behavior of Freemacs you must execute Mint functions that change those settings. Freemacs has two special functions, *edit-options* and *ef*, that make it easy for you to modify the editor.

The *edit-options* function, which modifies Freemacs variables, calls a buffer, *mint-edit*, in a special mode, Options. You use simple one-letter commands (n for next, p for previous, s for set, and ? for help) to inspect and possibly modify the values of the variables. The variables are similar to those for GNU Emacs given earlier in this chapter. Changes in the variables take effect immediately, so you can see the effects of the changes as you make them.

When you have finished customizing the Freemacs variables, you enter q to exit the *edit-options* function. If you then exit Freemacs, you are informed that the editor has been modified (if you made changes) and asked whether you would like to save the changes. If you answer yes, emacs.ed is modified.

In Freemacs everything is a function. Freemacs has three kinds of functions. The first kind is functions that return a value stored in a memory location, such as the variables just used to set *edit-options*. The second kind of function is a key binding. Instead of returning a value, these "functions" return a string that names another function and possibly a parameter for that function. The third kind of Freemacs function is what is normally thought of as a function, a subprogram that returns a value. All of these functions return a string. The syntax of the string determines the kind of function. Mint is a weird and wonderful language!

Customizing Freemacs may involve modifying the variables, modifying or adding to the key bindings, and modifying or adding to the functions. You have just seen how to do the first of these. The next section describes modifying key bindings and modifying functions, starting with key bindings.

Freemacs has the command **ef**, for edit function, which generates Mint code for any function that is already in the libraries. The code it generates is inserted into a special buffer called *mint-edit*. Now any buffer can be "compiled," in the same sense that GNU Emacs byte-compiles files. When Freemacs compiles, however, it directly modifies the editor. So if you use **ef** to generate the Mint code for binding keys, you can edit that code to change the binding and then compile with CONTROL-c CONTROL-c to change the bindings in Freemacs.

Here is what a typical key binding looks like. Note the spaces; they are required here.

```
Name:K.C-x 4 C-g
[*]F:ring-the-bell[*]
```

To change the key binding, you could modify either the name, `K.C-x 4 C-g`, or the function, `F:ring-the-bell` in this case, or both. For example, you can create a new key, CONTROL-x 4 CONTROL-q, and bind it to **capitalize-word** by changing *g* to *q* and *ring-the-bell* to *capitalize-word*, resulting in:

```
Name:K.C-x 4 C-q
[*]F:capitalize-word[*]
```

If you want to modify a group of keys, you can move them all into the *mint-edit* buffer with single command:

```
ESC x ef ENTER K. ENTER
```

Note that this **ef** command loads all functions starting with *K.*. This is a fairly slow process, so be patient. Or if you only want to edit a few keys, you can load them individually with **ef** commands like:

```
ESC x ef ENTER K.ESC x ENTER
```

The function name you give in response to the **ef** prompt is used as a match string. **ef** loads all functions that start with the given string. The first letter indicates the library when the binding is stored. *K* means KEYS.ED. The second character is *.* (a period) for keys and *:* (a colon) for interactive functions. If you give a name but no library symbol, all libraries are searched for functions matching that name.

Modifying the third kind of functions is just as easy: use **ef** to load them into *mint-edit*. The command ESC x ef ENTER F: ENTER (ENTER being a carriage return) loads all the functions from EMACS.ED (remember F for fundamental and : for interactive) into the buffer. It takes a few minutes to complete this process, so you might want to get in the proper frame of mind for Mint programming while you wait. Mint programming is tricky, and if you goof, the editor usually crashes when you test your function. Keep backup copies of EMACS.ED, KEYS.ED, and USER.ED in case you render Freemacs unusable!

The best reason for using **ef** to generate the Mint code for all the commands is so that you can study them and learn how they work. Save the *mint-edit* buffer to a file using the **write-file** command (CONTROL-x CONTROL-w), and study that file before you attempt to modify any of the functions in it. You also can save a list of the user-modifiable variables and the key bindings in the same way. These are all handy to have around.

Functions you may want to add to your USER.ED library are the functions you can generate using keyboard macros. To add them to Freemacs you must use the following steps:

1. Determine the set of keystrokes needed to add the functions.

2. Store the steps as a keyboard macro by entering CONTROL-x before you key in the macro and CONTROL-x after you key it in.

3. Test the macro with CONTROL-xe.

4. Name it with ESC x name-last-kybd-macro ENTER *name* ENTER.

5. Convert macro to Mint code in *mint-edit* with ESC x ef ENTER *name* ENTER.

Here is the Mint code for a keyboard macro that prints the word *test*:

```
Name:U:test
[*]#(Frun-kbd-macro,t<>e<>s<>t<>)[*]
```

Here is a code with some control key sequences in it:

```
Name:U:top_bot
[*]#(Frun-kbd-macro,Escape<><>b<>e<>g<>Return<>C-x<>C-x<>)[*]
```

To implement any changes or to add new functions, you must have the new Mint code in a buffer in mint mode. This could be the *mint-edit* buffer or another buffer you create for this purpose. Just enter the **find-file** command (CONTROL-x CONTROL-f) on a nonexistent file to create an empty buffer. Copy the functions you want to install to this buffer, change the buffer's mode to mint mode (use ESC x mint-mode ENTER), and then issuc the **done-editing** command (CONTROL-c CONTROL-c). To make the changes permanent, answer yes when Freemacs asks whether you want to save the modified editor.

A Sample Freemacs Initialization File

Here is the Freemacs equivalent of our standard initialization file. This simple Mint file has been named mine.min.

```
; mine.min, a simple file used to modify Freemacs

; Press CONTROL-c CONTROL-c (done-editing) to install these changes.
; Then answer 'y' to the prompt from save-all-libs to write the
; changes to disk.

; This function, when executed, will cause the functions
; defined in this file, and any other changes you have made,
; to be incorporated into your version of Freemacs. Note the
; [*] delimiters that surround the function. Also note the
; #, which tells Mint to evaluate this function.

[*]#(F:save-all-libs)[*]

; First we bind the key ESC-z to the function that runs a
; DOS shell.
Name:K.M-z
[*]F:suspend-emacs[*]

; Now we bind the key ^X^K to kbol, which doesn't exist yet.

Name:K.C-x C-k
[*]U:kbol[*]

; Next we create kbol, a kill to beginning of line function
; that will be stored in USER.ED (that's what the U: is for,
; the ':' means interactive). The function Fkill deletes to
; the special mark '^' which is always set at the beginning
; of the current line. This could be done with a keyboard
; macro, but Fkill is nicer.

Name:U:kbol
[*] #(Fkill,^) [*]
```

7

MicroEmacs

GNU Emacs, UniPress Emacs, and Freemacs are all written in interpreted functional languages, E-Lisp, MLisp, and Mint, respectively. And all of these Emacs enable you to use the same functional language as an extension language to extend and modify them. MicroEmacs and Epsilon are examples of Emacs not designed this way.

Customizing MicroEmacs

MicroEmacs is written in C and has a macro language that you can use to extend it. MicroEmacs' macro language is more like BASIC than Lisp. In fact, it doesn't use parentheses at all! It has the various commands, like GNU Emacs commands, that manipulate text, buffers, and windows within the editor. Micro-Emacs has more than 100 built-in commands.

Commands take a fixed number of arguments from zero to three. All arguments are character strings, but they might also be string constants, string variables, or strings returned by functions. The commands and functions interpret the strings as characters or as numbers, depending on the context. Numbers are stored as strings of digits.

MicroEmacs has BASIC-like *directives* that are used to build control structures. These control structures decide which lines are executed within a macro. Directives start with ! and must be the first nonblank item on a line. The !endm or end macro directive is used in our sample emacs.rc. There are directives for loops, directives for *if-then-else*, and even a directive for *goto*! BASIC programmers should feel right at home. There are also several types of *variables*.

Using Variables in MicroEmacs

Environmental variables are used to control different aspects of the editor. MicroEmacs' environment-variable names start with a dollar sign ($). The sample emacs.rc uses one called *$discmd* (for display command). *User variables* are string variables that you can use in your programs. Their names start with a percent sign (%). The *buffer variables* hold text from your buffer. These are associated with a single buffer and have the same name as the buffer preceded by a pound sign (#). Finally, *interactive variables* are a clever way the program prompts the user for information. Interactive variables start with the at sign (@).

Like Freemacs, all variables are stored as strings. Anywhere you can use a variable, you also can use a constant. Constants are expressed as strings in double quotation marks. Special characters within a constant are represented using the tilde (~) as an escape character. These special characters are listed in Table 7.2.

Any character that is not a special character but follows a tilde is passed unmodified. Numeric constants are strings, but they do not need the double quotation marks.

7

Table 7.2. Special Characters in MicroEmacs

Character Code	Meaning
~n	Newline
~r	Carriage return
~l	Linefeed
~~	Tilde
~b	Backspace
~f	Formfeed
~t	Tab
~"	Quote

Using Functions in MicroEmacs

Functions exist to manipulate all these variables. MicroEmacs has about 50 functions, including functions for mathematical equations, logic, bit manipulation, and string manipulation and comparison. Because all functions take strings as arguments and return a string, they may be combined in different ways. Following is an example of a condition involving logical functions, relational functions, environment variables, and two kinds of constants. This !if directive would be followed by lines containing MicroEmacs macro language statements to be executed if the conditions were met.

```
!if &and &seq $line "" $not &equ $curline 1
end-of-line
!endif
```

This reads: If the string in the environment variable *$line* (the current line) equals "" (the empty string), and the numeric environment variable *$curline* (the current line number) is not one, move the cursor to the end of the current line.

A Sample MicroEmacs Initialization File

MicroEmacs uses an initialization file called emacs.rc on MS-DOS systems and .emacsrc on UNIX systems. The MicroEmacs distribution comes with a sample emacs.rc for IBM PCs that binds some keys and sets up a number of named macros. These macros have numbers, rather than text names, and MicroEmacs has special functions to execute them. The function **execute-macro-10** is an example. You can have up to 40 of these numbered macros. They serve as a partial substitute for the named macros provided by the other Emacs.

```
; simple emacs.rc for MicroEmacs 3.10

; We turn off display in the echo area
set $discmd FALSE
; let the user know that the emacs.rc is running
; write-message "[Setting up....]"

; set up key bindings

; This key is bound to quick-exit by default, we rebind
; it to i-shell.

bind-to-key i-shell M-Z

; Now we bind a key to execute macro 40

bind-to-key execute-macro-40 ^X^K

; and create the function delete to beginning of line
; as named macro 40.

    40 store-macro
    set-mark
    beginning-of-line
    kill-region
!endm

; MicroEmacs does not have modes in the same manner as the
; others. Here we set a global mode that causes automatic
; line wrapping.

add-global-mode wrap

; Now we use a function to set the fill column. MicroEmacs
; uses more specialized functions and fewer environment
; variables than GNU Emacs

set-fill-column 69

; And re-enable display in the echo area by setting a
; variable.

set $discmd TRUE
```

Because MicroEmacs is written in C and designed to run on PCs, it is the most portable of Emacs. It is available on almost any reasonable machine except for an Apple. The Free Software Foundation currently is boycotting Apple; a text file that tells why is included in the GNU Emacs distribution. Regardless, if you often work on different machines, it is great to have the same editor on each one.

However, the DOS version of MicroEmacs is limited to medium-sized files. All the files you are viewing must fit into the regular memory. MicroEmacs has diverged from GNU Emacs in feel. This seems appropriate because MicroEmacs is used as an editor in a DOS environment, but many folks would rather use a more "GNUish" Emacs. If you need to edit larger files and you like the feel of GNU Emacs, check out the commercial version of Emacs, Epsilon. Of course, you have to be willing to pay about $200 list price.

Epsilon

Epsilon can edit any number and any size of files, limited only by your available disk space and patience. Editing can get pretty slow when you edit multimegabyte files on a DOS system. The DOS version of Epsilon can use EMS memory, if you have it, to speed up the process.

Epsilon is written in EEL, the "Epsilon Extension Language." EEL is a C subset, close enough to C that you hardly notice the difference. If you already know how to program in C, you should be comfortable in EEL. If you are not a C programmer, EEL is harder to learn than MLisp or MicroEmacs' macro language. E-Lisp is hard to learn because there is so much to it. Mint is hard to learn because it is Mint. EEL, like C or E-Lisp, is thorough but somewhat difficult to learn.

Customizing Epsilon

EEL, unlike the other languages discussed in this chapter, is compiled and strongly typed. Strongly typed languages require you to say what type (integer, string, and so on.) each variable is when you write the program. The other languages were interpreted languages, and their variables' type was determined at run time. Compiling makes a big difference in programming style. If you are more used to writing C programs than writing Lisp programs, EEL might seem much more natural than E-Lisp. If you've never programmed before, you probably will find it easier to do simple programs in E-Lisp or MLisp.

Usually, you do not need to program in EEL in order to customize Epsilon. There are two other ways to customize it. You can create a command file that modifies the editor when you run it, or you can modify the editor interactively and save the state of the modified editor in a state file. The first method is more limited, but it does allow you to rebind keys, create named keyboard macros, and create new prefix keys. The second method is similar to the way you can customize Freemacs. Because Epsilon's command-file method is close to the methods for the other Emacs variants, here is a command file for Epsilon.

A Sample Epsilon Initialization File

```
; Epsilon start-up--run this file using Epsilon's load-file
; command. First we rebind the ESC Z key to the Epsilon push
; command. You have to use A (for ALT) to define this, but
; ALT or ESC will work to run it.

(bind-to-key "push" "A-z")

; Now we create a function as a keyboard macro. In Epsilon
; we have to define a macro before we can bind it to a key.

(define-macro "kbol" "C-@C-AC-W")

; Next we define a key to invoke the kbol command.

(bind-to-key "kbol" "C-XC-K")
```

You cannot set variables or execute commands to change the default mode in a command file. To do that, you would use an EEL program or, more likely, change the editor interactively.

Using Epsilon State Files

After you have customized Epsilon using a command file, or more likely, interactively, you can save its *state* in a state file. When Epsilon starts, it reads a file called epsilon.sta. This file is similar to the libraries in Freemacs because it contains the commands, key bindings, and variable settings that Epsilon uses. Like Freemacs' libraries, but unlike command files, state files can be read only on start-up.

To create a state file, you type ESC-x write-state ENTER, ENTER meaning to hit the carriage return or ENTER key. Epsilon asks you to name the file. Epsilon comes with the stock state file named epsilon.sta for MS-DOS (or epsilon.st2 for OS/2 or espilon.stu for UNIX), but you can name your state file something different.

If you called your state file mine.sta (that would be mine.st2 for OS/2 and mine.stu for UNIX systems), when you start Epsilon you would use the command **epsilon -smine** to start it with your defaults. This mechanism enables several users to share an Epsilon and still have their own defaults.

7

If you want to save your defaults as epsilon.sta so that you don't have to use the -s option each time you start Epsilon, it is wise to copy the original epsilon.sta file to a safe place before replacing it. That way you can revert to the default settings whenever you want to.

Using EEL

It helps to look at an EEL program and to learn how you can extend Epsilon by creating new functions. Epsilon comes with source code, in EEL, for all its commands, and a tutorial on programming in EEL. It also has a debug mode to help you debug EEL code. Now, on to some examples.

Here is hello.el (we just couldn't resist!):

```
#include "eel.h"  /* EEL's standard definitions */

command hello()
{
  say("Hello World");
}
```

This prints "Hello World" in the echo area. Of course, it has to be compiled first and then loaded into Epsilon.

You compile EEL source files in MS-DOS with the program eel.exe (in UNIX, type /usr/bin/eel). Then load the resulting byte code file, hello.b (hello.bu in UNIX), into Epsilon with the **load bytes** command. Then, if you type ESC-x hello ENTER, Epsilon types "Hello World." You probably don't want to save this file in your state file.

Because EEL is a strongly typed language, you must declare your variables before you use them. Here is another variation on hello.el that uses a variable.

```
#include "eel.h"  /* EEL's standard definitions */
command hello()
{
    char temp[12];                      /* declare a local variable temp   */
    strcpy (temp ,"Hello World");       /* which is an array of characters */
                                        /* put "Hello World" in it.        */
    say("%s",temp);                     /* display it in the echo area     */
}
```

EEL has the same basic data types as C, but no floating point. It also has arrays, structures, and unions. It has pointers and typedef. It has assignment operators. If you don't know C, then learning to program in EEL also will help you learn the C language.

7

Someone on Usenet made the nasty comment that Epsilon was a failed C compiler that had been salvaged to create a text editor! It is far more than that, but EEL certainly does bear a strong resemblance to C. Of course, E-Lisp bears a strong resemblance to Common Lisp but is extended and modified for its special use. EEL also has specialized I/O and other Epsilon-specific functions. It is a good language for writing editor extensions.

Sprint

Borland International's Sprint is an Emacs descendant that offers (among other user interfaces) an interface that recognizes the Emacs command set. Sprint's integral programming language is C-like. Like other Emacs, this language enables you to completely customize Sprint's operation.

Because several books already have been written about Sprint (including one by coauthor Ralph Roberts), examples won't be used here in the interest of saving space. Sprint, however, is a good alternative to other Emacs on both MS-DOS and UNIX systems (the UNIX version of Sprint is available from Hunter Systems) if you need extensive formatting and printer support capabilities.

Conclusion

The explanations and examples in this chapter are a start in basic customization of Emacs. These are actions anyone can do. However, we encourage you to delve further into programming in Emacs, because there is almost nothing that cannot be done from within Emacs. No other editing software offers you this practically unlimited freedom.

The next chapters will move on to advanced topics. There are still many features that you have not yet learned.

7

Chapter 8

Advanced Topics

I n this chapter, you move beyond text processing and into more advanced realms of Emacs. It is human nature to master a new way of thinking by relating it to a well-known process. If you do this with Emacs, you will miss much of its true potential. Emacs is a good deal more than a normal text processor; it can't be compared to other text processors. After all, can you have thousands of files open at once in vi or WordPerfect? By this time, you probably are well aware of the difference and are excited about using Emacs in unlimited ways.

Emacs is a way of life, and with apologies to Jimmy Stewart and the classic movie, it is indeed a wonderful life.

Mail

Many UNIX systems are connected to the world through various networks or through the phone lines. You can send and receive electronic mail, or *E-mail*, to other users on your system, as well as to hundreds of thousands of people all over the world. Because electronic mail is so much easier than regular post, called "snail mail" in UNIX jargon, you may find yourself using it often.

Using UniPress Berkmail

GNU and UniPress Emacs manage both incoming and outgoing E-mail easily. UniPress features Berkmail, which is short for

Berkeley Mail, a program developed as part of BSD UNIX by the University of California at Berkeley. Berkmail is written to emulate Berkeley Mail.

To send mail within UniPress and GNU, type CONTROL-x m. You then are presented the word *To:* at the top of a newly created mail buffer. Enter the user name and electronic address of the person you are sending the message to. If he or she is on your local system, all you need is the user name, such as "jane" or "bob" or whatever. If the message is not local, the address needs to be more explicit, depending on the network used.

For example, if your system has access to the Internet, you could send mail to the authors of this book by typing author@cs.unca.edu (Ralph Roberts) or boyd@cs.unca.edu (Mark Boyd). The magic of UNIX and network communications would move the message from your machine to the University of North Carolina at Asheville's computer system, where you could retrieve and read it by calling your mail into Emacs.

Below the "To:" for UniPress (GNU works the same way) is a subject line. Enter the subject you are writing about (such as, "What a great book, guys," or "Did you know you left out..."). Below that, you can type the text of the message. When you are finished, type CONTROL-c only for UniPress to send the message on its electronic way.

To check for mail in UniPress Emacs, type CONTROL-x r. If there is mail, you are presented with a list of messages in a window. Another window displays the first message. While in a mail buffer, you can send a reply by typing the letter *r* in UniPress. UniPress automatically attaches the address and subject. You simply write your reply, then type CONTROL-c to send it. The letter *a* appears in front of the mail-messages subject line in your messages listing when your reply has been answered.

Various commands for movement in a list of unread messages are shown in Table 8.1.

Table 8.1. UniPress Berkmail Commands

Command	*Meaning*
p	Previous message
n	Next message
f	Scroll message in other window down
b	Scroll message in other window up
m	Start new message
r	Reply to message

8

Command	Meaning
s	Save message in window to a file
x	Exit from Berkmail

Like the rest of UniPress, Berkmail is a well-thought-out, logical system. If you use it, you'll find the commands both intuitive and standardized.

Using GNU Mail

As you saw previously, you start the mail system in GNU Emacs the same way as in UniPress. Type CONTROL-x m to get the mail buffer, or from UNIX's command line, type emacs -f mail. A "To:" and "Subject:" also appears, along with a few extra lines, such as "Cc:" (which means carbon copy). Typing other users' names and electronic addresses on the "Cc:" routes a copy of your message to them as well. In fact, you can have several names there, separated by commas, such as:

```
Cc: boyd@cs.unca.edu, author@cs.unca.edu
```

The same scheme works on the "To:" line also, both lines enabling you to send the message to more than one person. The bottom line in a newly created mail buffer is "—text follows this line—." Everything above this line is referred to as the mail *header*. Drop below the text line (using CONTROL-n moves you down a line at a time), and start the text of your message. When you are through entering and editing (you can use all GNU's standard editing commands in a mail buffer), type CONTROL-c CONTROL-c to send the message.

Here are the possible lines in a mail buffer header:

To: Users and mailing addresses to which the message
          is addressed.

Subject: What the message is about.

CC: Additional mailing addresses, but whose readers
          should not regard the message as addressed to
          them (carbon copy).

BCC: Additional mailing addresses to send the message
          to, but which should not appear in the header of
          the message actually sent (hidden carbons).

FCC: Name of a file (in UNIX mail file format) to
          which a copy of the message should be appended when
          it's sent--i.e., a way to mail a file and at the same
          time attach an explanatory message.

8

```
From:    Your valid electronic mailing address for replies.

Reply-To: Use if replies are to go to another address.

In-Reply-To: If replying to a message, this describes it.
```

The "To:," "CC:," "BCC:," and "FCC:" fields can appear any number of times, specifying the many places the message is to be sent.

Table 8.2 shows the commands used while you are in the mail buffer, as given in the GNU info file relating to this buffer.

Table 8.2. GNU Emacs Commands for Mail

Command Name	Key Binding	Meaning
mail-send	C-c C-s	Send the message, and leave the *mail* buffer selected.
mail-send-and-exit	C-c C-c	Send the message, and select some other buffer.
mail-to	C-c C-f C-t	Move to the To header field. Creates one if there is none.
mail-subject	C-c C-f C-s	Move to the Subject header field. Creates one if there is none.
mail-cc	C-c C-f C-c	Move to the CC header field. Creates one if there is none.
mail-signature	C-c C-w	Insert the file ~/.signature at the end of the message text ( ).
mail-yank-original	C-c C-y	Yank the selected message from Rmail. This command does nothing unless your send-message command was issued with Rmail.
mail-fill-yanked-message	C-c C-q	Fill all paragraphs of yanked old messages, each individually.

Using Rmail

GNU Emacs has an extensive mail management subsystem called *Rmail*. You enter it by typing ESC x rmail within Emacs or by typing emacs -f rmail from the UNIX (or XENIX) command line. Rmail then opens an Rmail buffer (not to be confused with the regular Mail buffer described previously). Rmail then reads your primary mail file (named RMAIL in your home directory), loads any new incoming messages from your electronic "inboxes" (part of the UNIX operating system), and reveals the first new message on the screen.

Rmail offers a set of commands for easy manipulation of messages, both old and new. We predict that after you get used to Rmail, you will do all your mail within Emacs and abandon the UNIX "mail" utility.

New messages are arranged sequentially and assigned a *message number* by Rmail. After a message has been read, you can either delete it or save it in the RMAIL file for later referral. Keeping and finding hundreds of messages in Rmail is easy. Typing CONTROL-x CONTROL-s while in Rmail saves the RMAIL file. You also are asked to save the file when exiting Emacs, even if you have quit Rmail without saving (by using the letter *q* for quit). In other words, Rmail is treated like any other modified buffer and you have a chance to save the files before leaving Emacs.

Rmail Basic Commands

The regular Emacs scrolling commands work in Rmail—that is, ESC v scrolls up, CONTROL-v scrolls down, ESC < takes you to the top of the message, and ESC > moves to the bottom. However, because you obviously do a lot of scrolling while reading messages, two one-key commands have been added to make this operation even less troublesome. Pressing SPC (the SPACEBAR) scrolls the text down; DEL (the DELETE key) scrolls the text up. Table 8.3 provides several commands for moving between messages as well.

Table 8.3. Commands to Manipulate Mail Messages in Rmail

Command Name	Key	Meaning
rmail-next-undeleted-message	n	Move to the next nondeleted message, skipping any intervening deleted messages.
rmail-previous-undeleted-message	p	Move to the previous nondeleted message.
rmail-next-message	ESC n	Move to the next message, including deleted messages.
rmail-previous-message	ESC p	Move to the previous message, including deleted messages.
rmail-show-message	j	Move to the first message. With argument N, move to message N.

continues

8

Table 8.3. Continued

Command Name	Key	Meaning
rmail-last-message	>	Move to the last message.
rmail-search	ESC s REGEXP	Move to the next message containing a match for REGEXP (regular expression). If REGEXP is empty, the last regexp is used again.

Deleting Messages

There are two kinds of *message deletion*. Deleting a message (see d in Table 8.4) removes it from the list of current messages and makes it "transparent" to several of Rmail's commands. Deleted messages are retained in the RMAIL file in your home directory. The **undelete** command (u) can retrieve them. *Expunging* a message (see e and x in Table 8.4) erases it totally from Rmail.

Table 8.4. GNU Emacs Rmail Deletion Commands

Command Name	Key Binding	Meaning
rmail-delete-forward	d	Delete the current message and the next nondeleted message.
rmail-delete-backward	C-d	Delete the current message, moving the previous nondeleted message.
rmail-undelete-previous-message	u	Undelete the current message, or go back to a deleted message and undelete it.
rmail-expunge	e or x	Expunge the Rmail file.

Using More Than One Mail File

Rmail reads new mail in your UNIX inbox into the RMAIL file, where it is added to the old mail stored there (that is, to nonexpunged messages). The regular UNIX mail files (/usr/mail/*your_user_name* in Sys V and /usr/spool/mail/*your_user_name* in Berkeley and XENIX) do not have provisions for keeping mail after it is read, nor all the commands to manipulate messages that Rmail boasts.

So new mail is read into the RMAIL file in a process called *getting* new mail when Rmail first starts. You can check for new messages at any time, by typing the letter *g*. Rmail then looks for new mail again.

In the spirit of openness in Emacs, you are not restricted to just one RMAIL file. You actually can have as many files as you like, even those tied to other electronic addresses, and edit them all with Rmail. If you worked for a software company, for example, you might have one address for technical questions, another for bug reports, and yet another for mail from personal friends. Being able to categorize and pre-sort your mail in this manner can be a great time-saver.

Table 8.5 shows the commands GNU Emacs provides for manipulating several inboxes and Rmail files.

Table 8.5. GNU Emacs Commands to Manipulate Multiple Rmail Inboxes

Command Name	Key Binding	Meaning
rmail-input	i FILE	Read FILE into Emacs and run Rmail on it.
set-rmail-inbox-list	ESC x set-mail-inbox-list ENTER FILES	Specify inbox file names for current Rmail file to get mail from.
rmail-get-new-mail	g	Merge new mail from current Rmail files' inboxes.
rmail-get-new-mail	C-u g FILE	Merge new mail from inbox file FILE.

Copying Messages to Files

At times you'll want to write a message you've received into a conventional file. There are two commands to handle this action: o and CONTROL-o. The first, the letter *o*, writes the message to a file in Rmail format (**rmail-output-to-rmail-file**). Pressing the CONTROL and o keys together (CONTROL-o) writes the message to a file in UNIX mail format (**rmail-output**). Both commands create a new file if one does not exist by that name or *append* the message to a file already in existence.

Either of these work fine, but consistency is important. If you use o to save messages, you should always use o. Inadvertently using CONTROL-o to save to an Rmail format file can cause a "simultaneous editing" warning when you attempt to save the buffer, and some text could be lost.

Using CONTROL-o rather than o would be better if you are saving messages to a file that other users access also. Some of them are no doubt using

8

other mail processing utilities that might be unable to recognize Rmail's. Again, consistency is the watchword.

Labels

Labels are used to retrieve a specific mail message in a file containing hundreds or even thousands of old messages. A label enables you to store messages by classes such as "business," "personal," or by any other word (label) that you want to use. Messages can have more than one label. Table 8.6 lists the commands GNU provides in Rmail for using labels.

Table 8.6. GNU Emacs Commands for Using Labels in Rmail

Command Name	Key Binding	Meaning
rmail-add-label	a LABEL	Assign the label LABEL to the current message.
mail-kill-label	k LABEL	Remove the label LABEL from the current message.
rmail-next-labeled-message	C-M-n LABELS	Move to the next message that has one of the labels LABELS.
rmail-previous-labeled-message	C-M-p LABELS	Move to the previous message that has one of the labels LABELS.
rmail-summary-by-labels	C-M-l LABELS	Make a summary of all messages containing any of the labels.

Several predefined labels are assigned automatically. They are shown in Table 8.7.

Table 8.7. GNU Emacs Predefined Labels in Rmail

Label	Meaning
unseen	The message has never been current. New mail messages are marked this way until Rmail is called and you read the message.
deleted	The message had been deleted but is still in the Rmail buffer. It can be retrieved by an **undelete** command (the letter *u*).
filed	The message has been copied to some other file. Both o and CONTROL-o automatically assign this label.

8

Label	Meaning
answered	An answer to the message has been sent using the r command.
forwarded	The message has been forwarded to other users with the f command.
edited	You've edited the message in Rmail.

Unlike labels you name and assign with the a key, the predefined labels cannot be removed.

Rmail Summaries

To help you keep track of stored mail messages, Rmail offers a *summary* feature. Summaries are reports generated by Rmail into a buffer. They consist of a single-line message with the message number, the date, who the message is from, any labels, and the subject. When the summary buffer is created, Rmail also provides movement and deletion commands. Table 8.8 lists the commands that generate a summary.

Table 8.8. GNU Emacs Commands to Create a Summary in Rmail

Command Name	Key Binding	Meaning
rmail-summary	h	Summarize all messages.
rmail-summary-by-labels	l LABELS	Summarize messages that have one or more of the specified labels.
rmail-summary-by-recipients	C-M-r RCPTS	Summarize messages that have one or more of the specified recipients.

Here is an example of an Rmail summary, generated with the **rmail-summary** command, using the RMAIL file belonging to coauthor Ralph Roberts:

```
 97  15-May            rms@gnu.ai.mit.edu   GNU Manifesto
 98  15-May            rms@gnu.ai.mit.edu   Unrelated question
 99  15-May  : biome!silvert@cs.dal.ca     emacs books
100  15-May  ER-DAEMON@oteen.cs.unca.e     Returned mail: Service unavailable
101  15-May  goldfish@concour.cs.conco     Desktop guide to EMACS
102  15-May  goldfish@concour.cs.conco     Re: Desktop guide to EMACS
103  15-May            rms@gnu.ai.mit.edu   Unrelated question
104  15-May            rms@gnu.ai.mit.edu   GNU Manifesto
105  15-May  ORNSTEIK%MYIPA%dupont.com     Desktop Guide to EMACS
```

8

```
106   15-May                         boyd  Re:  Garbo
107   15-May   robertsr%cs.unca.edu@RELA  Desktop Guide to EMACS
108   15-May       rms@gnu.ai.mit.edu  Unrelated question
109   15-May       rms@gnu.ai.mit.edu  docs
110   15-May   stevea@prodnet.la.locus.c  Re: EMACS
111   15-May           jbw@cs.bu.edu  Why do people use other Emacs?
112   15-May           jbw@cs.bu.edu  Re: Why do people use other Emacs?
113   16-May   archie@quiche.cs.mcgill.c  archie command: prog telebit
114   16-May                     boyd  Emacs, what else
115   16-May       rms@gnu.ai.mit.edu  Unrelated question
116   16-May       gumby@cygnus.com  Why do people use other Emacs?
117   16-May       rms@gnu.ai.mit.edu  Even more unrelated
118   16-May       rms@gnu.ai.mit.edu  Even more unrelated
119   16-May       rms@gnu.ai.mit.edu  Even more unrelated
120   16-May       paul@cygnus.com  Emacs support
121   16-May   to: paul@cygnus.com  Emacs support
122   17-May       rms@gnu.ai.mit.edu  docs
123   17-May                     boyd  book
```

The previous example probably exemplifies the utilitarian value of
Rmail for reading and tracking your mail messages far better than a whole
chap-ter on the subject. In a few weeks, you probably can amass hundreds of
messages, many of which have valuable information that you need later. Rmail's
summary message management features become extremely useful in such
cases.

Rmail adds even more to its flexibility by enabling you to edit the Rmail
Summary buffer in a number of ways. Table 8.9 shows the commands provided
for that message manipulation.

Table 8.9. GNU Emacs Commands for Editing Rmail Summaries

Command Name	Key Binding	Meaning
rmail-summary-goto-msg	j	Select the message described by the line that the point is on.
rmail-summary-next-all	C-n	Move to the next line and select its message in Rmail.
rmail-summary-previous-all	C-p	Move to the previous line and select its message.
rmail-summary-next-msg	n	Select the next nondeleted message. Skip lines marked "deleted" (deleted messages stay until they are "expunged").
rmail-summary-previous-msg	p	Move to previous line, skipping lines marked "deleted"; select line's message.

8

Command Name	Key Binding	Meaning
rmail-summary-delete-forward	d	Delete the current line's message, then move to the next nondeleted message.
rmail-summary-undelete	u	Undelete and select this message or the previous deleted message in the summary.
rmail-summary-scroll-msg-up	SPC	Scroll the other window (presumably Rmail) forward.
rmail-summary-scroll-msg-down	DEL	Scroll the other window backward.
rmail-summary-exit	x	Kill the summary window.
rmail-summary-quit	q	Exit Rmail.

Sending Mail with Rmail

Naturally, getting mail predisposes that you also send mail. Even while in Rmail, you can use GNU Emacs' Mail buffer, described earlier in this chapter. Just type CONTROL-x m and a mail buffer is opened with the heading of "To:" and "Subject" described in the earlier section on mail. Don't confuse this process with Rmail, the GNU Emacs subsystem we are discussing in this section. Your Rmail buffer remains open, of course, but the Mail buffer overlays it. When you have finished the message, typing CONTROL-c CONTROL-c sends it, closes the Mail buffer, and restores the Rmail buffer to your screen.

You have the option of invoking the Mail buffer with CONTROL-x 4 m, which opens a window on the screen and creates the Mail buffer there. Your Rmail buffer also remains on the screen, although it shrinks to accommodate the Mail buffer.

That's one way to send mail while you are in Rmail—by essentially dropping out temporarily to use the regular Emacs E-mail facilities. The second way is by using Rmail's own built-in commands for sending mail. These commands actually use the Mail buffer as well but are a bit more convenient. These commands are listed in Table 8.10.

Editing Within Rmail

Two commands, the letters *t* and *w*, enable you to edit while in Rmail.

Table 8.10. Rmail Commands to Send Mail

Command Name	Key Binding	Meaning
rmail-mail	m	Send a message.
rmail-continue	c	Continue editing an already started outgoing message.
rmail-reply	r	Send a reply to the current Rmail message.
rmail-forward	f	Forward current message to other users.

Rmail buffers are normally *read only*, which means that you cannot edit them. Typing the w command toggles you into editing mode, however. The Emacs movement, deletion, and other editing commands now may be used to modify the message. This facility can be handy if you want to add your own comments to a message before forwarding it to someone else, or to make additional notes before storing the message. Typing CONTROL-c CONTROL-c returns you to Rmail and saves your changes, and CONTROL-c CONTROL-] aborts, discarding any changes.

The other command, t, is useful as well. Anyone who has ever received or seen electronic mail sent by a UNIX system knows there are many often-cryptic header lines. Here's an example:

```
Received: from relay1.UU.NET by fletcher.cs.unca.edu (4.1/UNCA-CS/4-29-91)
    id AA07325; Wed, 15 May 91 18:53:45 EDT
Received: from prodnet.la.locus.com (LOCALHOST.UU.NET) by relay1.UU.NET
    with SMTP
    (5.61/UUNET-internet-primary) id AA02031; Wed, 15 May 91 18:53:42 -0400
Received: by orchard.locus.com (5.61-AIX-1.2/2.29 )
    from roulette.la.locus.com with SMTP
    (from stevea@prodnet.la.locus.com/stevea@prodnet.la.locus.com)
    id AA01382 for cs.unca.edu!robertsr; Wed, 15 May 91 15:39:20 -0700
Received: by prodnet.la.locus.com (5.61-AIX-1.2/0.07d) id AA237014 for
    robertsr@cs.unca.edu; Wed, 15 May 91 15:38:39 -0700
Date: Wed, 15 May 91 15:38:39 -0700
From: Steve Anderson <stevea@prodnet.la.locus.com>
Message-Id: <9105152238.AA237014@prodnet.la.locus.com>
To: robertsr@cs.unca.edu
Subject: Re: EMACS
Newsgroups: alt.msdos.programmer,comp.emacs
In-Reply-To: <1991May15.130326.22185@rock.concert.net>
References: <1991May14.202420.26958@cci632.cci.com>
    <NELSON.91May14222846@sun.clarkson.edu>
Organization: Locus Computing Corp, Los Angeles
Cc:
```

This message, in reply to a posting in the comp.emacs newsgroup, has a rather long heading, and many lines are less than interesting (OK, they're totally boring). Most UNIX mail systems show you all this before you get to the meat of the message—the actual message. It is not uncommon for the headers in a short mail message to be several lines longer than the text of the message. Rmail "cleans" the message for you by automatically displaying only the significant parts of the header. Here's the same message header as shown in Rmail:

```
Date: Wed, 15 May 91 15:38:39 -0700
From: Steve Anderson <stevea@prodnet.la.locus.com>
To: robertsr@cs.unca.edu
Subject: Re: EMACS
Newsgroups: alt.msdos.programmer,comp.emacs
In-Reply-To: <1991May15.130326.22185@rock.concert.net>
References: <1991May14.202420.26958@cci632.cci.com>
    <NELSON.91May14222846@sun.clarkson.edu>
Organization: Locus Computing Corp, Los Angeles
Cc:
```

This example of header lines is shorter and much less confusing. However, all the header lines are still in the Rmail buffer. You can toggle them on and off by typing t. When the extra lines are revealed, you then can type w to edit and delete any of the header lines.

In general, Rmail is considerably better than the generic mail system that came with your UNIX system. Because it is part of your favorite editor, Emacs, Rmail usually is easier to use and more convenient than stand-alone mail programs.

Emacs is a way of life, and the postman always beeps twice.

Printing

As you saw in Chapter 6, printing hard copy text (that is, printing on paper) is done by a separate text processing program that uses the formatting commands you embed with Emacs. Those commands vary with the text processor that the file is intended for. These separate text processing packages include the UNIX nroff and troff utilities, the TeX typesetting package, Scribe, GNU's own groff, psroff, Elan, and numerous others.

For a quickie note or memo, however, it would be convenient to print from Emacs and keep going. Both GNU and UniPress enable you to do this easily. To print the current buffer's contents with a UNIX lp device, type ESC x print-buffer. Page headings are automatically added that show the file name

8

and page number, which is convenient for long buffers that take many pages to print out. If you don't want a page header, use ESC lpr-buffer in GNU. To print only part of a buffer, mark a region and use the command ESC x print-region (or ESC lpr-region in GNU to print without page headings).

UniPress Emacs has the advantage of built-in PostScript support, for printing directly from UniPress to such PostScript lasers as the NEC SilentWriter (on which this book's original manuscript was printed), the Apple LaserWriter, and other high-end laser printers. You also can access and specify the printer fonts resident in these lasers.

Emacs As a Working Environment

Emacs often is used as a working environment on UNIX-based computers. Epsilon and Freemacs also can be used this way under MS-DOS. The Emacs starts as soon as the users log onto the computer. It runs until the users log off. In the GNU Emacs manual (page 22 of the Sixth Edition), Richard Stallman writes, "The recommended way to use GNU Emacs is to start it only once, just after you log in.... Usually you do not kill the Emacs until you are about to log out."

You already know several ways to use Emacs as more than a text editor. Using Dired mode, Emacs becomes a file-management tool. Using Rmail, you can read and send mail without leaving Emacs. These modes enable you to work within Emacs and use other UNIX or DOS utilities or application programs. In this section you learn about another way to use Emacs. Emacs can run other programs for you by running what GNU Emacs calls an *inferior shell*. In an inferior shell, you can do many of the same things you would do in a regular shell, including compiling programs. Working with inferior shells in Emacs enables you to work in an environment much like the Integrated Development Environment available in PC-based compilers.

Understanding Inferior Shells

8

You might think RMS (Richard Matthew Stallman) is putting down the shell by calling it "inferior," but "inferior" means only that the shell process runs under the Emacs process. This order gives the Emacs process special status with respect to the shell process. If the inferior shell is run interactively (communicates with the terminal), Emacs can control the shell and any processes running under the shell.

Using Emacs as a shell (as shown in Figure 8.1 with Epsilon), you can access the system from within the editor and even edit the results in the buffer.

```
e.1             emacs-in        emacsbk.ap1     gnu.text.2      secure.4
e.10            emacs-init      emacsbk.ap2     gnu.text.3      secure.5
e.11            emacs.book      emacsbk.ap3     gnu.text.4      service
e.12            emacs.co        emacsbk.ap4     gnuget          temp.spm
e.13            emacs.g         emacsbk.bac     gnuman.txt      toronto
e.14            emacs.guide     emacsbk.cov     gnuord          trash
e.5             emacs.help.ps   emacsbk.ins     gnutext.2       ue.tmp
e.6             emacs.hlp       emacsbk.pf      gnutext.tar     uedoc.tar
e.6~            emacs.magic     emacsbk.toc     head1           ukeys
e.7             emacs.mss       emark           head2           unifun
e.8             emacs.ol        emisc           linda.bk3       unipress
e.9             emacs.pro       enews           linda.bk4       unipress.tbl
e.ak            emacs.pub       epfun           linda.bk5       unipress.tmp
e.ap1           emacs.tut       escreen         linda.cmt       unipress.var
e.ap2           emacs.txt       eshell          linda.cor
e.ap3           emacs2          esources.2      linda.cov
e.ap4           emacs2.pro      esupport        linda.ins
$ adf
Filesystem                              MB Used  MB free   MB total   % full
/                                          140      322        462      30%
$


Epsilon 5.03 [Process] process:   100% *
```

Fig. 8.1. The result of listing the current directory, then checking to see how much disk space is left.

Emacs is not used to replace the shell (command interpreter) program, but acts as a user interface to the shell. There are two advantages to running an inferior shell interactively. The first advantage is that you don't have to leave Emacs to run other programs. You simply can open a window and work in that window. The second advantage is that you can, in GNU Emacs, use all Emacs' editing functions.

Both GNU Emacs and UniPress Emacs support interactive buffers running a shell, but in different ways. GNU Emacs has a command that enables you to use a shell within a window. UniPress Emacs has a command that enables you to use a window as a terminal that runs a shell. In both cases, the Emacs process must be executing simultaneously with the shell process. You actually can have many shell windows running their own processes. Only an Emacs running under a multitasking operating system, like UNIX, can have interactive shells. But there are other ways to use an inferior shell that do not require the Emacs process and the inferior shell to be running simultaneously. Emacs running under DOS as well as under UNIX can use these methods.

8

Understanding GNU Shells

GNU Emacs, UniPress Emacs, Epsilon, and Freemacs all have commands that take input from a buffer and send the shell's output to a buffer. Under DOS, the Emacs program cannot run at the same time as the shell program, but, as you shall see, these commands work just as well as they do on UNIX. The shell commands in GNU Emacs are covered first.

There are three GNU Emacs shell commands. The first is **shell**, which runs an interactive inferior shell, with all information flowing through the special Emacs buffer *shell*. The second is **shell-command** (ESC !). This command prompts you for a program name and then executes that program in a noninteractive inferior shell. The display output, if any, from that shell goes to *shell* or, with a numeric argument to the command, to the current buffer. Finally, there is **shell-command-on-region** (ESC |), which prompts you for a program name and then runs an inferior shell that executes that program *with the current region as its input*. The shell output normally is inserted in the *shell* buffer, but if you give this command a numerical argument (CONTROL-u ESC |), then the shell output replaces the region.

When you give the command **shell-command**, Emacs prompts you for a shell command line. It then runs that command line in an inferior shell, opens a window into the *shell* buffer, and inserts the output from the shell in that special buffer. If you give the command ls –l, the output data from a long directory listing of the current directory is placed in the *shell* buffer. You then can do whatever you want with that data. This is useful when you need to insert some system information in a file you are editing.

The other two shell commands have different uses. The **shell** command enables you to work in the interactive shell almost as though you weren't in Emacs, but all input and output is captured in a buffer. The **shell-command-on-region** command enables you to use many UNIX programs as *filters* on the region.

Understanding UniPress Shells

8

Two of these commands have different names in UniPress Emacs; one has a different function. The UniPress names are **ANSI-shell**, **shell-command**, and **filter-region**. The name ANSI-shell describes the action of this UniPress. It opens a window that acts as a terminal, an ANSI terminal. Any input typed into this window acts like input typed on that terminal. Any output written to the buffer appears on that "terminal's" screen, complete with all ANSI screen commands. ANSI terminals are a subset of a DEC VT100. This subset usually is defined as a terminal on UNIX systems, so you actually can run full-screen applications in it.

For example, you can run GNU Emacs in a UniPress Emacs ANSI- shell window. This process has some limitations because UniPress Emacs views the ANSI terminal's input before it is sent to the "terminal." A few Emacs commands that are still active in an ANSI-shell are processed by UniPress Emacs instead of being sent to the Emacs process running in the ANSI-shell. Most UniPress Emacs commands, including all the editing commands, are not active in an ANSI-shell. You can create multiple ANSI-terminal windows.

Using Shells

GNU Emacs' *shell* buffer also acts as a terminal, but in a much different manner. The window runs in a special mode, called *shell mode*. It remains as an editing window, but it does have a special command for sending input to the shell. The mode doesn't act like a terminal when it receives output; it acts like an Emacs window. Shell mode has some interesting commands for inferior shells. These commands enable you to use GNU Emacs to manage the processes running in the inferior shell and the input and output of those processes. Two commands help make inputting to the shell easier.

The first command is **copy-last-shell-input** (CONTROL-c CONTROL-y). This command copies the last shell input and inserts it into the *shell* buffer, but does not insert the newline because that would cause it to be sent to the shell. This is a simple history recall mechanism that enables you to edit the previous command and then re-execute it. In shell mode, hitting ENTER (the carriage return) enters the current line as input to the shell. The **send-shell-input** command is bound to the ENTER key. The **copy-last-shell-input** command makes it easy for you take advantage of **send-shell-input** command. You could simply move the point back to any line, do any editing you want, and hit ENTER to execute that line. Of course, that action would change the com-mand as it appeared in the buffer, which **copy-last-shell-input** wouldn't do.

There are three commands for managing output in the *shell* buffer. The first, **show-output-from-shell** (CONTROL-c CONTROL-r), moves the point and the window so that the output from the last command given appears at the top of the window. This is handy if the last command produced many lines of output.

If you don't want the output from a shell command, you can use the second command, **kill-output-from-shell** (CONTROL-c CONTROL-o), to delete all output since the last input. If you enter new type into the shell buffer and then decide you don't want it, you can use the third command,

8

kill-shell-input (CONTROL-c CONTROL-u), to get rid of everything you entered since the last output.

Finally, shell mode provides a limited form of job control. It has five commands that deal with interrupting, signaling, or exiting the shell or the processes running under it. These commands are shown in Table 8.11.

Table 8.11. Commands to Perform Job Control in Shell Mode

Command Name	Key Binding	Meaning
interrupt-shell-subjob	C-c C-c	Interrupt this shell's current subprocess.
kill-shell-subjob		Send a kill signal to the *shell* buffer's current subprocess.
quit-shell-subjob	C-c C-|	Send a quit signal to the *shell* buffer's current subprocess.
shell-send-eof	C-c C-d	Send eof to the subshell (or to the program running under it).
stop-shell-subjob	C-c C-z	Stop the shell's current subprocess.

These commands replace some of the control you lose by running a shell in the *shell* buffer. Three of these commands are bound to the CONTROL key you would enter if you were simply in the shell, prefixed by CONTROL-c. They are CONTROL-c CONTROL-c, CONTROL-c CONTROL-d, and CONTROL-c CONTROL-z. Many computer systems use CONTROL-c as an interrupt key. The UNIX csh, ksh, tcsh, and zsh shells use CONTROL-z to suspend the shell's current process. And CONTROL-d is the UNIX end-of-file signal. In each case, Emacs intercepts the regular key (CONTROL-c, CONTROL-d, or CONTROL-z) before it can get to the shell, so you must use an Emacs command instead. GNU Emacs makes the keys you need for those commands easy to remember if you use the normal keys prefixed by CONTROL-c.

There are two commands that send signals to the process running in *shell*. They are **kill-shell-subjob** and **quit-shell-subjob**. These commands partially replace the shell's **kill** command. The **kill** command is used to send many kinds of signals to processes running under the shell. GNU Emacs' commands have less control, but they handle the two most commonly used signals, **kill** and **quit**.

Even with all of these commands, you can't run anything that requires more than simple line-oriented input and output in the *shell* buffer. Emacs enables you to send only the current line, using the **send-shell-input** command. This is sent as a line terminated by linefeed, to the shell or subprocess. Output from the process is inserted, in front of the point, in the buffer. No screen positioning is supported. This is the price you must pay for being able to edit in the *shell* buffer. Of course, this style of communication works well for running compilers, linkers, and even debuggers, all of which are strictly line-oriented on most UNIX systems.

GNU Emacs also keeps track of the working directory for the *shell* buffer's shell by looking for **cd**, **pushd**, and **popd**, the shell commands for changing the current directory, at the start of lines input by **send-shell-command**. This enables you to use the working directory as the default directory when you specify files. GNU Emacs also enables you to rename the *shell* buffer, using the **rename-buffer** command. After you have renamed it, you can create a new *shell* buffer. This process can be repeated to supply as many shell mode buffers as you need, all running simultaneously and having different working directories.

In yet another example of the power of Emacs, we issued a **find / -print** UNIX command and got the results shown in Figure 8.2.

```
$ find / -print
/
/dev
/dev/root
/dev/rroot
/dev/swap
/dev/rswap
/dev/scratch
/dev/rscratch
/dev/recover
/dev/rrecover
/dev/d1057all
/dev/rd1057all
/dev/dsk
/dev/dsk/f0d8t
/dev/dsk/f0d8dt
/dev/dsk/f0d9t
/dev/dsk/f0d9dt
/dev/dsk/f1d8t
/dev/dsk/f1d8dt
/dev/dsk/f1d9t
/dev/dsk/f1d9dt
/dev/dsk/f0q9dt
Epsilon 5.03 [Process] process:  0% *
```

Fig. 8.2. Part of a list of all the files on the mounted file system (thousands!) inserted into the current buffer.

UniPress' **filter-region** command and GNU Emacs' **shell-command-on-region** enable you to use the current region as input to a process and to either capture its output in a special buffer or use the output to replace the region. The latter case is where the **filter-region** command gets its name. The concept of programs that act as filters is an important part of the design of most UNIX system utilities. This command enables you to use those utilities on any part of any Emacs buffer.

Understanding Emacs and DOS Shell Processes

On DOS systems, Freemacs attempts to be as GNUish as is physically possible. It succeeds remarkably well, but shell commands are one feature for which DOS is inherently limited. You can't have a *shell* buffer or ANSI-shell window without at least two processes: one to run the buffer or window and the other to run in the buffer or window. The best you can do in DOS is to redirect the output of a subprocess into a window or use the contents of a region as input to a process. You also can do both of these actions simultaneously. DOS systems cannot update the Emacs display while running shell commands, because the Emacs process is not running, so you won't see the changes in the buffer until after the command has completed.

Although DOS has only a single process that can run different programs in sequence, it does enable that process to have its input and output redirected. That way, a program's input can come from a file, rather than from the keyboard, and the process' output can go to a file, rather than to the screen. This is called I/O *redirection*. I/O redirection is used in UNIX to pipe the I/O from an inferior shell process into an Emacs process buffer. In UNIX this can take place interactively with both processes running.

With DOS, this process must take place sequentially. First the Emacs program is running, then it is suspended while the subprocess runs, and then the Emacs program is resumed. If the Emacs program sets up a temporary file containing a copy of the region before the subprocess is run, the subprocess can use this file as input. If the subprocess' output is redirected to a temporary file, then when the Emacs program is restarted, it can insert this file in a buffer or use it to replace the region.

Freemacs has the same three shell command names as GNU Emacs, but Freemacs' **shell** and **shell-command** are the same command. They are both equivalent to the **shell-command** in GNU Emacs. They enable you to run a DOS program and capture its output in a buffer. If you give one of these commands without a numeric argument, the output from the subprocess goes to a special buffer called *shell-output*. With a numeric argument, the output goes to the current buffer. The **shell-command** command is bound to ESC-!.

8

You can use CONTROL-u ESC-!, in which CONTROL-u is the numeric prefix, when you want output to the current buffer. Epsilon has the same names as UniPress Emacs and, when running under DOS, the same limitations as Freemacs.

Freemacs and Epsilon also have **shell-command-on-region** (ESC |), which prompts you for a program name and then runs that program with the current region as its input. The output from the program is inserted in the *shell-output* buffer. If you give this command a numerical argument (CONTROL-u ESC |), the program's output replaces the region. In this case, it is a **filter-region** command. Many DOS utilities are designed to act as filters; in fact, many DOS utilities are ports of the corresponding UNIX filter utilities. Freemacs or Epsilon, when used with filters like **grep** or **sort** (not the **sort** that comes with DOS, but the more powerful one that comes from GNU and has been ported to DOS), can give a DOS user much of the feel and versatility of a UNIX system.

Compile and Tag Commands

The original purpose of Emacs was to serve as a programmers' editor, and Emacs has many properties that support this purpose. This section covers two important features with which Emacs supports programmers: the **compile** command and the **tag** commands.

PC users who are programmers often complain that UNIX systems do not offer the features of the Integrated Development Environments (IDEs) available on PCs. Actually, if those users had tried developing large applications, they might have discovered how restrictive those IDEs are! But PC IDEs certainly are ideal for simple things, like entering, compiling, and debugging small C programs. Emacs, of course, provides much of the same convenience in a way that supports work done with large programs as well as with small programs.

The programming language editing modes make Emacs a powerful and easy-to-use program editor. The **compile** command, which you will look at next, makes Emacs into an IDE for UNIX programmers, an integrated environment that works well for both small and large programming projects. The **tag** commands, which end this section, supplement the **compile** command and the programming language editing modes. These commands give the Emacs user the ability to handle large programming projects.

8

Compiling Programs

There are two commands used when compiling programs with external compilers: **compile** and **kill-compiler**. The default for the **compile** command is to run a make process, using the current buffer's default directory, in an asynchronous inferior shell. An asynchronous process is one that runs independently of the process that started it. This is a batch process rather than a interactive process like the **shell** command runs. The error messages from **make** appear in the *compilation* buffer as the compilation proceeds. When you give the **compile** command, Emacs opens a new window for this buffer. This window is not made into the current window, and it may be closed without affecting the compilation process. However, it is updated as error messages come in. You can watch the progress of the compilation in this window as you do other things in other windows. The **kill-compile** command can be used to abort **make** if it becomes evident there is no point in continuing.

Having the *compilation* buffer updated even when it isn't being displayed supports UNIX-style compiling. Unlike DOS IDEs that force you to wait until the compile is completed or aborted before you can look at the sources that have erred, Emacs enables you to fix the early errors before the **make** is finished. The information you need to find those errors is inserted in the *compilation* buffer when the compiler finds the errors. Emacs uses that information to display the code where errors have been found using the **next-error** command.

The **next-error** command, bound to CONTROL-x ‘, brings the *compilation* buffer back in one window as it brings the file where the next error occurred up in another window. The point is placed on the line where the error was found, and the corresponding error message is scrolled to the top of the window into the *compilation* buffer. You can edit the file with the error or simply note where it occurred. Each time you enter the **next-error** command, you see not only the next error message, but also the actual file where that error was found and the location in that file where that error was discovered. This works even if hundreds of source files are being compiled. In fact, because the compilation is continuing while you edit files where errors have already been found, this method works best with complicated programs involving many files. Fixing errors at the same time that you are using the compiler to discover other errors is an efficient process.

Two related commands, **grep** and **kill-grep**, run the grep regular expression pattern matcher on a file or set of files. Grep works much like the regular expression pattern-matcher built into Emacs. It outputs all the lines in a file containing strings that match a given regular expression. The **grep** command's output goes to the *compilation* buffer. The **kill-grep** command is used to abort the grep process when the appropriate match has been found. The *compilation* buffer behaves the same with these commands as it does with the **compile** command. The **next-error** command becomes a **next-match** command. Now you can step through all occurrences of an RE found in a set of files. You can check the first matches while grep searches for others. If the **next-error** command is given a numeric argument, it goes back to the first error (or match) that was found instead of going on to the next one.

Big programs involving hundred of files can be difficult to work with because it is almost impossible to keep track of which files have which functions in them. The **grep** command helps you find a function and all references to it in other files, but it takes too long to do the search if many files are involved. Tags provide an efficient and effective way to track these functions' locations. Tags are labels for locations in files kept in a special file.

Using Tags

The tags functions use a special file, created by the program etags. This file contains information about the locations of functions in files. The shell command **etags** *input_file_list* creates a file called Tags in the current directory. The *input_file_list* contains the space-separated names of all the files you want to include in the Tags file. The format of this file depends on the version of etags you are using, but basically it contains the names of all the functions found in the files in *input_file_list* and enough information for Emacs to find each function quickly. The contents of this file are collectively called a tag table. Etags is compatible with E-Lisp, FORTRAN, TeX, and LaTeX "functions." It automatically recognizes each type of file, so you do not have to tell it what to look for.

Tag files do not have to be named Tags and do not have to be in the default directory of the current buffer. Emacs has the command **visit-tag-table**, which selects a named tag file. Several of the tags commands also prompt you for a file name. If you do not select a tag table file, the file called Tags in the default directory for the current buffer is used. Table 8.12 lists the commands GNU Emacs can carry out on a tag table (other Emacs have a similar but limited set of functions for handling tags).

As you see, quite a lot can be done! With Emacs and tags, you can learn your way around a program made up of many files as easily and as rapidly as you can a small program consisting of only a few files.

8

Table 8.12. Commands to Manipulate Tags

Command Name	Key Binding	Meaning
find-tag	ESC .	Finds the first instance of TAG. With a numeric argument, finds the next instance of the last tag you specified.
find-tag-other-window	C-x 4 .	Like find-tag, but this command displays the file where the tag is located in another window.
tags-search		Does an RE search for the same RE in each file.
tags-query-replace		Performs the same query-replace on each file.
tags-loop-continue		Restarts the last-executed tag's command (one of those listed previously) from the current location of the point.
next-file		Visits the next file in the selected tag table. With a numeric argument, it visits the first file.
list-tags		Displays all the tags defined in a particular file.
tags-apropos		Displays all the tags with names that match an RE.

Emulations

Yet another benefit about an extremely flexible program like Emacs is that it can be made to resemble almost any other editor in operation and in keystrokes. Like a chameleon, it can change its appearance to match the surroundings. In fact, Borland International originally advertised its Emacs-derived Sprint word processing package as "the Chameleon." Sprint comes with user interfaces that enable it to mimic the operation of such lesser packages as Word, WordPerfect, WordStar, and Multimate, yet keeps the advantages of the Emacs philosophy. This works in both the DOS and the UNIX versions of Sprint. There is even a pure Emacs user interface.

GNU Emacs provides several emulations oriented toward the packages found on larger UNIX and VMS systems. The rest of this topic concerns those emulations, as described in the GNU Emacs manual.

8

Understanding the EDT (DEC VMS Editor)

Emulation of Digital Equipment Corporation's EDT text editor is turned on by typing ESC x edt-emulation-on. ESC x edt-emulation-off restores normal Emacs command bindings.

Most of the EDT emulation commands are keypad keys, and most Emacs key bindings are still available. The EDT emulation rebindings are done in the global keymap, so there is no problem with switching buffers or major modes while in EDT emulation.

Understanding Gosling Emacs

You can turn on emulation of Gosling Emacs (which is what UniPress Emacs is based on) by typing ESC x set-gosmacs-bindings. Many keys have to be redefined, especially those using the CONTROL-x and ESC prefixes, to work as they do in Gosmacs. ESC x set-gnu-bindings rebinds your keys to the definitions they originally had. It also is possible to run Mocklisp code written for Gosling Emacs.

Using vi (Berkeley UNIX Editor)

The vi editor is provided with almost every UNIX system sold these days. It is much simpler than Emacs, and many people are already well-practiced in its use. You can make Emacs act like vi by typing ESC x vi-mode. This is a major mode that replaces the previously established major mode.

Another vi emulator that many contend more thoroughly resembles real vi can be called by typing ESC x vip-mode. To get from emulated vi command mode back to ordinary Emacs, type CONTROL-z.

Fun!

Just the day-to-day use of Emacs is a lot of fun. Because Emacs is the work of Richard Stallman and many other free spirits, rather than some stuffy corporate development team, it also has humor embedded in it. Following are just a few of the amusing diversions you can find in GNU and, to lesser extent, other Emacs.

8

Using the Dissociated Press

Have you ever grown weary after a long day of punching out text for some boring company report, school term paper, or the like? Of course you have, we all have. Want to get even with all those lines of text, all that yawn-producing prose? Indulge yourself! Let it all go! Call up the Dissociated Press and scramble the heck out of that sucker! You'll feel much better. The results are often highly hilarious.

The Dissociated Press, a feature of GNU Emacs, is invoked by typing ESC x dissociated-press. Here's an example generated using the preceding paragraph.

```
Hing out text thatte heck outer long day ong day of puncing
prose. Indull haveport, schompany report, sciated
Presssociatedissou'll fed Pressults are ofte you have, we along
dayve you ever grown some borint have, we all Dissociated
Punching out, school often hat yawn-produchind sch better. The ll
have. Want up the Dissociated! Let it alts are oft all go! Call
urse you'll feel me boring compandulge yourselften highly hines
of text for somble boring companyawn-producing prose. paper, or
the term pape. Want to get alll hecke? Of that sucker! You'll
feer. The resulong day of put Of course you come boring company
reporm paper, or thoor the ll up the likever grown wear grown
weary af text, schooroducing prose. Issociated Prm pany repress
and scrall those lines of yoursel much better. yourself! the
hecourse you hany report, scing prose. The resul te. Inday of
punche Dissociated Producing prourse you'llge your the it all go!
Calll have. Indulge paper often highly hilarxt all grown weary
afthosese you'll term paper, oducing prose you everout of text
of thatedurse you hall have. Want tourself! report to get even
alle the out of thave, we all have, we all school term
paproducing Press amble the prose. Inday of puny repou'lll go!
Call up those term paper, out of that sucke? Of course ter long
day You'll that yawn-prose like? Of course yof text, like?
```

Try using a numerical argument, both negative and positive, for differing results. We used ESC 1 ESC x dissociated-press in generating the preceding paragraph.

Feel free to let us know which paragraph (the original or the dissociated) you found to be the clearest in meaning and the most succinct. Thank you (we think)!

Playing the Towers of Hanoi

A classic test in artificial intelligence programming for several decades has been the Towers of Hanoi game. Because GNU Emacs uses a variant of Lisp, which is a declarative-type language used for artificial intelligence, you should not be surprised that the Towers of Hanoi works in GNU Emacs, nor that it is included in the standard distribution.

When you invoke Hanoi by typing ESC x hanoi, Emacs shows you how to solve the game, using animation to move disks among the three posts. All the disks are of graduated size, from large to small. The object is to get all the disks stacked on one pole, the largest on the bottom and the smallest on the top. At no time can a larger disk be placed on top of a smaller one. It's a heck of a lot more complicated than it sounds. Figure 8.3 shows GNU Emacs running the Towers of Hanoi in animation mode. It's fascinating to watch GNU solve the problem.

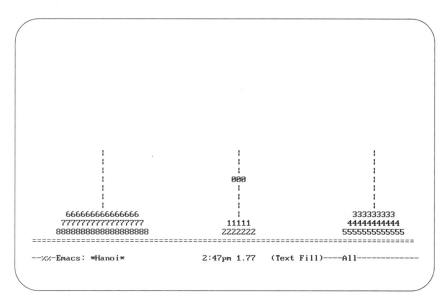

Fig. 8.3. The Towers of Hanoi is a game often used to demonstrate artificial intelligence.

The default is three disks, but try it by typing ESC 9 ESC x hanoi. Emacs may take a while to solve that one. This little exercise may seem silly at first glance, but when you attempt to figure out all the permutations Emacs is considering in solving the Towers of Hanoi, you should be solidly sold on its power!

Spook, Are You Listening, Spook?

There is an intelligence-gathering agency of the Federal Government called the National Security Agency. They run satellites, microwave taps, and many other communication intercept devices to keep track of whatever information they keep track of. One of their areas of information tracking is electronic traffic over the various networks, including telephone and computer networks. They are especially interested in international traffic.

Intelligence people often are called "spooks." The NSA spooks, having billions of words pour through their computers every day, can't possibly eavesdrop on every conversation or message. So they have their computers look for certain key words, the use of which "red flags" (a term not so significant now with the fall of the Soviet empire) messages for human attention.

Someone, just to irritate the NSA, wrote a little function called "spook.el," which is included with GNU. The function generates a number of these key words. When you finish a message, just type ESC x spook, and several words designed to make the bells go off at NSA are inserted into your message.

We certainly do not advocate their usage, but here's a sampling:

```
"nuclear Nazi Ortega NSA terrorist Rule Psix spy Mossad Noriega
Cocaine Kennedy genetic ammunition $400 million in gold bullion
Nancy Reagan."
```

By the way, you may first need to load the function into Emacs by typing ESC x load-library ENTER spook ENTER.

Playing Doctor, Doctor

Is your work driving you crazy? Well, GNU Emacs can be your psychiatrist too. Just type ESC x doctor. This function also demonstrates artificial intelligence. Carry on a conversation with the doc for a while, and you might start forgetting you are talking to Emacs. Here's a typical session (the human response is in bold):

```
I am the psychotherapist. Please, describe your problems.
Each time you are finished talking, type RET twice.

I am very tired today.

Why do you say you are very tired today?

I have been working a lot.
```

Is it because of your plans that you say you have been working a lot?

Yes, that's it!

Maybe your life have something to do with this.

I guess it could.

What makes you believe you guess it could?

Because I am a hard worker?

Is it because you are a hard worker that you came to me?

Yes, I believe that is the reason.

Does it bother you that is the reason?

No.

Why not?

Other Fun

There's lots more. For example, with getris.el (available widely on Internet and Usenet now), you can play the Tetris game in Emacs. To play Tetris, type the following:

```
ESC x load-library
getris.el
ESC x getris
```

and instructions for the game will appear. Yow, which comes built in GNU Emacs (type ESC x yow), says wild Ziggy-like things in the echo area. And there is much, much more, just like there is in almost every phase of Emacs.

8

Part

Reference Section

Frequently Asked

Questions

by Joe Wells

We are going to turn this chapter over to Joe Wells in just a moment. He kindly has volunteered to answer some frequently asked questions about Emacs.

One of the greatest resources for help in the wonderful world of Emacs is the Internet and Usenet, that magnificent collection of computers that literally span the globe. By subscribing to such newsgroups as comp.emacs, gnu.emacs.announce, gnu.emacs.bug!, gnu.emacs.gnews!, gnu.emacs.help, gnu.emacs.lisp.manual, gnu.emacs.sources, gnu.emacs.vm.bug!, gnu.emacs.vm.info!, gnu.emacs.vms!, and gnu.epoch.misc, you are treated to hundreds of questions and answers each month about Emacs. You also can ask your own questions and get instant responses from various experts.

Of course, these experts (who so freely volunteer their time and expertise) might get a bit miffed if people were to keep asking the same basic questions. Joe Wells, a doctoral student at Boston University, has helped alleviate that problem by putting together a list of the most frequently asked questions about Emacs. He gets help from many people, and he makes new versions available from time to time. Here is his latest.

Take it away, Joe, and thanks again for sharing with all of us!

The FAQ

Here is a list of frequently asked questions (FAQ) about GNU Emacs, along with their answers. The FAQ is posted to reduce the noise level in the gnu.emacs.help newsgroup (also the help-gnu-emacs mailing list) resulting from question repetition. It is cross-posted to comp.emacs because so many news readers do not receive the gnu.* newsgroups.

Feel free to suggest new questions or answers, wording changes, deletions, and so forth. Include either "FAQ" or "frequently asked questions" in the subject of messages you send to me about the FAQ.

Please do not send questions to me because you do not want to disturb others or you think I would know the answer. I have assembled the FAQ mainly because I do not have time to answer questions individually. I do not mind people asking me for copies of the FAQ, but in practice such requests tend to get ignored for months at a time.

And finally, enjoy!

—Joe Wells (jbw@cs.bu.edu)

P.S. I would love to see someone write a comprehensive description of the key binding situation that covers all the different situations. This situation seems to be the issue consuming the most bandwidth.

Notation Used in the Answers

You can skip this section on notation if you are reasonably familiar with GNU Emacs. Some of these questions actually are not frequently asked, but knowing them is important for understanding the answers to the rest of the questions.

1. What do things like this mean: C-a (or CONTROL-a), M-C-a (or META-CONTROL-a), CR (or ENTER), and so on?

   - C-a (or CONTROL-a) means while holding down the CONTROL key press the a key. The ASCII code that this key binding sends generally is the value that would be sent by pressing just the a key minus 96 or 64. Either way, it is a number from 0 to 31.

   - M-a (or META-a) means while holding down the META key press the a key. The ASCII code this sends is the sum of the

ASCII code that would be sent by pressing just the a key and 128.

- M-C-a (or META-CONTROL-a) means while holding down both the CONTROL key and the META key press the a key. CONTROL-META-a is a synonym for META-CONTROL-a.

- CR (or ENTER) means press the carriage return key. CR is the same as CONTROL-m. This sends ASCII code 13.

- LFD means press the LINEFEED key. LFD is also the same as CONTROL-j. This sends ASCII code 10. Under UNIX, ASCII code 10 is more often called "newline."

- DEL (or DELETE) means press the DELETE key. DEL is the same as CONTROL-?. This sends ASCII code 127.

- ESC means press the ESCAPE key. ESC is the same as CONTROL-[. This sends ASCII code 27.

- SPC (or SPACEBAR) means press the SPACEBAR key. This sends ASCII code 32.

- TAB means press the TAB key. TAB is the same as CONTROL-i. This sends ASCII code 9.

To read more about the keys and key combinations on-line, type `CONTROL-h i m emacs ENTER m characters ENTER`, and `CONTROL-h i m emacs ENTER m keys ENTER`.

2. What do you mean when you write things like this: type `META-x INFO`?

You hold down the META key (or the ESC key if you don't have a META key), type `x`, and then type `INFO`. The space between x and INFO can be ignored; only SPC or SPACEBAR means press the SPACEBAR.

3. What if I don't have a META key?

Instead of typing META-a, you can type ESC a. In fact, Emacs converts META-a internally into ESC a anyway.

4. What if I don't have an ESCAPE key?

Type CONTROL-[instead. This should send ASCII code 27 just like an ESCAPE key would.

5. What does `META-x` *command* mean?

`META-x` *command* means type `META-x`, then type the name of the

9

command, then press ENTER. META-x is simply the default key sequence that invokes the command **execute-extended-command**. This command enables you to run any Emacs command if you can remember the command's name. If you can't remember the command's name, you can type TAB and SPACEBAR for completion, and ? for a list of possibilities. An Emacs "command" is any "interactive" Emacs function.

> **Note:** Your system administrator may have bound other key sequences to invoke **execute-extended-command**. A function key labeled "DO" is a good candidate for this.

To run noninteractive Emacs functions, use META-ESC instead, and type a Lisp form that invokes the function (see question 82).

6. What do things like this mean: etc/SERVICE, src/config.h, lisp/default.el?

These are the names of files that are part of the GNU Emacs distribution. The GNU Emacs distribution is divided into several subdirectories; the important subdirectories are named "etc," "lisp," and "src." If you use GNU Emacs but don't know where it is kept on your system, start Emacs, and then type CONTROL-h v exec-directory ENTER. The directory name this displays is the full path name of the etc directory of your installed GNU Emacs distribution.

Some of these files are available individually by FTP or e-mail (see question 17).

7. What do the abbreviations FSF, LPF, OSF, GNU, RMS, FTP, BTW, and GPL stand for?

FSF	Free Software Foundation
LPF	League for Programming Freedom
OSF	Open Software Foundation
GNU	GNU's Not UNIX
RMS	Richard Matthew Stallman
FTP	File Transfer Protocol
BTW	By the way
GPL	GNU General Public Licence

9

Avoid confusing the FSF, the LPF, and the OSF. The LPF opposes look-and-feel copyrights and software patents. The FSF aims to make high-quality free software available for everyone. The OSF is a commercial organization that wants to provide an alternative, standardized version of UNIX not controlled by AT&T.

> ▶ **Note:** The word *free* in the title of the Free Software Foundation refers to freedom, not zero dollars. Anyone can charge any price for GPL-covered software. However, in practice, the freedom enforced by the GPL leads to low or nonexistent prices because you always can get the software cheaper from someone else, and everyone has the right to resell or give away GPL-covered software.

Sources of Information and Help

8. I'm just starting GNU Emacs; how do I do basic editing?

   Type `CONTROL-h t` to invoke the self-paced tutorial. Typing just `CONTROL-h` enters the help system.

> ▶ **Note:** Your system administrator may have changed CONTROL-h to act like DEL. You can use `META-x help-for-help` instead to invoke help. To discover what key (if any) invokes help on your system, type `META-x where-is ENTER help-for-help ENTER`. This command prints a comma-separated list of key sequences in the echo area. Ignore the last character in each key sequence listed. Each of the resulting key sequences invokes help.
>
> Emacs' help facility works best if help is invoked by a single key. The variable *help-char* should hold the value of this character. (The default key to invoke help is CONTROL-h, but you can change it to whatever you like.)

9

9. How do I find out how to do something in GNU Emacs?

   There are several methods for finding out how to do things in Emacs. You should become familiar with the on-line documentation for Emacs. The complete text of the Emacs manual is available on-line in a hypertext format from the "Info" manual reader. Type CONTROL-h i to invoke Info. You can order a hard copy of the manual from the FSF (see question 12).

   You can get a printed reference card listing commands and keys to invoke them. You can order one from the FSF for $1 (or 10 for $5), or you can print your own from the etc/refcard.tex file in the Emacs distribution.

   You can list the commands whose names contain a certain word (actually that match a regular expression) using the **command-apropos** command. Type CONTROL-h a to invoke this command.

   You can list the functions and variables whose names contain a certain word using the **apropos** command. META-x apropos invokes this command.

   There are many other commands in Emacs for getting help and information. To get a list of these commands, type CONTROL-h CONTROL-h CONTROL-h.

   > **Note:** You may find that **command-apropos** and **apropos** are extremely slow on your system. This is fixed in Emacs 19. If you can't wait that long, there is a fast-apropos.el file available that contains the fix. This file also contains a **super-apropos** command that lists all the functions and variables whose documentation strings contain a certain word.

10. Where can I get GNU Emacs on the net (or by regular mail)?

    Look in the files etc/DISTRIB and etc/FTP for information on nearby archive sites. If you don't already have GNU Emacs, see question 17 for how to get these two files.

    The latest version is always available through anonymous File Transfer Protocol (FTP) at MIT (prep.ai.mit.edu:/pub/gnu/emacs-18.57.tar.Z).

11. Where can I get help in installing GNU Emacs?

    Look in the file etc/SERVICE for names of companies and individuals who sell you this type of service. An up-to-date version of the SERVICE

9

file is available on prep.ai.mit.edu. See question 17 for how to retrieve this file. Appendix B has a comprehensive list of support personnel as well.

12. How do I get a printed copy of the GNU Emacs manual?

    You can order a printed copy of the GNU Emacs manual from the FSF for $20. For six or more manuals, the price is $13 each.

    The full TeX source for the manual also comes in the "man" directory of the Emacs distribution, if you're daring enough to try to print out this 300-page manual yourself. If you order it from the FSF, the price may be tax-deductible as a business expense.

    If you absolutely have to print your own copy and you don't have TeX, you can get a PostScript version through anonymous FTP (ab20.larc.nasa.gov:/pub/docs/emacs-18.57.PS.Z, size: 466K; also cs.ubc.ca:/src/gnu/manuals_ps/emacs-18.57.ps.Z, which requests that you confine any major FTPing to late evenings or early mornings their time—pacific time zone, GMT-8).

    If you don't have TeX, you can convert the Texinfo sources into troff, nroff, or psroff format with the texi2roff program, available from anonymous FTP (tut.cis.ohio-state.edu:/pub/gnu/texi2roff/ texi2roff.shar.Z).

    Carl Witty <cwitty@cs.stanford.edu> writes:

    The Emacs manual also is available on-line in the Info system, which is available by typing CONTROL-h i. In this form, it has hypertext links and is easy to browse or search; many people prefer it to the printed manual.

13. Has someone written a GNU Emacs Lisp package that does *XXX*?

    Probably. A listing of Emacs Lisp packages, called the Lisp Code Directory, is being maintained by Dave Brennan <brennan@dg-rtp.dg.com>. You can search through this list for information that might help you.

    This list is file LCD-datafile.Z in the Emacs Lisp Archive (see question 14). The files lispdir.el.Z and lispdir.doc.Z in the archive contain information to help you use the list.

14. Where can I get GNU Emacs Lisp packages that don't come with Emacs?

    First, check the Lisp Code Directory to find the name of the package you are looking for (see question 13). Then check local archives and

9

the Emacs Lisp Archive to find a copy of the relevant files. Then, if you still haven't found it, you can send e-mail to the author asking for a copy.

You can access the Emacs Lisp Archive from anonymous FTP (tut.cis.ohio-state.edu:/pub/gnu/emacs/elisp-archive/). Fetch the file README.Z first.

> **Note:** Any files with names ending in ".Z" are compressed; use "binary" mode in FTP to retrieve them. Also use binary mode whenever you retrieve any files with names ending in ".elc."

15. How do I submit code to the Emacs Lisp Archive?

Send submissions for the archive to Dave Sill <de5@ornl. gov>. If you have FTP access, the submission can be deposited in the directory /pub/gnu/emacs/elisp-archive/incoming on tut.cis.ohio-state.edu.

Whenever possible, submissions should contain an LCD-datafile entry, because this reduces administrative overhead for the maintainers. Before submitting anything, read the file guidelines.Z, available in the archive.

The format of an LCD-datafile entry is this:

```
Name¦Author¦Contact¦Description¦Date¦Version¦Archive
```

Here is an example:

```
1char¦Bard Bloom¦bard@theory.lcs.mit.edu¦Help fixing typos.
¦90-07-13¦¦~/misc/1char.el.Z
```

16. Where can I get documentation on GNU Emacs Lisp?

Obtain the *GNU Emacs Lisp Reference Manual* for Emacs 18 under UNIX. It is available from the FSF for $50 (or five for $200). The latest revision available for FTP is edition 1.03, dated January 28, 1991. Within Emacs, you can type CONTROL-h f to get the documentation for a function, and CONTROL-h v for a variable. Also, as a popular USENET saying goes, "Use the Force, Read the Source."

You also can get the Texinfo source for the manual if you are daring enough to try to print this 550-page manual yourself. This is available in the Emacs Lisp Archive and also from anonymous FTP (prep.ai.mit.edu:/pub/gnu/elisp.tar.Z).

9

A set of pregenerated Info files comes with the Texinfo source for the Emacs Lisp manual, so you don't have to format it yourself for on-line use. (You can create the Info files from the Texinfo source.) See question 22 for details on how to install these files on-line.

17. What informational files are available for GNU Emacs?

    This isn't a frequently asked question, but it should be! A variety of informational files about GNU Emacs and relevant aspects of the GNU project are available for you to read.

    The following files are available in the etc directory of the GNU Emacs distribution, and the latest versions are available individually through anonymous FTP (prep.ai.mit.edu:/pub/gnu/etc/):

    - APPLE—Why the FSF doesn't support GNU Emacs on Apple computers

    - DISTRIB—GNU Emacs availability information, including the popular "Free Software Foundation Order Form"

    - FTP—How to get GNU Software by Internet FTP or by UUCP

    - GNU—The GNU Manifesto INTERVIEW—Richard Stallman discusses his public-domain UNIX-compatible software system with *BYTE* editors

    - MACHINES—Status of GNU Emacs on various machines and systems

    - MAILINGLISTS—GNU project electronic mailing lists

    - SERVICE—GNU service directory

    - SUN-SUPPORT—Includes the popular "Using Emacstool with GNU Emacs"

    These files also are available in the etc directory of the GNU Emacs distribution:

    - DIFF—Differences between GNU Emacs and Twenex Emacs

    - CCADIFF—Differences between GNU Emacs and CCA Emacs

    - GOSDIFF—Differences between GNU Emacs and Gosling (Unipress) Emacs

    - COPYING—GNU Emacs general Ppublic license

    - NEWS—GNU Emacs News, a history of user-visible changes

9

- LPF—Why you should join the League for Programming Freedom

- FAQ—GNU Emacs Frequently Asked Questions (you're reading a version of it)

- OPTIONS—A complete explanation of start-up option handling

These files are available through anonymous FTP (prep.ai.mit. edu:/pub/gnu/):

- TASKS—GNU task list standards

- TEXT—GNU coding standards

In addition, all the preceding files are available directly from the FSF by e-mail. Of course, try to get them from a local source first.

These additional files are available from the FSF by e-mail:

- GNU's Bulletin, January, 1991—this file includes:

GNU'S Who
What Is the Free Software Foundation?
What Is Copyleft?
GNUs Flashes
Free Software Support
"Protect Your Freedom to Write Programs"
        by Richard Stallman
GNU Project Status Report
"Help Keep Government Software Free"
        by Richard Stallman
GNU Documentation
GNU Wish List
GNU Software Available Now
Contents of the Emacs Tape
Contents of the Compiler Tape
Contents of the X11 Tapes
VMS Emacs and Compiler Tapes
How to Get GNU Software
Free Software for MS-DOS
GNUish MS-DOS Project
Freemacs, an Extensible Editor for MS-DOS
GNU in Japan
Thank GNUs
FSF Order Form

9

- Legal issues about contributing code to GNU

- GNU Project Status Report

18. What is the current address of the FSF?

Snail mail address:
Free Software Foundation, Inc.
675 Massachusetts Ave.
Cambridge, MA 02139 USA
Phone number: 617-876-3296

E-mail addresses:
gnu@prep.ai.mit.edu (probably read by Len Tower)
gnulists@prep

19. What is the current address of the LPF?

Snail mail address:
League for Programming Freedom
1 Kendall Square, Number 143
Post Office Box 9171
Cambridge, MA 02139 USA
Phone number: 617-243-4091

E-mail address:
league@prep.ai.mit.edu

20. Where can I get the up-to-date GNU stuff?

The most up-to-date official GNU stuff normally is kept on
prep.ai.mit.edu and is available for anonymous FTP. See the files etc/
DISTRIB and etc/FTP for more information. (To get copies of these
files, see question 17.)

21. Where can I get the latest VM, Supercite, GNUS, Calc, Calendar, Ispell,
or Patch?

- VM
  Author: Kyle Jones <kyle@uunet. uu. net>
  Mailing lists: info-vm-request@uunet.uu.net
                   info-vm@uunet.uu.net
                   bug-vm-request@uunet.uu.net
                   bug-vm@uunet.uu.net
  Anonymous FTP:
  Latest released version: 4.41
  tut.cis.ohio-state.edu:/pub/gnu/emacs/elisp-archive/packages/vm-
  4.41.tar.Z ab20.larc.nasa.gov:/pub/vm/vm-4. 41.tar.Z

9

Beta.test.version: 5.31
ab20.larc.nasa.gov:/pub/vm/{vm-5. 31,timer}.tar.Z

- Supercite
  Author: Barry Warsaw <warsaw@warsaw.nlm.nih.gov>
  Mailing lists: supercite@warsaw.nlm.nih.gov
                   supercite-request@warsaw.nlm.nih.gov
  Anonymous FTP:
  Latest version: 2.1
  durer.cme.nist.gov:/pub/gnu/elisp/supercite-2.1.shar. 0{1,2}
  E-mail:
  To: library@cme.nist.gov Subject: help
  NOTE: Superyank is an old version of Supercite.

- GNUS
  Author: Masanobu Umeda <umerin@mse.kyutech.ac.jp>
  Anonymous FTP:
  Latest version: 3.13
  tut.cis.ohio-state.edu: /pub/gnu/emacs/elisp-archive/packages
  /gnus-3.13.tar.Z

- Calc
  Author: Dave Gillespie <daveg@csvax.cs.caltech.edu>
  Anonymous FTP:
  Latest released version: 1.07
  csvax.cs.caltech.edu:/pub/calc-1.07.tar.Z
  Beta test version: 1.08
  csvax.cs.caltech.edu:/pub/calc-1.08beta1.tar.Z

- Calendar/Diary
  Author: Ed Reingold <reingold@cs.uiuc.edu>
  Latest version: 4
  E-mail:
  To: reingold@cs.uiuc.edu Subject: send-emacs-cal body: your
  best internet e-mail address

- Ispell
  Latest version: 2.0.02
  Anonymous FTP:
  tut.cis.ohio-state.edu:/pub/gnu/ispell/*

- Patch
  Author: Larry Wall <lwall@jpl-devvax.jpl.nasa.gov>
  Latest version: 2.0 patchlevel 12u3
  This is the version that supports the new "unified" diff format.
  Anonymous FTP: prep.ai.mit.edu:/pub/gnu/patch-2.0.12u3.tar.Z

9

22. How do I install a piece of Texinfo documentation?

    First create Info files from the Texinfo files with the makeinfo program. The **texinfo-format-buffer** command is currently obsolete. Makeinfo is available as part of the latest Texinfo package (prep.ai.mit.edu:/pub/gnu/texinfo-2.05.tar.Z). It also comes with Emacs, but several include files are missing. For information about the Texinfo format, read the Texinfo manual that comes with Emacs. This manual also comes installed in Info format, so you can read it on-line. Neither **texinfo-format-buffer** nor the makeinfo program installs the resulting Info files in Emacs' Info tree.

    To install Info files:

    1. Move the files to the info directory in the installed Emacs distribution. See question 6 if you don't know where that is.

    2. Edit the file info/dir in the installed Emacs distribution, and add a line for the top-level node in the Info package that you are installing. If you want to install Info files and you don't have the necessary privileges, you have two options:

       Info files don't actually need to be installed. You can feed a file name to the **Info-goto-node** command (invoked by pressing g in Info mode) by typing the name of the file in parentheses. This goes to the node named "Top" in that file. For example, to view an Info file named *XXX* in your home directory, you can type this:

       ```
       CONTROL-h i g (~/XXX) ENTER
       ```

       You can create your own Info directory. You can tell Emacs where the Info directory is by setting the value of the variable *Info-directory* to its path name. For example, to use a private Info directory that is a subdirectory of your home directory named Info, you can type this:

       ```
       (setq Info-directory (expand-file-name "~/Info"))
       ```

       You need a top-level Info file named dir in this directory. You can include the system-wide Info directory in your private Info directory with symbolic links or by copying it.

23. Can I view Info files without using GNU Emacs?

    Yes, the info and xinfo programs do this. You can get info as part of the latest Texinfo package (see question 22). The xinfo program is available separately (prep.ai.mit.edu:/pub/gnu/xinfo-1.01.01.tar.Z).

9

24. What is the legal meaning of the GNU copyleft?

RMS writes:

The legal meaning of the GNU copyleft is less important than the spirit, which is that Emacs is a free software project and that work pertaining to Emacs also should be free software. "Free" means that all users have the freedom to study, share, change, and improve Emacs. To make sure everyone has this freedom, pass along source code when you distribute any version of Emacs or a related program, and give the recipients the same freedom that you enjoyed. If you still want to find out about the legal meaning of the copyleft, ask yourself whether this means you are not paying attention to the spirit.

25. What are appropriate messages for gnu.emacs.help/gnu.emacs.bug/comp.emacs?

The file etc/MAILINGLISTS discusses the purpose of each GNU mailing list. (See question 17 on how to get a copy.) For those that are gatewayed with newsgroups, it lists both the newsgroup name and the mailing list address. Comp.emacs is used for discussion of Emacs programs in general. This includes GNU Emacs along with various other implementations like JOVE, MicroEmacs, Freemacs, MG, Unipress, CCA, and so on. Many people post GNU Emacs questions to comp.emacs because they don't receive any of the gnu newsgroups. Arguments have been made both for and against posting GNU-Emacs-specific material to comp.emacs. You have to decide for yourself.

26. How do I "unsubscribe" to this mailing list?

If you are receiving a GNU mailing list named "*XXX*," you might be able to "unsubscribe" to it by sending a request to the address *XXX*-`request@prep.ai.mit.edu`. However, this doesn't work if you are not listed on the main mailing list, but receive the mail from a distribution point instead. In that case, you have to track down the distribution point at which you are listed. Inspecting the "Received:" headers on the mail messages may help, along with liberal use of the "EXPN" and "VRFY" sendmail commands through "`telnet <site-address> smtp.`" Ask your postmaster for help.

27. What is the LPF and why should I join it?

The LPF opposes the expanding danger of software patents and look-and-feel copyrights. Write to league@prep.ai.mit.edu for more information. You can get papers describing the LPF's views by anonymous FTP (prep.ai.mit.edu:/pub/lpf/*) or by anonymous UUCP (osu-cis!~/lpf/*).

9

GNU Emacs, All Its Variants, and Other Editors

28. Where does the name "Emacs" come from?

    Emacs originally was an acronym for Editor MACroS. The first Emacs was a set of macros written by Richard Stallman and Guy Steele for the editor TECO (Text Editor and COrrector—originally Tape Editor and COrrector) on a PDP-10. (Amusing fact: many people have told me that TECO code looks a lot like line noise. See alt.lang.teco if you are interested.)

29. What is the latest version of GNU Emacs?

    GNU Emacs 18.57.

30. When will GNU Emacs 19 be available?

    Good question. I don't know. For that matter, neither do the developers. It undoubtedly will be available sometime in the 1990s.

31. What will be different about GNU Emacs 19?

    From the latest "GNU's Bulletin":

    Version 19 approaches release, counting among its new features: before and after change hooks, source-level Lisp debugging, X selection processing, including clipboard selections, scroll bars, support for European character sets, floating point numbers, per-buffer mouse commands, interfacing with the X resource manager, mouse-tracking, Lisp-level binding of function keys, and multiple X windows ("screens" to Emacs). Thanks go to Alan Carroll and the people who worked on Epoch for generating initial feedback to a multi-windowed Emacs. Emacs 19 supports two styles of multiple windows, one with a separate screen for the minibuffer, and another with a minibuffer attached to each screen. A couple of other features of Emacs 19 are buffer allocation, which uses a new mechanism capable of returning storage to the system when a buffer is killed, and a new input system—all input now arrives in the form of Lisp objects. Other features being considered for later releases of Emacs 19 include: associating property lists with regions of text in a buffer, multiple font, color, and pixmaps defined by those properties, different visibility conditions for the regions, and for various windows showing one buffer, hooks to be run if point or mouse moves outside a certain range, incrementally saving undo history in a file; static

9

menu bars, and better pop-up menus. Mention of these two items disappeared from the latest "GNU's Bulletin":

- Incremental syntax analysis for various programming languages (Leif).

- A more sophisticated emacs client/server model, which would provide network transparent Emacs widget functionality.

32. Is there an Emacs that has better mouse and X window support?

Emacs 18 has some limited X Window System support, but there are problems. Emacs 19 will have amazing mouse and window support. Right now, there is a modified version of Emacs 18.55 called "Epoch," which has greatly improved mouse and window support. The latest version of Epoch is available by anonymous FTP (cs.uiuc.edu:/pub/epoch-files/epoch/epoch-3.2b; b stands for beta).

> **Note:** Epoch works only with the X Window System; it does not work on ordinary terminals.

33. How do I get Emacs for my PC?

GNU Emacs won't run on a PC directly under MS-DOS. There have been reports of people running GNU Emacs under a special program under MS-DOS on 286 or 386 machines, but I don't know the details. You can try a variety of similar programs such as MG, MicroEmacs, and Freemacs. Russ Nelson <nelson@sun.soe.clarkson.edu>, the author, describes Freemacs:

- Freemacs is free, and it was designed from the start to be programmable.

- Freemacs is the only IBM-PC editor that tries to be like GNU Emacs.

- Freemacs can edit only files less than 64K in length.

- Freemacs doesn't have undo.

Carl Witty <cwitty@cs.stanford.edu> describes Freemacs:

Better is Freemacs, which follows the tradition of ITS and GNU Emacs by having a full, Turing-complete extension language which is incompatible with everything else. In fact, it's even closer to ITS Emacs than GNU Emacs is, because Mint (Freemacs' extension language) is absolutely illegible without weeks of study, much like TECO.

The latest version of Freemacs is 16a. You can get Freemacs several ways:

Anonymous FTP:
simtel20.army.mil:PD:<MSDOS. FREEMACS>
grape.ecs.clarkson.edu:/pub/msdos/freemacs/

E-mail:
Address: archive-server@sun.soe.clarkson.edu body: help

Snail mail:
Russell Nelson
11 Grant St.
Potsdam, NY 13676

Send $15 for the copying fee, and specify the preferred floppy disk format: 5$\frac{1}{4}$-inch, 360K, or 3$\frac{1}{2}$-inch, 720K.

There is a mailing list for Freemacs. To subscribe, send e-mail:

listserv@clvm.bitnet body: SUBSCRIBE FREEMACS Firstname Lastname

MicroEmacs is programmable in a BASIC-like language. The author is Daniel Lawrence <dan@midas.mgmt.purdue.edu, nwd@j.cc.purdue.edu, dan@mdbs.uucp>. Many of the key bindings are different from those in GNU Emacs. The latest version is 3.10, available by anonymous FTP (durer.cme.nist.gov).

Another Emacs for small machines is JOVE (Jonathan's Own Version of Emacs). The latest official version is 4.14. There appears to be a newer version. People rumored to be working on JOVE include Mark Moraes at cs.toronto.edu and Bill Marsh <bmarsh@cod.nosc.mil>. It is available by anonymous FTP (cs.rochester.edu:/pub/jove.tar.4.14.Z).

Yet another Emacs is "mg," which used to stand for MicroGNUEmacs but now just stands for "mg." It also is available by anonymous FTP (snow.white.toronto.edu).

34. Where can I get Emacs for my Atari ST?

The latest version for the ST is available by anonymous FTP (cs.uni-sb.de:/pub/atari/emacs/).

35. Where can I get Emacs with NeWS support?

Chris Maio's NeWS support package for GNU Emacs is available by anonymous FTP (columbia.edu/pub/ps-emacs.tar.Z, tut.cis.ohio-state.edu:/pub/gnu/emacs/ps-emacs.tar.Z).

9

Binding Keys to Commands

36. Why does my key binding fail?

    Most likely, it fails because ESC [(the ESCAPE key) is already defined. Evaluate this form first:

    ```
    (define-key esc-map "[" nil)
    ```

37. Why doesn't this terminal or window-system setup code work in my .emacs file, although it works just fine after Emacs starts up?

    This is because you're trying to do something in your .emacs file that needs to be postponed until after the terminal/window-system setup code is loaded. This is a result of the order in which things are done during the start-up of Emacs. To postpone the execution of Emacs Lisp code until after the terminal/window-system setup, set the value of the variable *term-setup-hook* or *window-setup-hook* to be a function that does what you want. See etc/OPTIONS for a complete explanation of what Emacs does every time it is started. Here is a simple example of how to set *term-setup-hook*:

    ```
    (setq term-setup-hook
    (function
     (lambda ()
       (if (string-match "^vt220" (or (getenv "TERM") ""))
           ;; Make vt220's "Do" key behave like META-x:
     (define-key CSI-map "29~" 'execute-extended-command)))))
    ```

38. How do I use function keys under X Windows?

    This depends on whether you are running Emacs inside a terminal emulator window or allowing Emacs to create its own X window. You can tell which you are doing by noticing whether Emacs creates a new window when you start it. The following description applies only when Emacs has its own X window.

    If compiled on a Sun, Emacs recognizes these X "keysyms" that are normally on a Sun keyboard:

    F1 through F9
    L1 through L10 (same as F11 through F20)
    R1 through R15 (same as F21 through F35)
    Break (the ALTERNATE key is given this keysym)
    Up, Down, Right, Left (the arrow keys, R??, R??, R??, and R??)

    When Emacs sees one of the arrow keys, it behaves as though a CONTROL key had been pressed instead, like this:

9

UP becomes CONTROL-p DOWN, which becomes CONTROL-n
RIGHT, which becomes CONTROL-f LEFT, which becomes
CONTROL-b.

The rest of the keys work like Sun function keys. Each function key
generates a key sequence that looks like ESC [### z, in which ###
is replaced by a number. The key sequences are identical to those
generated by Sun's keyboard under SunView. Any function key not
previously listed generates ESC [-1 z.

If not compiled on a Sun, the function keys appear to Emacs in a way
remarkably similar to the keys of a DEC LK201 keyboard (used on
some VT series terminals). The arrow keys work the same as in the
preceding explanation. These X keysyms are recognized:

F1 through F20
Help (treated same as F15)
Menu (treated same as F16, is the LK201 DO key)
Find Insert (LK201 INSERT HERE key)
Select Up, Down, Right, Left (LK201 arrow keys)

These keysyms are supposed to be recognized, but they are not due to
a bug:

Prior (LK201 PREV SCREEN key)
Next (LK201 NEXT SCREEN key)

And finally, the Delete keysym generates the DEL character
(CONTROL-?) rather than the key sequence given by the LK201
REMOVE key. Each function key generates a key sequence that looks
like ESC [##~, in which a number replaces ##. The key sequences are
identical to those generated by an LK201 keyboard. Any function key
not previously listed generates ESC [-1 z.

For the complete list of the numbers generated by the function keys,
look in the file src/x11term.c. If you are running Emacs on a Sun
machine, even if your X display is running on a non-Sun machine (for
example, X terminal), you get the setup described previously for Suns.
The determining factor is what type of machine Emacs is running on,
not what type of machine your X display is on. You can use
xmodmap to change your X keysym assignments to get keys previously listed, but that may mess up other programs. If you have
function keys not listed previously and you don't want to use
xmodmap to change their names, you might want to make a modification to your Emacs. Johan Vromans <jv@mh.nl> explains:

9

There are a number of tricks that can be helpful. The most elegant solution, however, is to use the function **x-rebind-key**. This function is commented out in the source for good reasons—it's buggy. It is easy to replace this function with the function **epoch:rebind-key** from the Epoch distribution. After implementing this, all keyboard keys can be configured to send user-definable sequences; for example:

```
(x-rebind-key "KP_F1" 0 "\0330P")
```

This sequence has the keypad key PF1 send the sequence \eOP, just like an ordinary VTxxx terminal.

39. How do I tell what characters my function keys emit?

   Use this function by Randal L. Schwartz <merlyn@iwarp.intel.com>:

```
(defun see-chars ()
 "Displays characters typed, terminated by a 3-second
   timeout."
 (interactive)
 (let ((chars "")
  (inhibit-quit t))
   (message "Enter characters, terminated by 3-second
    timeout. ")
   (while (not (sit-for 3))
(setq chars (concat chars (list (read-char)))
 quit-flag nil))  ; quit-flag maybe set by C-g
   (message "Characters entered: %s" (key-description
    chars)))))
```

40. Why does Emacs spontaneously go into "I-search:" mode?

   Your terminal (or something between your terminal and the computer) is sending CONTROL-s and CONTROL-q for flow control, and Emacs is receiving these characters and interpreting them as commands. (The CONTROL-s character normally invokes the **isearch-forward** command).

   For a more detailed discussion, read the file PROBLEMS in the Emacs distribution.

41. What do I do if my terminal is sending CONTROL-s and CONTROL-q for flow control and I can't disable it?

   Use this piece of Emacs Lisp:

```
(set-input-mode nil t)
```

42. How do I make Emacs use CONTROL-s and CONTROL-q for flow control rather than for commands?

   Same answer as previous question.

43. Why does Emacs never see CONTROL-s and CONTROL-q through my network connection?

    Eirik Fuller <eirik@theory.tn.cornell.edu> writes:

    Some versions of rlogin (and possibly telnet) do not pass flow control characters to the remote system to which they connect. On such systems, Emacs on the remote system cannot disable flow control on the local system. One way to cure this is to disable flow control on the local host (the one running rlogin, not the one running rlogind) using the **stty** command, before starting the rlogin process. On many systems, `stty start u stop u` does this. Sometimes `rlogin -8` avoids this problem. Some versions of tcsh prevent even this from working. One way around this is to start another shell before starting rlogin, and issue the **stty** command to disable flow control from that shell.

44. How do I use commands bound to CONTROL-s and CONTROL-q (or any key) if these keys are filtered out?

    I suggest swapping CONTROL-s with CONTROL-\ and CONTROL-q with CONTROL-^:

    ```
    (swap-keys ?\CONTROL-s ?\CONTROL-\\)
    (swap-keys ?\CONTROL-q ?\CONTROL-^)
    ```

    See question 45 for the implementation of **swap-keys**.

45. How do I swap two keys?

    When Emacs receives a character, you can make Emacs behave as though it received another character by setting the value of **keyboard-translate-table**. The following Emacs Lisp does this for you, enabling you to swap keys. After arranging for Emacs to evaluate this Lisp, you can evaluate (`swap-keys ?A ?B`) to swap A and B.

⊘ **Caution!** The value of CONTROL-g (which is 7) is still hard coded in one place in the minibuffer code. Thus, swapping CONTROL-g with another key may cause minor problems.

```
(defun swap-keys (key1 key2)
  "Swap keys KEY1 and KEY2 using map-key. "
  (map-key key1 key2)
  (map-key key2 key1))

(defun map-key (from to)
  "Make key FROM behave as though key TO were typed instead. "
  (setq keyboard-translate-table
    (concat keyboard-translate-table
```

```
(let* ((i (length keyboard-translate-table))
  (j from)
  (k i)
  (str (make-string (max 0 (- j (1- i)))
  ?X)))
  (while (<= k j)
    (aset str (- k i) k)
    (setq k (1+ k)))
 str)))
(aset keyboard-translate-table from to)
(let ((i (1- (length keyboard-translate-table))))
  (while (and (>= i 0) (eq (aref keyboard-translate-table
  i) i))
(setq i (1- i)))
  (setq keyboard-translate-table
      (if (eq i -1) nil (substring keyboard-translate-table 0 (1+ i)))))))
```

46. Why does the BACKSPACE key invoke help?

    The BACKSPACE key (on every keyboard I've used) sends ASCII
    code 8. CONTROL-h sends the same code. In Emacs, by default
    CONTROL-h invokes **help-command**. The easiest solution to this
    problem is to use CONTROL-h (and BACKSPACE) for help and
    DELETE for deleting the previous character. For some people this
    solution may be problematic:

    1. They normally use BACKSPACE outside of Emacs for deleting
       the previous character typed. This can be solved by making
       DELETE the command for deleting the previous character
       outside of Emacs. This command does the following on many
       UNIX systems:

       ```
       stty erase '^?'
       ```

    2. They may prefer using the BACKSPACE key for deleting the
       previous character because it is more conveniently located on
       the keyboard or because they don't have a separate DELETE
       key. In this case, the best solution is to swap CONTROL-h and
       DELETE:

       ```
       (swap-keys ?\CONTROL-h ?\CONTROL-?)
       ```

    See question 45 for the implementation of **swap-keys**.

47. How do I type DELETE on PC terminal emulators?

    Someone whose name I forgot wrote:

    Most PCs have deficient keyboards that don't have both BACKSPACE
    and DELETE keys. Whether CONTROL-h (backspace) or DEL is
    generated by the BACKSPACE key varies from one terminal emulator

to another. If you're lucky, you can reconfigure the keyboard so that it generates DEL. If not, you have to hunt to figure out what keystroke will do it—possibilities include various shifted and controlled versions of BACKSPACE, the DEL key on the numeric keypad (which might depend on SHIFT or NUMLOCK), or perhaps CONTROL-?. If this is too difficult, you may want to swap the DELETE key with some other key. See question 46.

48. Can I make my COMPOSE key behave like a META key?

    In general, no. However, the LK201 keyboard does send a code for COMPOSE key up and key down, so if you're on an X workstation you might have luck using the xmodmap program.

49. How do I turn on the arrow keys for VT-style terminals?

    Put this in your .emacs file:

    ```
    (setq term-setup-hook
    (function
     (lambda ()
       (if (fboundp 'enable-arrow-keys)  (enable-arrow-keys)))))
    ```

    We put this in our lisp/default.el file, so users don't have to worry about it:

    ```
    (or term-setup-hook
        (setq term-setup-hook
          (function
    (lambda ()
      (and (fboundp 'enable-arrow-keys)
        (eq 'backward-paragraph (lookup-key esc-map "["))
      (enable-arrow-keys))))))
    ```

Building, Installing, and Porting Emacs, and Machine/OS-Specific Bugs

50. Why do I get an "f68881_used undefined" error when I build Emacs on my Sun 3?

    Barry A. Warsaw <warsaw@cme.nist.gov> writes:

    Some of the code being linked on the "ld" line of Emacs' **build** command has been compiled with the -f68881 option. The most common reason is that you're linking with X libraries that built with the -f68881 option set. You need to either remove all dependencies to the 68881 (which may mean a recompile of the X libraries with

9

-fswitch or -fsoft option), or link emacs with the 68881 start-up file /usr/lib/Mcrt1.o. Make this change to src/ymakefile:

change

```
#define START_FILES crt0.o
```

to

```
#define START_FILES crt0.o /usr/lib/Mcrt1.o
```

The order of these start files is critical.

51. How do I get Emacs running on VMS under DECwindows?

Hal R. Brand <BRAND@addvax.llnl.gov> is said to have a VMS save set with a ready-to-run VMS version of Emacs for X Windows. It is available by anonymous FTP (addvax.llnl.gov). Johan Vromans <jv@mh.nl> writes:

Getting Emacs to run on VMS with DECwindows requires a number of changes to the sources. Fortunately, this has been done already. Joshua Marantz <josh@viewlogic.com> did most of the work for Emacs 18.52, and the mods were ported to 18.55 by Johan Vromans <jv@mh.nl>. Also included is the handling of DEC's LK201 keyboard. You need to apply the changes to a fresh Emacs 18.55 distribution on a UNIX system, and then you can copy the sources to VMS to perform the compile/link/build. The set of changes has been posted a number of times in the past 12 months, so it should be widely available.

52. Why does Emacs ignore my X resources (my .Xdefaults file)?

Try compiling Emacs with the XBACKWARDS macro defined. There is a bug in some implementations of XGetDefault that do not correspond to the documentation or the header files.

53. What should I do if I have trouble building Emacs?

RMS writes:

If you try to build Emacs and it does not run, the first thing to do is look in the file called PROBLEMS to see if a solution is given there. If none is given, then send a report by mail to bug-gnu-emacs@prep.ai.mit.edu. Please do not send it to help-gnu-emacs@prep.ai.mit.edu. Sending to help-gnu-emacs (which has the effect of posting on gnu.emacs.help) is undesirable because it takes the time of an unnecessarily large group of people, most of whom are just users and have no idea how to fix these problems. However, bug-gnu-emacs reaches a much smaller group of people who are more likely to know what to do and have expressed a wish to receive more messages about Emacs than the others.

Weird and Confusing Problems

54. Does Emacs have problems with files larger than 8 megs?

    Most installed versions of GNU Emacs use 24-bit signed integers (and 24-bit pointers!) internally. This limits the file size that Emacs can handle to 8388608 bytes.

    Leonard N. Zubkoff <lnz@lucid.com> writes:

    Putting the following two lines in src/config.h before compiling Emacs allows for 26-bit integers and pointers:

    ```
    #define VALBITS 26
    #define GCTYPEBITS 5
    ```

    See question 55 for an explanation.

55. Why does Emacs use 24-bit integers and pointers?

    David Gillespie <daveg@csvax.cs.caltech.edu> writes:

    Emacs is largely written in a dialect of Lisp; Lisp is a freely typed language in the sense that you can put any value of any type into any variable, or return it from a function, and so on. So each value must carry a "tag" along with it identifying what kind of thing it is; for example, integer, pointer to a list, pointer to an editing buffer, and so on. Emacs uses standard 32-bit integers for data objects, taking the top 8 bits for the tag and the bottom 24 bits for the value. So integers (and pointers) are somewhat restricted compared to true C integers and pointers. Emacs uses 8-bit tags because that's a little faster on byte-oriented machines, but there are only enough tags to require 6 bits. See question 54 to find how to recompile Emacs with 6-bit tags and 26-bit integers and pointers if space is at a premium for you.

56. Why does Emacs start up using the wrong directory?

    Most likely, you have an environment variable named PWD that is set to a value other than the name of your current directory. This is most likely caused by using two different shell programs. ksh and some versions of csh set and maintain the value of the PWD environment variable, but sh doesn't. If you start sh from ksh, change your current

9

directory inside sh, and then start Emacs from inside sh; PWD has the wrong value but Emacs will use this value. See the etc/OPTIONS file for more details. Perhaps an easier solution is not to use two shells. The chsh program often can be used to change one's default log-in shell.

57. How do I edit a file with "$" in its name?

When you enter a file name in the minibuffer, Emacs attempts to expand a "$" followed by a word as an environment variable. To suppress this behavior, type $$ instead.

58. Why does Shell mode lose track of the shell's current directory?

Emacs has no way of knowing when the shell actually changes its directory. This is an intrinsic limitation of UNIX. Emacs tries to guess by recognizing **cd** commands. If you type cd followed by a directory name with a variable reference (cd $HOME/bin) or with a shell meta character (cd ../lib*), Emacs fails to correctly guess the shell's new current directory. A number of fixes and enhancements to Shell mode for this problem have been written; check the Emacs Lisp Archive (question 14).

59. Why doesn't Emacs expand my aliases when sending mail?

First, you must separate multiple addresses with commas. Second, Emacs normally reads the .mailrc file only once per session, when you start to compose your first mail message. If you edit .mailrc, you can type the **build-mail-aliases** command (META-ESC) to make Emacs reread .mailrc.

60. Why doesn't setting the variable *default-directory* always work?

There is a separate value of *default-directory* for each Emacs buffer. The value in the current buffer is the one that is used.

61. Why doesn't my change to *load-path* work?

If you added file names with tildes (~) in them to your *load-path*, you'll need to do something like this:

```
(setq load-path (mapcar 'expand-file-name load-path))
```

62. Why does the cursor always go to the wrong column when I move up or down one line?

You have inadvertently typed the **set-goal-column** command (CONTROL-x CONTROL-n), which sets the "goal-column" to the column where the cursor was. To undo this, type CONTROL-u CONTROL-x CONTROL-n.

If you make this mistake frequently, you might want to unbind this command by doing one of these two actions:

```
(define-key ctl-x-map "\CONTROL-n" nil)
(put 'set-goal-column 'disabled t)
```

63. Why does Emacs hang with message "Unknown XMenu" with X11R4?

    Many different X errors can produce this message. Here is the solution to one problem:

    X11 Release 4 now enforces some conditions in the X protocol that were previously allowed to pass unnoticed. You need to put the X11R4 server into X11R3 bug compatibility mode for Emacs' Xmenu code to work. You can do this with the command **xset bc**.

64. Why doesn't **display-time** show the load average in the mode line anymore?

    In GNU Emacs 18.56, a change was made in the **display-time** code. Formerly, in version 18.55, Emacs used a program named **loadst** to notify Emacs of the change in time every minute. **loadst** also sent Emacs the system load average if it was installed with sufficient privilege to get that information (or was on a system where no such privilege was needed). Emacs then displayed this information in the mode line. In version 18.56, this code was changed to use a program named **wakeup**.

    Wakeup doesn't send Emacs any information; its only purpose is to send Emacs something every minute, thus invoking the **filter** function in Emacs once a minute. The **filter** function in Emacs does all the work of finding the time, date, and load average. However, getting the load average requires the privilege to read kernel memory on most systems. Because giving Emacs this privilege would destroy any security a system might have, for almost everyone this is not an option. In addition, Emacs does not have the built-in code to get this information on the systems that have special system calls for this purpose, even though **loadst** had code for this. The solution I use is to get the files lisp/display-time.el and etc/loadst.c from version 18.55 and use those with 18.57. (I have heard a rumor that **loadst** disappeared because of the legal action Unipress threatened against IBM.)

9

> **Caution!** Do not install Emacs **setgid kmem** unless you wish to destroy any security your system might have!

If you are using Emacs 18.55 or earlier, or the solution I described previously, read further:

The most likely cause of the problem is that **loadst** can't read the special file /dev/kmem. To properly install **loadst**, it should be either **setuid** to the owner of /dev/kmem, or **setgid** to the group to which /dev/kmem belongs. In either case, /dev/kmem should be readable by its owner or its group. Another possibility is that your version of UNIX doesn't have the load average data available in /dev/kmem. Your version of UNIX might have a special system call to retrieve this information (for example, **inq_stats** under UMAX), and **loadst** might not have been enhanced to cope with this.

65. Why doesn't GNUS work anymore through NNTP?

There is a bug in NNTP version 1.5.10.(NNTP is a networking program.) When multiple requests are sent to the NNTP server, the server handles only the first one before blocking and waiting for more input, which never comes. NNTP version 1.5.11 claims to fix this. You can work around the bug inside Emacs like this:

```
(setq nntp-maximum-request 1)
```

I also have a patch you can use for NNTP 1.5.10 based on the timeout code that was in 1.5.9. However, try to upgrade to 1.5.11 first.

66. Why does **ispell** sometimes ignore the local dictionary?

You need to update the version of **ispell** to 2.0.02. A patch is available by anonymous FTP (tut.cis.ohio-state.edu:/pub/gnu/ispell/patch2.Z). You also need to change a line in ispell.el from

```
(defconst ispell-version "2.0.01") ;; Check against output of
   "ispell -v."
```

to

```
(defconst ispell-version "2.0.02") ;; Check against output of
   "ispell -v."
```

67. How do I get rid of the CONTROL-m (line-return) junk in my Shell buffer?

For tcsh, put this in your .cshrc (or .tcshrc) file:

```
if ($?EMACS) then
    if ($?tcsh) unset edit
    stty nl endif
```

Or put this in your .emacs_tcsh file:

```
unset edit stty nl
```

Alternatively, you can use csh in your Shell buffers rather than tcsh. One way is:

```
(setq explicit-shell-file-name "/bin/csh")
```

Another is to do this in your .cshrc (or .tcshrc) file:

```
setenv ESHELL /bin/csh
```

68. Does GNU Emacs have a vulnerability to Trojan horses?

    Yes. (Trojan horses are innocent-appearing programs that have harmful routines hidden in them.) Your site should put this in lisp/site-init.el before building Emacs:

    ```
    (setq inhibit-local-variables t)
    ```

    If Emacs already has been built, the expression should be put in lisp/default.el instead. The security hole that would otherwise be left open is described in the "File Variables" section of the manual (and Info tree).

69. How do I recover my mail files after RMAIL munges (changes) their format?

    You may have noticed that RMAIL has a disturbing way of eating your mbox file and producing instead an RMAIL file in an entirely different format. To remedy this, Ken Manheimer <klm@cme.nist.gov> wrote a package called **rmail-to-vm** that does a nice job of recovering mail files, even entire directories of mail files.

> ⊘ **Caution!** The last version I used didn't correctly handle the number of spaces after the day of the month in the date portion of the "From " line message separator. So you may have to add an extra space by hand after days with only one digit in them, or else Mail will think several messages are just one.

9

Configuring Emacs for Yourself

70. How do I set up a .emacs file properly?

See the section of the manual on the .emacs file, inside the section on customization. To reach this section of the on-line Info manual, type this:

```
CONTROL-h i m emacs ENTER g init SPC file ENTER
```

 Caution! In general, new Emacs users should not have .emacs files, because they cause confusing nonstandard behavior. Then the new users send questions to help-gnu-emacs asking why Emacs isn't behaving as documented.

71. How do you debug a .emacs file?

First start Emacs with the **−q** command line option. Then, in the *scratch* buffer, type the following:

```
(setq debug-on-error t) CONTROL-j
(load-file "~/.emacs") CONTROL-j
```

If you have an error in your .emacs file, the debugger is invoked when the error occurs. If you don't know how to use the debugger, do (setq stack-trace-on-error t) instead.

 Caution! This does not discover errors caused by an attempt to do something that requires a loaded terminal/window-system initialization code. See question 37.

72. How do I turn on abbrevs by default just in mode *XXX*?

Put this in your .emacs file:

```
(condition-case ()
   (read-abbrev-file nil t)
 (file-error nil))

(setq XXX-mode-hook
(function
 (lambda ()
   (setq abbrev-mode t))))
```

9

73. How do I turn on Auto-Fill mode by default?

To turn on Auto-Fill mode just once for one buffer, you type META-x
`auto-fill-mode`. To turn it on for every buffer in, for example, Text
mode, do this:

```
(setq text-mode-hook 'turn-on-auto-fill)
```

If you want Auto-Fill mode on in all major modes, do this:

```
(setq-default auto-fill-hook 'do-auto-fill)
```

74. How do I make Emacs use a certain major mode for certain files?

If you want to use *XXX* mode for all files that end with the extension
. *YYY*, the following sequence does it for you:

```
(setq auto-mode-alist (cons '("\\. YYY\\'" . XXX-mode)
   auto-mode-alist))
```

Otherwise, put this somewhere in the first line of any file you want to
edit in *XXX* mode:

```
-*-XXX-*-
```

75. What are the valid X resource settings (that is, stuff in the .Xdefaults
file)?

See the Emacs man page, or the etc/OPTIONS file.

76. How do I stop Emacs from beeping on a terminal?

Martin R. Frank <martin@cc.gatech.edu> writes:

Tell Emacs to use the visible bell rather than the audible bell, and set
the visible bell to nothing. Put this in your TERMCAP environment
variable:

```
. . . :vb=: . . .
```

And evaluate this:

```
(setq visible-bell t)
```

77. How do I turn down the bell volume in Emacs running under X
Windows?

Under Epoch you can do:

```
(setq epoch::bell-volume 20)
```

Under normal GNU Emacs you must modify the XTfeep function in
src/x11term.c, and change the number 50 to –50:

9

```
XTfeep ()
{
  BLOCK_INPUT_DECLARE ();
#ifdef XDEBUG
  fprintf (stderr, "XTfeep\n");
#endif
  BLOCK_INPUT ();
  XBell (XXdisplay,50);  /* change this 50 to -50 */
  UNBLOCK_INPUT ();
}
```

Then `xset b 0` turns off Emacs' beeping. After `xset b BASE`:

```
XBell (disp,  VAL) beeps with volume BASE - (BASE*VAL)/100 +
  VAL, XBell (disp, -VAL) beeps with volume BASE -
  (BASE*VAL)/100.
```

78. How do I make Emacs send 8-bit characters to my terminal?

Johan Widen <jw@sics.se> writes:

A patch for emacs-18.55 is available by FTP and mail-server from sics.se. Anonymous FTP: site: sics.se [192.16.123.90] file: archive/emacs-18. 55-8bit-diff.

E-mail:
To: mail-server@sics.se body: send emacs-18.55-8bit-diff.

79. How do I change *load-path*?

In general, you should only *add* to the *load-path*. You can add directory */XXX/YYY* to the *load-path* like this:

```
(setq load-path (append load-path '("/XXX/YYY/")))
```

To do this relative to your home directory, use:

```
(setq load-path (append load-path (list (expand-file-name
  "~/YYY/"))))
```

Emacs Lisp Programming

80. What dialect of Lisp is Emacs Lisp?

It's the dialect of Lisp called Emacs Lisp (no joke!). People also call it elisp or e-lisp. (NOTE: The term "Elisp" is trademarked by someone else.)

9

81. How close is Emacs Lisp to Common Lisp?

    Not very close. GNU Emacs Lisp is case-sensitive, uses dynamic scoping, doesn't have packages, doesn't have multiple return values, doesn't have reader macros, and so on. For people used to Common Lisp, some of the functions in Common Lisp that are not in Emacs Lisp by default are provided in the file lisp/cl.el. There is a Texinfo manual describing these functions in man/cl.texinfo.

82. How do I execute a piece of Emacs Lisp code?

    There are a number of ways to execute (called *evaluate*) an Emacs Lisp "form" (A form is a common structure in E-Lisp):

    - If you want it evaluated every time you run Emacs, put it in a file named .emacs in your home directory.

    - You can type the form in the *scratch* buffer, and then type `CONTROL-j` after it. The result of evaluating the form is inserted in the buffer.

    - In an Emacs-Lisp mode, typing `META-CONTROL-x` evaluates a top-level form before or around the point.

    - Typing `CONTROL-x CONTROL-e` in any buffer evaluates the Lisp form immediately before the point and prints its value in the echo area.

    - Typing `META-ESC` or `META-x eval-expression` enables you to type a Lisp form in the minibuffer which is evaluated.

    - You can use `META-x load-file` to have Emacs evaluate all the Lisp forms in a file. (To do this from Lisp, use the function **load** instead.)

83. How do I make a set of operations fully local to a region?

    Use **narrow-to-region** inside of **save-restriction**.

84. How can I highlight a region?

    There are ways to get highlighting in GNU Emacs 18.57, but they all require patching the C code of Emacs and rebuilding. They are also slow, and the highlighting disappears if you scroll or redraw the screen. One patch is by Kenichi Handa <handa@etl.go.jp>. You can highlight regions in a variety of ways in Epoch. GNU Emacs 19 will have everything you need, but it won't be out soon.

9

85. How do I change Emacs' idea of the tab character's length?

    Use:

    ```
    (setq default-tab-width 10)
    ```

86. What is the difference between `(interactive "P")` and `(interactive "p")`?

    The value that is a result of "P" can be a list, a symbol, or an integer; the value that is a result of "p" is always an integer:

Prefix Keys Typed	Result of "P"	Result of "p"
nothing	nil	1
"M-1"	1	1
"C-u 1"	1	1
"M--"	'_	−1
"C-u −"	'_	−1
"C-u"	(4)	4
"C-u C-u"	(16)	16

Carrying Out Common Tasks

87. How do I insert ">" characters in the beginning of every line in a buffer?

    Type `META-x replace-regexp ENTER ^ ENTER > ENTER`. (`replace-regexp` can be shortened to `repl TAB r`.)

    To do this only in the region, type `CONTROL-x n META-x replace-regexp ENTER ^ ENTER > ENTER CONTROL-x w`. (You're going to remember that, right?)

88. How do I insert "_ ^H" characters (an underscore followed by a backspace) before each character in a paragraph to get an underlined paragraph?

    ```
    META-x underline-region
    ```

89. How do I repeat a command as many times as possible?

    Make a keyboard macro that invokes the command, and then type `META-0 CONTROL-x e`.

9

Caution! Any messages your command prints in the echo area are suppressed.

90. How do I search for or delete unprintable (8-bit or control) characters?

    To search for a single character that appears in the buffer as, for example, \237, you can type CONTROL-s CONTROL-q 2 3 7. (This assumes the value of **search-quote-char** is 17 (CONTROL-q).)

    Searching for ALL unprintable characters is best done with a "regexp" search. The easiest regexp to use for the unprintable chars is the complement of the regexp for the printable chars. Regexp for the printable chars is [\t\n\r\f -~]. Therefore, the regexp for the unprintable chars is [^\t\n\r\f -~].

    To type some of these special characters (\t, \n, \r, \f) as an interactive argument to **isearch-forward-regexp** or **re-search-forward**, you need to use CONTROL-q. So to search for unprintable characters using **re-search-forward**:

    ```
    META-x re-search-forward ENTER [^ TAB CONTROL-q CONTROL-j
    CONTROL-q ENTER CONTROL-q CONTROL-l SPC -~] ENTER
    ```

    Using **isearch-forward-regexp**:

    ```
    META-CONTROL-s [^ TAB ENTER CONTROL-q ENTER CONTROL-q
    CONTROL-l SPC -~]
    ```

    To delete all unprintable characters, simply use a **replace-regexp**:

    ```
    META-x replace-regexp ENTER [^ TAB CONTROL-q CONTROL-j
    CONTROL-q ENTER CONTROL-q CONTROL-l SPC -~] ENTER ENTER
    ```

    Notes:

    - With isearch, you can type ENTER to get a quoted CONTROL-j. (Not a quoted CONTROL-m.)

    - You don't need to quote TAB with either isearch or typing something in the minibuffer. Here are the Emacs Lisp forms of the previous regexps:

      ```
      ;; regexp matching all printable characters:
      "[\t\n\r\f -~]"
      ```

9

```
;; regexp matching all unprintable characters:
"[^\t\n\r\f -~]"

;; alternative regexps for all unprintable characters:
"[\-@-\-h\-k\-n-\-_\-?-\377]"
"[\000-\010\013\016-\037\177-\377]"

(To use "[\000-\010\013\016-\037\177-\377]" interac-
tively, type:

[ -q 000 - -q 010 -q 013 -q 016 - -q
037 -q 177 - -q 377 ]

)
```

91. How do I control Emacs' case sensitivity when searching and replacing?

    For searching, the value of the variable *case-fold-search* determines whether they are case-sensitive:

    ```
    (setq case-fold-search nil) ; make searches case-sensitive
    (setq case-fold-search t)   ; make searches case-insensitive
    ```

    Similarly for replacing, the variable *case-replace* determines whether replacements preserve case.

92. How do I tell Emacs to automatically indent a new line to the indentation of the previous line?

    Use `META-x indented-text-mode`. (This is a major mode.)

    If you have Auto-Fill mode on (minor mode), you can tell Emacs to prefix every line with a certain character sequence, the *fill prefix*. Type the prefix at the beginning of a line, position the point after it, and then type the **set-fill-prefix** command (CONTROL-x) to set the fill prefix. Thereafter, auto-filling automatically puts the fill prefix at the beginning of new lines, and the **fill-paragraph** command (META-q) maintains any fill prefix when refilling the paragraph.

93. How do I make Emacs "typeover" or "overwrite" when I type rather than always inserting?

    Use `META-x overwrite-mode` (minor mode).

94. How do I determine which parenthesis matches the one I'm looking at?

    If you're looking at a right parenthesis (or brace or bracket), you can delete it and reinsert it. Emacs blinks the cursor on the matching

9

parenthesis. The **forward-sexp** command (META-CONTROL-f) and the **backward-sexp** command (META-CONTROL-b) skip over balanced parentheses, so you can see which parentheses match. (You can train the commands to skip over balanced brackets and braces at the same time by modifying the syntax table.)

Here is some Emacs Lisp that makes the % key show the matching parenthesis, as in vi. In addition, if the cursor isn't over a parenthesis, it simply inserts a % like normal. (This code is by an unknown contributor.)

```
(global-set-key "%" 'match-paren)

(defun match-paren (arg)
  "Go to the matching parenthesis if on parenthesis otherwise insert %. "
  (interactive "p")
  (cond ((looking-at "\\s\(") (forward-list 1) (backward-char 1))
    ((looking-at "\\s\)") (forward-char 1) (backward-list 1))
    (t (self-insert-command (or arg 1)))))
```

95. How do I make the cursor stay in the same column when I go up and down, even if the line is too short?

   Use META-x picture-mode. (This is a minor mode, in theory anyway.)

96. How do I read news under Emacs?

   There are at least three news-reading packages that operate inside Emacs. The rnews package comes with Emacs. GNUS and Gnews come separately. By the way, rnews will be replaced with GNUS in Emacs 19.

   Note that rnews does not work with NNTP. Both GNUS and Gnews handle reading news over NNTP. I think both also can read from a local news spool. GNUS also supports reading mail stored in MH folders or articles saved by GNUS. People have complained that GNUS uses a lot of CPU time (it does). Some people have complained that Gnews is slower than GNUS. GNUS is written (mostly) by Masanobu Umeda. His latest e-mail address is umerin@mse.kyutech.ac.jp. The latest version is GNUS 3.13. There is a newsgroup for discussion of GNUS called gnu.emacs.gnus. This newsgroup is gatewayed with the mailing list info-gnus-english; to subscribe send mail to info-gnus-english-request@cis.ohio-state.edu. There is also a mailing list called info-gnus, which includes discussion in Japanese. Gnews was written by Matthew Wiener. There is a newsgroup for Gnews called gnu.emacs.gnews.

9

97. In C mode, can I show just the lines that will be left after #ifdef commands are handled by the compiler?

    Use META-x `hide-ifdef-mode`. (This is a minor mode.)

    You may have to (load "hideif") first. If you want to do this regularly, put this in your .emacs file:

    ```
    (autoload 'hide-ifdef-mode "hideif" nil t)
    ```

    (Yes, I know, this should be in lisp/loaddefs.el already.)

98. Is there an equivalent to the "." (dot) command of vi? ("." is the redo command in vi. It redoes the last insertion or deletion.)

    No, not really. You can type the **repeat-complex-command** command (CONTROL-x ESC) to reinvoke commands that used the minibuffer to get arguments. In **repeat-complex-command**, you can type META-p and META-n to scan through all the different complex commands you've typed. To repeat something on each line, I recommend using keyboard macros.

99. How do I use the **emacstool** function under SunView?

    The file etc/SUN-SUPPORT includes the document "Using Emacstool with GNU Emacs." Also read the man page for **emacstool** (etc/emacstool.1).

100. How do I make Emacs show the current line (column) number on the mode line?

    There is no "correct" way to constantly display the current line (or column) number on the mode line in Emacs 18. Emacs is not a line-oriented editor and has no idea which "lines" of the buffer are displayed in the window. It would require a lot of work at the C-code level to make Emacs keep track of this. Emacs 19 probably will be able to do this, but not with great efficiency. To find out what line of the buffer you are on right now, do META-x `what-line`. Typing CONTROL-x 1 also tells you what line you are on, provided the buffer isn't separated into "pages" with CONTROL-l characters. In that case, it tells you only what line of the current "page" you are on.

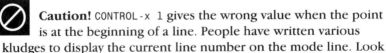 **Caution!** CONTROL-x 1 gives the wrong value when the point is at the beginning of a line. People have written various kludges to display the current line number on the mode line. Look in the Lisp Code Directory. (See question 13.)

9

101. How do I tell Emacs to iconify itself?

You need to modify C source and recompile—or get Epoch instead. For those interested, I have a patch to enable Emacs to iconify itself.

102. How do I use regexps (regular expressions) in Emacs?

This is documented in the Emacs manual. To read the manual section on-line, type CONTROL-h i m emacs ENTER m regexps ENTER.

Caution! Unlike in UNIX grep, sed, and so on, a complement character set ([^...]) can match a newline, unless newline is mentioned as one of the characters not to match.

9

GNU Emacs Reference

G NU Emacs is undeniably the world's most powerful text editing program generally available. It is published by the Free Software Foundation, 675 Massachusetts Avenue, Cambridge, MA 02139, and its cost is nothing.

The files that comprise GNU Emacs (you get the complete source with it also) are several megabytes in length. The FSF (Free Software Foundation) offers Emacs—and much more— on tapes that can be read by various UNIX systems. The foundation does charge for the tape and the labor of copying it, but not for the programs. Contact the FSF at the preceding address for pricing.

The best way to get GNU, if your system is on the Internet, is by anonymous FTP (file transfer protocol) from prep.ai.mit.edu, a computer at the Massachusetts Institute of Technology that serves as the primary electronic distribution site for GNU. There is no charge for connection. The latest version is 18.57. GNU Emacs also is available on hundreds of other computers worldwide on the Internet. You'll have no trouble finding it.

The following list shows how to get Emacs on a system connected to the Internet.

1. Type `ftp prep.ai.mit.edu`, and the system responds:

   ```
   Connected to prep.ai.mit.edu.
   220 aeneas FTP server (Version 4.136 Mon Oct 31
     23:18:38 EST 1988) ready.
   Name (prep.ai.mit.edu:robertsr):
   ```

10

2. Enter anonymous as name, and the system responds:

   ```
   331 Guest login ok, send ident as password.
   Password:
   ```

3. Enter your user name as the password (such as "robertsr"), and the system tells you:

   ```
   230 Guest login ok, access restrictions apply.
   ```

4. Type cd pub/gnu to change to the GNU directory.

5. Type dir emacs* to see which Emacs files are available. The system responds:

```
200 PORT command successful.
150 Opening data connection for /bin/ls (128.109.185.12,1896) (0 bytes).
-rw-r--r--    22828    May 19   1989   emacs-18.54-apollo-README
-rw-r--r--  1416681    May 19   1989   emacs-18.54-apollo-binary-SR10.1.tar.Z
-rw-r--r--   715617    May 19   1989   emacs-18.54-apollo-binary-SR9.7.tar.Z
-rw-r--r--   523623    May 19   1989   emacs-18.54-apollo-update.tar.Z
-rw-r--r--  3988838    Jan 26  16:14   emacs-18.57.tar.Z
-rw-r--r--   225323    Apr  5   1989   emacs.diff-18.44-18.45.Z
-rw-r--r--    35702    Apr  5   1989   emacs.diff-18.45-18.46.Z
-rw-r--r--    19382    Apr  5   1989   emacs.diff-18.46-18.47.Z
-rw-r--r--   115927    Apr  5   1989   emacs.diff-18.47-18.48.Z
-rw-r--r--    24326    Apr  5   1989   emacs.diff-18.48-18.49.Z
-rw-r--r--   577167    Apr  5   1989   emacs.diff-18.49-18.50.Z
-rw-r--r--   468899    Apr  5   1989   emacs.diff-18.50-18.51.Z
-rw-r--r--   545949    Apr  5   1989   emacs.diff-18.51-18.52.Z
-rw-r--r--    38576    Apr  5   1989   emacs.diff-18.52-18.53.Z
-rw-r--r--    70153    Apr 26   1989   emacs.diff-18.53-18.54.Z
-rw-r--r--   104213    Aug 23   1989   emacs.diff-18.54-18.55.Z
-rw-r--r--   372135    Mar 22  18:19   emacs.dvi.Z
226 Transfer complete.
remote: emacs*
1375 bytes received in 0.44 seconds (3 Kbytes/s)
```

6. Determine the most recent version of Emacs. At this time, it is the file emacs-18.57.tar.Z (you want the highest version number).

7. Type binary to set your ftp program up for a binary transfer.

8. Type get emacs-18.57.tar.Z.

9. When the transfer is finished (the system tells you), type quit to break the connection to prep.ai.mit.edu. The Emacs compressed tar file now is in your working directory.

If your system is not connected to the Internet, you can still use UUCP (UNIX to UNIX copy protocol). All your system needs is a modem hooked to the phone line and the capacity for UUCP transfers. You then can avail yourself of Ohio State University's free 24-hour service to copy the GNU files to your system by phone.

Select the correct command from the following list, based on the baud rate your modem uses. The following settings are entered into the uucp configuration file using /etc/uuinstall on most UNIX systems. After the entry is made, any user can call the system by typing cu osu-cis.

```
osu-cis Any ACU 19200 1-614-292-5112 in:--in:--in: Uanon
osu-cis Any ACU 9600 1-614-292-1153 in:--in:--in: Uanon
osu-cis Any ACU ##00 1-614-292-31## ""
\r\c Name? osu-cis nected \c
  GO \d\r\d\r\d\r in:--in:--
in: Uanon
  Micom port selector, at 1200, 2400, or 9600 bps.
  Replace ##'s above with 12, 24, or 96 (both speed and phone number).
```

Following is a list of the GNU-how-to-get file current as of January 26, 1991. Always look for the current version so you can program your uucp request correctly. Use this information to transfer:

Source is prep.ai.mit.edu:pub/gnu/emacs-18.57.tar.Z of 26 Jan 1991.

Root is ~/gnu/emacs/18.57/emacs-18.57.tar.Z-part-??, pieces aa-bn [40 pieces].

Part -bn is 88,838 bytes long.

Diffs available are ~/gnu/emacs/

diff-18.50-18.51.Z	468,899
diff-18.51-18.52.Z	545,949
diff-18.52-18.53.Z	38,576
diff-18.53-18.54.Z	70,153
diff-18.54-18.55.Z	104,213

No patches have been distributed since 18.55.

More information is available in the GNU.how-to-get file, which is widely distributed on various networks.

However you get it, GNU Emacs is well worth having. Refer to Chapter 2 for more information on how to get GNU and other flavors of Emacs.

Keys

All versions of Emacs are infinitely customizable. We can't just give you a list of key combinations and say these are always true, because 48 people could have modified your version of Emacs. Certainly you will want to rearrange the keys to better suit your own needs and preferences. This chapter, however, gives you a starting point. This shows how the keys initially are bound in GNU Emacs 18.57. The names of commands in Emacs are usually self-explanatory, like beginning-of-line (now bound to the CONTROL and a keys). Use Table 10.1 as a starting point in verifying and changing your keys around. With the **help-for-help** command, you can generate a list like this one.

Table 10.1. GNU Emacs Global Commands and Their Key Bindings

Key Bindings	Commands
C-@	set-mark-command
C-a	beginning-of-line
C-b	backward-char
C-c	mode-specific-command-prefix
C-d	delete-char
C-e	end-of-line
C-f	forward-char
C-g	keyboard-quit
C-h	help-command
TAB	indent-for-tab-command
LFD	newline-and-indent
C-k	kill-line
C-l	recenter
ENTER	newline
C-n	next-line
C-o	open-line
C-p	previous-line
C-q	quoted-insert
C-r	isearch-backward
C-s	isearch-forward
C-t	transpose-chars
C-u	universal-argument
C-v	scroll-up
C-w	kill-region
C-x	Control-X-prefix
C-y	yank
C-z	suspend-emacs

Key Bindings	Commands
ESC	ESC-prefix
C-]	abort-recursive-edit
C-_	undo
SPC to ~	self-insert-command
DEL	delete-backward-char
C-h v	describe-variable
C-h w	where-is
C-h t	help-with-tutorial
C-h s	describe-syntax
C-h n	view-emacs-news
C-h C-n	view-emacs-news
C-h m	describe-mode
C-h l	view-lossage
C-h i	info
C-h f	describe-function
C-h d	describe-function
C-h k	describe-key
C-h c	describe-key-briefly
C-h b	describe-bindings
C-h a	command-apropos
C-h C-w	describe-no-warranty
C-h C-d	describe-distribution
C-h C-c	describe-copying
C-h ?	help-for-help
C-h C-h	help-for-help
C-x C-a	add-mode-abbrev
C-x C-b	list-buffers
C-x C-c	save-buffers-kill-emacs
C-x C-d	list-directory
C-x C-e	eval-last-sexp
C-x C-f	find-file
C-x C-h	inverse-add-mode-abbrev
C-x TAB	indent-rigidly

10

continues

10

Table 10.1. Continued

Key Bindings	Commands
C-x C-l	downcase-region
C-x C-n	set-goal-column
C-x C-o	delete-blank-lines
C-x C-p	mark-page
C-x C-q	toggle-read-only
C-x C-r	find-file-read-only
C-x C-s	save-buffer
C-x C-t	transpose-lines
C-x C-u	upcase-region
C-x C-v	find-alternate-file
C-x C-w	write-file
C-x C-x	exchange-point-and-mark
C-x C-z	suspend-emacs
C-x ESC	repeat-complex-command
C-x $	set-selective-display
C-x '	expand-abbrev
C-x (	start-kbd-macro
C-x)	end-kbd-macro
C-x +	add-global-abbrev
C-x –	inverse-add-global-abbrev
C-x .	set-fill-prefix
C-x /	point-to-register
C-x 0	delete-window
C-x 1	delete-other-windows
C-x 2	split-window-vertically
C-x 4	ctl-x-4-prefix
C-x 5	split-window-horizontally
C-x ;	set-comment-column
C-x <	scroll-left
C-x =	what-cursor-position
C-x >	scroll-right
C-x [	backward-page

10

Key Bindings	Commands
C-x]	forward-page
C-x ^	enlarge-window
C-x `	next-error
C-x a	append-to-buffer
C-x b	switch-to-buffer
C-x d	dired
C-x e	call-last-kbd-macro
C-x f	set-fill-column
C-x g	insert-register
C-x h	mark-whole-buffer
C-x i	insert-file
C-x j	register-to-point
C-x k	kill-buffer
C-x l	count-lines-page
C-x m	mail
C-x n	narrow-to-region
C-x o	other-window
C-x p	narrow-to-page
C-x q	kbd-macro-query
C-x r	copy-rectangle-to-register
C-x s	save-some-buffers
C-x u	advertised-undo
C-x w	widen
C-x x	copy-to-register
C-x {	shrink-window-horizontally
C-x }	enlarge-window-horizontally
C-x DEL	backward-kill-sentence
ESC C-@	mark-sexp
ESC C-a	beginning-of-defun
ESC C-b	backward-sexp
ESC C-c	exit-recursive-edit
ESC C-d	down-list

continues

Table 10.1. Continued

Key Bindings	Commands
ESC C-e	end-of-defun
ESC C-f	forward-sexp
ESC C-h	mark-defun
ESC TAB	lisp-complete-symbol
ESC LFD	indent-new-comment-line
ESC C-k	kill-sexp
ESC C-n	forward-list
ESC C-o	split-line
ESC C-p	backward-list
ESC C-s	isearch-forward-regexp
ESC C-t	transpose-sexps
ESC C-u	backward-up-list
ESC C-v	scroll-other-window
ESC C-w	append-next-kill
ESC ESC	eval-expression
ESC C-\	indent-region
ESC SPACEBAR	just-one-space
ESC !	shell-command
ESC $	spell-word
ESC %	query-replace
ESC '	abbrev-prefix-mark
ESC (	insert-parentheses
ESC)	move-past-close-and-reindent
ESC ,	tags-loop-continue
ESC –	negative-argument
ESC .	find-tag
ESC /	dabbrev-expand
ESC 0 to ESC 9	digit-argument
ESC ;	indent-for-comment
ESC <	beginning-of-buffer
ESC =	count-lines-region
ESC >	end-of-buffer

Key Bindings	Commands
ESC @	mark-word
ESC O	Prefix Command
ESC [	backward-paragraph
ESC \	delete-horizontal-space
ESC]	forward-paragraph
ESC ^	delete-indentation
ESC a	backward-sentence
ESC b	backward-word
ESC c	capitalize-word
ESC d	kill-word
ESC e	forward-sentence
ESC f	forward-word
ESC g	fill-region
ESC h	mark-paragraph
ESC i	tab-to-tab-stop
ESC j	indent-new-comment-line
ESC k	kill-sentence
ESC l	downcase-word
ESC m	back-to-indentation
ESC q	fill-paragraph
ESC r	move-to-window-line
ESC t	transpose-words
ESC u	upcase-word
ESC v	scroll-down
ESC w	copy-region-as-kill
ESC x	execute-extended-command
ESC y	yank-pop
ESC z	zap-to-char
ESC |	shell-command-on-region
ESC ~	not-modified
ESC DEL	backward-kill-word
C-x 4 C-f	find-file-other-window
C-x 4 .	find-tag-other-window

continues

10

Table 10.1. Continued

Key Bindings	Commands
C-x 4 a	add-change-log-entry-other-window
C-x 4 b	switch-to-buffer-other-window
C-x 4 d	dired-other-window
C-x 4 f	find-file-other-window
C-x 4 m	mail-other-window
ESC O A	previous-line
ESC O B	next-line
ESC O C	forward-char
ESC O D	backward-char
ESC O M	open-line
ESC O P	beginning-of-line
ESC O Q	end-of-line
ESC O R	isearch-forward
ESC O S	kill-line
ESC O n	delete-char
ESC O p	yank
ESC O q	backward-word
ESC O s	forward-word
ESC O w	backward-paragraph
ESC O y	forward-paragraph

Commands and Variables

There are many more commands than there are key combinations. New commands and variables can be added to Emacs at any time.

Being familiar with available commands and variables helps you tremendously in customizing and achieving the true versatility of Emacs. To get a complete list of the commands and variables that are now part of your version of GNU, type:

```
META-x apropos ENTER \w
```

This list, like the following examples from Emacs 18.57, is very useful. Peruse it often to find commands that you might not have known before. Experiment and turn them into old friends—that will make your work easier!

Commands

Table 10.2 lists the commands that come with the standard distribution version of Emacs 18.57 with key bindings as applicable. After GNU is installed on your system, it is subject to modification, and you often will find many more commands added by users. When no key binding is listed, the command is not bound to a key by default.

Table 10.2. GNU Emacs Commands

Command Name	Key Binding	Meaning
Buffer-menu-2-window		Select this line's buffer, with previous buffer in second window.
Buffer-menu-backup-unmark		Move up and cancel all requested operations on buffer on line above.
Buffer-menu-buffer		Return buffer described by this line of buffer menu.
Buffer-menu-delete		Mark buffer on this line to be deleted by M-x Buffer-menu-execute command.
Buffer-menu-delete-backwards		Mark buffer on this line to be deleted by M-x Buffer-menu-execute command.
Buffer-menu-execute		Save and/or delete buffers marked with M-x Buffer-menu-save or M-x Buffer-menu-delete commands.
Buffer-menu-mark		Mark buffer on this line for being displayed by M-x Buffer-menu-select command.
Buffer-menu-mode		Major mode for editing a list of buffers.
Buffer-menu-not-modified		Mark buffer on this line as unmodified (no changes to save).

continues

10

Table 10.2. Continued

Command Name	Key Binding	Meaning
Buffer-menu-other-window		Select this line's buffer in other window, leaving buffer menu visible.
Buffer-menu-save		Mark buffer on this line to be saved by M-x Buffer-menu-execute command.
Buffer-menu-select		Select this line's buffer; also display buffers marked with ">."
Buffer-menu-this-window		Select this line's buffer in this window.
Buffer-menu-unmark		Cancel all requested operations on buffer on this line.
Control-X-prefix	C-x	Prefix command (definition is a Lisp vector of subcommands).
ESC-prefix		Prefix command (definition is a Lisp vector of subcommands).
Helper-describe-bindings		Describe local key bindings of current mode.
Helper-help		Provide help for current mode.
Info-split		Split an info file into an indirect file plus bounded-size subfiles.
Info-tagify		Create or update Info-file tag table in current buffer.
Info-validate		Check current buffer for validity as an Info file.
LaTeX-mode		Major mode for editing files of input for LaTeX.
Snarf-documentation		Used during Emacs initialization, before dumping runnable Emacs.
TeX-mode		Major mode for editing files of input for TeX or LaTeX.
abbrev-expansion		Return the string that ABBREV expands into in the current buffer.
abbrev-mode		Toggle abbrev mode.

Command Name	Key Binding	Meaning
abbrev-prefix-mark	ESC '	Mark current point as the beginning of an abbrev.
abbrev-symbol		Return the symbol representing abbrev named ABBREV.
abort-recursive-edit	C-]	Abort the command that requested this recursive edit or minibuffer input.
accept-process-output		Allow any pending output from subprocesses to be read by Emacs.
accessible-keymaps		Find all keymaps accessible via prefix characters from KEYMAP.
add-change-log-entry		Find change log file and add an entry for today.
add-change-log-entry-other-window	C-x 4 a	Find change log file in other window, and add an entry for today.
add-global-abbrev	C-x +	Define global (all modes) abbrev for last word(s) before point.
add-mode-abbrev	C-x C-a	Define mode-specific abbrev for last word(s) before point.
add-name-to-file		Give FILE additional name NEWNAME. Both args strings.
advertised-undo	C-x u	Undo some previous changes.
after-find-file		Called after finding a file and by the default revert function.
all-completions		Search for partial matches to STRING in ALIST.
and		Eval args until one of them yields NIL, then return NIL.
append		Concatenate arguments and make the result a list.
append-next-kill	ESC C-w	Cause following command, if kill, to append to previous kill.
append-to-buffer	C-x a	Append to specified buffer the text of the region.
append-to-file		Append the contents of the region to the end of file FILENAME.

continues

Table 10.2. Continued

Command Name	Key Binding	Meaning
append-to-register		Append region to text in register REG.
apply		Call FUNCTION, passing remaining arguments to it.
apropos		Show all symbols whose names contain match for REGEXP.
aref		Return the element of ARRAY at index INDEX.
arrayp		T if OBJECT is an array (string or vector).
aset		Store into the element of ARRAY at index INDEX the value NEWVAL.
ash		Return VALUE with its bits shifted left by COUNT.
ask-user-about-lock		Ask user what to do when he wants to edit FILE but it is locked by USER.
ask-user-about-supersession-threat		Ask a user who is about to modify an obsolete buffer what to do.
assoc		Return non-nil if ELT is the car of an element of LIST. Comparison done with equal.
assq		Return non-nil if ELT is the car of an element of LIST. Comparison done with eq.
atom		T if OBJECT is not a cons cell. This includes nil.
auto-fill-mode		Toggle auto fill mode.
auto-save-file-name-p		Return non-nil if FILENAME can be yielded by make-auto-save-file-name.
auto-save-mode		Toggle auto-saving of contents of current buffer.
autoload		Define FUNCTION to autoload from FILE.
back-to-indentation	ESC m	Move point to the first non-whitespace character on this line.

Command Name	Key Binding	Meaning
backtrace		Print a trace of Lisp function calls currently active.
backtrace-debug		Set the debug-on-exit flag of eval frame LEVEL levels down to FLAG.
backup-buffer		Make a backup of the disk file visited by the current buffer, if appropriate.
backup-file-name-p		Return non-nil if FILE is a backup file name (numeric or not).
backward-char	C-b, ESC O D	Move point left ARG characters (right if ARG is negative). (For example, to move back five characters, type ESC 5 C-b.)
backward-delete-char		Delete the previous ARG characters (or the following ARG characters, with negative ARG).
backward-delete-char-untabify		Delete characters backward, changing tabs into spaces.
backward-kill-paragraph		Kill back to start of paragraph.
backward-kill-sentence	C-x DEL	Kill back from point to start of sentence.
backward-kill-sexp		Kill the syntactic expression preceding the cursor.
backward-kill-word	ESC DEL	Kill characters backward until encountering the end of a word.
backward-list	ESC C-p	Move backward across one balanced group of parentheses.
backward-page	C-x [	Move backward to page boundary. With arg, repeat, or go forward if negative.
backward-paragraph	ESC [, ESC O w	Move backward to start of paragraph. With arg, do it arg times.
backward-prefix-charsmeme		Move point backward over any number of chars with syntax "prefix."
backward-sentence	ESC a	Move backward to start of sentence. With arg, do it arg times.

continues

Table 10.2. Continued

Command Name	Key Binding	Meaning
backward-sexp	ESC C-b	Move backward across one balanced expression.
backward-to-indentation		Move backward ARG lines and position at first nonblank character.
backward-up-list	ESC C-u	Move backward out of one level of parentheses.
backward-word	ESC b, ESC O q	Move backward until encountering the end of a word.
barf-if-buffer-read-only		Signal a buffer-read-only error if the current buffer is read-only.
basic-save-buffer		Save the current buffer in its visited file, if it has been modified.
batch-byte-compile		Run byte-compile-file on the files remaining on the command line.
batch-info-validate		Run Info-validate on the files remaining on the command line.
batch-texinfo-format		Run texinfo-format-buffer on the files remaining on the command line.
baud-rate		Return the output baud rate of the terminal.
beep		Beep, or flash the screen.
beginning-of-buffer	ESC <	Move point to the beginning of the buffer; leave mark at previous position.
beginning-of-defun	ESC C-a	Move backward to next beginning-of-defun.
beginning-of-line	C-a, ESC O P	Move point to beginning of current line.
blink-matching-open		Move cursor momentarily to the beginning of the sexp before point.
bobp		Return t if point is at the beginning of the buffer.
bolp		Return t if point is at the beginning of a line.
boundp		T if SYMBOL's value is not void.

Command Name	Key Binding	Meaning
buffer-enable-undo		Start keeping undo information for buffer BUFFER (default is current buffer).
buffer-file-name		Return name of file BUFFER is visiting, or NIL if none.
buffer-flush-undo		Make BUFFER stop keeping undo information.
buffer-list		Return a list of all buffers.
buffer-local-variables		Return alist of variables that are buffer-local in BUFFER.
buffer-menu		Make a menu of buffers so you can save, delete, or select them.
buffer-modified-p		Return t if BUFFER is modified since file last read in or saved.
buffer-name		Return the name of BUFFER, as a string.
buffer-size		Return the number of characters in the current buffer.
buffer-string		Return the contents of the current buffer as a string.
buffer-substring		Return the contents of part of the current buffer as a string.
bufferp		T if OBJECT is an editor buffer.
bury-buffer		Put BUFFER at the end of the list of all buffers.
byte-compile-file		Compile a file of Lisp code named FILENAME into a file of byte code.
byte-recompile-directory		Recompile every .el file in DIRECTORY that needs recompilation.
c-backward-to-start-of-if		Move to the start of the last "unbalanced" if.
c-indent-command		Indent current line as C code, or in some cases insert a tab character.
c-indent-line		Indent current line as C code.
c-macro-expand		Display the result of expanding all C macros occurring in the region.

continues

10

Table 10.2. Continued

Command Name	Key Binding	Meaning
c-mode		Major mode for editing C code.
calculate-c-indent		Return appropriate indentation for current line as C code.
calculate-c-indent-within-comment		Return the indentation amount for line, assuming that the current line is part of a block comment.
calculate-lisp-indent		Return appropriate indentation for current line as Lisp code.
calendar		Display three-month calendar in another window.
call-interactively		Call FUNCTION, reading args according to its interactive calling specs.
call-last-kbd-macro	C-x e	Call the last keyboard macro that you defined with C-x (.
call-process		Call PROGRAM in separate process.
call-process-region		Send text from START to END to a process running PROGRAM.
cancel-debug-on-entry		Undo effect of debug-on-entry on FUNCTION.
capitalize		One arg, a character or string. Convert it to capitalized form and return that.
capitalize-region		Convert the region to uppercase. In programs, wants two arguments.
capitalize-word	ESC c	Capitalize the following word (or ARG words), moving over.
car		Return the car of CONSCELL. If arg is nil, return nil.
car-safe		Return the car of OBJECT if it is a cons cell, or else nil.
catch		(catch TAG BODY...) performs BODY allowing nonlocal exits using (throw TAG).
cd		Make DIR become the current buffer's default directory.

Command Name	Key Binding	Meaning
cdr		Return the cdr of CONSCELL. If arg is nil, return nil.
cdr-safe		Return the cdr of OBJECT if it is a cons cell, or else nil.
center-line	ESC s	Center the line point is on, within the width specified by "fill-column."
center-paragraph	ESC S	Center each line in the paragraph at or after point.
center-region		Center each line starting in the region.
char-after		One arg, POS, a number. Return the character in the current buffer.
char-equal		T if args (both characters (numbers)) match. May ignore case.
char-or-string-p		T if OBJECT is a character (a number) or a string.
char-syntax		Return the syntax code of CHAR, described by a character.
char-to-string		Convert arg CHAR to a string containing that character.
clear-abbrev-table		Undefine all abbrevs in abbrev table TABLE, leaving it empty.
clear-rectangle		Blank out rectangle with corners at point and mark.
clear-visited-file-modtime		Clear out records of last mod time of visited file.
command-apropos	C-h a	Like apropos but list only symbols that are names of commands.
command-execute		Execute CMD as an editor command.
command-history-mode		Major mode for examining commands from command-history.
commandp		T if FUNCTION makes provisions for interactive calling.
compare-windows		Compare text in current window with text in next window.

continues

10

Table 10.2. Continued

Command Name	Key Binding	Meaning
compile		Compile the program including the current buffer. Default: run "make."
completing-read		Read a string in the minibuffer, with completion.
concat		Concatenate arguments and make the result a string.
cond		(cond CLAUSES...) tries each clause until one succeeds.
condition-case		Regain control when an error is signaled.
cons		Create a new cons, give it CAR and CDR as components, and return it.
consp		T if OBJECT is a cons cell.
continue-process		Continue process PROCESS. May be process or name of one.
convert-mocklisp-buffer		Convert buffer of Mocklisp code to real Lisp that GNU Emacs can run.
coordinates-in-window-p		Return non-nil if POSITIONS (a list, (SCREEN-X SCREEN-Y)) is in WINDOW.
copy-alist		Return a copy of ALIST.
copy-file		Copy FILE to NEWNAME. Both args strings.
copy-keymap		Return a copy of the keymap KEYMAP.
copy-marker		Return a new marker pointing at the same place as MARKER.
copy-rectangle-to-register	C-x r	Copy rectangular region into register REG.
copy-region-as-kill	ESC w	Save the region as if killed, but don't kill it.
copy-sequence		Return a copy of a list, vector, or string.
copy-syntax-table		Construct a new syntax table and return it.

10

Command Name	Key Binding	Meaning
copy-to-buffer		Copy to specified buffer the text of the region.
copy-to-register	C-x x	Copy region into register REG.
count-lines		Return number of newlines between START and END.
count-lines-page	C-x l	Report number of lines on current page, and how many are before or after point.
count-lines-region	ESC =	Print number of lines in the region.
count-matches		Print number of matches for REGEXP following point.
create-file-buffer		Create a suitably named buffer for visiting FILENAME, and return it.
ctl-x-4-prefix	C-x 4	Prefix command (definition is a Lisp vector of subcommands).
current-buffer		Return the current buffer as a Lisp buffer object.
current-column		Return the horizontal position of point. Beginning of line is column 0.
current-global-map		Return the current global keymap.
current-indentation		Return the indentation of the current line.
current-local-map		Return current buffer's local keymap, or nil if it has none.
current-time-string		Return the current time, as a human-readable string.g
current-window-configuration		Return an object representing Emacs' current window configuration.
dabbrev-expand	ESC /	Expand previous word "dynamically."
debug		Enter debugger. Return if user says "continue."
debug-on-entry		Request FUNCTION to invoke debugger each time it is called.
default-value		Return SYMBOL's default value.

continues

10

Table 10.2. Continued

Command Name	Key Binding	Meaning
defconst		(defconst SYMBOL INITVALUE DOCSTRING) defines SYMBOL as a constant variable.
define-abbrev		Define an abbrev in TABLE named NAME, to expand to EXPANSION or call HOOK.
define-abbrev-table		Define TABNAME (a symbol) as an abbrev table name.
define-abbrevs		Define abbrevs according to current visible buffer contents.
define-global-abbrev		Define ABBREV as a global abbreviation for EXPANSION.
define-key		Args KEYMAP, KEY, DEF. Define key sequence KEY, in KEYMAP, as DEF.
define-mail-alias		Define NAME as a mail-alias that translates to DEFINITION.
define-mode-abbrev		Define ABBREV as a mode-specific abbreviation for EXPANSION.
define-prefix-command		Define SYMBOL as a prefix command.
defmacro		(defmacro NAME ARGLIST [DOCSTRING] BODY...) defines NAME as a macro.
defun		(defun NAME ARGLIST [DOCSTRING] BODY...) defines NAME as a function.
defvar		(defvar SYMBOL INITVALUE DOCSTRING) defines SYMBOL as an advertised variable.
delete-auto-save-file-if-necessary		Delete the auto-save file name for the current buffer (if it has one).
delete-backward-char	DEL	Delete the previous ARG characters (following, with negative ARG).
delete-blank-lines	C-x C-o	On blank line, delete all surrounding blank lines leaving just one.
delete-char	C-d, ESC O n	Delete the following ARG characters (previous, with negative ARG).

10

Command Name	Key Binding	Meaning
delete-extract-rectangle		Return and delete contents of rectangle with corners at START and END.
delete-file		Delete specified file. One argument, a file name string.
delete-horizontal-space	ESC \	Delete all spaces and tabs around point.
delete-indentation	ESC ^	Join this line to previous and fix up whitespace at join.
delete-matching-lines		Delete lines containing matches for REGEXP.
delete-non-matching-lines		Delete all lines except those containing matches for REGEXP.
delete-other-windows	C-x 1	Make WINDOW (or the selected window) fill the screen.
delete-process		Delete PROCESS: kill it and forget about it immediately.
delete-rectangle		Delete (don't save) text in rectangle with point and mark as corners.
delete-region		Delete the text between point and mark.
delete-window	C-x 0	Remove WINDOW from the display. Default is selected window.
delete-windows-on		Delete all windows showing BUFFER.
delq		Delete by side effect any occurrences of ELT as a member of LIST.
describe-bindings	C-h b	Show a list of all defined keys, and their definitions.
describe-copying	C-h C-c	Display info on how you may redistribute copies of GNU Emacs.
describe-distribution	C-h C-d	Display info on how to obtain the latest version of GNU Emacs.
describe-function	C-h f, C-h d	Display the full documentation of FUNCTION (a symbol).
describe-key	C-h k	Display documentation of the function KEY invokes. KEY is a string.

continues

10

Table 10.2. Continued

Command Name	Key Binding	Meaning
describe-key-briefly	C-h c	Print the name of the function KEY invokes. KEY is a string.
describe-mode	C-h m	Display documentation of current major mode.
describe-no-warranty	C-h C-w	Display info on all the kinds of warranty Emacs does NOT have.
describe-syntax	C-h s	Describe the syntax specifications in the syntax table.
describe-variable	C-h v	Display the full documentation of VARIABLE (a symbol).
digit-argument	ESC 0–9	Part of the numeric argument for the next command.
ding		Beep, or flash the screen.
directory-file-name		Return the file name of the directory named DIR.
directory-files		Return a list of names of files in DIRECTORY.
dired	C-x d	"Edit" directory DIRNAME—delete, rename, print, etc., some files in it.
dired-noselect		Like M-x dired but returns the dired buffer as value, does not select it.
dired-other-window	C-x 4 d	"Edit" directory DIRNAME. Like C-x d but selects in another window.
disable-command		Require special confirmation to execute COMMAND from now on.
disassemble		Print disassembled code for OBJECT on (optional) STREAM.
discard-input		Discard the contents of the terminal input buffer.
display-buffer		Make BUFFER appear in some window but don't select it.
display-completion-list		Display in a buffer the list of completions, COMPLETIONS.
display-time		Display current time and load level in mode line of each buffer.

Command Name	Key Binding	Meaning
dissociated-press		Dissociate the text of the current buffer.
do-auto-save		Auto-save all buffers that need it.
doctor		Switch to *doctor* buffer and start giving psychotherapy.
documentation		Return the documentation string of FUNCTION.
documentation-property		Return the documentation string that is SYMBOL's PROP property.
dot		Return value of point, as an integer.
dot-marker		Return value of point, as a marker object.
dot-max		Return the maximum permissible value of point in the current buffer.
dot-min		Return the minimum permissible value of point in the current buffer.
down-list	ESC C-d	Move forward down one level of parentheses.
downcase		One arg, a character or string. Convert it to lower case and return that.
downcase-region	C-x C-l	Convert the region to lower case. In programs, wants two arguments.
downcase-word	ESC l	Convert following word (or ARG words) to lower case, moving over.
dump-emacs		Dump current state of Emacs into executable file FILENAME.
edit-abbrevs		Alter abbrev definitions by editing a list of them.
edit-abbrevs-mode		Major mode for editing the list of abbrev definitions.
edit-abbrevs-redefine		Redefine abbrevs according to current buffer contents.
edit-and-eval-command		Prompting with PROMPT, let user edit COMMAND and eval result.

continues

10

Table 10.2. Continued

Command Name	Key Binding	Meaning
edit-options		Edit a list of Emacs user option values.
edit-picture		Switch to Picture mode, in which a quarter-plane screen model is used.
edit-tab-stops		Edit the tab stops used by tab-to-tab-stop.
edit-tab-stops-note-changes		Put edited tab stops into effect.
edt-emulation-on		Begin emulating DEC's EDT editor.
electric-buffer-list		Vaguely like ITS lunar select buffer.
electric-c-brace		Insert character and correct line's indentation.
electric-c-semi		Insert character and correct line's indentation.
electric-c-terminator		Insert character and correct line's indentation.
electric-command-history		Major mode for examining and redoing commands from command-history.
elt		Return element of SEQUENCE at index N.
emacs-lisp-mode		Major mode for editing Lisp code to run in Emacs.
emacs-version		Return string describing the version of Emacs that is running.
emc-restore		Restore Emacs configuration from optional FILE or emc-file.
emc-restore-wconfigs		Restore Emacs window configuration ring from optional FILE or emc-wconfigs-file.
emc-save		Save Emacs configuration to optional FILE or emc-file.
emc-save-wconfigs		Save Emacs window configuration ring to optional FILE or emc-wconfigs-file.

Command Name	Key Binding	Meaning
emc-window-list		Return a list of Lisp window objects for all Emacs windows.
enable-arrow-keys		Enable the use of the VT100 arrow keys for cursor motion.
enable-command		Allow COMMAND to be executed without special confirmation from now on.
end-kbd-macro	C-x)	Finish defining a keyboard macro.
end-of-buffer	ESC >	Move point to the end of the buffer; leave mark at previous position.
end-of-defun	ESC C-e	Move forward to next end of defun.
end-of-line	C-e, ESC O Q	Move point to end of current line.
enlarge-window	C-x ^	Make current window ARG lines bigger.
enlarge-window-horizontally	C-x }	Make current window ARG columns wider.
eobp		Return t if point is at the end of the buffer.
eolp		Return t if point is at the end of a line.
eq		T if the two args are the same Lisp object.
eql		T if the two args are the same Lisp object.
equal		T if two Lisp objects have similar structure and contents.
erase-buffer		Delete the entire contents of the current buffer.
error		Signal an error, making error message by passing all args to "format."
eval		Evaluate FORM and return its value.
eval-current-buffer		Execute the current buffer as Lisp code.
eval-defun		Evaluate defun that point is in or before.

continues

10

10

Table 10.2. Continued

Command Name	Key Binding	Meaning
eval-expression	ESC ESC	Evaluate EXPRESSION and print value in minibuffer.
eval-last-sexp	C-x C-e	Evaluate sexp before point; print value in minibuffer.
eval-minibuffer		Return value of Lisp expression read using the minibuffer.
eval-print-last-sexp		Evaluate sexp before point; print value into current buffer.
eval-region		Execute the region as Lisp code.
exchange-dot-and-mark		Put the mark where point is now, and point where the mark is now.
exchange-point-and-mark	C-x C-x	Put the mark where point is now, and point where the mark is now.
execute-extended-command	ESC x	Read function name, then read its arguments and call it.
execute-kbd-macro		Execute MACRO as string of editor command characters.
exit-minibuffer		Terminate this minibuffer argument.
exit-recursive-edit	ESC C-c	Exit from the innermost recursive edit or minibuffer.
expand-abbrev	C-x '	Expand the abbrev before point, if it is an abbrev.
expand-file-name		Convert FILENAME to absolute, and canonicalize it.
expand-region-abbrevs		For abbrev occurrence in the region, offer to expand it.
extract-rectangle		Return contents of rectangle with corners at START and END.
fboundp		T if SYMBOL's function definition is not void.
featurep		Return t if FEATURE is present in this Emacs.
file-attributes		Return a list of attributes of file FILENAME.
file-directory-p		Return t if file FILENAME is the name of a directory as a file.

10

Command Name	Key Binding	Meaning
file-exists-p		Return t if file FILENAME exists. (This does not mean you can read it.)
file-locked-p		Return nil if the FILENAME is not locked.
file-modes		Return mode bits of FILE, as an integer.
file-name-absolute-p		Return t if file FILENAME specifies an absolute path name.
file-name-all-completions		Return a list of all completions of file name FILE in directory DIR.
file-name-as-directory		Return a string representing file FILENAME interpreted as a directory.
file-name-completion		Complete file name FILE in directory DIR.
file-name-directory		Return the directory component in file name NAME.
file-name-nondirectory		Return file name NAME sans its directory.
file-name-sans-versions		Return FILENAME sans backup versions or strings.
file-newer-than-file-p		Return t if file FILE1 is newer than file FILE2.
file-nlinks		Return number of names file FILENAME has.
file-readable-p		Return t if file FILENAME exists and you can read it.
file-symlink-p		If file FILENAME is the name of a symbolic link, return the name of the file to which it is linked; otherwise, return nil.
file-writable-p		Return t if file FILENAME can be written or created by you.
fill-individual-paragraphs		Fill each paragraph in region according to its individual fill prefix.
fill-paragraph	ESC q	Fill paragraph at or after point.

continues

10

Table 10.2. Continued

Command Name	Key Binding	Meaning
fill-region	ESC g	Fill each of the paragraphs in the region.
fill-region-as-paragraph		Fill region as one paragraph: break lines to fit fill-column.
fillarray		Store each element of ARRAY with ITEM. ARRAY is a vector or string.
find-alternate-file	C-x C-v	Find file FILENAME, select its buffer, kill previous buffer.
find-backup-file-name		Find a file name for a backup file, and suggestions for deletions.
find-file	C-x C-f	Edit file FILENAME.
find-file-noselect		Read file FILENAME into a buffer and return the buffer.
find-file-other-window	C-x 4 C-f, C-x 4 f	Edit file FILENAME, in another window.
find-file-read-only	C-x C-r	Edit file FILENAME but don't save without confirmation.
find-tag	ESC .	Find tag (in current tag table) whose name contains TAGNAME.
find-tag-other-window	C-x 4 .	Find tag (in current tag table) whose name contains TAGNAME.
fixup-whitespace		Fixup white space between objects around point.
flush-lines		Delete lines containing matches for REGEXP.
fmakunbound		Make SYMBOL's function definition be void.
following-char		Return the character following point, as a number.
format		Format a string out of a control-string and arguments.
fortran-mode		Major mode for editing FORTRAN code.
forward-char	C-f, ESC O C	Move point right ARG characters (left if ARG negative).

10

Command Name	Key Binding	Meaning
forward-line		If point is on line i, move to the start of line i + ARG.
forward-list	ESC C-n	Move forward across one balanced group of parentheses.
forward-page	C-x]	Move forward to page boundary. With arg, repeat, or go back if negative.
forward-paragraph	ESC], ESC O y	Move forward to end of paragraph. With arg, do it arg times.
forward-sentence	ESC e	Move forward to next sentence-end. With argument, repeat.
forward-sexp	ESC C-f	Move forward across one balanced expression.
forward-to-indentation		Move forward ARG lines and position at first nonblank character.
forward-word	ESC f, ESC O s	Move point forward ARG words (backward if ARG is negative).
fset		Set SYMBOL's function definition to NEWVAL, and return NEWVAL.
ftp-find-file		FTP to HOST to get FILE, logging in as USER with password PASSWORD.
ftp-write-file		FTP to HOST to write FILE, logging in as USER with password PASSWORD.
funcall		Call first argument as a function, passing remaining arguments to it.
function		Quote a function object.
function-key-sequence		Return key sequence for function key that is on this terminal.
fundamental-mode		Major mode not specialized for anything in particular.
garbage-collect		Reclaim storage for Lisp objects no longer needed.
gdb		Run gdb on program FILE in buffer *gdb-FILE*.
generate-new-buffer		Create and return a buffer named NAME if one does not already exist.

continues

10

Table 10.2. Continued

Command Name	Key Binding	Meaning
get		Return the value of SYMBOL's PROPNAME property.
get-buffer		Return the buffer named NAME (a string).
get-buffer-create		Like get-buffer but creates a buffer named NAME and returns it if none already exists.
get-buffer-process		Return the (or, a) process associated with BUFFER.
get-buffer-window		Return a window currently displaying BUFFER, or nil if none.
get-file-buffer		Return the buffer visiting file FILENAME (a string).
get-file-char		Don't use this yourself.
get-largest-window		Return the largest window in area.
get-lru-window		Return the window least recently selected or used for display.
get-process		Return the process named NAME, or nil if there is none.
get-register		Return contents of Emacs register named CHAR, or nil if none.
getenv		One arg VAR, a string. Return the value of environment variable VAR, as a string.
global-key-binding		Return the definition for command KEYS in current global keymap only.
global-set-key		Give KEY a definition of COMMAND.
global-unset-key		Remove global definition of KEY.
goto-char		One arg, a number. Set point to that number.
goto-line		Goto line ARG, counting from line 1 at beginning of buffer.
grep		Run grep, with user-specified args, and collect output in a buffer.
hack-local-variables		Parse, and bind or evaluate as appropriate, any local variables.

Command Name	Key Binding	Meaning
hanoi		Towers of Hanoi diversion. Argument is number of rings.
help-command	C-h	Prefix command (definition is a list whose cdr is an alist of subcommands).
help-for-help	C-h ?, C-h C-h	You have typed C-h, the help character. Type a Help option.
help-with-tutorial	C-h t	Select the Emacs learn-by-doing tutorial.
how-many		Print number of matches for REGEXP following point.
identity		Return the argument unchanged.
if		(if C T E...) if C yields non-NIL do T, else do E...
indent-according-to-mode		Indent line in proper way for current major mode.
indent-c-exp		Indent each line of the C grouping following point.
indent-code-rigidly		Indent all lines of code, starting in the region, sideways by ARG columns.
indent-for-comment	ESC ;	Indent this line's comment to comment column, or insert an empty comment.
indent-for-tab-command		Indent line in proper way for current major mode.
indent-new-comment-line	ESC LFD, ESC j	Break line at point and indent, continuing comment if presently within one.
indent-region	ESC C-\	Indent each nonblank line in the region.
indent-relative		Space out to under next indent point in previous nonblank line.
indent-relative-maybe		Indent a new line like previous nonblank line.
indent-rigidly	C-x TAB	Indent all lines starting in the region sideways by ARG columns.

10

continues

10

Table 10.2. Continued

Command Name	Key Binding	Meaning
indent-sexp		Indent each line of the list starting just after point.
indent-to		Indent from point with tabs and spaces until COLUMN is reached.
indent-to-column		Indent from point with tabs and spaces until COLUMN is reached.
indented-text-mode		Major mode for editing indented text intended for humans to read.
info	C-h i	Enter Info, the documentation browser.
input-pending-p		T if command input is currently available with no waiting.
insert		Any number of args, strings, or chars. Insert them after point, moving point forward.
insert-abbrev-table-description		Insert before point a description of abbrev table named NAME.
insert-abbrevs		Insert after point a description of all defined abbrevs.
insert-before-markers		Any number of args, strings or chars. Insert them after point.
insert-buffer		Insert after point the contents of BUFFER.
insert-buffer-substring		Insert before point a substring of the contents buffer BUFFER.
insert-char		Insert COUNT (second arg) copies of CHAR (first arg).
insert-file	C-x i	Insert contents of file FILENAME into buffer after point.
insert-file-contents		Insert contents of file FILENAME after point.
insert-kbd-macro		Insert in buffer the definition of kbd macro NAME, as Lisp code.
insert-parentheses	ESC (	Put parentheses around next ARG sexps. Leave point after open-paren.

Command Name	Key Binding	Meaning
insert-rectangle		Insert text of RECTANGLE with upper left corner at point.
insert-register	C-x g	Insert contents of register REG. REG is a character.
insert-string		Mocklisp-compatibility insert function.
int-to-string		Convert INT to a string by printing it in decimal, with minus sign if negative.
integer-or-marker-p		T if OBJECT is an integer or a marker (editor pointer).
integerp		T if OBJECT is a number.
interactive		Specify a way of parsing arguments for interactive use of a function.
interactive-p		Return t if function in which this appears was called interactively.
intern		Return the symbol whose name is STRING.
intern-soft		Return the symbol whose name is STRING, or nil if none exists yet.
interrupt-process		Interrupt process PROCESS. May be process or name of one.
inverse-add-global-abbrev	C-x –	Define last word before point as a global (mode-independent) abbrev.
inverse-add-mode-abbrev	C-x C-h	Define last word before point as a mode-specific abbrev.
isearch-backward	C-r	Do incremental search backward.
isearch-backward-regexp		Do incremental search backward for regular expression.
isearch-forward	C-s, ESC O R	Do incremental search forward.
isearch-forward-regexp	ESC C-s	Do incremental search forward for regular expression.
ispell-buffer		Check spelling of every word in the buffer.
ispell-complete-word		Complete word at or before point.

continues

10

Table 10.2. Continued

Command Name	Key Binding	Meaning
ispell-region		Check spelling of every word in the region.
ispell-word		Check spelling of word at or before point.
just-one-space	ESC SPC	Delete all spaces and tabs around point, leaving one space.
justify-current-line		Add spaces to line point is in, so it ends at fill-column.
kbd-macro-query	C-x q	Query user during kbd macro execution.
keep-lines		Delete all lines except those containing matches for REGEXP.
key-binding		Return the definition for command KEYS in current keymaps.
key-description		Return a pretty description of key-sequence KEYS.
keyboard-quit	C-g	Signal a quit condition.
keymapp		Return t if ARG is a keymap.
kill-all-abbrevs		Undefine all defined abbrevs.
kill-all-local-variables		Eliminate all the buffer-local variable values of the current buffer.
kill-buffer	C-x k	One arg, a string or a buffer. Get rid of the specified buffer.
kill-comment		Kill the comment on this line, if any.
kill-emacs		Exit the Emacs job and kill it. ARG means no query.
kill-line	C-k, ESC O S	Kill the rest of the current line; if no nonblanks there, kill through newline.
kill-local-variable		Make VARIABLE no longer have a separate value in the current buffer.
kill-paragraph		Kill to end of paragraph.
kill-process		Kill process PROCESS. May be process or name of one.

Command Name	Key Binding	Meaning
kill-rectangle		Delete rectangle with corners at point and mark; save as last killed one.
kill-region	C-w	Kill between point and mark.
kill-ring-save		Save the region as if killed, but don't kill it.
kill-sentence	ESC k	Kill from point to end of sentence.
kill-sexp	ESC C-k	Kill the syntactic expression following the cursor.
kill-some-buffers		For each buffer, ask whether to kill it.
kill-word	ESC d	Kill characters forward until encountering the end of a word.
latex-mode		Major mode for editing files of input for LaTeX.
ledit-mode		Major mode for editing text and stuffing it to a Lisp job.
length		Return the length of vector, list, or string SEQUENCE.
let		(let VARLIST BODY...) binds variables according to VARLIST then executes BODY.
let*		(let* VARLIST BODY...) binds variables according to VARLIST then executes BODY.
lisp-complete-symbol	ESC TAB	Perform completion on Lisp symbol preceding point.
lisp-indent-line		Indent current line as Lisp code.
lisp-interaction-mode		Major mode for typing and evaluating Lisp forms.
lisp-mode		Major mode for editing Lisp code for Lisps other than GNU Emacs Lisp.
lisp-send-defun		Send the current defun to the Lisp process made by M-x run-lisp.
list		Return a newly created list whose elements are the arguments (any number).

continues

10

10

Table 10.2. Continued

Command Name	Key Binding	Meaning
list-abbrevs		Display a list of all defined abbrevs.
list-buffers	C-x C-b	Display a list of names of existing buffers.
list-command-history		List history of commands typed to minibuffer.
list-directory	C-x C-d	Display a list of files in or matching DIRNAME, a la "ls."
list-matching-lines		Show all lines following point containing a match for REGEXP.
list-options		Display a list of Emacs user options, with values and documentation.
list-processes		Display a list of all processes.
list-tags		Display list of tags in file FILE.
listp		T if OBJECT is a list. This includes nil.
load		Execute a file of Lisp code named FILE.
load-average		Return the current 1-minute, 5-minute, and 15-minute load averages.
load-file		Load the file FILE of Lisp code.
load-library		Load the library named LIBRARY.
local-key-binding		Return the definition for command KEYS in current local keymap only.
local-set-key		Give KEY a local definition of COMMAND.
local-unset-key		Remove local definition of KEY
lock-buffer		Lock FILE, if current buffer is modified.
logand		Return bitwise and of all the arguments (numbers).
logior		Return bitwise or of all the arguments (numbers).
lognot		Return the bitwise complement of ARG.
logxor		Return bitwise exclusive-or of all the arguments (numbers).

Command Name	Key Binding	Meaning
looking-at		T if text after point matches regular expression PAT.
lookup-key		In keymap KEYMAP, look up key sequence KEY. Return the definition.
lpr-buffer		Print buffer contents as with UNIX command "lpr."
lpr-region		Print region contents as with UNIX command "lpr."
lsh		Return VALUE with its bits shifted left by COUNT.
macroexpand		If FORM is a macro call, expand it.
mail	C-x m	Edit a message to be sent. Argument means resume editing (don't erase).
mail-other-window	C-x 4 m	Like "mail" command, but display mail buffer in another window.
make-abbrev-table		Create a new, empty abbrev table object.
make-auto-save-file-name		Return file name to use for auto-saves of current buffer.
make-backup-file-name		Create the non-numeric backup file name for FILE.
make-command-summary		Make a summary of current key bindings in the buffer *Summary*.
make-keymap		Construct and return a new keymap, a vector of length 128
make-list		Return a newly created list of length LENGTH, with each element being INIT.
make-local-variable		Make VARIABLE have a separate value in the current buffer.
make-marker		Return a newly allocated marker which does not point at any place.
make-sparse-keymap		Construct and return a new sparse-keymap list.
make-string		Return a newly created string of length LENGTH, with each element being INIT.

continues

10

Table 10.2. Continued

Command Name	Key Binding	Meaning
make-symbol		Return a newly allocated uninterned symbol whose name is NAME.
make-symbolic-link		Make a symbolic link to FILENAME, named LINKNAME. Both args strings.
make-syntax-table		Construct a new syntax table and return it.
make-temp-name		Generate temporary name (string) starting with PREFIX (a string).
make-variable-buffer-local		Make VARIABLE have a separate value for each buffer.
make-vector		Return a newly created vector of length LENGTH, with each element being INIT.
makunbound		Make SYMBOL's value be void.
manual-entry		Display the UNIX manual entry for TOPIC.
mapatoms		Call FUNCTION on every symbol in OBARRAY.
mapcar		Apply FUNCTION to each element of LIST, and make a list of the results.
mapconcat		Apply FN to each element of SEQ, and concat the results as strings.
mark		Return this buffer's mark value as integer, or nil if no mark.
mark-c-function		Put mark at end of C function, point at beginning.
mark-defun	ESC C-h	Put mark at end of defun, point at beginning.
mark-end-of-sentence		Put mark at end of sentence. Arg works as in forward-sentence.
mark-marker		Return this buffer's mark, as a marker object.
mark-page	C-x C-p	Put mark at end of page, point at beginning.
mark-paragraph	ESC h	Put point at beginning of this paragraph, mark at end.

10

Command Name	Key Binding	Meaning
mark-sexp	ESC C-@	Set mark ARG sexps from point.
mark-whole-buffer	C-x h	Put point at beginning and mark at end of buffer.
mark-word	ESC @	Set mark ARG words away from point.
marker-buffer		Return the buffer that MARKER points into, or nil if none.
marker-position		Return the position MARKER points at, as a character number.
markerp		T if OBJECT is a marker (editor pointer).
match-beginning		Return the character number of start of text matched by last regexp searched for.
match-data		Return list containing all info on what the last search matched.
match-end		Return the character number of end of text matched by last regexp searched for.
max		Return largest of all the arguments (which must be numbers.)
memq		Return non-nil if ELT is an element of LIST. Comparison done with EQ.
message		Print a one-line message at the bottom of the screen.
mh-rmail		Inc(orporate) new mail (no arg) or scan a MH mail box (arg given).
mh-smail		Send mail using the MH mail system.
min		Return smallest of all the arguments (which must be numbers.)
minibuffer-complete		Complete the minibuffer contents, as far as possible.
minibuffer-complete-and-exit		Complete the minibuffer contents and maybe exit.
minibuffer-complete-word		Complete the minibuffer contents, at most a single word.

continues

Table 10.2. Continued

Command Name	Key Binding	Meaning
minibuffer-completion-help		Display a list of possible completions of the current minibuffer contents.
minibuffer-depth		Return current depth of activations of minibuffer, a non-negative integer.
minibuffer-window		Return the window used for minibuffers.
ml-arg		Argument #N to this mocklisp function.
ml-if		Is the if function for mocklisp programs
ml-interactive		True if this mocklisp function was called interactively.
ml-nargs		# arguments to this mocklisp function.
ml-provide-prefix-argument		Evaluate second argument, using first argument as prefix arg value.
mod		Return remainder of first arg divided by second.
mode-specific-command-prefix	C-c	Prefix command (definition is a list whose cdr is an alist of sub-commands.)
modify-syntax-entry		Set syntax for character CHAR according to string S.
modula-2-mode		This is a mode intended to support program development in Modula-2.
momentary-string-display		Momentarily display STRING in the buffer at POS.
move-marker		Position MARKER before character number NUMBER in BUFFER.
move-past-close-and-reindent	ESC)	Move past next), delete indentation before it, then indent after it.
move-to-column		Move point to column COLUMN in the current line.
move-to-window-line	ESC r	Position point relative to window.

Command Name	Key Binding	Meaning
name-last-kbd-macro		Assign a name to the last keyboard macro defined.
narrow-to-page	C-x p	Make text outside current page invisible.
narrow-to-region	C-x n	Restrict editing in this buffer to the current region.
natnump		T if OBJECT is a non-negative number.
nconc		Concatenate any number of lists by altering them.
negative-argument	ESC–	Begin a negative numeric argument for the next command.
newline RET		Insert a newline. With arg, insert that many newlines.
newline-and-indent	LFD	Insert a newline, then indent according to major mode.
news-post-news		Begin editing a new USENET news article to be posted.
next-complex-command		Inserts the next element of "command-history" into the minibuffer.
next-error	C-x '	Visit next compilation error message and corresponding source code.
next-file		Select next file among files in current tag table.
next-line	C-n, ESC O B	Move cursor vertically down ARG lines.
next-window		Return next window after WINDOW in canonical ordering of windows.
nlistp		T if OBJECT is not a list. Lists include nil.
normal-mode		Choose the major mode for this buffer automatically.
not		T if OBJECT is nil.
not-modified	ESC ~	Mark current buffer as unmodified, not needing to be saved.

continues

10

Table 10.2. Continued

Command Name	Key Binding	Meaning
nreverse		Reverse LIST by modifying cdr pointers. Return the beginning of the reversed list.
nroff-mode		Major mode for editing text intended for nroff to format.
nth		Return the Nth element of LIST.
nthcdr		Take cdr N times on LIST, return the result.
null		T if OBJECT is nil.
numberp		T if OBJECT is a number.
occur		Show all lines following point containing a match for REGEXP.
occur-mode		Major mode for output from M-x occur.
occur-mode-goto-occurrence		Go to the line this occurrence was found in, in the buffer it was found in.
one-window-p		Return non-nil if there is only one window.
open-dribble-file		Start writing all keyboard characters to FILE.
open-line	C-o, ESC O M	Insert a newline and leave point before it.
open-network-stream		Open a TCP connection for a service to a host.
open-rectangle		Blank out rectangle with corners at point and mark, shifting text right.
open-termscript		Start writing all terminal output to FILE as well as the terminal.
or		Eval args until one of them yields non-NIL, then return that value.
other-buffer		Return most recently selected buffer other than BUFFER.
other-window	C-x o	Select the ARGth different window.
outline-mode		Set major mode for editing outlines with selective display.

Command Name	Key Binding	Meaning
overwrite-mode		Toggle overwrite mode.
parse-partial-sexp		Parse Lisp syntax starting at FROM until TO; return status of parse at TO.
picture-mode		Switch to Picture mode, in which a quarter-plane screen model is used.
plain-TeX-mode		Major mode for editing files of input for plain TeX.
plain-tex-mode		Major mode for editing files of input for plain TeX.
point		Return value of point, as an integer.
point-marker		Return value of point, as a marker object.
point-max		Return the maximum permissible value of point in the current buffer.
point-max-marker		Return a marker to the end of the currently visible part of the buffer.
point-min		Return the minimum permissible value of point in the current buffer.
point-min-marker		Return a marker to the beginning of the currently visible part of the buffer.
point-to-register	C-x /	Store current location of point in a register.
pop-mark		Pop off mark ring into the buffer's actual mark
pop-to-buffer		Select buffer BUFFER in some window, preferably a different one.
pos-visible-in-window-p		Return t if position POS is currently on the screen in WINDOW.
postnews		Begin editing a new USENET news article to be posted.
preceding-char		Return the character preceding point, as a number.
prefix-numeric-value		Return numeric meaning of raw prefix argument ARG.
prepend-to-buffer		Prepend to specified buffer the text of the region.

continues

10

10

Table 10.2. Continued

Command Name	Key Binding	Meaning
prepend-to-register		Prepend region to text in register REG.
previous-complex-command		Inserts the previous element of "command-history" into the minibuffer.
previous-line	C-p, ESC O A	Move cursor vertically up ARG lines.
previous-window		Return previous window before WINDOW in canonical ordering of windows.
primitive-undo		Undo N records from the front of the list LIST.
prin1		Output the printed representation of OBJECT, any Lisp object.
prin1-to-string		Return a string containing the printed representation of OBJECT.
princ		Output the printed representation of OBJECT, any Lisp object.
print		Output the printed representation of OBJECT, with newlines around it.
print-buffer		Print buffer contents as with UNIX command "lpr -p."
print-help-return-message		Display or return message saying how to restore windows after help command.
print-region		Print region contents as with UNIX command "lpr -p."
process-buffer		Return the buffer PROCESS is associated with.
process-command		Return the command that was executed to start PROCESS.
process-exit-status		Return the exit status of PROCESS or the signal number that killed it.
process-filter		Return the filter function of PROCESS; nil if none.
process-id		Return the process id of PROCESS.

10

Command Name	Key Binding	Meaning
process-kill-without-query		Say no query needed if PROCESS is running when Emacs is exited.
process-list		Return a list of all processes.
process-mark		Return the marker for the end of the last output from PROCESS.
process-name		Return the name of PROCESS, as a string.
process-send-eof		Make PROCESS see end-of-file in its input.
process-send-region		Send current contents of region as input to PROCESS.
process-send-string		Send PROCESS the contents of STRING as input.
process-sentinel		Return the sentinel of PROCESS; nil if none.
process-status		Return the status of PROCESS—a symbol, one of these: run, for a process that is running; stop, for a process stopped but continuable; exit, for a process that has exited; signal, for a process that has a fatal signal; open, for a network stream connection that is open; closed, for a network stream connection that is closed; nil, if arg is a process name and no such process exists.
processp		Return t if OBJECT is a process.
prog1		Eval arguments in sequence, then return the FIRST arg's value.
prog2		Eval arguments in sequence, then return the SECOND arg's value.
progn		Eval arguments in sequence, and return the value of the last one.
prolog-mode		Major mode for editing Prolog code for Prologs.
provide		Announce that FEATURE is a feature of the current Emacs.

continues

10

Table 10.2. Continued

Command Name	Key Binding	Meaning
psychoanalyze-pinhead		Zippy goes to the analyst.
purecopy		Make a copy of OBJECT in pure storage.
push-mark		Set mark at LOCATION (point, by default) and push old mark on mark ring.
put		Store SYMBOL's PROPNAME property with value VALUE.
pwd		Show the current default directory.
query-replace	ESC %	Replace some occurrences of FROM-STRING with TO STRING.
query-replace-regexp		Replace some things after point matching REGEXP with TO-STRING.
quietly-read-abbrev-file		Read abbrev definitions from file written with write-abbrev-file.
quit-process		Send QUIT signal to process PROCESS. May be process or name of one.
quote		Return the argument, without evaluating it. (quote x) yields x.
quoted-insert	C-q	Read next input character and insert it.
random		Return a pseudo-random number.
rassq		Return non-nil if ELT is the cdr of an element of LIST. Comparison done with EQ.
re-search-backward		Search backward from point for match for regular expression REGEXP.
re-search-forward		Search forward from point for regular expression REGEXP.
read		Read one Lisp expression as text from STREAM, return as Lisp object.
read-abbrev-file		Read abbrev definitions from file written with write-abbrev-file.

Command Name	Key Binding	Meaning
read-buffer		One arg PROMPT, a string. Read the name of a buffer and return as a string.
read-char		Read a character from the command input (keyboard or macro).
read-command		One arg PROMPT, a string. Read the name of a command and return as a symbol.
read-file-name		Read file name, prompting with PROMPT and completing in directory DIR.
read-file-name-internal		Internal subroutine for read-file-name. Do not call this.
read-from-minibuffer		Read a string from the minibuffer, prompting with string PROMPT.
read-from-string		Read one Lisp expression which is represented as text by STRING.
read-input		Read a string from the minibuffer, prompting with string PROMPT.
read-key-sequence		Read a sequence of keystrokes and return as a string.
read-minibuffer		Return a Lisp object read using the minibuffer.
read-no-blanks-input		Args PROMPT and INIT, strings. Read a string from the terminal, not allowing blanks.
read-quoted-char		Like "read-char," except that if the first character read is an octal digit, two more octal digits are read and the character represented by those three digits is returned.
read-string		Read a string from the minibuffer, prompting with string PROMPT.
read-variable		One arg PROMPT, a string. Read the name of a user variable and return.
recent-auto-save-p		Return t if buffer has been auto-saved since last read in or saved.

continues

10

Table 10.2. Continued

Command Name	Key Binding	Meaning
recent-keys		Return string of last 100 chars read from terminal.
recenter	C-l	Center point in window and redisplay screen. With ARG, put point on line ARG.
recover-file		Visit file FILE, but get contents from its last auto-save file.
recursion-depth		Return the current depth in recursive edits.
recursive-edit		Invoke the editor command loop recursively.
redraw-display		Clear the screen and output again what is supposed to appear on it.
regexp-quote		Return a regexp string which matches exactly STRING and nothing else.
region-beginning		Return position of beginning of region, as an integer.
region-end		Return position of end of region, as an integer.
register-to-point	C-x j	Move point to location stored in a register.
reindent-then-newline-and-indent		Reindent current line, insert newline, then indent the new line.
rename-auto-save-file		Adjust current buffer's auto save file name for current conditions.
rename-buffer		Change current buffer's name to NEWNAME (a string).
rename-file		Rename FILE as NEWNAME. Both args strings.
repeat-complex-command	C-x ESC	Edit and re-evaluate last complex command, or ARGth from last.
repeat-matching-complex-command		Edit and re-evaluate complex command with name matching PATTERN.
replace-buffer-in-windows		Replace BUFFER with some other buffer in all windows showing it.

Command Name	Key Binding	Meaning
replace-match		Replace text matched by last search with NEWTEXT.
replace-regexp		Replace things after point matching REGEXP with TO-STRING.
replace-string		Replace occurrences of FROM-STRING with TO-STRING.
require		If FEATURE is not present in Emacs—that is, (featurep FEATURE) is false—load FILENAME. FILENAME is optional and defaults to FEATURE.
reverse		Reverse LIST, copying. Return th beginning of the reversed list.
revert-buffer		Replace the buffer text with the text of the visited file on disk.
rmail		Read and edit incoming mail.
rmail-input		Run RMAIL on file FILENAME.
rnews		Read USENET news for groups for which you are a member and add or delete groups.
rotate-yank-pointer		Rotate the yanking point in the kill ring.
rplaca		Set the car of CONSCELL to be NEWCAR. Return NEWCAR.
rplacd		Set the cdr of CONSCELL to be NEWCDR. Return NEWCDR.
run-hooks		Take hook names and run each one in turn. Major mode functions use this.
run-lisp		Run an inferior Lisp process, input and output via buffer *lisp*.
run-prolog		Run an inferior Prolog process, input and output via buffer *prolog*.
run-scheme		Run an inferior Scheme process.
save-buffer	C-x C-s	Save current buffer in visited file if modified. Versions described below.
save-excursion		Save point (and mark), execute BODY, then restore point and mark.

continues

10

Table 10.2. Continued

Command Name	Key Binding	Meaning
save-restriction		Execute the body, undoing at the end any changes to current buffer's restrictions.
save-some-buffers	C-x s	Save some modified file-visiting buffers. Asks user about each one.
save-window-excursion		Execute body, preserving window sizes and contents.
scan-lists		Scan from character number FROM by COUNT lists.
scan-sexps		Scan from character number FROM by COUNT balanced expressions.
scheme-mode		Major mode for editing Scheme code.
screen-height		Return number of lines on screen available for display.
screen-width		Return number of columns on screen available for display.
scribe-mode		Major mode for editing files of Scribe (a text formatter) source.
scroll-down	ESC v	Scroll text of current window downward ARG lines; or near full screen if no ARG.
scroll-left	C-x <	Scroll selected window display ARG columns left.
scroll-other-window	ESC C-v	Scroll text of next window upward ARG lines; or near full screen if no ARG.
scroll-right	C-x >	Scroll selected window display ARG columns right.
scroll-up	C-v	Scroll text of current window upward ARG lines; or near full screen if no ARG.
search-backward		Search backward from point for STRING.
search-forward		Search forward from point for STRING.
select-window		Select WINDOW. Most editing will apply to WINDOW's buffer.

Command Name	Key Binding	Meaning
selected-window		Return the window that the cursor now appears in and commands apply to.
self-insert-and-exit		Terminate minibuffer input.
self-insert-command		Insert this character. Prefix arg is repeat-count.
send-region		Send current contes of region as input to PROCESS.
send-string		Send PROCESS the contents of STRING as input.
send-string-to-terminal		Send STRING to the terminal without alteration.
sendnews		Begin editing a new USENET news article to be posted.
sequencep		T if OBJECT is a sequence (list or array).
server-start		Allow this Emacs process to be a server for client processes.
set		Set SYMBOL's value to NEWVAL, and return NEWVAL.
set-auto-mode		Select major mode appropriate for current buffer.
set-buffer		Set the current buffer to the buffer or buffer name supplied as argument.
set-buffer-auto-saved		Mark current buffer as auto-saved with its current text.
set-buffer-modified-p		Mark current buffer as modified or unmodified according to FLAG.
set-comment-column	C-x ;	Set the comment column based on point.
set-default		Set SYMBOL's default value to VAL. SYMBOL and VAL are evaluated.
set-file-modes		Set mode bits of FILE to MODE (an integer).
set-fill-column	C-x f	Set fill-column to current column, or to argument if given.

continues

10

Table 10.2. Continued

Command Name	Key Binding	Meaning
set-fill-prefix	C-x .	Set the fill-prefix to the current line up to point.
set-goal-column	C-x C-n	Set the current horizontal position as a goal for C-n and C-p.
set-gosmacs-bindings		Rebind some keys globally to make GNU Emacs resemble Gosling Emacs.
set-input-mode		Set mode of reading keyboard input.
set-mark		Set this buffer's mark to POS. Don't use this function!
set-mark-command	C-@	Set mark where point is, or jump to mark.
set-marker		Position MARKER before character number NUMBER in BUFFER.
set-process-buffer		Set buffer associated with PROCESS to BUFFER (a buffer, or nil).
set-process-filter		Give PROCESS the filter function FILTER; nil means no filter.
set-process-sentinel		Give PROCESS the sentinel SENTINEL; nil for none.
set-register		Set contents of Emacs register named CHAR to VALUE.
set-screen-height		Tell redisplay that the screen has LINES lines.
set-screen-width		Tell redisplay that the screen has COLS columns.
set-selective-display	C-x $	Set selective-display to ARG; clear it if no arg.
set-syntax-table		Select a new syntax table for the current buffer.
set-variable		Set VARIABLE to VALUE. VALUE is a Lisp object.
set-visited-file-name		Change name of file visited in current buffer to FILENAME.
set-window-buffer		Make WINDOW display BUFFER as its contents.

10

Command Name	Key Binding	Meaning
set-window-configuration		Restore the configuration of Emacs' windows and buffers to the state scified by CONFIGURATION.
set-window-dot		Make point value in WINDOW be at position POS in WINDOW's buffer.
set-window-hscroll		Set number of columns WINDOW is scrolled from left margin to NCOL.
set-window-point		Make point value in WINDOW be at position POS in WINDOW's buffer.
set-window-start		Make display in WINDOW start at position POS in WINDOW's buffer.
setcar		Set the car of CONSCELL to be NEWCAR. Return NEWCAR.
setcdr		Set the cdr of CONSCELL to be NEWCDR. Return NEWCDR.
setplist		Set SYMBOL's property list to NEWVAL, and return NEWVAL.
setq		(setq SYM VAL SYM VAL ...) sets each SYM to the value of its VAL.
setq-default		Set SYMBOL's default value to VAL. VAL is evaluated; SYMBOL is not.
setup-terminal-keymap		Set up keymap MAP to forward to function-keymap according to TRANSLATIONS.
shell		Run an inferior shell, with I/O through buffer *shell*.
shell-command	ESC !	Execute string COMMAND in inferior shell; display output, if any.
shell-command-on-region	ESC |	Execute string COMMAND in inferior shell with region as input.
show-buffer		Make WINDOW display BUFFER as its contents.
shrink-window		Make current window ARG lines smaller.
shrink-window-horizontally	C-x {	Make current window ARG columns narrower.

continues

10

Table 10.2. Continued

Command Name	Key Binding	Meaning
signal		Signal an error. Args are SIGNAL-NAME, an associated DATA.
single-key-description		Return a pretty description of command character KEY.
sit-for		Perform redisplay, then wait for ARG seconds or until input is available.
skip-chars-backward		Move point backward, stopping after a char not in CHARS, or at position LIM.
skip-chars-forward		Move point forward, stopping before a char not in CHARS, or at position LIM.
sleep-for		Pause, without updating display, for ARG seconds
sort		Sort LIST, comparing elements using PREDICATE.
sort-columns		Sort lines in region alphabetically by a certain range of columns.
sort-fields		Sort lines in region lexicographically by the ARGth field of each line.
sort-lines		Sort lines in region alphabetically; argument means descending order.
sort-numeric-fields		Sort lines in region numerically by the ARGth field of each line.
sort-pages		Sort pages in region alphabetically; argument means descending order.
sort-paragraphs		Sort paragraphs in region alphabetically; argument means descending order.
sort-regexp-fields		Sort the region lexicographically as specifed by RECORD-REGEXP and KEY.
spell-buffer		Check spelling of every word in the buffer.
spell-region		Like spell-buffer but applies only to region.

Command Name	Key Binding	Meaning
spell-string		Check spelling of string supplied as argument.
spell-word	ESC $	Check spelling of word at or before point.
split-line	ESC C-o	Split current line, moving portion beyond point vertically down.
split-window		Split WINDOW, putting SIZE lines in the first of the pair.
split-window-horizontally	C-x 5	Split current window into two windows side by side.
split-window-vertically	C-x 2	Split current window into two windows, one above the other.
standard-syntax-table		Return the standard syntax table.
start-kbd-macro	C-x (	Record subsequent keyboard input, defining a keyboard macro.
start-process		Start a program in a subprocess. Return the process object for it.
stop-process		Stop process PROCESS. May be process or name of one.
store-match-data		Set internal data on last search match from elements of LIST.
string-equal		T if two strings have identical contents.
string-lessp		T if first arg string is less than second in lexicographic order.
string-match		Return index of start of first match for REGEXP in STRING, or nil.
string-to-char		Convert arg STRING to a character, the first character of that string.
string-to-int		Convert STRING to an integer by parsing it as a decimal number.
string<		T if first arg string is less than second in lexicographic order.
string=		T if two strings have identical contents.

continues

10

Table 10.2. Continued

Command Name	Key Binding	Meaning
stringp		T if OBJECT is a string.
subrp		T if OBJECT is a built-in function.
subst-char-in-region		From START to END, replace FROMCHAR with TOCHAR each time it occurs.
substitute-command-keys		Return the STRING with substrings of the form M-x COMMAND.
substitute-in-file-name		Substitute environment variables referred to in STRING.
substitute-key-definition		Replace OLDDEF with NEWDEF for any keys in KEYMAP now defined as OLDDEF.
substring		Return a substring of STRING, starting at index FROM and ending before TO.
suppress-keymap		Make MAP override all buffer-modifying commands to be undefined.
suspend-emacs	C-z, C-x C-z	Stop Emacs and return to superior process. You can resume.
swap-bs-del		Accept single optional argument. If no argument, or nil, swap values.
switch-to-buffer	C-x b	Select buffer BUFFER in the current window.
switch-to-buffer-other-window	C-x 4 b	Select buffer BUFFER in another window.
symbol-function		Return SYMBOL's function definition.
symbol-name		Return SYMBOL's name, a string.
symboplist		Return SYMBOL's property list.
symbol-value		Return SYMBOL's value.
symbolp		T if OBJECT is a symbol.
syntax-table		Return the current syntax table.
syntax-table-p		Return t if ARG is a syntax table.
system-name		Return the name of the machine you are running on, as a string.
tab-to-tab-stop	TAB, ESC i	Insert spaces or tabs to next defined

Command Name	Key Binding	Meaning
TAB,		tab-stop column.
tabify		Convert multiple spaces in region to tabs when possible.
tag-table-files		Return a list of files in the current tag table.
tags-apropos		Display list of all tags in tag table REGEXP matches.
tags-loop-continue	ESC ,	Continue last M-x tags-search or M-x tags-query-replace command.
tags-query-replace		Query-replace-regexp FROM with TO through all files listed in tag table
tags-search		Search through all files listed in tag table for match for REGEXP.
telnet		Open a network login connection to host named HOST (a string).
terminal-emulator		Under a display-terminal emulator in BUFFER, run PROGRAM on arguments ARGS.
terpri		Output a newline to STREAM (or value of standard-output).
tex-mode		Major mode for editing files of input for TeX or LaTeX.
texinfo-format-buffer		Process the current buffer as texinfo code, into an Info file.
texinfo-format-region		Convert the the current region of the Texinfo file to Info format.
texinfo-mode		Major mode for editing texinfo files.
text-char-description		Return a pretty description of file-character CHAR.
text-mode		Major mode for editing text intended for humans to read.
this-command-keys		Return string of the keystrokes that invoked this command.
throw		(throw TAG VALUE) throws to the catch for TAG and returns VALUE from it.

continues

10

Table 10.2. Continued

Command Name	Key Binding	Meaning
toggle-read-only	C-x C-q	Change whether this buffer is visiting its file read-only.
top-level		Exit all recursive editing levels.
transpose-chars	C-t	Interchange characters around point, moving forward one character.
transpose-lines	C-x C-t	Exchange current line and previous line, leaving point after both.
transpose-paragraphs		Interchange this (or next) paragraph with previous one.
transpose-sentences		Interchange this (next) and previous sentence.
transpose-sexps	ESC C-t	Like ESC t but applies to sexps.
transpose-words	ESC t	Interchange words around point, leaving point at endf them.
try-completion		Return common substring of all completions of STRING in ALIST.
turn-on-auto-fill		Unconditionally turn on auto fill mode.
underline-region		Underline all nonblank characters in the region.
undo	C-_	Undo some previous changes.
undo-boundary		Mark a boundary between units of undo.
undo-more		Undo back N undo-boundaries beyond what was already undone recently.
undo-start		Move undo-pointer to front of undo records.
unexpand-abbrev		Undo the expansion of the last abbrev that expanded.
universal-argument	C-u	Begin a numeric argument for the following command.
unlock-buffer		Unlocks the file visited in the current buffer.
untabify		Convert all tabs in region to multiple spaces, preserving columns.

10

Command Name	Key Binding	Meaning
ununderline-region		Remove all underlining (overstruck underscores) in the region.
unwind-protect		Do BODYFORM, protecting with UNWINDFORMS.
up-list		Move forward out of one level of parentheses.
upcase		Convert one arg, a character or string, to uppercase, and return that form.
upcase-region	C-x C-u	Convert the region to uppercase. In programs, wants two arguments.
upcase-word	ESC u	Convert following word (or ARG words) to upper case, moving over.
use-global-map		Selects KEYMAP as the global keymap.
use-local-map		Selects KEYMAP as the local keymap.
user-full-name		Return the full name of the user logged in, as a string.
user-login-name		Return the name under which user logged in, as a string.
user-real-login-name		Return the name of the user's real uid, as a string.
user-real-uid		Return the real uid of Emacs, as an integer.
user-uid		Return the effective uid of Emacs, as an integer.
user-variable-p		Return t if VARIABLE is intended to be set and modified by users.
vconcat		Concatenate arguments and make the result a vector.
vector		Return a newly created vector with your arguments (any number) as its elements.
vectorp		T if OBJECT is a vector.
verify-visited-file-modtime		Return t if last mod time of BUF's visited file matches what BUF records.

continues

Table 10.2. Continued

Command Name	*Key Binding*	*Meaning*
vertical-motion		Move to start of screen line LINES lines down.
vi-mode		Major mode that acts like the vi editor.
view-buffer		View BUFFER in View mode, returning to previous buffer when done.
view-emacs-news	C-h n, C-h C-n	Display info on recent changes to Emacs.
view-file		View FILE in View mode, returning to previous buffer when done.
view-lossage	C-h l	Display last 100 input keystrokes.
view-mode		Major mode for viewing text but not editing it.
view-register		Display what is contained in register named REGISTER.
vip-mode		Begin emulating the vi editor. This is distinct from "vi-mode."
visit-tags-table		Tell tags commands to use tag table file FILE.
waiting-for-user-input-p		Return non-NIL if emacs is waiting for input from the user.
what-cursor-position	C-x =	Print info on cursor position (on screen and within buffer).
what-line		int the current line number (in the buffer) of point.
what-page		Print page and line number of point.
where-is	C-h w	Print message listing key sequences that invoke specified command.
where-is-internal		Return list of key sequences that currently invoke command DEFINITION.
while		(while TEST BODY...), if TEST yields non-NIL, executes the BODY forms and repeats.

10

Command Name	Key Binding	Meaning
widen	C-x w	Remove restrictions from current buffer, allowing full text to be seen and edited.
window-buffer		Return the buffer that WINDOW is displaying.
window-dot		Return current value of point in WINDOW.
window-edges		Return a list of the edge coordinates of WINDOW.
window-height		Return the number of lines in WINDOW (including its mode line).
window-hscroll		Return the number of columns by which WINDOW is scrolled from left margin.
window-point		Return current value of point in WINDOW.
window-start		Return position at which display currently starts in WINDOW.
window-width		Return the number of columns in WINDOW.
windowp		Return t if OBJ is a window.
with-output-to-temp-buffer		Binding "standard-output" to buffer named BUFNAME, execute BODY then display that buffer.
word-search-backward		Search backward from point for STRING, ignoring differences in punctuation.
word-search-forward		Search forward from point for STRING, ignoring differences in punctuation.
write-abbrev-file		Write all abbrev definitions to file of Lisp code.
write-char		Output character CHAR to stream STREAM.
write-file	C-x C-w	Write current buffer into file FILENAME.

continues

10

Table 10.2. Continued

Command Name	Key Binding	Meaning
write-region		Write current region into specified file.
x-color-p		Return t if the display is a color X terminal.
x-debug		ARG non-nil means that X errors should generate a coredump.
x-flip-color		Toggle the background and foreground colors.
x-get-background-color		Return the color of the background, as a string
x-get-border-color		Return the color of the border, as a string.
x-get-cursor-color		Return the color of the cursor, as a string.
x-get-cut-buffer		Return contents of cut buffer of the X window system, as a string.
x-get-default		Get default for X-window attribute ATTRIBUTE from the system.
x-get-foreground-color		Return the color of the foreground, as a string.
x-get-mouse-color		Return the color of the mouse cursor, as a string.
x-get-mouse-event		Get next mouse event out of mouse event buffer (com-letter (x y)).
x-mouse-events		Return number of pending mouse events from X windosystem.
x-proc-mouse-event		Pull a mouse event out of the mouse event buffer and dispatch the appropriate function to act on this event.
x-set-background-color		Set background color to COLOR.
x-set-bell		For X window system, set audible vs visible bell.
x-set-border-color		Set border color to COLOR.

Command Name	Key Binding	Meaning
x-set-border-width		Set width of border to WIDTH, in the X window system.
x-set-cursor-color		Set text cursor color to COLOR.
x-set-font		Set the font to be used for the X window.
x-set-foreground-color		Set foreground (text) color to COLOR.
x-set-internal-border-width		Set width of internal border to WIDTH, in the X window system.
x-set-mouse-color		Set mouse cursor color to COLOR.
x-store-cut-buffer		Store contents of STRING into the cut buffer of the X window system.
y-or-n-p		Ask user a "y or n" question. Return t if answer is "y."
yank	C-y, ESC O p	Reinsert the last stretch of killed text.
yank-pop	ESC y	Replace just-yanked stretch of killed-text with a different stretch.
yank-rectangle		Yank the last killed rectangle with upper left corner at point.
yes-or-no-p		Ask user a "yes or no" question. Return t if answer is "yes."
yow		Return or display a Zippy quotation.
zap-to-char	ESC z	Kill up to (but not including) ARGth occurrence of CHAR.

Variables

Table 10.3 lists most of the variables that come in the distribution version of Emacs 18.57. As with the command table, in almost any installation that has been on the system for a while, you will find many additional variables, and you also can create many of your own. Emacs' capacity for customization is, after all, its strongest point.

10

Table 10.3. GNU Emacs Variables

Variable	Meaning
CSI-map	The CSI-map maps the CSI function keys on the VT100 keyboard.
SS3-map	SS3-map maps the SS3 function keys on the VT100 keyboard.
abbrev-all-caps	Set non-nil means expand multiword abbrevs all caps if abbrev was so.
abbrev-file-name	Default name of file to read abbrevs from.
abbrev-mode	Non-nil turns on automatic expansion of abbrevs when inserted.
abbrev-start-location	Buffer position for expand-abbrev to use as the start of the abbrev.
abbrev-start-location-buffer	Buffer that abbrev-start-location has been set for.
abbrev-table-name-list	List of symbols whose values are abbrev tables.
abbrevs-changed	Set non-nil by defining or altering any word abbrevs.
auto-fill-hook	Function called (if non-nil) after self-inserting a space at column beyond fill-column.
auto-mode-alist	Alist of file name patterns vs corresponding major mode functions.
auto-save-default	T says by default do auto-saving of every file-visiting buffer.
auto-save-interval	Number of keyboard input characters between auto-saves.
auto-save-visited-file-name	T says auto-save a buffer in the file it is visiting, when practical.
backup-by-copying	Non-nil means always use copying to create backup files.
backup-by-copying-when-linked	Non-nil means use copying to create backups for files with multiple names.
backup-by-copying-when-mismatch	Non-nil means create backups by copying if this preserves owner or group.
blink-matching-paren	Non-nil means show matching open-paren when close-paren is inserted.

Variable	*Meaning*
blink-matching-paren-distance	If non-nil, is maximum distance to search for matching open-paren.
blink-paren-hook	Function called, if non-nil, whenever a char with close-paren syntax is self-inserted.
buffer-auto-save-file-name	Name of file for auto-saving current buffer.
buffer-backed-up	Non-nil if this buffer's file has been backed up.
buffer-file-name	File being visited, or NIL if none. Name of file visited in current buffer, or nil if not visiting a file.
buffer-offer-save	Non-nil in a buffer means offer to save the buffer on exit.
buffer-read-only	Non-nil if this buffer is read-only.
buffer-saved-size	Length of current buffer when last read in, saved, or auto-saved.
buffer-undo-list	List of undo entries in current buffer.
c-argdecl-indent	Indentation level of declarations of C function arguments.
c-auto-newline	Non-nil means automatically newline before and after braces.
c-brace-imaginary-offset	Imagined indentation of a C open brace that actually follows a statement.
c-brace-offset	Extra indentation for braces, compared with other text in same context.
c-continued-brace-offset	Extra indent for substatements that start with open braces.
c-continued-statement-offset	Extra indent for lines not starting new statements.
c-indent-level	Indentation of C statements with respect to containing block.
c-label-offset	Offset of C label lines and case statements relative to usual indentation.
c-mode-abbrev-table	Abbrev table in use in C-mode buffers.
c-mode-map	Keymap used in C mode.
c-mode-syntax-table	Syntax table in use in C-mode buffers.

continues

10

Table 10.3. Continued

Variable	Meaning
c-tab-always-indent	Non-nil means TAB in C mode should always reindent the current line.
case-fold-search	Non-nil if searches should ignore case.
case-replace	Non-nil means query-replace shod preserve case in replacements.
command-history	List of recent commands that read arguments from terminal.
command-line-args	Args passed by shell to Emacs, as a list of strings.
command-line-processed	T once command line has been processed.
command-switch-alist	Alist of command-line switches.
comment-column	Column to indent right-margin comments to.
comment-end	String to insert to end a new comment.
comment-indent-hook	Function to compute desired indentation for a comment.
comment-multi-line	Non-nil means ESC LFD should continue same comment.
comment-start	String to insert to start a new comment, or nil if no comment syntax defined.
comment-start-skip	Regexp to match the start of a comment plus everything up to its body.
compile-command	Last shell command used to do a compilation; default for next compilation.
completion-auto-help	Non-nil means automatically provide help for invalid completion input.
completion-ignore-case	Non-nil means don't consider case significant in completion.
completion-ignored-extensions	Completion ignores file names ending in any string in this list.
ctl-arrow	Non-nil means display control chars with up arrow.
ctl-x-4-map	Keymap for subcommands of C-x 4.
ctl-x-map	Default keymap for C-x commands.

10

Variable	Meaning
current-prefix-arg	The value of the prefix argument for this editing command.
cursor-in-echo-area	Non-nil means put cursor in minibuffer after any message displayed there.
debug-end-pos	Don't ask.
debug-on-error	Non-nil means enter debugger if an error is signaled.
debug-on-next-call	Non-nil means enter debugger before next eval, apply, or funcall.
debug-on-quit	Non-nil means enter debugger if quit is signaled (C-g, for example).
debugger	Function to call to invoke debugger.
default-abbrev-mode	Default abbrev-mode for buffers that do not override it.
default-case-fold-search	Default case-fold-search for buffers that do not override it.
default-ctl-arrow	Default ctl-arrow for buffers that do not override it.
default-directory	Name of default directory of current buffer. Should end with slash.
default-fill-column	Default fill-column for buffers that do not override it.
default-left-margin	Default left-margin for buffers that do not override it.
default-major-mode	Major mode for new buffers. Defaults to fundamental-mode.
default-mode-line-format	Default mode-line-format for buffers that do not override it.
default-tab-width	Default tab-width for buffers that do not override it.
default-truncate-lines	Default truncate-lines for buffers that do not override it.
defining-kbd-macro	Non-nil means store keyboard input into kbd macro being defined.
delete-auto-save-files	Non-n means delete a buffer's auto-save file.

continues

Table 10.3. Continued

Variable	Meaning
delete-exited-processes	Non-nil means delete processes immediately when they exit.
dired-kept-versions	When cleaning directory, number of versions to keep.
dired-listing-switches	Switches passed to "ls" for Dired. MUST contain the "l" option.
disabled-command-hook	Value is called instead of any command that is disabled.
display-time-day-and-date	Non-nil means M-x display-time should display day and date as well as time
display-time-interval	Seconds between updates of time in the mode line.
display-timc-mail-file	File name of mail inbox file, for indicating existence of new mail.
echo-keystrokes	Nonzero means echo unfinished commands after this many seconds of pause.
edit-abbrevs-map	Keymap used in edit-abbrevs.
edit-tab-stops-buffer	Buffer whose tab stops are being edited—in case the variable tab-stop-list is unique to that buffer.
edit-tab-stops-map	Keymap used in edit-tab-stops.
emacs-build-time	Time at which Emacs was dumped out.
emacs-version	Version numbers of this version of Emacs.
emc-file	Default file into which to save Emacs session data.
emc-start-file	Last file to read in each time the default Emacs configuration is loaded.
emc-wconfigs-file	Default file into which to save Emacs window configuration ring data.
enable-recursive-minibuffers	Non-nil means to allow minibuffers to invoke commands which use recursive minibuffers.
esc-map	Default keymap for ESC (meta) commands.
exec-directory	Directory that holds programs that come with GNU Emacs.

10

Variable	Meaning
exec-path	List of directories to search programs to run in subprocesses.
executing-kbd-macro	Currently executing keyboard macro (a string); nil if none executing.
executing-macro	Currently executing keyboard macro (a string); nil if none executing.
features	A list of symbols which are the features of the executing emacs.
file-precious-flag	Non-nil means protect against I/O errors while saving files.
fill-column	Column beyond which automatic line-wrapping should happen.
fill-prefix	String for filling to insert at front of newline, or nil for none.
find-file-hooks	List of functions to be called after a buffer is loaded from a file.
find-file-not-found-hooks	List of functions to be called for find-file on nonexistent file.
find-file-run-dired	Non-nil says run dired if find-file is given the name of a directory.
function-keymap	Keymap containing definitions of keypad and function keys.
fundamental-mode-abbrev-table	The abbrev table of mode-specific abbrevs for Fundamental mode.
gc-cons-threshold	Number of bytes of consing between garbage collections.
global-abbrev-table	The abbrev table whose abbrevs affect all buffers.
global-map	Default global keymap mapping Emacs keyboard input into commands.
global-mode-string	String displayed by mode-line-format's "%m" specification.
goal-column	Semipermanent goal column for vertical motion, as set by C-x C-n, or nil.
help-char	Character to recognize as meaning Help.

continues

10

Table 10.3. Continued

Variable	Meaning
help-form	Form to execute when character help-char is read.
help-map	Keymap for characters following the Help key.
indent-line-function	Function to indent current line.
indent-region-function	Function which is short cut to indent each line in region with Tab.
indent-tabs-mode	Indentation can insert tabs if this is non-nil.
inhibit-default-init	Non-nil inhibits loading the "default" library.
inhibit-local-variables	Non-nil means query before obeying a file's local-variables list
inhibit-quit	Non-nil inhibits C-g quitting from happening immediately.
inhibit-startup-message	Non-nil inhibits the initial startup messages.
initial-major-mode	Major mode command symbol to use for the initial scratch buffer.
insert-default-directory	Non-nil means when reading a file name start with default dir in minibuffer.
inverse-video	Non-nil means use inverse-video.
kept-new-versions	Number of newest versions to keep when a new numbered backup is made.
kept-old-versions	Number of oldest versions to keep when a new numbered backup is made.
keyboard-translate-table	String used as translate table for keyboard input, or nil.
kill-emacs-hook	Function called, if non-nil, whenever kill-emacs is called.
kill-ring	List of killed text sequences.
kill-ring-max	Maximum length of kill ring before oldest elements are thrown away.
kill-ring-yank-pointer	The tail of the kill ring whose car is the last thing yanked.
last-abbrev	The abbrev-symbol of the last abbrev expanded.
last-abbrev-location	The location of the last abbrev expanded.

Variable	Meaning
last-abbrev-text	The exact text of the last abbrev expanded.
last-command	The last command executed. Normally a symbol with a function definition.
last-command-char	Last terminal input character that was part of a command, as an integer.
last-input-char	Last terminal input character, as an integer.
last-kbd-macro	Last kbd macro defined, as a string; nil if none defined.
ledit-go-to-lisp-string	Shell commands to execute to resume Lisp job.
ledit-go-to-liszt-string	Shell commands to execute to resume Lisp compiler job.
ledit-save-files	Non-nil means Ledit should save files before transferring to Lisp.
left-margin	Column for the default indent-line-function to indent to.
list-directory-brief-switches	Switches for list-directory to pass to "ls" for brief listing.
list-directory-verbose-switches	Switches for list-directory to pass to "ls" for verbose listing.
list-matching-lines-default-context-lines	Default number of context lines to include around a list-matching-lines.
load-in-progress	Non-nil if inside of load.
ad-path	List of directories to search for files to load.
local-abbrev-table	Local (mode-specific) abbrev table of current buffer.
lpr-switches	List of strings to pass as extra switch args to lpr when it is invoked.
mail-aliases	Alias of mail address aliases.
mail-archive-file-name	Name of file to write all outgoing messages in, or nil for none.
mail-header-separator	Line used to separate headers from text in messages being composed.
mail-interactive	Non-nil means when sending a message wait for and display errors.

continues

10

10

Table 10.3. Continued

Variable	Meaning
mail-self-blind	Non-nil means insert BCC to self in messages to be sent.
mail-use-rfc822	If non-nil, use a full, hairy RFC822 parser on mail addresses.
mail-yank-ignored-headers	Delete these headers from old message when it's inserted in a reply.
major-mode	Symbol for current buffer's major mode.
make-backup-files	Create a backup of each file when it is saved for the first time.
manual-formatted-dir-prefix	Prefix for directories containing formatted manual pages.
manual-formatted-dirlist	List of directories containing formatted manual pages.
manual-program	Program to run to print man pages.
mark-ring	The list of saved former marks of the current buffer.
mark-ring-max	Maximum size of mark ring. Start discarding off end if gets this big.
max-lisp-eval-depth	Limit on depth in eval, apply and funcall before error.
max-specpdl-size	Limit on number of Lisp variable bindings and unwind-protects before error.
meta-flag	Non-nil means treat 0200 bit in terminal input as Meta bit.
meta-prefix-char	Meta-prefix character code. Meta-foo as command input.
mh-lib	Directory of MH library.
mh-progs	Directory containing MH commands.
minibuffer-completion-confirm	Non-nil => demand confirmation of completion before exiting minibuffer.
minibuffer-completion-predicate	Holds PREDICATE argument to completing-read.
minibuffer-completion-table	Alist or obarray used for completion in the minibuffer.

Variable	Meaning
minibuffer-help-form	Value that help-form takes on inside the minibuffer.
minibuffer-local-completion-map	Keymap to use when reading from the minibuffer with completion.
minibuffer-local-map	Default keymap to use when reading from the minibuffer.
minibuffer-local-must-match-map	Keymap to use when reading from the minibuffer with completion and an exact match of one of the completions is required.
minibuffer-local-ns-map	The keymap used by the minibuf for local bindings when spaces are not to be allowed in the input string
minibuffer-scroll-window	Non-nil means it is the window that C-M-v in minibuffer should scroll.
minor-mode-alist	Alist saying how to show minor modes in the mode line.
mocklisp-arguments	While in a mocklisp function, the list of its unevaluated args.
me-line-buffer-identification	Mode-line control for identifying the buffer being displayed.
mode-line-format	Template for displaying mode line for current buffer.
mode-line-inverse-video	Non-nil means use inverse video, or other suitable display mode, for the mode line.
mode-line-modified	Mode-line control for displaying whether current buffer is modified.
mode-line-process	Mode-line control for displaying info on process status.
mode-name	Pretty name of current buffer's major mode (a string).
mode-specific-map	Keymap for characters following C-c.
mouse-map	Keymap for mouse commands from the X window system.
news-inews-program	Program to post news.
news-path	The root directory below which all news files are stored.

continues

Table 10.3. Continued

Variable	Meaning
next-screen-context-lines	Number of lines of continuity when scrolling by screenfuls.
no-redraw-on-reenter	Non-nil means no need to redraw entire screen after suspending.
noninteractive	Non-nil means Emacs is running without interactive terminal.
obarray	Symbol table for use by intern and read.
only-global-abbrevs	T means user plans to use global abbrevs only.
overlay-arrow-position	Marker for where to display an arrow on top of the buffer text
overlay-arrow-string	String to display as an arrow. See also overlay-arrow position.
overwrite-mode	Non-nil if self-insertion should replace existing text.
page-delimiter	Regexp describing line-beginnings that separate pages.
paragraph-ignore-fill-prefix	Non-nil means the paragraph commands are not affected by fill-prefix.
paragraph-separate	Regexp for beginning of a line that separates paragraphs.
paragraph-start	Regexp for beginning of a line that starts OR separates paragraphs.
parse-sexp-ignore-comments	Non-nil means forward-sexp, etc., should treat comments as whitespace.
polling-period	Interval between polling for input during Lisp execution.
pop-up-windows	Non-nil means display-buffer should make new windows.
prefix-arg	The value of the prefix argument for the next editing command.
print-escape-newlines	Non-nil means print newlines in strings as backslash-n.
print-length	Maximum length of list to print before abbreviating. "nil" means no limit.
process-connection-type	Control type of device used to communicate with subprocesses.

10

Variable	Meaning
process-environment	List of strings to append to environment of subprocesses that are started.
pure-bytes-used	Number of bytes of sharable Lisp data allocated so far.
purify-flag	Non-nil means loading Lisp code in order to dump an executable.
query-replace-help	Help message while in query-replace.
quit-flag	Non-nil causes eval to abort, unless inhibit-quit is non-nil.
register-alist	Alist of elements (NAME . CONTENTS), one for each Emacs regist.
require-final-newline	T says silently put a newline at the end whenever a file is saved.
reset-terminal-on-clear	Non-nil means re-init terminal modes for clear screen as on entry to Emacs.
revert-buffer-function	Function to use to revert this buffer, or nil to do the default.
rmail-default-dont-reply-to-names	A regular expression specifying part of the value of the default value of the variable rmail-dont-reply-to-names. The other part is the user's name.
rmail-delete-after-output	Non-nil means automatically delete a message that is copied to a file.
rmail-dont-reply-to-names	A regular expression specifying names to prune in replying to messages.
rmail-file-name	Name of user's primary mail file.
rmail-ignored-headers	Gubbish header fields one would rather not see.
rmail-primary-inbox-list	List of files which are inboxes for user's primary mail file ~/RMAIL.
rmail-spool-directory	Name of directory used by system mailer for delivering new mail.
save-abbrevs	Non-nil means save word abbrevs too when files are saved.
scroll-step	The number of lines to try scrolling a window by when point moves out.

continues

10

Table 10.3. Continued

Variable	Meaning
search-delete-char	Character to delete from incremental search string.
search-exit-char	Character to exit incremental search.
search-exit-option	Non-nil means random control characters terminate incremental search.
search-last-regexp	Last string searched for by a regexp search command.
search-last-string	Last string searched for by a non-regexp search command.
search-quote-char	Character to quote special characters for incremental search.
search-repeat-char	Character to repeat incremental search forward.
search-reverse-char	Character to repeat incremental search backward.
search-slow-speed	Highest terminal speed at which to use "slow" style incremental search.
search-slow-window-lines	Number of lines in slow search display windows.
search-yank-line-char	Character to pull rest of line from buffer into search string.
search-yank-word-char	Character to pull next word from buffer into search string.
sclective-display	T enables selective display.
selective-display-ellipses	T means display ... on previous line when a line is invisible.
send-mail-function	Function to call to send the current buffer as mail.
sendmail-program	Program used to send messages.
sentence-end	Regexp describing the end of a sentence.
shell-file-name	File name to load inferior shells from.
shell-prompt-pattern	Regexp used by Newline command in shell mode to match subshell prompts.
split-height-threshold	display-buffer would prefer to split the largest window if this large.

10

Variable	Meaning
stack-trace-on-error	Non-nil means automatically display a backtrace buffer.
standard-input	Stream for read to get input from.
standard-output	Function print uses by default for outputting a character.
system-type	Symbol indicating type of operating system you are using.
tab-stop-list	List of b stop positions used by tab-to-tab-stops.
tab-width	Distance between tab stops (for display of tab characters), in columns.
tags-file-name	File name of tag table.
temp-buffer-show-hook	Non-nil means call as function to display a help buffer.
temporary-goal-column	Current goal column for vertical motion.
term-file-prefix	If non-nil, Emacs startup does (load (concat term-file-prefix (getenv "TERM"))).
term-setup-hook	Function to be called after loading terminal-specific lisp code.
text-mode-abbrev-table	Abbrev table used while in text mode.
text-mode-syntax-table	Syntax table used while in text mode.
top-level	Form to evaluate when Emacs starts up.
this-command	The command now being executed.
track-eol	Non-nil means vertical motion starting at the end of a line should keep to ends of lines.
trim-versions-without-asking	If true, deletes excess backup versions silently.
truncate-lines	Non-nil means do not display continuation lines.
truncate-partial-width-windows	Non-nil means truncate lines in all windows less than full screen wide.
undo-high-threshold	Don't keep more than this much size of undo information.
undo-threshold	Keep no more undo information once it exceeds this size.

continues

Table 10.3. Continued

Variable	*Meaning*
unread-command-char	Character to be read as next input from command input stream, or -1 if none.
values	List of values of all expressions which were read, evaluated, and printed.
version-control	Control use of version numbers for backup files.
visible-bell	Non-nil means try to flash the screen to represent a bell.
vms-stmlf-recfm	Non-nil means write new files with record format "stmlf."
window-min-height	Delete any window less than this tall (including its mode line).
window-min-width	Delete any window less than this wide.
window-system	A symbol naming the window-system under which Emacs is running.
window-system-version	Version number of the window system Emacs is running under.
write-file-hooks	List of functions to be called before writing out a buffer to a file.
x-mouse-abs-pos	Current x-y position of mouse relative to root window.
x-mouse-item	Encoded representation of last mouse click, corresponding to numerical entries in x-mouse-map.
x-mouse-pos	Current x-y position of mouse by row, column as specified by font

Chapter

11

UniPress Emacs Reference

U niPress is a descendant of Gosling Emacs. As you've seen through the course of this book, UniPress certainly is similar to GNU, although it works differently in some instances. UniPress Emacs is a commercial product available for many kinds of computing platforms. Contact UniPress Software, 2025 Lincoln Highway, Edison, NJ 08817 for more information, or phone 1-800-222-0550, or fax 1-908-287-4929.

Keys

All versions of Emacs can be infinitely customized. We can't just give you a list of key combinations and say they are always true, because many people could have modified your version of Emacs. You probably will want to rearrange the keys to better suit your own needs and preferences. Use Table 11.1, however, as a starting point. This table lists the initial bindings of keys in the current version of UniPress Emacs. By typing ESC x help and choosing the k option, you can get a current list of the key bindings.

11

**Table 11.1. UniPress Emacs Global Commands
and Their Key Bindings**

Key Binding	Command
C-@	set-mark
C-a	beginning-of-line
C-b	backward-character
C-c	exit-emacs
C-d	delete-next-character
C-e	end-of-line
C-f	forward-character
C-g	illegal-operation
C-h	delete-previous-character
C-i	tab
NEWLINE	#newline-and-indent
C-k	kill-to-end-of-line
C-l	redraw-display
ENTER	newline
C-n	next-line
C-o	newline-and-backup
C-p	previous-line
C-q	quote-character
C-r	search-reverse
C-s	search-forward
C-t	transpose-characters
C-u	argument-prefix
C-v	next-page
C-w	delete-to-killbuffer
C-x	C-x-prefix
C-x-C-b	list-all-buffers
C-x-C-c	exit-emacs
C-x-C-d	describe-word-in-buffer
C-x-C-e	compile-it
C-x-C-f	find-file
C-x-C-i	indent-region
C-x-C-k	kill-command-execution

Key Binding	Command
C-x-C-l	current-line-number
C-x-ENTER	write-modified-files
C-x-C-n	next-command-error
C-x-C-o	switch-to-recent-buffer
C-x-C-p	previous-error
C-x-C-r	read-file
C-x-C-s	write-current-file
C-x-C-u	undo
C-x-C-v	visit-file
C-x-C-w	write-named-file
C-x-C-x	exchange-dot-and-mark
C-x-C-z	shrink-window
C-x-!	execute-shell-command
C-x-(	start-remembering
C-x-)	stop-remembering
C-x-1	delete-other-windows-nicely
C-x-2	split-window-nicely
C-x-:	set-paragraph-style
C-x-;	set-comment-style
C-x-<	shift-comment-left
C-x->	shift-comment-right
C-x-D	close-current-frame
C-x-K	delete-current-frame
C-x-N	next-frame
C-x-P	previous-frame
C-x-[	gen-on
C-x-]	gen-off
C-x-b	switch-to-buffer
C-x-d	delete-window-nicely
C-x-e	execute-keyboard-macro
C-x-h	mark-whole-buffer
C-x-i	info

continues

11

Table 11.1. Continued

Key Binding	Command
C-x-j	join-lines
C-x-l	goto-line
C-x-m	send-mail
C-x-n	next-window
C-x-p	previous-window
C-x-r	mail
C-x-t	toggle-application-subsystem
C-x-z	enlarge-window
C-x-|	filter-region
C-x-C-?	kill-to-beginning-of-sentence
C-y	yank-from-killbuffer
C-z	scroll-one-line-up
ESC	ESC-prefix
ESC-C-f	fill-with-exdent
ESC-NEWLINE	expand-inline-file-name
ESC-C-k	kill-comment-line
ESC-ENTER	goto-current-indent
ESC-C-r	dit-ruler
ESC-C-t	switch-context
ESC-C-v	page-next-window
ESC-C-w	delete-region-to-buffer
ESC-C-y	yank-buffer
ESC-ESC	eval-mlisp
ESC-C-^	case-region-invert
ESC-C-_	help
ESC-SPACEBAR	set-mark
ESC-!	line-to-top-of-window
ESC-(	backward-parenthesis
ESC-)	forward-parenthesis
ESC-,	beginning-of-window
ESC--	meta-minus
ESC-.	end-of-window

Key Binding	*Command*
ESC-0 to ESC-9	meta-digit
ESC-;	goto-or-create-comment
ESC-<	beginning-of-file
ESC->	end-of-file
ESC-?	apropos
ESC-J	justify-paragraph
Keypad-Comma	next-page
Keypad-Period	end-of-line
Keypad-0	beginning-of-line
Keypad-1	backward-word
Keypad-2	next-line
Keypad-3	forward-word
Keypad-4	backward-character
Keypad-5	argument-prefix
Keypad-6	forward-character
Keypad-7	previous-page
Keypad-8	previous-line
Keypad-9	next-page
UP	previous-line
DOWN	next-line
RIGHT	forward-character
LEFT	backward-character
HOME	beginning-of-window
ESC-\	delete-white-space
ESC-]	forward-paragraph
ESC-^	case-word-invert
ESC-a	backward-sentence
ESC-b	backward-word
ESC-c	case-word-capitalize
ESC-d	delete-next-word
ESC-e	forward-sentence
ESC-f	forward-word

continues

11

Table 11.1. Continued

Key Binding	Command
ESC-h	delete-previous-word
ESC-i	indent-line
ESC-j	fill-paragraph
ESC-k	kill-to-end-of-sentence
ESC-l	case-word-lower
ESC-m	point-Menu
ESC-n	next-recent-buffer
ESC-o	update-all-frames
ESC-p	previous-recent-buffer
ESC-q	query-replace
ESC-r	replace-string
ESC-s	center-line
ESC-t	transpose-word
ESC-u	case-word-upper
ESC-v	previous-page
ESC-w	copy-region-to-killbuffer
ESC-x	execute-extended-command
ESC-z	scroll-one-line-down
ESC-{	backward-paragraph
ESC-}	forward-paragraph
ESC C-~	make-buffer-unmodified
ESC C-?	delete-previous-word
C-]	abort-recursive-edit
C-_	point-help
SPACE to ,	self-insert
–	minus
. to /	self-insert
0 to 9	digit
: to ~	self-insert

Commands and Variables

The following commands are found in the distribution version of the current UniPress Emacs. You can get the description shown in Table 11.2 plus much more by typing ESC x help d and entering the name of the command. Or, if you don't know the full name, type ESC x help a and enter a partial string—UniPress then gives you all commands and variables in that string.

11

Table 11.2. UniPress Emacs Commands

Command Name	Meaning
abbrev-expansion	Returns abbreviation's expansion to abbrev hook.
abbrev-mode	Allows expansion of trigger phrases.
abbrev-word-in-buffer	Creates an abbrev for the word before dot.
abort-recursive-edit	Aborts the current recursive edit, if any.
abort-transient-edit	Aborts transient edit in current buffer.
active-process	Returns the name of the currently active process.
add-tag	Adds line defining a function to tangible.
add-to-child-menu	Renamed add-to-node-child-menu.
add-to-menu	Renamed add-to-node-menu.
add-to-node-child-menu	The command add-to-node-child-menu <node-name> adds the given name at the front of the child menu in the current mode.
add-to-node-menu	The command add-to-node-menu <node-name> adds the given name at the front of the menu in the current node, before the child menu if there is one.
align-center	Inserts a given string and centers it on a line with given width.
align-close-paren-with-open	Controls placement of automatically aligned closed parenthesis.
align-right	Inserts a given string so that it is right-justified on a line of given width.
annotate-selection	Inserts description of selection.

continues

Table 11.2. Continued

Command Name	Meaning
announcement-message	Returns current announcement message.
ansi-shell	Runs a shell in raw input mode.
append-body	Appends the body around or before dot to the end of a given buffer.
append-matching-bodies	Appends all bodies passing given conditions to the end of a given buffer.
append-node-to-script	Appends the current node to the script in the buffer.
append-region-to-buffer	Adds region between dot and mark to buffer end.
append-region-to-file	Adds region to end of named file.
append-region-to-killbuffer	Appends the text that lies between dot and mark.
append-string-to-buffer	Appends given string to end of given buffer.
append-to-file	Adds current buffer to end of file.
application-subsystem	Contains name of current buffer's application subsystem.
apropos	Lists function/variable names containing keyword.
argc	Returns number of arguments passed to Emacs.
argument-prefix	Supplies prefix argument for following command.
argv	Returns Nth argument given Emacs when invoked.
array-size	Returns the number of entries in the given array.
ask-user-about-exit	Asks user to confirm exit and to dispose of modified files.
auto-arg	Sets local key bindings, turns auto-arg on.
auto-context	If 1, adjusts context on each command; if 2, adjusts context on key time out.
auto-execute	An obsolete synonym for auto-major-mode.
auto-fill-hook	Calls all buffers in auto-fill-mode to end a line and start a new one.

11

Command Name	Meaning
auto-fill-mode	Turns paragraph filling on and off.
auto-load	Loads named functions from the named file.
auto-major-mode	Calls function when file name matches a pattern.
auto-minor-mode	Executes a minor mode when files matching given prefix or suffix are visited.
auto-other-mode	Calls function when file name matches a pattern.
auto-write-abbrev-file	File where abbrevs are written on exit.
autoload	Creates named function from the named file.
avoid-trailing-blanks	Permits deletion of blanks after tabs.
await-process-input	Makes Emacs sleep until process creates output.
backup-before-writing	Emacs backs up files automatically.
backup-by-copying-when-linked	Specifies whether linked files should be backed up by copying.
backup-by-copying	Specifies whether files should be backed up by copying.
backward-balanced-paren-line	Moves backward to find unmatched "(".
backward-body	Moves dot to the beginning of the previous body.
backward-c-function-body	Moves dot to beginning of current C function definition.
backward-character	Moves dot backward one character.
backward-kill-char	Deletes previous character.
backward-kill-word	Deletes previous word.
backward-paragraph	Moves dot to beginning of current or earlier paragraph.
backward-paren	Moves cursor backward to first unmatched "(".
backward-sentence	Moves dot to beginning of current sentence.
backward-word	Moves dot to beginning of previous word.
baud-rate	Returns baud rate of communication line.

continues

Table 11.2. Continued

Command Name	Meaning
begin-comment-string	Users can return comments from syntax table.
beginning-of-file	Moves dot to first character in current buffer.
beginning-of-line	Moves dot to first character in current line.
beginning-of-node-menu	Puts dot at the beginning of the current node's menu.
beginning-of-paragraph	Moves dot to beginning of current or earlier paragraph.
beginning-of-selection	Moves to beginning of current selection.
beginning-of-window	Moves dot to beginning of window.
beginning-of-word	Moves dot to the beginning of the current word.
berkmail	The berkmail library is based on a mailer used at the University of California.
bind-to-key	Binds a function to the given key(s).
binding-of-key	Names function and function type bound to given keystroke sequence.
bit&=	Variable = bitwise AND of variable and expression.
bit&	Returns bitwise logical AND of its arguments.
bottom-mini-window	Moves the miniwindow to the bottom of this frame.
box-region	Encloses the region in a box comment.
box-comments	The box-comments package contains commands used to box and unbox comments in C.
break-character-position	Lists position in file of MLisp code to debug.
break-file-name	Returns the name of the break file.
break-string-forward	Moves dot until it reaches one of the given string argument characters.
break-string-reverse	Moves dot backward until it reaches one of its given string arguments.

Command Name	Meaning
brief-recursive-edit-description	Displays brief message about recursive edit. (Obsolete?)
buffer-apropos	Lists buffer names containing given string.
buffer-creation-hook	Invokes buffer-creation-hook every time a new buffer is created.
buffer-deletion-hook	Invokes the buffer-deletion-hook every time a buffer is deleted.
buffer-exists	Returns 1 if string names existing buffer.
buffer-file-name	Returns file name associated with given buffer, null string if none.
buffer-info	Returns printable buffer statistics.
buffer-is-modified	Returns 1 if the buffer is modified and 0 if not modified .
buffer-is-scratch	Returns 1 if the given buffer is a scratch buffer.
buffer-is-visible	Returns 1 if current buffer is in visible window.
buffer-name-arg	The command buffer-name-arg <argnum> <prompt> <default> returns the buffer-name given as an argument to the caller.
buffer-not-modified	An obsolete synonym for make-buffer-unmodified.
buffer-size	Returns number of characters in current buffer.
buffer-to-resource	Stores the contents of the given resource in the current buffer.
buffer-to-string	Returns contents of given buffer as a string.
buffer-to-temp-ps-file	Copies the given buffer to a temporary file.
buffer-window-flags	Stores buffer-specific window flags.
buffer	Returns and displays information on buffers.
c++macs-mode	This invokes c++macs-mode on the current buffer.

11

continues

Table 11.2. Continued

Command Name	Meaning
c=	Sets case-fold-search when creating new buffers.
c2ps-view	Interprets the current buffer as c-code that is to be viewed as postscript.
call-interactively	Runs function as if it were used interactively.
can-one-line-opt	Tells Emacs display driver to redraw the current line.
capitalize-word	Capitalizes first letter, others lowercase.
capword	Package that contains the commands used to change the case of a letter.
case-flip-character	Changes case of letter underneath cursor.
case-fold-search	Allows you to choose whether or not to consider the case of words in searches.
case-region-capitalize	Capitalizes every word in region.
case-region-invert	Makes uppercase lowercase, and vice versa.
case-region-lower	Changes uppercase in region to lowercase.
case-region-upper	Changes lowercase in region to uppercase.
case-string-lower	The command case-string-lower <string> returns a lowercased copy of the given string.
case-string-upper	The command case-string-upper <string> returns an uppercased copy of the given string.
case-word-capitalize	Capitalizes the first letter in the current word.
case-word-lower	Changes the entire word around or before dot to lowercase.
case-word-upper	Changes the entire word on or before dot to uppercase.
cd	Sets path name as current working directory.
center-line	Centers the current line between the left and right margins.
change-current-process	Makes the given process become the current process.

Command Name	Meaning
change-directory	Changes current directory, but only under Emacs.
channel-list-editor	Sets up current buffer to edit a list of open channels.
char-is-graphic	Returns nonzero if a character has a graphic representation.
char-to-string	Turns number to character with the ASCII value.
check-for-abort	Raises an error if C-g has been typed, returns otherwise.
checkpoint-frequency	Number of keystrokes between checkpoints.
checkpoint	Causes automatic backup of modified files.
child-menu-to-node-list	Creates a list in the given buffer of the nodes.
clock	Displays current time on the mode line, notifies you of incoming mail, etc.
close-all-frames	Closes all frames, including the current one.
close-current-frame	Closes (iconifies) the current frame.
cmacs-mode	Starts mode for editing C text.
comm-buffers	Finds common lines in two sorted buffers.
command-read-hook	Called whenever Emacs is reading a command sequence.
comment-begin-fill-hook	Cleans and sorts for fill-paragraph.
comment-begin-re	A regular expression that matches a comment-begin.
comment-begin	Used to introduce new comments.
comment-column	Sets column where comments start.
comment-end-re	A regular expression that matches a comment-end.
comment-end	Used to end new comments.
comment-indent-hook	Tells fill-paragraph how to indent each line.
comments	The comments package contains generic comment-handling functions.

continues

Table 11.2. Continued

Command Name	Meaning
compare-windows	Compares the contents of two windows. Stops at first difference.
compile-it	Executes shell command, remembers it for next time.
compile-library	Compiles the given library without executing it.
compile-message-format	Sets the error-message-format used by compile-it.
compile-mlisp-debugging-hooks	Lets MLisp add debugging data to compilation.
concat	Returns concatenation of its string arguments.
confirm-delete-buffer	An obsolete synonym for delete-current-buffer.
confirm-delete-file	An obsolete synonym for delete-current-file.
confirm-exit	Determines whether user really wants to exit.
confirm-use-menu	If 1, confirm uses menus to ask for yes/no, or, if 0, proceeds without asking.
confirm	Accepts yes/no answer; returns 1 for y, 0 for n.
continue-process-leader	Continues leader of named process' group.
continue-process	Resumes process halted by stop-process.
copy-current-buffer	Copies the current buffer to a given buffer.
copy-matching-bodies	Copies the bodies that match a given test to the end of the specified buffer.
copy-rectangular-region	Copies a rectangle to a given buffer.
copy-region-to-buffer	Copies the region to the named buffer.
copy-region-to-file	Writes region to named file.
copy-region-to-killbuffer	Copies region to kill buffer, no changes made.
count-chars-buffer	Returns the number of characters in a buffer.
count-chars-region	Returns the number of characters in the region.
count-lines-buffer	Returns the number of lines in the buffer.

Command Name	Meaning
count-lines-region	Returns the number of lines in the region.
create-boxed-comment	Puts whatever text you type in a transient window into box.
create-database	Creates an empty database with the given name.
create-dbox-frame	Creates a frame that is dBox-style.
create-directory	Makes subdirectory in named directory.
create-doc-frame	Creates a new frame with the default Main-class.
ctlchar-with-^	Determines how control characters are displayed.
current-buffer-name	Returns name of current buffer as a string.
current-buffer-to-temp-file	Copies current buffer to a temp file with an arbitrarily chosen name.
current-column	Returns column number of the cursor's position.
current-date	Returns current system date in DD-MMM-YY format.
current-directory	Returns the current directory.
current-file-name	Gets file name associated with current buffer.
current-frame	Returns the index of the current frame.
current-global-keymap	Returns name of current global keymap.
current-indent	Lists column of line's first nonspace character.
current-line-number	Returns the number of the line on which the cursor is located.
current-local-abbrev-table	Returns name of current local abbrev table.
current-local-keymap	Returns name of current local keymap.
current-numeric-time	Returns time of day in seconds since 1-Jan-1970.
current-process	Returns the name of the process that is currently being considered.
current-syntax-table	Returns name of current syntax table.

11

continues

Table 11.2. Continued

Command Name	Meaning
current-time	Returns current time of day.
current-timezone	Returns the current time zone as a string.
current-window	Returns the number of the current window.
cut-region-to-frame	Displays contents of region in a new frame.
database-directory	Directory where system-wide databases are kept.
database	Returns database search lists for this session.
dBox-class	Makes any frame started up hereafter "dBoxEmacsWindow".
debox-region	Removes boxed comments.
debug	The debug package is the MLisp part of the debugging facility.
declare-buffer-specific	Defines buffer-specific values for variables.
declare-global	Globally binds each unbound variable in list.
default-begin-fill-hook	The default for begin-fill-hook.
default-case-fold-search	Sets case-fold-search when creating new buffers.
default-comment-column	Sets comment-column when creating new buffers.
default-compile-it-command	Command executed by compile-it if no prefix arg is given.
default-confirm	Prompts for confirmation in the minibuffer.
default-displayed-tab-size	Sets displayed-tab-size when creating new buffers.
default-editor-abort	Reassures user and invokes abort-recursive-edit to stop the edit.
default-editor-exit	Cleans up, offers to save, and invokes editor to leave the edit.
default-error-hook	Sets as the default @error-hook. Invoked when an error is detected.
default-global-keymap	An obsolete synonym for @normal-mode-keymap.
default-indent-hook	The default for indent-hook.

Command Name	Meaning
default-left-margin	Sets left-margin when creating new buffers.
default-mode-line-format	Sets mode-line-format when creating new buffers.
default-needs-checkpointing	Sets needs-checkpointing for new buffers.
default-prefix-string	Sets prefix-string when creating new buffers.
default-read-only	Sets read-only when creating new buffers.
default-right-margin	Sets right-margin when creating new buffers.
default-tab-size	An obsolete synonym for default-displayed-tab-size.
default-visit-file-hook	Invokes dired if file is a directory rather than normal-mode.
default-wrap-long-lines	Sets wrap-long-lines when creating new buffers.
default	Profile that is loaded for users who don't have Emacs profiles in their own directory.
define-buffer-macro	Defines contents of current buffer as a macro.
define-global-abbrev	Defines abbreviation for all buffers.
define-hooked-global-abbrev	Associates named function with defined abbrev.
define-keyboard-macro	Names and saves keyboard macro.
define-keymap	Creates empty keymap, which user must name.
define-local-abbrev	Sets expansion for current buffer.
define-region-as-macro	Defines a new macro whose body is between the dot and mark.
define-special-keys	Clears special key list, sets up some defaults, and programs its arguments.
define-string-macro	Uses string in minibuffer as macro.
defun	Defines a new MLisp function.
delete-blank-lines	Deletes blank lines around dot.
delete-body	The command delete-body <buffer> deletes the body around or before dot.

11

continues

Table 11.2. Continued

Command Name	Meaning
delete-buffer-frame	The command delete-buffer-frame deletes the current buffer's primary frame.
delete-buffer	The command delete-buffer [<buffer-name>] deletes the given buffer, defaulting to the current buffer if no buffer name is given.
delete-current-buffer	Deletes the current buffer.
delete-current-file	Asks before deleting file associated with current buffer.
delete-current-line	Deletes the line that dot is on.
delete-directory	Deletes named directory and all files in it.
delete-file	Attempts to unlink (delete) named file.
delete-frame	The command delete-frame <index> deletes the frame with the given index.
delete-from-ring	Deletes the value of the given variable from the ring.
delete-keymap	Eliminates a named keymap.
delete-matching-bodies	Deletes bodies that pass test.
delete-menu-item	Renamed to delete-node-menu item.
delete-mini-window	Deletes the frame's miniwindow.
delete-next-character	Deletes character following dot.
delete-next-word	Deletes from dot to the end of the word.
delete-node-menu-item	The command delete-node-menu-item <item> deletes the menu item and its associated text.
delete-other-windows	Removes all but the current window.
delete-previous-character	Deletes character to left of cursor.
delete-previous-word	Deletes from dot to beginning of word.
delete-region-to-buffer	Deletes a region to a given buffer.
delete-search-list	Deletes named search list.
delete-selection	Deletes all characters in the current selection.
delete-some-buffers	Asks before deleting buffers.

Command Name	Meaning
delete-spaces-inside-tabs	When set to 1, tries to delete unnecessary spaces.
delete-subprocess-files	Deletes intermediate files created for subprocesses and compiles.
delete-subsystem-window	Deletes subsystem window that looks at given buffer.
delete-syntax-table	Deletes a named syntax table.
delete-this-menu-item	Renamed to delete-this-node-menu-item.
delete-this-node-menu-item	Removes the menu item around or after dot.
delete-to-killbuffer	Deletes region, but allows for its retrieval.
delete-transient-window	Deletes the transient window most recently created on the current buffer.
delete-white-space	Deletes all white space on either side of dot.
delete-window-nicely	Deletes window, returns space so other window's text doesn't move.
delete-window	Removes the current window.
describe-command	Describes a named command.
describe-current-buffer	Prints info on current buffer in the minibuffer.
describe-current-file	Presents a summary of the current file's characteristics.
describe-editor-subsystem	Describes the buffer's active editor subsystem.
describe-function	Displays the Info entry for a named function.
describe-key	Describes function bound to given key.
describe-keymap	Describes key bindings in the given keymap.
describe-library	Edits description of the current library.
describe-local-bindings	Describes bindings in the current local keymap.
describe-major-mode	Describes current buffer's active major mode.
describe-recursive-edit	An obsolete synonym for describe-editor-subsystem.

continues

Table 11.2. Continued

Command Name	Meaning
describe-variable	Describes a named variable.
describe-word-in-buffer	Prints description of word nearest cursor.
describe-word	Displays the database entry describing the given word.
description-search-list	The search list used to find descriptions of words in a buffer.
desword-update-entry	Updates word description entry being edited.
digit	Permits integer arguments; noninteractive.
dired-mode-hook	Invoked by dired-mode (hence, by dired).
dired-mode	Sets buffer as dired listing buffer, or reverts it to previous mode.
dired	Provides facilities for listing and editing a directory.
dispatch-on-input	dispatch-on-input
display-file-percentage	Controls expansion of "%P" in mode-line format.
display-font	Displays all the characters available in the named font in the current font.
display-in-frame	Displays the given buffer in the given frame.
display-in-subsystem-window	Opens a subsystem window on the given buffer.
display-is-bitmap	Zero if this display is an ASCII terminal and 1 otherwise.
display-line-numbers	Puts line numbers on the left side of the display.
display-statistics	Shows statistics used to debug display driver.
display-tildes	Gives character to be displayed in column one of textless lines.
displayed-tab-size	Number of characters between tab stops.
do-inside-comment	Executes arguments on comment text only.
do-recursive-edit	Tool for writing MLisp code that does recursive edits.

Command Name	Meaning
don't-step-through	Turns off "stepping through" a named function.
dot-in-code	Sets major mode and returns 1 if now in code.
dot-in-comment	Invokes the proper major mode for the current context, and returns 1 if dot is in comment.
dot-in-quote	Returns nonzero if dot is inside a simple quoted string.
dot-is-visible	Returns the number of the display line within the window where dot lies.
dot-percent	Returns an integer between 0 and 100 that expresses how far down in the buffer the dot lies.
dot-to-center	Shifts buffer position in the window so that the dot is in the center.
dot-to-centre	An obsolete synonym for dot-to-center.
dot-to-left-margin	Moves the window so that the dot is at the left margin.
dot-to-mouse	Moves dot to the position of the mouse.
dot-to-right-margin	Moves the window so that the dot is at the right margin.
dot	Returns buffer name, dot's position in buffer.
drag-dot	Dot tracks mouse cursor as long as button is down.
drag-frozen-modeline	Toggles window's frozen state and drags mode line.
drag-modeline	Drags mode line as long as mouse button is held down.
drag-text	Drags text as long as mouse button is down.
draw-current-buffer	Bound to C-x C-l, it draws the graphic view of the current buffer.
dump-stack-trace	Puts MLisp stack trace in "Stack trace" buffer.

continues

11

Table 11.2. Continued

Command Name	Meaning
dump-syntax-table	Places listing of syntax table into buffer.
echo-argument	Number of seconds of delay before echoing a prefix argument in the minibuffer.
echo-keystrokes	Number of seconds of delay before echoing a partially typed keystroke sequence.
echo-string	Used in /hoard/master/src/keyecho.c.
edit-abbrev-list	Offers the given abbrev list to the user for editing.
edit-block-comment	Deboxes, narrows, and recursively edits comment.
edit-boxed-comment	Puts the contents of boxed comment in recursive edit.
cdit-current-buffer-name	Edits the name of the current buffer.
edit-current-file-name	Edits the current file name.
edit-description-search-list	Interactively edits the description search list.
edit-elec-mlisp-mode-options	Recursively edits variables pertaining to elec-mlisp mode.
edit-embedded-mlisp	Edits resource in current buffer named MLisp, if any.
edit-entry-hook	User-defined hook invoked on entry to main and recursive edits.
edit-environment-variable	Recursively edits value of environment variable.
edit-exit-hook	User-defined.
edit-file-name	Edits the name of the current file in a transient window.
edit-frame-settings	Calls a temporary window at the top of the current frame.
edit-function-definition	Shows the source code for the given function.
edit-key-bindings	Allows you to examine (and edit) local and global key bindings.
edit-keyboard-macro	Edits the body of the named keyboard macro in a transient window.

Command Name	*Meaning*
edit-keystroke-history	Edits the last several dozen keys you typed.
edit-level	Returns a string with the edit level.
edit-library	The command edit-library <library-name> runs a visit-file on the given library.
edit-local-key-bindings	Allows you to examine (and change) key bindings in effect for the current buffer.
edit-macro	Edits named macro in a buffer.
edit-major-mode-options	Places current major-mode's options in a transient window for editing.
edit-minor-modes	Interactively edits the minor mode options.
edit-options	Recursively edits all variables with names containing a string.
edit-ruler	Interactively modifies tab and margin settings.
edit-search-lists	Edits database search list(s).
edit-session-options	Offers controls affecting the session.
edit-subsystem-options	Offers the active subsystem's control panel.
edit-tab-stops	Modifies current tab stop settings.
edit-variable	Edits variable value in transient window.
edit-word-description	Enters a recursive edit on the database entry describing a given word.
editor-subsystem	Default buffer subsystem. Sets key bindings and available commands.
egrep	The command egrep and fgrep are the counterparts to the UNIX filtering commands egrep and fgrep.
elec-c-assume	Nonzero if function body's "{" lie in column one.
elec-c-auto-close-paren	If 1, typing left parenthesis inserts matching right parenthesis.
elec-c-indent-width	An obsolete synonym for fixed-tab-width.
elec-c-magic-brace	Controls whether "{" opens a template block.

continues

11

Table 11.2. Continued

Command Name	Meaning
elec-c-magic-comma	Controls whether "," also inserts space.
elec-c-magic-semi	Controls whether ";" opens a newline.
elec-c-mode-icon	Specifies the icon to be used for the elec-c major mode.
elec-c-mode	Starts mode for editing C text.
elec-c	This library contains the major mode for entering and editing C code.
elec-lisp-mode	Starts editing environment for writing Lisp.
elec-mlisp-mode-icon	Names icon assigned to MLisp windows. Defaults to "clown".
elec-mlisp-mode	Starts editing environment for writing MLisp.
electric-c-mode	An obsolete synonym for elec-c-mode.
electric-lisp-mode	An obsolete synonym for elec-lisp-mode.
electric-mlisp-mode	An obsolete synonym for elec-mlisp-mode.
emacs-editor	Places the current buffer in Emacs editor mode.
emacs-helper-bin-dir	Directory containing auxiliary utilities used by MLisp packages.
emacs-process-id	Returns the process id for the Emacs session (not for any subshells).
emacs-version	Describes current Emacs version.
enable-eipc	If true, allows eipc connections to be made to this Emacs session.
end-comment-string	Returns end comment string from syntax table.
end-of-data	Moves dot to the end of the data page.
end-of-file	Moves cursor to end of current buffer.
end-of-line	Moves dot to end of current line.
end-of-paragraph	Moves dot to end of current or next paragraph.
end-of-selection	Moves to end of current selection.
end-of-window	Moves dot to end of current window.
end-of-word	Moves dot to the end of the current word.

Command Name	Meaning
enlarge-frame-height	Enlarges the height of the frame in terms of the client coordinate system.
enlarge-frame-width	Enlarges the width of the frame in terms of the client coordinate system.
enlarge-window	Enlarges current window by one line.
enter-major-mode	Cleans up after previous major mode and sets up a new one.
enter-minor-mode	Turns minor modes on and off.
eolp	Returns 1 if dot is at end of line.
eot-process	Sends end-of-transmission to process.
erase-buffer	Deletes all text from current buffer.
erase-region	Deletes text between mark and dot.
error-and-exit	Forces an error and exit from a recursive edit.
error-message-format	Format compiling commands use for errors.
error-message	Raises error condition and displays message.
error-occurred	Executes MLisp expressions, catching errors.
eval-mlisp	Reads a line of mlisp from the user and evaluates it.
examine-collapsed-buffer	Displays only lines indented less than specified amount.
examine-comment-style	Sets comment style options.
examine-context-and-display	Updates the display after examining the current context.
examine-context	Sets context mode for context in which dot lies (comment/code).
examine-paragraph-style	Automatically sets left-margin and prefix-string variables.
exchange-dot-and-mark	Swaps positions of the dot and the mark.
exchange-region-with-killbuffer	Exchanges contents of region with kill buffer.
execute-defun	Executes current defun.
execute-embedded-mlisp	Execute resource named MLisp that has been embedded in a resource.

continues

11

Table 11.2. Continued

Command Name	Meaning
execute-extended-command	Calls function that is not bound to a key.
execute-keyboard-macro	Causes execution of keyboard macro.
execute-mlisp-buffer	Parses and compiles current buffer as MLisp.
execute-mlisp-line	An obsolete synonym for execute-mlisp-string.
execute-mlisp-string	Executes string as set of MLisp expressions.
execute-mlisp-word-in-buffer	Executes the MLisp function whose name lies around dot.
execute-mlisp	Executes MLisp by writing and loading current file.
execute-resource	The command execute-resource <resource-name> evaluates the contents of the given resource in the current buffer.
execute-shell-command	Executes shell command, output to buffer.
execute-string	Does characters in string as if typed on keys.
exit-edit	An obsolete synonym for exit-emacs.
exit-emacs-immediately	Exit Emacs, but query first whether unsaved buffers should be saved.
exit-emacs	Ends Emacs session.
exit-recursive-edit	Successfully exits recursive edit.
exit-transient-edit	Aborts transient edit active in current buffer.
expand-file-name	Expands file name into absolute path name.
expand-inline-file-name	Insert file name into buffer.
expand-mlisp-variable	Inserts MLisp variable name into a buffer.
expand-mlisp-word	Inserts function name into a buffer.
expert-user	Limits the display of unneeded help messages.
explode-nodes-to-scripts	Distributes all the nodes in the current info database into separate buffers.
extend-database-search-list	Adds database file at head of search list.

Command Name	Meaning
extend-to-column	Adds blanks to the line end to put dot at column.
extend-to-tab-stop	Moves dot to the next tab stop, adding white space if necessary.
fast-confirm	If fast-confirm is nonzero, acts on first character typed, otherwise waits.
fast-filter-region	Passes region as input to host OS command.
fetch-database-entry	Puts matching database entry in current buffer.
fetch-help-database-flags	Determines what help database information is placed in the buffer.
fetch-resource	Insert given resource in given buffer at dot.
file-directory-name	Returns directory name prefix of given path.
file-exists	Returns 1, 0, −1, depending on status of file.
file-is-directory	Returns 1 if given file is a directory; else 0.
file-leaf-name	Returns leaf file name of given path.
file-modtime	Returns time when file was previously modified.
file-name-arg	The command file-name-arg <argnum> <prompt> <default> returns as a string the file-name.
files-should-end-with-newline	If ON, Emacs tries to make sure files end with newline.
fill-for-context	Fills comment paragraph or code according to context.
fill-paragraph	Sets paragraph so no lines go past right margin.
fill-region	Makes region into one paragraph.
fill-to-end-of-buffer	Fills the text from dot to the end of the buffer.
fill-with-exdent	Fills current paragraph, exdenting before the dot.
filter-region-command	Displays the previous string sent as a command to the filter-region command.
filter-region	Filters a region through a UNIX command.

continues

Table 11.2. Continued

Command Name	Meaning
find-file	Edits the given file in a new buffer.
find-token	The command find-token <token> searches forward for the given token.
finish-selection	Calls the PostScript function finish-selection.
first-command-error	Goes back to the first error of a process buffer.
first-line-of	Returns the first line of a string.
fit-comment	Adjusts a comment line by prefix-argument spaces or to tab stop.
fit-frame-to-region	Resizes the current frame so it fits around the region as closely as possible.
fixed-tab-width	Sets of columns moved by tab-to-fixed-stop.
flash-close-paren	Causes pairs of open and close parentheses to blink on the screen.
flush-lines	Deletes all lines matching specified regular expression.
flush-mail	Kills the mail process and deletes the buffers.
flush-terminal-output	Sends to the terminal device the characters queued by recent calls to send-string-terminal.
focus-track-frame	If nonzero, forces window system's input focus to waiting Emacs frame.
following-char	Shows ASCII of following character.
font-dir	Holds the name of the directory in which fonts are to be found.
for-all-other-frames	Progns its arguments in all frames except the current frame.
for-each-line-in-buffer	Executes argument for each line in the buffer.
for-each-minibuffer-keymap	Executes arguments once for each minibuffer keymap.
for-each-selected-buffer	Performs action for each buffer that passes the test.

11

Command Name	Meaning
forth-mode	Provides an environment for forth programs, including interactive "forth listener."
forth	Starts an interactive forth listener.
forward-balanced-paren-line	Moves dot over parenthetical expressions.
forward-body	Moves dot to the beginning of the next body.
forward-c-function	Moves dot after the current C function definition.
forward-character	Moves dot forward one character.
forward-paragraph	Moves dot to end of current or next paragraph.
forward-paren	Moves cursor forward to first unmatched ")".
forward-sentence	Moves dot to first character of next sentence.
forward-word	Moves dot to end of current or next word.
frame-is-open	Returns 1 if the current frame is open, 0 otherwise.
frame-is-visible	Returns nonzero if the current frame is visible, zero if it is not visible.
frame-label-mode	Renamed to frame-label-editor.
frame-layout-editor	Allows editing of the current frame layout.
frame-settings-editor	Presents current frame settings for editing.
frame-to-bottom	Moves given frame underneath all other frames.
frame-to-top	Moves given frame on top of all other frames.
freeze-window	Causes the current window to become frozen.
full-emacs-version	Returns info about Emacs version as a string.
full-recursive-edit-description	Displays message in window about recursive edit. (Obsolete?)
full-stack-trace	Shows the MLisp call stack similarly to the way dump-stack-trace does, except in more detail.
function-from-arg	Defines a new function.

continues

Table 11.2. Continued

Command Name	*Meaning*
function-type	Returns the type of named function as a string.
fundamental-mode	Provides an environment for text processing.
fuzzy-search-threshold	Gives the percent similarity (as returned by simil).
gen-off	Stops generating MLisp code from keystrokes typed to the generation buffer.
generate	The generate package provides an interface for the MLisp-from-keystrokes.
get-dot-x	Returns frame column of dot as of last frame update.
get-dot-y	Returns frame row of dot as of last frame update.
get-frame-buffer	Returns name of buffer associated with current buffer.
get-frame-client-height	Returns the number of active screen lines.
get-frame-client-width	Returns the number of active screen columns.
get-frame-font-name	Returns the name of the current frame's current font.
get-frame-shape	Gets a string that can be passed to set-frame-shape to set and later restore a given frame shape.
get-function-comment	Returns the comment preceding an Emacs function.
get-icon-label	Returns a string containing the label of the current frame's icon.
get-mouse-word	Returns word around the mouse pointer.
get-selection	Returns selection around dot.
get-tty-buffer	Reads name of existing buffer from minibuffer.
get-tty-character	Returns character from terminal as integer.
get-tty-command	Reads name of Emacs command from minibuffer.
get-tty-file	Reads the name of a file from the minibuffer.

Command Name	Meaning
get-tty-key	The command get-tty-key <key> returns keystroke sequence sent.
get-tty-keys	Accepts typed keystrokes and returns a string.
get-tty-string	Prompts for a string from the terminal.
get-tty-variable	Prompts for name of declared variable.
get-tty-word	Reads a word from the tty.
get-window-layout	Returns the window layout of the current frame.
get-word-in-buffer	Returns as a string the word around or before the dot.
global-binding-of-key	Returns global binding of named function.
global-delete-lines	Deletes all lines matching specified regular expression.
global-mode-string	String referenced by "%M" in mode-line-format .
global-rebind	Replaces function bindings in global keymap.
goto-character	Moves cursor to given character position.
goto-current-indent	Moves to the first nonblank column in the line, skipping the prefix string.
goto-line	Moves the cursor to a given line.
goto-mark	Moves the dot to the given mark.
goto-marker	Makes marker visible in current window.
goto-menu-key	Moves dot to the given menu item.
goto-menu	The command goto-menu <menu-name> visits the info node that stores the given menu.
goto-named-mark	Moves the dot to the given mark.
goto-or-create-comment	Moves to comment on current line, or creates empty one if none.
goto-percent	Moves dot to the given percentage of the buffer.
goto-tag-in-buffer	Interprets word around dot as a tag and goes to that tag.

11

continues

Table 11.2. Continued

Command Name	Meaning
goto-tag	Visits file containing named function.
goto-window	Moves the cursor to the specified window.
grab-the-line	Brings back previous string as input.
graph-view	Views the contents of the buffer as coordinate pairs.
grep-function-call	Searches a set of files for references to Emacs functions.
grep-token	Searches a set of files for a given token.
grep	Searches files for pattern, returns lines.
guard-window	Causes the current window to become guarded.
hard-pathnames	If true, causes path names to be fully expanded.
help-?	Calls help within Info: ?
help-^1	Moves within a <space>.
help-Adv	Some advanced info commands: l, d, and f.
help-on-command-completion-error	If 1, lists terms to help complete command.
help-p	Moving between nodes: p and n.
help-q	Exits Info and returns to Emacs; type q for Quit.
help	Provides help in using Emacs features.
hide-selection	Undoes the effect of show-selection; makes selection look like other text.
how-to-invoke	Lists keystroke, if any, named function is bound to.
icon-dx	Gives amount to change x-coordinate of successive icons. Used by tidy-icons.
icon-dy	Gives amount to change x-coordinate of successive icons. Used by tidy-icons.
icon-x	Gives x-coordinate where icons should be placed. Used by tidy-icons.
icon-y	Gives y-coordinate where icons should be placed. Used by tidy-icons.

Command Name	Meaning
ignore-hangup	When 1, Emacs ignores HANGUP interrupt signals.
illegal-operation	Forces error; returns Emacs to user level.
in-command-context	Temporarily restores the context most recently saved by save-command-context.
in-window-manager	True if Emacs is running under a window manager.
incremental-search	Instantly searches forward for characters.
indent-line	Indents current line according to mode and context.
indent-lisp-function	Indents current defun appropriately.
indent-lisp-region	Indents current region appropriately.
indent-region	Shifts region left/right by number of spaces.
index-nodes-by-time	The command index-nodes-by-time <index-node> generates an index of nodes whose names match the given regular expression.
index-nodes-containing-re	The command index-nodes-containing-re <index-node> <re> generates an index of nodes whose names match the given regular expression.
index-nodes-matching-re	The command index-nodes-matching-re <index-node> <regexp> generates an index of nodes whose names match the given regular expression.
index-nodes-of-author	The command index-nodes-of-author <index-node> <author> generates an index of nodes whose names match the given regular expression.
info-abort-edit	Stops editing the current node, without saving any changes.
info-buffer	Holds the buffer name of the info-browser.
info-check-compile	Compiles the current node if it has been updated.
info-describe-function	Visit info node that describes the given function.

continues

11

Table 11.2. Continued

Command Name	Meaning
info-describe-variable	Visits info node that describes the given variable.
info-edit-mode	Prepares the current buffer for editing as an info node.
info-edit-recent-nodes	Displays a list of the most recently visited nodes.
info-emacs-tutorial	Invoke info, go to node (Emacs)tutorial.
info-execute-node	Executes the OnEntry action of the given node without fully visiting it.
info-get-resource	Returns the given resource as a string.
info-go-back	Goes back to the previous node in the list of visited nodes.
info-go-footnote	A node may contain links to other nodes.
info-go-here	Revisits the current node.
info-go-menu-item	The command info-go-menu-item <menu-item> visits the node associated with the given menu.
info-go-menu-path	Follows a sequence of menu choices.
info-go-named-button	Goes to the node associated with the button whose name is given.
info-go-node	The command info-go-node <nodespec> visits the given node in the active info browser.
info-go-simil	Finds menu item most similar to the given string and offers to take you there.
info-list-buffers	Visits an info node that presents the buffer list for editing.
info-list-recent-nodes	Displays a list of the most recently visited nodes.
info-mode	Sets up the current buffer to act as an info browser.
info-node-list-mode	Used for dealing with lists of nodes in info.
info-quit	Tries to restore the user's context as it was when the most recent info was called.

Command Name	Meaning
info-root-node	Gives the node component of the root (top) node.
info-toggle-author	Switches between authoring mode and browsing mode.
info-toggle-edit	Switches between editing and authoring/browsing.
info	Reads on-line Emacs documentation.
init-input-character-map	Restores the input mapping to the default mapping.
init-tab-stops	Makes tab-stops in current buffer have tabs every (abs fixed-tab-width) columns.
insert-character	Inserts ASCII value of number as character.
insert-crypted-file	Decrypts an encrypted file and inserts it into the buffer at the dot position.
insert-file	Inserts contents of named file at dot.
insert-filter	Inserts procedure to manipulate process output.
insert-or-typeout	Displays an evaluation of its arguments in a typeout window.
insert-string	Inserts string into current buffer before dot.
insert-tab	Inserts a tab character into the buffer.
int-process-leader	Sends interrupt signal to process' group leader.
int-process	Sends an interrupt signal to the active process.
interactive-shell-name	Names the shell program to be started by shell functions.
interactive-shell-options	First argument to interactive shell processes.
interactive-shell-prompt-re	Regular expression matching your interactive shell prompt.
invisible-argc	Secretly returns the number of arguments passed to Emacs.
invisible-argv	Secretly returns the Ith argument passed to Emacs.

continues

Table 11.2. Continued

Command Name	Meaning
invoke-put-entry	Invokes the "put-entry" function for this description search list.
is-bound	Returns 1 if all named variables are bound.
is-directory	An obsolete synonym for file-is-directory.
is-first-line	Returns nonzero if dot lies in the first line in the buffer.
is-function-bound	Returns 1 if function exists; 0 if not.
is-last-line	Returns nonzero if dot lies in the last line in the buffer.
is-top-window	Returns 1 if current window is topmost; else 0.
isearch-backward	Performs incremental search backward.
isearch-forward	Performs incremental search forward.
join-lines	Joins the current and next lines.
justify-line	Justifies current line to right margin.
justify-paragraph	Extends lines in paragraph to reach right margin.
keep-lines	Deletes lines not matching specified regular expression.
key-binding-editor	Prepare buffer for editing key bindings.
key-timeout-hook	Calls the function that is to do something on key timeout.
key-timeout-interval	Gives number of deciseconds allowed before the key-timeout-hook is invoked.
key-update-hook	Hook invoked when the display is updated just before reading a command.
keymap-dispatch-on-input	Reads a subsystem command and executes.
keypad-standard-bindings	Internal function that sets up default bindings for the keypad.
keys-to-string	Returns readable representation of the given keystroke sequence.
kill-boxed-region	Deletes the boxed region to the kill buffer.
kill-char	Moves next character to kill buffer.
kill-command-execution	Interrupts executing asynchronous command.

Command Name	Meaning
kill-comment-line	Deletes comment on current line.
kill-comment	Kills comment around or after dot.
kill-current-line	Deletes the current line.
kill-process-leader	Sends kill signal to leader of process' group.
kill-process	Sends kill signal to named process.
kill-rectangular-region	Deletes the rectangular region to the retangle kill buffer.
kill-region	An obsolete synonym for delete-to-killbuffer.
kill-to-beginning-of-sentence	Moves beginning of sentence to kill buffer.
kill-to-end-of-line	Deletes from dot to end of the line.
kill-to-end-of-sentence	Moves end of current sentence to kill buffer.
kill-to-pos	Delete to the position affected by command.
killring	Maintains a ring of kill buffers.
last-error-message	Returns the message associated with the last error that occurred.
last-key-struck	Returns ASCII value of last key struck.
last-shell-command	The last command executed in the current buffer by execute-shell-command.
learn	Beginner's tutorial for Emacs.
left-margin	Holds the value of left margin for text formatting.
left-offset	Offset between left edges of text and screen.
library-search-path	Default path for libraries to be loaded.
line-contains-re	Returns nonzero if the current line contains a string that matches the given regular expression.
line-to-bottom-of-window	Moves current line to bottom of window.
line-to-top-of-window	Moves current line to top of current window.
lint	Executes "make lint" and sets up error log for next-command-error.
lisp-comment-mode	Turns on mode for editing lisp comments.

continues

Table 11.2. Continued

Command Name	*Meaning*
lisp-hanging-indent	If lisp-hanging-indent is zero, the mode indents every 4 spaces.
lisp-kill-output	Erases output from last MLisp process command.
lisp-mode	Calls up elec-lisp-mode.
lisp	Starts interactive lisp process in "lisp" buffer.
list-abbrevs	Inserts a list of abbreviations into the current buffer.
list-all-bindings	List local and global bindings in a typeout window or in current buffer.
list-all-buffers	Lists data on all buffers in use.
list-all-files	Displays information in a typeout window on all buffers associated with files.
list-all-links	Lists all node links.
list-autoloaded-functions	Lists functions that will be sought in MLisp libraries when first used.
list-automode-actions	Lists currently installed automode actions and their triggering patterns.
list-buffer-names	Lists all buffer names open in this session.
list-buffers	Provides a list of all existing buffers and information about each.
list-channels	Pops up a list of all channels associated with this session.
list-database-keys	Places into buffer a list of keys in database.
list-databases	Lists all defined database search lists.
list-defuns	Displays names of MLisp functions defun'ed in current buffer.
list-fonts	Has been renamed to list-open-fonts.
list-frame-layout	Offers frame layout description in a typeout window or at dot.
list-frame-settings	Inserts a list of settings for the current frame into a buffer.
list-info-nodes	The command list-info-nodes <RE pattern> displays a list of the Info nodes in the current buffer.

11

Command Name	Meaning
list-key-bindings	Lists all keystrokes and associated functions of both global and local keymaps.
list-keymaps	Lists the defined keymaps into a buffer.
list-lines-context	Controls number of extra lines surrounding list-lines.
list-lines	Lists lines containing regular expression.
list-links-in-this-node	Generates a list of all the nodes that this node refers to.
list-loaded-libraries	Displays the libraries loaded during this session.
list-local-bindings	Lists all bindings specific to the current buffer.
list-marks	Shows a list of all marks.
list-menu-keys	Displays menu items for the current buffer and their key bindings.
list-modified-buffers	Displays information on all modified non-scratch buffers.
list-modified-files	Displays information on all modified file buffers.
list-mouse-keys	View bindings of all mouse keys on your system.
list-open-fonts	Lists open fonts.
list-options	Lists all the currently assigned variables containing the given string.
list-processes	Lists all processes.
list-special-keys	Displays a list of all special keys.
list-syntax-tables	Lists the names of all syntax tables in use.
listener-mode	Sets up current buffer to act as an eipc listener.
literal-character-mode	If true, causes all characters to be displayed, including newline and tab.
local-bind-to-key	Binds function and such to keys in current buffer.

continues

Table 11.2. Continued

Command Name	Meaning
local-binding-of-key	Returns function for locally bound key.
local-name-keyboard-macro	Names and binds local keyboard macro.
local-rebind	Replaces keys in local keymap for local buffer.
looking-at	Returns 1 if string matches text after dot.
macro-to-string	Returns the body of the given macro as a string.
mail-node-script	Sends a mail message containing the node script in info-script-buffer to the given address.
mail	Lets you read and reply to mail in Emacs.
major-code-mode	Major mode used in "code context" in current buffer.
major-comment-mode	Major mode used to edit comments in buffer.
major-mode-from-file-name	Returns the name of the major mode action that will be executed for a file or buffer.
major-mode	Major mode used in current buffer.
make-buffer-typein	Places the current buffer in typein mode.
make-buffer-unmodified	Sets buffer-is-modified to 0.
make-emacs-description-buffer	Sets up to describe word search for database access.
make-mini-window	Turns any window into a miniwindow.
make-tag-table	An obsolete synonym for tag-files.
make-typein-frame	Makes the current frame the session-wide typein frame.
makefile-mode	Sets up the current buffer for editing Makefiles.
manual-entry	Fetches UNIX manual page for given topic.
map-file-name	Generates a file name from a base name and template.
map-input-character	Maps an input character to a different character.
map-standard-key	An obsolete synonym for setq-default.

Command Name	Meaning
mark-boxed-region	Allows you to mark a boxed region.
mark-c-function-body	Marks body of C function containing or after the dot.
mark-child-menu	Has been renamed to mark-node-child-menu.
mark-comment	Establishes region around nearest comment.
mark-data	Sets dot and mark around data portion of the buffer.
mark-defun	Marks a Lisp or MLisp "defun".
mark-entire-c-function	Marks C function definition and header.
mark-insertions	If not 0, sets region around yanked text.
mark-line	Sets dot and mark around line.
mark-node-body	Marks the current node body.
mark-node-child-menu	Sets region around current node's child menu.
mark-paragraph	Places dot at beginning and mark at end of current paragraph.
mark-to-mouse	Moves the mark to the position of the mouse.
mark-whole-buffer	Marks current buffer's contents as a region.
mark-word	Sets dot and mark around word.
mark	Returns buffer and position of mark.
memory-allocation-statistics	Places memory allocation statistics into a buffer.
memory-in-use	Returns the number of memory blocks being used by this Emacs session.
menu-available-major-modes	Selects major mode for current buffer from a list of available modes.
menu-buffer-operations	Offers choice of operations on current buffer.
menu-confirm	Pops up a menu-box with yes/no options in it.
menu-edit-options	Pops up a menu with a list of classes of options that you may edit.

11

continues

Table 11.2. Continued

Command Name	Meaning
menu-elec-mlisp-mode	Pops up menu of elec-mlisp mode options.
menu-file-operations	Offers choice of operations on the current file.
menu-help	Help for people having trouble with menus.
menu-major-mode	Invokes special menu for current major mode, if there is one.
menu-normal-mode	A synonym for menu-session.
menu-session	Presents the Emacs top-level menu.
menu-subsystem	Offers the active subsystem's menu of operations.
menu-switch-to-frame	Activates the chosen frame.
menu-window-operations	Offers choice of operations on the current window.
message-for	Briefly displays a message.
message	Displays named expressions in minibuffer.
meta-digit	Supplies numeric argument to bound functions.
meta-minus	Lists number argument, flips function operation.
meta-prefix-char	ASCII value of key used as META and META-prefix.
min	Lists smallest MLisp integer expression.
mini-buffer	Returns name of the current frame's minibuffer.
minibuf-key-bind-hook	Rebinds specified keys for the local keymap in the minibuffer.
minibuf	Sets up key bindings in the minibuffer.
minus	Enables operation of meta-minus function.
mlambda	Defines a unique function.
mlisp	Starts an interactive mlisp interpreter.
mode-line-format	Format of current buffer's mode line.
mode-string	String referenced by "%m" in mode-line-format.
modified	Lists files with unsaved changes in this Emacs session.

Command Name	Meaning
modify-syntax-entry	Modifies entries in the current syntax table.
morse	The command morse <string> returns the given string as a series of beeps and boops.
mouse-change-font	Changes session font to font whose name is around mouse pointer.
mouse-delete-window	Deletes the window under the dot.
mouse-drag-cursor	Dictates cursor shape used for dragging different objects.
mouse-drag-window	Moves window up and down in relation to others in the same frame.
mouse-frame-x	Stores the current frame's last mouse x-coordinate.
mouse-frame-y	Stores the current frame's last mouse y-coordinate.
mouse-mark-region	Sets mark where button is down, drags dot until button is up.
mouse-modeline-cursor	Tells Emacs which cursor to use when mouse lies over a mode line.
mouse-prefix-string	String prepended to mouse button input.
mouse-set-collapse-column	Hides lines indented farther right than the mouse.
mouse-split-window	Splits current window at position of mouse.
mouse-text-cursor	Tells Emacs which mouse cursor to use when the mouse lies in text.
mouse-to-frame	Moves the mouse to where it was when the current frame was last current.
mouse-warp	Factor to multiply mouse movements by. Used by mouse-drag-text.
move-body	Moves the current body to a given buffer and deletes what was there.
move-child-nodes	Moves the current node's child nodes to the given nodeset.
move-dot-to-x-y	Moves cursor to x,y coordinates on the screen.
move-frame-down	Moves the current frame down one unit.

11

continues

Table 11.2. Continued

Command Name	Meaning
move-frame-left	Moves the current frame left one unit.
move-frame-right	Moves the current frame right one unit.
move-frame-up	Moves the current frame up one unit.
move-matching-bodies	Moves bodies that pass <test> to the end of a given buffer.
move-mode-line-up	Moves mode line and resizes windows. To use, drag mode line with mouse.
move-modeline-up	An obsolete synonym for move-mode-line-up.
move-node-and-children	Moves this node and all its children to the given nodeset.
move-rectangular-region	Copies a rectangle into the given buffer, deleting the original.
move-this-node	Moves the current node to the given nodeset.
move-to-column	Moves dot as close as it can to given column.
move-to-comment-column	Moves cursor to pre-set comment column.
move-to-head-of-search-list	Ensures database is at head of search list.
move-to-tab-stop	Moves to next tab stop or end of line, whichever comes first.
narrow-bounds-body	Narrows the virtual buffer bounds to enclose the body around or before dot.
narrow-bounds-c-function	Narrows region to the C function definition.
narrow-bounds-data	Narrows the bounds to enclose the data segment of the current buffer.
narrow-bounds-defun	Narrows region to include only current defun.
narrow-bounds-line	Narrows the virtual buffer bounds to the current line.
narrow-bounds-region	Narrows virtual buffers bounds, executes arguments.
narrow-region	Restricts window to current region.

Command Name	Meaning
needs-checkpointing	Tells whether a given buffer needs checkpointing.
new-undo	An obsolete synonym for undo.
newline-and-backup	Starts new line above this line.
newline-and-indent	Inserts new line indented same as previous line.
newline	Inserts a new line into the current buffer.
next-command-error	Visits site of next error in command output log.
next-comment-line	Moves to next line; executes goto-or-create-comment.
next-error	Puts dot in file on line where error occurred.
next-font	Moves to the next font listed in Emacs' list of fonts open in this session.
next-line	Moves dot to the next line.
next-page	Moves forward one page in the buffer.
next-recent-buffer	Switches to the next buffer in the recent buffer list.
next-screen-line	Moves to the next line on the screen, hopping over window boundaries.
next-terminal	Moves dot to next terminal in line.
next-window	Moves cursor to lower window and buffer.
next-word	Moves dot to the beginning of the next word in the current buffer.
no-auto-arg	Removes auto-arg bindings, turns auto-arg off.
node-list-to-menu	The command node-list-to-menu <list-buffer> inserts menu items into the current buffer at the dot.
non-blank-lines-in-buffer	Computes number of nonblank display lines buffer will consume.
non-interactive-process-icon	Contains name or index of icon used for noninteractive process frames.

11

continues

Table 11.2. Continued

Command Name	Meaning
non-interactive-shell-name	Names shell to use for noninteractive processes.
non-interactive-shell-options	First argument to noninteractive shell processes.
normal-mode	Changes current buffer to normal mode.
normalize-all-nodes	Removes redundant file specs from links to nodes in the same file.
normalize-this-node	Removes redundant nodeset names in links to nodes in the same nodeset.
nroff-mode	Environment for editing text with nroff/troff.
number-of-abbrev-tables	Returns the number of abbrev tables currently defined.
number-of-frames	Returns the number of frames that currently exist.
number-of-replacements	Returns number of occurrences replaced by the last replace-string command.
number-of-terminals	Returns the number of terminals associated with this Emacs session.
number-of-windows	Returns the number of windows currently in use.
offer-default-shell-command	Determines whether a default is offered to a shell command.
open-all-frames	Opens all frames, including the current one.
open-rectangular-region	Creates a retangle region between the mark and the dot.
option-list-editor	Called to edit a list of options.
order-child-nodes	Sets the next and previous links in the nodes.
outline-selection	A NeWS-only function that draws a black line around the current selection.
output-threshold	Controls how often output gets sent to the terminal.
overlay-top-window	Creates an overlay window of the given size.

Command Name	Meaning
overview	overview \<destination frame\> displays in the destination frame labeled stamps of all frames.
overwrite-mode	Write over characters in an existing buffer rather than inserting new ones.
page-next-window	Moves buffer in lower window ahead one page.
paint-view	Views a buffer as a description of a set of graphic objects.
panel-view	Interprets the contents of a buffer as a control panel.
paragraph-column	Column in which first line of paragraph will be placed.
paragraph-delimiters	The regular expression that defines the ends of paragraphs.
paren-flash-interval	Time spent "flashing" a matching open parenthesis.
paren-pause	Searches for matching open parenthesis.
parse-error-messages-in-region	Searches region for errors, sets up next-error.
pass-interactiveness	Passes state of caller's interactiveness to given function.
pass-mlisp-args	Passes given arguments to the given function when it is called.
pass-prefix-argument	Passes prefix arguments of calling function to given function.
path-of	Returns path of file in current directory.
pause-emacs	Temporarily goes to shell running Emacs.
pending-input	Sends 1 if unread input is pending from terminal.
peruse-buffer	Displays a buffer in typeout window.
pop-mark	Sets mark to value of top mark on mark stack.
pop-out-of-emacs	Saves modified files, pauses Emacs.

continues

11

11

Table 11.2. Continued

Command Name	Meaning
pop-to-buffer	Moves to named buffer, ties it to a new window.
pop-to-compilation-buffer	Pops up a window on the last buffer in which a compilation command was run.
pop-up-frame-dy	Amount to change the y-coordinate of successive frames by.
pop-up-frame-height	Height of pop-up-frames.
pop-up-frame-width	Width of pop-up-frames.
pop-up-frame-x	X-location of most recently created frame.
pop-up-frame-y	Y-location of most recently created frame.
pop-up-message	Displays a message so that the user will notice it, under the mouse by default.
pop-up-process-windows	If 1, starts new window for displaying messages.
pop-up-region	Displays the region in a pop-up-window so the user will notice it.
pop-up-windows	When 1, buffer commands start new windows.
pop-window-layout	Pops the window layout for this frame from stack or given buffer.
popd	Goes to the last stacked directory, pops it off the stack.
postscript-mode	Supports PostScript programmers using Emacs.
pr-newline	Sends current line to process as input.
preceding-char	Returns ASCII value of character preceding dot.
preferred-window-line	Line number where dot should be in current window.
prefix-argument-loop	Argument prefix sets number of function executions.
prefix-argument-provided	1 if current function has a numeric argument.
prefix-argument	Controls number of executions of MLisp function.

Command Name	Meaning
prefix-string-re	Regular expression version of prefix-string.
prefix-string	New line inserted when right margin is passed.
preparing-to-dump	True if Emacs has been invoked with the d option; false otherwise.
prepend-region-to-buffer	Copies region to top of buffer.
prepend-string-to-buffer	The command prepend-string-to-buffer \<buffer\> \<string\> prepends the string to the given buffer without permanently switching it.
previous-command	Shows ASCII of previous command keystroke.
previous-comment-line	Moves to previous line; executes goto-or-create-comment.
previous-line	Moves dot to the previous line.
previous-page	Moves backward one page in the buffer.
previous-screen-line	Moves up one line of the screen, skipping over window boundaries.
previous-window	Moves cursor to above window and buffer.
previous-word	Moves dot to beginning of previous word.
print-buffer	print-buffer \<buffer-name\> prints the given buffer on the default printer.
print-current-buffer	Prints the current buffer on the printer according to the primary view.
print-postscript-command	Command postscript-view buffers are piped through on the way to the printer.
print-postscript-header-file	File to prepend to any postscript printed by Emacs.
print-region	Prints the region on the default printer according to the buffers view.
print-text-command	String that directs text to a printer.
print-text-header-file	File to prepend to any text printed by Emacs.
print	Prints the value of a named variable.
printcap-mode	Sets up current buffer to edit UNIX printcap files.

continues

Table 11.2. Continued

Command Name	Meaning
process-buffer-size	Maximum size to which process' buffer can grow.
process-history-limit	Number of past commands available to history mechanism.
process-id	Returns identifier of named process.
process-leader-id	Returns process id of process group's leader.
process-output	Returns process output as a string.
process-status	Reports on status of a named process.
process-tty-editing-chars	If 1, process windows respond to tty driver characters.
progn	Executes expressions and returns value of last evaluated expression.
provide-prefix-argument	Executes the named function n times.
ps-autoload	The command ps-autoload <library> <symbolname> loads the given PS library into the display.
ps-common-directory	Names a common directory that the display server and Emacs can both access.
ps-common-file	Names a file that can be accessed by both the display server and Emacs.
ps-load	The command ps-load <library> loads the given PS library into the display server.
ps-pass-file	If nonzero, the server and Emacs will pass information via a text file.
push-back-character	Causes next character to be read from keyboard.
push-back-string	Causes string to be next characters read.
push-back-word-in-buffer	Sends current word to MLisp functions.
push-frame-settings	Pushes frame settings onto frame settings stack or specified buffer.
push-to-shell	Starts inferior shell and waits for it to finish.
push-window-layout	Pushes the window layout to stack or specified buffer.
pushd	Goes to a directory, pushing the old one onto the directory stack.

Command Name	*Meaning*
put-database-entry	Stores current buffer as database entry.
put-resource	The command put-resource <resource> <buffer> copies the contents of the current region to the given buffer.
pwd	Prints current working directory in mode line.
query-replace-string	Asks before replacing one string with another.
quick-index-nodes	Generates a node whose menu lists the nodes whose names match the given regular expression.
quick-redisplay	When 1, Emacs updates only your current window.
quietly-read-abbrev-file	Reads abbrevs from file; no errors displayed.
quit-process-leader	Sends quit signal to leader of process' group.
quit-process	Sends quit signal to named process.
quote-character	Inserts a character without interpreting it.
quote-postscript-string	Returns <string> as a postscript string constant.
raw-where-is-bound	The command raw-where-is-bound <function-name> returns the raw keystroke sequence to which the given function is bound.
raw-where-is-globally-bound	The command raw-where-is-globally-bound <function-name> returns the raw keystroke sequence to which the given function is bound.
raw-where-is-locally-bound	The command raw-where-is-locally-bound <function-name> returns the raw keystroke sequence to which the given function is bound.
re-isearch-backward	Regular expression incremental search backward.
re-isearch-forward	Regular expression incremental search (forward).
re-query-replace-string	Searches for string with regular expression.

11

continues

Table 11.2. Continued

Command Name	*Meaning*
re-replace-string	Replaces strings with regular expression characters.
re-search-forward	Searches forward for regular expression.
re-search-reverse	Searches backward for regular expression.
read-abbrev-file	Reads and defines abbrevs from named file.
read-crypted-file	The command read-crypted-file <file-name> <password> decrypts the given file into the current buffer.
read-file	Reads named file into the current buffer.
read-node-script	Reads the node script in the current buffer into the info database.
read-only-mode	Places the current buffer in the minor-mode so it only can be read.
read-only	If 1, no changes to the buffer are allowed.
recompute-all-tags	Refinds all tags in tagfile.
recursion-depth	Returns depth of nesting within recursive edit.
recursive-edit-aborted	Tells post-operatively whether a recursive edit was aborted.
recursive-edit	Edits a function during its execution.
redraw-display	Clears the screen and rewrites it.
region-around-match	Sets dot and mark around matching string.
region-size	Returns the number of characters between the dot and the mark.
region-to-process	Sends characters in region to a process.
region-to-string	Returns region as a string.
remap-minibuf	Sets up certain key bindings for each minibuffer.
remembering-keystrokes	Returns nonzero if keyboard macro is being recorded.
remote-shell-icon	Gives the index or name of icon used for frames containing remote shells.
remove-all-local-bindings	Removes all locally defined key bindings.
remove-binding	Removes global binding of keystroke sequence.

Command Name	*Meaning*
remove-database-entry	Removes an entry from the given database.
remove-from-search-list	Removes given database from search list.
remove-local-abbrev-table	Removes any local abbrev table.
remove-local-binding	Removes local binding of given key.
remove-local-map	Removes the current buffer's keymap.
rename-buffer	Changes the name of an existing buffer.
rename-current-buffer	The command rename-current-buffer <string> changes current buffer name to <string>.
rename-current-file	Changes current file name in both buffer and file system.
render-frame-image	Draws an image of the current frame in the given destination frame.
replace-case	If 1, alters case of new string to match old.
replace-obsolete-names	Replaces obsolete functions and variables with current synonyms.
replace-region-from-killbuffer	Irrevocably replaces contents of region with contents of kill buffer.
replace-string	Replaces string with another throughout file.
replaying-keyboard-macro	Returns nonzero if a keyboard macro is being played back.
reset-filter	Removes a filter bound to a process in a buffer.
resource-to-buffer	Replaces contents of given buffer with resource for this buffer.
resource-to-string	The command resource-to-string <resource> returns the body of the given buffer as a string.
restart-subsystem	Re-executes the start-program of the current buffer's subsystem.
restore-command-context	Reverts to the frame, window, and dot saved by the most recent save-command-context.
restore-frame-settings	The command restore-frame-settings [<buffer-name>] restores frame settings from stack or given buffer.

11

continues

Table 11.2. Continued

Command Name	Meaning
restore-session	Restores the session saved in the named file.
restore-window-layout	Restores the frozen/guarded state of a window.
return-prefix-argument	Sets numeric argument for next function called.
return-to-shell	Returns to a shell, suspending Emacs.
reverse-incremental-search	Instantly searches backward for characters.
revert-file	Refills buffer with new copy of associated file.
revert-to-default	Returns variable to its default setting.
review-message	Repeats last message shown.
right-margin	Sets column position of right margin.
ring-size	The command ring-size <var-exp> returns the number of values in the ring specified by <var-exp>.
rmail	Reads your mail into Emacs and provides an environment to manipulate it.
rotate-ring	rotate-ring <var-exp> <count> rotates ring <var-exp> by <count> slots.
rtext-view	Sets up the current buffer so that executing the buffer via C-x C-l will draw its formatted text in the canvas.
ruler	Displays and modifies tab and margin settings for the current buffer.
save-command-context	Notes the current frame, window, and dot as the command.
save-context	Saves the current window layout in a given layout mode.
save-crypted-file	Encrypts the current buffer to the associated filename.
save-excursion-nicely	The command save-excursion-nicely <expressions> saves the current buffer and executes its arguments, then returns to that buffer and position.

Command Name	Meaning
save-excursion	Saves buffer state, allows operations elsewhere.
save-file-info	The command save-file-info <buffer-name> generates a piece of MLisp code that describes each buffer and the file associated with it.
save-frame-layout-in-resource	Saves current frame settings in FrameSettings resource.
save-frame-settings-in-resource	Saves settings of current frame in resource named FrameSettings.
save-frame-settings	The command save-frame-settings [<buffer-name>] saves the settings for the current frame on stack or in given buffer.
save-input-redirection	Saves the currently executing string and stops execution.
save-rectangular-region	Copies the current rectangle to the rectangle kill buffer.
save-restriction	Saves current buffer's region restriction.
save-search	Save context of search, execute arguments, and restore context.
save-session	Records frame layout, non-scratch buffers, etc., about the session.
save-window-excursion	Saves states of all windows.
save-window-layout	Saves the window layout in a given buffer.
save-window	Remembers which window is current, executes its arguments, and returns to the remembered window.
score-on-exit	Displays a report of session resource usage statisics when you exit.
score	Displays a report of session resource usage statistics.
scratch-buffer-name	Returns name of new scratch buffer based on key.
scratch-file-name	Returns a unique scratch file name.

continues

Table 11.2. Continued

Command Name	Meaning
script-child-nodes	Appends the child nodes to the dbbuild script in the buffer named in info script-buffer.
scroll-left	Scrolls the view in the current window to the left by the number of columns given.
scroll-one-line-down	Moves buffer one line down through the window.
scroll-overlap	Specifies the percentage of the window that should remain visible when scrolling.
scroll-right	Scrolls the view in the current window to the right by the number of columns given.
scroll-step	The number of lines to be the page length.
scroll-text-down	Scrolls text down.
scroll-text-up	Scrolls the text, leaving the cursor on the same screen line.
search-forward	Searches forward for matching string.
search-reverse	Searches backward for string.
select-blink-fill	Tells whether selection is blinked by high-lighting or outlining.
select-blink-interval	Specifies how long selection should blink.
select-blinks	Buffer-specific; defaults to a value of 1.
select-flash-interval	Specifies, in deciseconds, how long cursor is to sit at other end of selection.
select-flashes	A global variable whose default value is 0.
select-line	Selects line that the dot is on.
select-paragraph	Selects the paragraph around or before the dot.
select-region	Selects the current region.
select-word	A synonym for mark-word.
self-insert-and-exit	Inserts the invoking character into the buffer, then exits Emacs.
self-insert	Places typed character into buffer.
send-int-signal	Sends interrupt to subprocess.

Command Name	Meaning
send-mail	Lets you send mail from within Emacs.
send-quit-signal	Sends QUIT signal to subprocess.
send-string-to-terminal	Sends string argument to terminal.
sending-process	Gives name of invoking process to process filter.
sense-comment-context	Returns the name of the mode appropriate to the context in which the dot lies.
sense-dot-in-comment	Returns 1 if the dot is within a comment block.
sentence-delimiters	Defines the ends of sentences.
session-attach-hook	Invoked when a display is first attached to a session.
session-detach-hook	Invoked when the session is detached from a display.
session-entry-hook	User-defined.
session-exit-hook	Invokes some defined MLisp function upon exiting the Emacs session.
session-program-name	Returns name of program with which session started.
set-attach-hook	Installs hook function to be invoked when session is attached to a display.
set-auto-fill-hook	Associates specific command with buffer.
set-begin-fill-hook	The internal function set-begin-fill-hook <function-name> sets the current buffer's begin-fill-hook variable to the name of the given function.
set-buffer-apropos-hook	Sets function used for each buffer-apropos match.
set-buffer-creation-hook	Sets up the hook to be invoked just before a new buffer is created.
set-buffer-deletion-hook	Sets up the hook to be invoked just before a new buffer is deleted.
set-buffer-frame-label	Sets the label of the buffer's primary frame.
set-buffer-icon-image	Sets the icon image for the current buffer.

continues

Table 11.2. Continued

Command Name	Meaning
set-channel-input-mode	Specifies how a channel treats its Emacs input.
set-checkpoint-hook	Installs a function that is executed upon every checkpoint.
set-command-read-hook	Installs function to invoke just before reading keyboard command character.
set-comment-column	Sets comment column to prefix-arg or current column.
set-comment-delimiters	Sets comment delimiters to argument strings.
set-comment-markers	Sets the variables comment-begin-marker and comment-end-marker.
set-comment-style	Infers comment style from nearby example.
set-confirm-hook	Sets a function to be invoked before a user is asked to confirm an action.
set-default-frame-class	Arranges that all frames created after invoking will be of a given PS class.
set-default-frame-font-name	Sets the default font to be used in any frames created after this one.
set-default-frame-mapped	Tells whether any frames started up after this will be visible or not.
set-default	Sets default value for variable.
set-description-search-list	Changes to named description search list.
set-detach-hook	Installs a hook function that is invoked when the session is detached from a display.
set-eipc-filter	Installs a function to handle output from unexpected processes.
set-eipc-sentinel	Installs a function to handle output from unexpected processes.
set-enter-emacs-hook	Calls function if starting Emacs/recursive edit.
set-error-message-format	Sets the error-message-format variable.
set-exit-emacs-hook	Calls function if exiting Emacs/recursive edit.
set-font-fixed-pitch	Defines font as fixed-pitch or non-fixed-pitch.

11

Command Name	Meaning
set-frame-buffer	The command set-frame-buffer <buffer-name> associates the given buffer with the current frame.
set-frame-font-name	Sets font for the current frame.
set-frame-type	Defines the current frame as either a text (0) or graphic (1) frame.
set-function-apropos-hook	Sets a function to be invoked every time the user requests infomation about a function.
set-help-key	The help key gets help on whatever sub-system is active.
set-help-typeout-hook	Invokes function when help output is generated.
set-incomplete-hook	Obsolete.
set-indent-hook	Sets @indent-hook to named function.
set-key-timeout-hook	Sets a function to be invoked every time a user doesn't do anything for the number of deciseconds specified in the key-timeout-interval.
set-keymap-hook	Sets a function to be invoked whenever the current local keymap is triggered.
set-left-offset	Specifies the offset between the left edge of the text and the left edge of the screen.
set-mark	Sets mark at dot within the buffer.
set-mini-string	Allows the user to set the mini-string.
set-minibuf-entry-hook	Installs a function to be executed upon entry to a minibuffer.
set-mode-menu	Installs a menu as the "Major Mode" submenu.
set-morse-speed	Sets speed at which morse code transmits in words per minute.
set-mouse-drag-hook	Sets a function to be invoked each time the mouse is clicked, then dragged.
set-named-mark	Allows you to place markers in a buffer so that you can refer to them by name.
set-paragraph-delimiters	Sets the paragraph delimiting sequences.

11

continues

Table 11.2. Continued

Command Name	Meaning
set-paragraph-style	Sets paragraph style options according to current paragraph.
set-prefix-string	Sets prefix-string and prefix-string-re variables.
set-primary-frame-label	Has been renamed to set-buffer-frame-label.
set-primary-icon-image	Has been renamed to set-buffer-icon-image.
set-process-filter	Installs the given function as a process filter.
set-process-sentinel	Installs function as a process sentinel.
set-screen-columns	Sets the number of screen columns Emacs will use.
set-screen-lines	Sets the number of screen lines Emacs will use.
set-single-step-hook	Sets a function to be invoked in the debugger when single-step is turned on.
set-variable-apropos-hook	Sets a function to be invoked each time the user requests an apropos list.
set-visit-file-hook	Sets a function to be invoked each time a file is written.
set-window-flags	Allows setting and clearing of window flags.
set-window-height	Changes the height of the current text window to the given number of lines.
set-window-layout	Configures the windows in the current text frame according to the given string.
set-window-min-height	Sets the minimum height allowable for a window.
set-window-popup-hook	Sets the window popup hook.
set	Changes value of Emacs variable.
setq-default	Sets default value of a variable.
setq-option-default	Behaves exactly like setq-default, except that the setting is made only if the variable is not already bound.
setq	Assigns new value to variable in MLisp function.
shell-cd-follows	If nonzero, cd's within shell windows change Emacs' working directory.

Command Name	*Meaning*
shell-command-use-temp-file	Puts shell command output in temp file instead of buffer.
shell-goto-current-indent	The noninteractive function shell-goto-current-indent will place dot just after the shell prompt.
shell-hook	Defined by user, invoked by shell command.
shell-icon	Specifies icon for frames whose primary buffers are shells.
shell-prompt-template	Sets the template for the prompt used in shell buffers.
shell-set-environment-command	Accepts the name of an environment variable and a string to which it should be set.
shell-uses-new-line-discipline	Returns nonzero if shell requires new line discipline.
shell-uses-setenv	Returns a nonzero value if the given shell uses the setenv command to set the environment.
shift-comment-left	Moves the current comment line left by prefix-arg spaces.
shift-comment-right	Moves the current comment line right by prefix-arg spaces.
show-error	Puts dot at point in file where error occurred.
show-function-in-error	Makes error messages show calling function name.
show-line-number-in-mode-line	If 1, %L in mode line expands to line number.
show-paragraph-style-options	Shows values of paragraph style-related variables.
show-selection	Highlights current selection.
show-time-in-mode-line	If 1, %T in mode line expands to current time.
shrink-frame-height	Shrinks the height of the frame in terms of the client coordinate system.
shrink-frame-width	Shrinks the width of the frame in terms of the client coordinate system.

11

continues

Table 11.2. Continued

Command Name	*Meaning*
shrink-window	Shrinks the current window by one line.
signal-to-process-leader	Sends the given signal to the leader of the given process' group.
signal-to-process	Sends the given signal to a process.
silently-kill-processes	Kills subprocesses without questioning on exit.
simil	The command simil <string-1> <string-2> computes the similarity between the two strings.
simulate-keyboard-input	Stuffs a string into the current terminal exactly as if it was typed there.
simulate-minibuf-input	Allows you to specify string for minibuffer input.
single-frame-terminal	Stuffs the given string into the current terminal exactly as if it had been typed by the user.
single-step-handler	Used by MLisp debugging functions.
single-step	If 1, functions execute one step at a time.
sit-for	Updates display and pauses for n/10 seconds.
skip-blanks-backward	Moves dot back past spaces and tabs preceding it.
skip-blanks-forward	Moves dot ahead past spaces and tabs following it.
sleep-for	Makes Emacs not update screen for n seconds.
slide-to-column	Inserts white space to move dot to given column.
slide-to-tab-stop	Inserts white space so dot lies at the next tab stop on the current line.
smail	Allows you to send electronic mail.
span-string-forward	Moves the dot as long as it is adjacent to one of the given characters in the string argument.

Command Name	*Meaning*
span-string-reverse	Moves the dot backwards as long as it is adjacent to one of the characters within the set.
spell	Scans the current buffer for spelling errors.
split-current-window	Splits window into two smaller windows.
split-height-threshhold	An obsolete synonym for split-height-threshold.
split-height-threshold	Size of smallest window that can be split.
split-to-buffer	Pops up a new window of the current buffer prefix-argument lines high.
split-window-nicely	Splits current window without redrawing it.
srccom	An obsolete synonym for compare-windows.
stack-limit	Maximum number of recursions MLisp permits.
stack-trace-on-error	If 1, dumps MLisp stack into buffer on error.
start-editor-window	Starts an editor window on the given buffer and executes its body arguments.
start-filtered-process	Starts filter, output to buffer, calls function.
start-generating-mlisp	Starts generating MLisp code from keystrokes.
start-interactive-lisp	Starts interactive "lisp listener" in buffer.
start-interactive-program	Runs the given program in an interactive process.
start-interactive-shell	Starts interactive shell in given buffer.
start-process	Uses home shell to start a named process.
start-selection	Sets the mouse to begin selecting a region starting at the current point.
start-sync-process	Executes synchronous shell command, output in buffer.
startup-hook	Executes commands upon starting Emacs session.
stats-on-exit	If nonzero, causes statistics to be displayed upon session exit.
std-key	Internal to keypad-standard-bindings.

11

continues

Table 11.2. Continued

Command Name	Meaning
step-through	Sets up single-step handler for MLisp function.
stick-frame-on-top-of-this-one	Reshapes the given frame so that it sits above the current frame.
stop-generating-mlisp	Stops generating MLisp code from keystrokes.
stop-process-leader	Halts the leader of an active process' group.
stop-process	Pauses a process.
stop-remembering	Ends the definition of the keyboard macro.
string-contains-re	Returns nonzero if string contains match for regular expression.
string-search	Looks for a given string.
string-to-buffer	Replaces given buffer with given string.
string-to-char	Returns integer value of first char in string.
string-to-field	Sets the contents of the given field to the given string.
string-to-process	Sends a string to a process.
string-to-re	Returns a regular expression that matches the argument string.
string-to-resource	Places the given string into the given buffer.
strip-paragraph	Removes prefix strings from a paragraph.
strip-prefix-from-region	Strips prefix string from each line in region.
subarray	Creates and returns an array that is a subrange of the given array.
subsys-again	Reads the next character and processes it.
subsys-default	Bound to all "ordinary" keys.
subsys-end	Terminates the currently active dynamic subsystem.
subsys-get-response	Returns as a string the next keystrokes typed using the current local keymap.
swapd	Swaps two directories on the stack.
switch-context	Toggles between application subsystem and editor subsystem.

Command Name	Meaning
switch-to-buffer-menu	Pops up a menu containing a list of all buffers.
switch-to-buffer	Associates named buffer with current window.
switch-to-file	An obsolete synonym for visit-in-this-window.
synonym-function	Declares new name for an existing function.
synonym-variable	Declares new name for an existing variable.
sys_4.1bsd	Is true if Emacs is being run under 4.1bsd UNIX, otherwise false.
sys_macintosh	Is true if Emacs is running on a Macintosh, otherwise false.
sys_sysiii	Is true if Emacs is being run under system III UNIX, otherwise false.
sys_unisoft	Is true if Emacs is being run under the Unisoft operating system.
sys_v7	Is true if Emacs is being run under system 7 UNIX, otherwise false.
sys_vms	Is true if Emacs is being run on a VMS system, otherwise false.
system-name	Returns name of the system running Emacs.
tab-class	Causes any frames started up hereafter to be "TabEmacsWindow".
tab-size	An obsolete synonym for displayed-tab-size.
tab-stops-template	Returns as a string a tab stops template with tabs every n columns.
tab-to-fixed-stop	Moves to the next tab column.
tab-to-tab-stop	Inserts blanks to move dot to next tab column.
tab	Slides text after dot to next tab stop by inserting white space.
tabs-use-only-spaces	If 1, tab uses spaces, not tabs (actually affects slide-to-col primitive).
tag-current-file	Recomputes the tag pointers for the current file.

continues

Table 11.2. Continued

Command Name	Meaning
tag-file	The command tag-file <file> adds a slot in the file's entry in the current tag table for all taggable locii in the given file.
tag-files	Builds tagfile for all functions in named files.
tag-regexp	Can be set to a regular expression that matches lines to be tagged.
talk-answer-automatically	If nonzero, incoming calls will be answered.
talk-defer-display	If nonzero, makes talk windows appear only after callee answers.
talk-log-conversations	If nonzero, causes talk session to be recorded in a file.
talk-log-directory	Directory in which talk session logs are stored.
talk-split-windows	If nonzero, talk sessions have two windows each; otherwise they get only one.
temp-use-buffer	Switches to named buffer; no new windows.
temp-use-file	Temporarily switches to a buffer visiting the given file.
termcap-mode	Sets up current buffer to edit termcap entries.
terminal-device	Returns the name of the device that Emacs is using to control your terminal.
terminal-driver-name	Returns the name of the terminal driver module Emacs is using to control the current terminal.
terminal-is-slow	Nonzero if terminal is using slow baud rate.
terminal-type	Returns the terminal type as a string.
terminal-width	Contains the set width of the terminal screen connected to Emacs.
test-abbrev-expand	Tests, returns string/numeric values of abbrev.
test-comment-style	For debugging do-inside-comment.
text-mode-icon	Gives name or index of icon for frames whose primary buffer is in text mode.

11

11

Command Name	Meaning
text-mode	Implements an environment for standard text applications.
this-command	Associates its integer value with a function.
tidy-frames	Moves all the frames to nice positions.
tidy-icons	Moves all the icons to nice positions.
tip	Opens an interactive command listener (shell window) on a remote host by connecting to it via the UNIX command "tip."
to-col	An obsolete synonym for slide-to-column.
toggle-application-subsystem	Switches between the buffer's application subsystem and the editor subsystem.
toggle-cursor	Turns the text cursor on and off.
toggle-mode-line	Turns the current window's mode line on and off.
toggle-typein-frame	Installs/uninstalls global typein frame at top of screen.
top-mini-window	Moves the miniwindow to the top of this frame.
top-window	Moves cursor to top window on screen.
track-eol-on-^N-^P	If 1, cursor stays at end of line while moving.
transient-edit-recursive	If nonzero, transient edits enter a recursive edit.
transient-pop-up-frame	If nonzero, transient edits get their own frames.
transpose-line	Switches current line with line above.
transpose-windows	Swaps the current window with the next window.
transpose-word	Switches current word with previous one.
troff-mode	Environment for editing text with nroff/troff.
tty-mode-rare	Allows (or not) C-g keyboard interrupt.
tty-name	Returns full path name of terminal device as string.
typeout-end-prompt	String, mode line for typeout window bottom.

continues

Table 11.2. Continued

Command Name	Meaning
typeout-max-size	Maximum possible height of transient window.
typeout-more-prompt	String, mode line for larger typeout buffer.
typeout-pop-up-frame	If nonzero, transient browser windows get their own frames.
typeout-text	Concatenates its arguments and displays them in a typeout window in a scratch buffer.
umask-for-checkpoints	An obsolete synonym for checkpoint-permissions.
undo-boundary	Separates commands that may be undone later.
undo-last	Reverses the effects of the last buffer-modifying command.
undo-more	Undoes command effects after invoking undo-last.
undo	Removes the effects of previous commands.
unfreeze-all-windows	Unfreezes all windows on screen.
unkill	Restore last deleted text.
unlink-checkpoint-files	If 1, checkpoint file unlinked when saving file.
update-buffer-frame	Updates the given buffer's primary frame.
update-dot-x-y	Recomputes the values returned by get-dot-x and get-dot-y to make sure the dot is in the right place.
update-frame	The command update-frame <frame> updates the specified frame in the same manner as does update-current-frame.
update-primary-frame	Has been renamed to update-buffer-frame.
use-abbrev-table	Sets local abbrev table to the given name.
use-async-processes	Enables/disables asynchronous process use.
use-default-menu-style	If 1, force use of default menu style over system menu interface.
use-file	Ensures that the current buffer is associated with the given file.

Command Name	Meaning
use-global-map	Uses named keymap as global keymap.
use-ins/del-line/char	Tells whether to insert/delete lines and characters or just redraw the line.
use-local-map	Associates given keymap with current buffer.
use-memory-file	If 1, saves visible files' names on exit.
use-named-mark	Uses the named mark as the mark for the current buffer.
use-old-buffer	Associates existing buffer with current window.
use-placard-window	Placard window—a "permanent" window at top of screen.
use-scratch-buffer	Executes arguments in unique, empty scratch buffer.
use-spaces-in-to-col	An obsolete synonym for tabs-use-only-spaces.
use-syntax-table	Associates syntax table with current buffer.
use-transient-window	Opens a transient window on the given buffer.
use-typeout-window	Puts output from arguments in transient window.
users-full-name	Returns user's full name as a string.
users-id	Returns user's numeric uid, as in /etc/passwd.
users-login-name	Returns the user's login name as a string.
variable-apropos	Runs apropos on variables only.
visible-bell	When 1, replaces audible bell with screen flash.
visit-crypted-file	The command visit-crypted-file <file-name> <password> visits an encrypted file.
visit-file-hook	Default visit-file hook. Called every time visit-file is invoked.
visit-function	Recursively edits function definition.
visit-in-other-frame	Pops up a new frame and visits the given file in a window.

continues

11

Table 11.2. Continued

Command Name	Meaning
visit-in-other-window-in-this-frame	Takes over a window in the current frame or creates a new window in it.
visit-in-other-window	Pops up a new window and visits the given file in it.
visit-in-this-frame	Visits the given file in some window in the current frame.
visit-in-this-window	Places named file in current window.
visit-tag-table	Allows use of tagfile named other than ".tags".
watch-during-replace-string	If 1, display updated after each string replaced.
where-is-bound	Returns raw keystroke sequence bound to function.
where-is-globally-bound	Shows raw keystroke sequence globally bound to function.
where-is-locally-bound	Shows raw keystroke sequence locally bound to function.
while	Executes expressions while test-clause is true.
whist	Generates a log entry under the history section in a header.
widen-region	Removes region restriction from current window.
window-bottom-to-line	Resizes the current window so that the mode line lies on the line given.
window-edit-mode	Binds C-n and C-p so they move between windows, and C-o and C-k.
window-height	Lists number of visible text lines in window.
window-line-widths	Returns a string describing the line widths in the current window.
window-popup-hook	Hook invoked when a new window is created.
window-width	Returns number of columns in current window.
window	Window manipulation with a minimum of screen repainting.

Command Name	Meaning
windows-mode-line	Returns the screen line on which the mode line of the current window lies.
with-all-nodes	Progns its args on each node in the current info database.
with-each-body	The command with-each-body <args> evaluates args in each of the bodies in the current buffer.
with-each-child-node	Evaluates its arguments with the contents of each child node in turn in the current buffer.
with-each-leaf-node	Evaluates its arguments in each leaf node in the tree below the current node.
with-each-tree-node	The command with-each-tree-node <enter> <exit> recursively descends, depth- first, the tree rooted at the current node.
with-editor-command-keymap	Executes its arguments in the appropriate keymap.
with-editor-typein-keymap	The commands with-editor-typein-keymap and with-editor-command-keymap execute their arguments with the editor keymap.
with-global-map	Temporarily makes a map the global map and does something with it.
with-local-map	The command with-local-map <keymapname> temporarily makes the keymap given by the local keymap.
with-matching-bodies	The command with-matching-bodies <test> <args> evaluates args in each of the nodes in which the test returns zero.
with-meta-keymap	Creates a local copy of the META keymap for the current keymap and does something.
with-node	The command with-node <node> <args> evaluates its args while editing the given node, creating it if necessary.
with-region-full-lines	Moves dot and mark so that they enclose entire lines, then does something that frees the region.

11

continues

Table 11.2. Continued

Command Name	Meaning
with-this-body	The command with-this-body <args> evaluates its args with virtual buffer bounds narrowed.
with-this-node	Evaluates its arguments with the current node in edit-mode.
with-update-inhibited	Progns its arguments while the current frame is inhibited from updating itself.
word-delimiter	Defines what ends all words.
working-directory	Returns path name of current working directory.
wrap-long-lines	Toggles whether or not lines that are too long are continued on the next line.
write-abbrev-file	Writes all defined abbreviations into file.
write-crypted-file	Writes an encrypted buffer into named file.
write-file-exit	Writes modified buffers to files, exits Emacs.
write-modified-files	Writes modified buffers into associated files.
write-named-file	Writes contents of current buffer into file.
write-some-modified-files	Writes each modified file buffer to its associated file as directed.
writeregion	The writeregion package implements only one function, write-region-to-file.
xon/xoff-flow-control	If 1, C-s and C-q treated as flow controls, ignored.
yank-buffer	Inserts named buffer into current one at dot.
yank-from-killbuffer	Inserts contents of kill buffer at dot.
yank-rectangular-region	Yanks the last rectangle from the rectangle kill buffer.
zoom-current-window	Enlarges the current window to fill the screen.

Table 11.3 shows the variables found in the distribution version of the current UniPress Emacs. You can get the descriptions shown in the table plus much more by typing ESC x help d and then entering the name of the variable. Or, if you don't know the full name, type ESC x help a and enter a partial string—UniPress then gives you all commands and variables in that string.

11

Table 11.3. UniPress Emacs Variables

Variable	Meaning
auto-fill-mode	Is on if nonzero.
buffer-deletion-hook	Contains name of the function called when a buffer is deleted.
buffer-frame	Gives index of frame associated with this buffer.
command-read-hook	Contains name of buffer-specific command-read-hook.
context-sensor	Contains the buffer-specific name of the function that senses context.
editor-abort-action	Names function to be bound to abort key when editor is active.
editor-browse-action	Gives buffer-specific name of function that prepares current buffer for browsing.
editor-class-name	Names the type of object that is being edited.
editor-client-frame	Names the frame associated with this editor buffer.
editor-client-window-layout	Holds output of get-window-layout.
editor-description	Gives rough description of the current buffer's current editor subsystem.
editor-exit-description	Is set by a subsystem to describe what happens when they exit.
editor-fetch-action	Names function that puts an object for the editor in the current buffer.
editor-is-browsing	Is nonzero if current editor is browsing.
editor-object-description	Describes the object currently being edited.
editor-object-name	Names the object that is currently being edited.
editor-save-action	Names the save function for this editor.

continues

11

Table 11.3. Continued

Variable	Meaning
editor-save-description	Describes what happens when the editor-save-action is invoked.
editor-saved-keymap	Saves keymap that was current when the editor subsystem was invoked.
editor-saved-mode-line	Stores mode line that was current when editor was started.
editor-was-browsing	Is nonzero if this transient window was started as a browser.
error-hook	Contains name of the function to be invoked when an error is detected.
fill-code-action	Contains name of the function to be called when dot lies in code.
fill-comment-action	Contains name of function that knows how to justify comments.
frame-label	Contains the string displayed somewhere around the edge of each frame.
frame-label-mode	Is on if nonzero.
icon-image	Contains the name of the icon associated with this buffer.
indent-hook	Holds function to be executed when indenting.
info-activate-nodes	Tells whether to run certain resources upon first entering a node.
info-authoring	If nonzero, script nodes won't be executed and resources won't be signalled.
info-editing	Is nonzero while editing a node, zero otherwise.
info-frame	Contains the index of the frame in which the current browser was started.
info-last	Gives name of the last node visited.
info-last-how	Gives the relationship of the node last accessed to this one.
info-next	Info-mode variable that stores the name of the next node in the list.
info-previous	Info-mode variable that gives the name of the previous node in current list.

Variable	*Meaning*
info-up	Contains the name of the node above the one in the current tour.
info-was-authoring	Is nonzero if info-authoring was true when the current node was last placed in the editing mode.
key-timeout-hook	Contains name of buffer-specific key-timeout-hook.
key-update-hook	Gives name of buffer-specific key-update-hook.
mark-body-hook	Gives name of current buffer's mark-body-hook.
pop-up-client-buffer	Contains name of buffer that was current when this was created.
pop-up-client-frame	Gives the name of the frame that was current when this was created.
resource-page-marker	Is set to the location of the beginning of the resource page.
subsys-start-program	Gives name of a function that restores current buffer's subsystem.
visit-file-hook	Gives name of current buffer's visit-file-hook.

11

Epsilon Reference

E psilon is an advanced programmer's editor that has a standard Emacs set of commands. It features extreme customizability and concurrent executions of most programs with input and output captured in a window. Epsilon has automatic, programmable C language indentation (checking). It also has multilevel undo with full redo. There are no built-in limits on the number of files or windows, and you can edit files larger than available memory using EMS or automatic disk paging. Epsilon is available for DOS, SCO UNIX or XENIX, interactive 386/ix UNIX, and OS/2.

Keys

All versions of Emacs can be infinitely customized. We can't just give you a list of key combinations and be sure they are always the same, because many different people could have modified your version of Emacs. You probably will want to rearrange the keys to suit your own needs and preferences. Use Table 12.1, however, as a starting point. The table lists the initial bindings in the current version of Epsilon. You can generate a similar list on your own system at any time by typing:

```
Esc x wall-chart
```

The following table lists the Epsilon commands and their key bindings. With our conventions, C-x would mean to hold down the CONTROL key and press the x key. When typing ALT-&, press the ALTERNATE (META) key and, because the ampersand (&) key is a shifted key, let up and press the SHIFT and the & key together.

Table 12.1. Epsilon Emacs Global Commands and Their Key Bindings

Key Binding	Command
C-@	set-mark
C-a	beginning-of-line
C-b	backward-character
C-c	stop-process
C-d	delete-character
C-e	end-of-line
C-f	forward-character
C-g	abort
C-h	backward-delete-character
C-i	indent-previous
C-j	maybe-break-line
C-k	kill-line
C-l	center-window
C-m	enter-key
C-n	down-line
C-o	open-line
C-p	up-line
C-q	quoted-insert
C-r	reverse-incremental-search
C-s	incremental-search
C-t	transpose-characters
C-u	argument
C-v	next-page
C-w	kill-region
C-y	yank
C-z	scroll-up
C-[	alt-prefix
C-^	ctrl-prefix

12

Key Binding	Command
C-_	help
\<space\>	maybe-break-line
! to ~	normal-character
C-?	backward-delete-character
C-a-b	backward-level
C-a-f	forward-level
C-a-h	backward-kill-word
C-a-i	indent-under
C-a-k	kill-level
C-a-r	reverse-regex-search
C-a-s	regex-search
C-a-w	append-next-kill
C-a-\	indent-region
C-a-^	ctrl-prefix
ALT-%	query-replace
ALT-&	replace-string
ALT-)	find-delimiter
ALT-*	regex-replace
ALT-,	beginning-of-window
ALT-–	argument
ALT-.	end-of-window
ALT-0 to ALT-9	argument
ALT-<	goto-beginning
ALT->	goto-end
ALT-?	help
ALT-@	set-mark
ALT-a to ALT-z	case-indirect
ALT-[	backward-paragraph
ALT-\	delete-horizontal-space
ALT-]	forward-paragraph
ALT-a	backward-sentence
ALT-b	backward-word
ALT-c	capitalize-word

continues

Table 12.1. Continued

Key Binding	Command
ALT-d	kill-word
ALT-e	forward-sentence
ALT-f	forward-word
ALT-h	mark-paragraph
ALT-k	kill-sentence
ALT-l	lowercase-word
ALT-m	to-indentation
ALT-q	fill-paragraph
ALT-s	center-line
ALT-t	transpose-words
ALT-u	uppercase-word
ALT-v	previous-page
ALT-w	copy-region
ALT-x	named-command
ALT-y	yank-pop
ALT-z	scroll-down
ALT-{	scroll-left
ALT-}	scroll-right
ALT-~	change-modified
F1	help
F2	named-command
F3	load-bytes
F4	bind-to-key
F5	where-is
F6	what-is
F7	cd
F8	set-variable
F9	undo
F10	redo
C-F2	compare-windows
C-F3	write-state
C-F4	last-kbd-macro
C-F5	next-video

Key Binding	Command
C-F6	set-show-graphic
C-F7	copy-to-file
C-F8	show-variable
C-F9	undo-changes
C-F10	redo-changes
Alt-F5	set-video
C-l	center-window
C-m	enter-key
INS	overwrite-mode
END	end-of-window
DOWN	down-line
PGDN	next-page
LEFT	backward-character
RIGHT	forward-character
HOME	beginning-of-window
UP	up-line
PGUP	previous-page
DEL	delete-character
C-END	goto-end
C-DOWN	forward-sentence
C-PGDN	shrink-window
C-LEFT	backward-word
C-RIGHT	forward-word
C-HOME	goto-beginning
C-UP	backward-sentence
C-PGUP	enlarge-window
ALT-n--	argument
ALT-n-*	regex-replace
ALT-n-b	backward-kill-word
ALT-END	next-window
ALT-DOWN	forward-paragraph
ALT-PGDN	shrink-window-horizontally

12

continues

Table 12.1. Continued

Key Binding	Command
ALT-LEFT	beginning-of-line
ALT-RIGHT	end-of-line
ALT-HOME	previous-window
ALT-UP	backward-paragraph
ALT-PGUP	enlarge-window-horizontally
ALT-DEL	backward-kill-level
C-x C-b	bufed
C-x C-c	exit
C-x C-d	kill-window
C-x C-e	push
C-x C-f	find-file
C-x C-i	indent-rigidly
C-x C-m	start-process
C-x C-n	next-error
C-x C-o	delete-blank-lines
C-x C-r	redo-changes
C-x C-s	save-file
C-x C-t	transpose-lines
C-x C-u	undo-changes
C-x C-v	visit-file
C-x C-w	write-file
C-x C-x	exchange-point-and-mark
C-x C-z	exit-level
C-x C-[	alt-prefix
C-x C-^	ctrl-prefix
C-x (	start-kbd-macro
C-x)	end-kbd-macro
C-x ,	pluck-tag
C-x .	goto-tag
C-x 0	kill-window
C-x 1	one-window

Key Binding	Command
C-x 2	split-window
C-x 5	split-window-vertically
C-x =	show-point
C-x @	enlarge-window-horizontally
C-x a to C-x z	case-indirect
C-x ^	enlarge-window
C-x b	select-buffer
C-x c	compare-windows
C-x d	dired
C-x e	last-kbd-macro
C-x f	set-fill-column
C-x g	goto-line
C-x i	insert-file
C-x k	kill-buffer
C-x l	count-lines
C-x m	make
C-x n	next-window
C-x o	next-window
C-x p	previous-window
C-x r	redo
C-x s	save-all-buffers
C-x u	undo
C-x w	write-region
C-x C-ALT-i	tabify-region
C-x C-ALT-^	ctrl-prefix
C-x ALT-,	select-tag-file
C-x ALT-.	tag-files
C-x ALT-a to C-x ALT-z	case-indirect
C-x ALT-i	untabify region
C-x ALT-n	name-kbd-macro

12

Commands and Variables

Table 12.2 lists the commands and variables present in the current distribution version of Epsilon. You can, of course, customize the editor as much as you want, thanks to Epsilon's customization facilities and its built-in EEL programming language.

Table 12.2. Epsilon Emacs Commands

Command/Variable Name	Meaning
abort	Abort the command currently executing.
alt-prefix	Do the next key as an ALT key.
append-next-kill	Don't discard the kill buffer.
apropos	List commands dealing with a topic.
argument	Set argument or multiply it by four.
auto-fill-mode	Toggle automatic line breaking.
backward-character	Move point back.
backward-delete-character	Delete before point.
backward-kill-level	Kill a bracketed expression backward.
backward-kill-word	Kill the word before point.
backward-level	Move point before a bracketed expression.
backward-paragraph	Go back one paragraph.
backward-sentence	Go back one sentence.
backward-word	Go back one word.
beginning-of-linc	Go to the start of the line.
beginning-of-window	Go to the upper left corner.
bind-to-key	Put a named command on a key.
bufed	Manipulate a list of buffers.
c-mode	Do automatic indentation for C-like languages.
capitalize-word	Uppercase first character.
case-indirect	Do the reverse-case binding of the invoking key.
cd	Change the current directory.
center-line	Center line horizontally.
center-window	Vertically center the current window.

Command/Variable Name	Meaning
change-modified	Change the modified status of the buffer.
change-name	Change the name of a command, variable, and so on.
clear-tags	Forget all the tags in the current tag file.
compare-windows	Find next difference between current and next windows.
copy-rectangle	Copy the current rectangle to a kill buffer.
copy-region	Copy the region to a kill buffer.
copy-to-file	Copy buffer contents to a file.
count-lines	Show the number of lines in the buffer.
create-prefix-command	Define a new prefix key.
create-variable	Define a new EEL variable.
ctrl-prefix	Do the next key as a CONTROL key.
delete-blank-lines	Remove blank lines around point.
delete-character	Delete the character after point.
delete-horizontal-space	Delete white space near point.
delete-name	Delete a command, variable, and so on.
delete-rectangle	Delete the characters in the current rectangle.
describe-command	Give help on the named command.
describe-key	Give help for the command on a key.
diff	List differences between current and next windows.
dired	Edit the contents of a directory.
do-c-indent	Tabbing command in C mode.
down-line	Move point to the next line.
end-kbd-macro	Stop defining a keyboard macro.
end-of-line	Go to the end of the line.
cnd-of-window	Go to last character in window.
enlarge-window	Current window enlarges by one line.
enlarge-window-horizontally	Enlarge window by one column.
enter-key	Insert a newline character.

continues

Table 12.2. Continued

Command/Variable Name	Meaning
exchange-point-and-mark	Swap point and mark.
exit	Exit the editor.
exit-level	Exit the current recursive edit.
fill-paragraph	Fill the current paragraph.
fill-region	Fill the current region.
find-delimiter	Show the matching left delimiter.
find-file	Put a file in the current window.
forward-character	Go forward one character.
forward-level	Move point past a bracketed expression.
forward-paragraph	Go to the next paragraph.
forward-sentence	Go to the end of the sentence.
forward-word	Move past the next word.
fundamental-mode	Turn off any special key definitions.
goto-beginning	Go to the beginning of the buffer.
goto-end	Go to the end of the buffer.
goto-line	Go to a certain line by number.
goto-tag	Ask for the name of a command, then go there.
help	Get documentation on commands.
incremental-search	Search for a string as you type it.
indent-previous	Indent based on the previous line.
indent-region	Indent from point to mark using the command on TAB.
indent-rigidly	Move all lines in the region left or right by a fixed amount.
indent-under	Indent to the next text on the previous line.
insert-binding	Make a command to reestablish a key's current binding.
insert-file	Insert the specified file before point.
insert-macro	Make a command to define a macro again later.
kill-buffer	Make a specified buffer not exist.
kill-level	Kill a bracketed expression.

Command/Variable Name	*Meaning*
kill-line	Kill to end of line.
kill-rectangle	Kill the rectangular area between point and mark.
kill-region	Kill the text between point and mark.
kill-sentence	Kill to the end of sentence.
kill-window	Delete the current window.
kill-word	Kill the word after point.
last-kbd-macro	Execute the last keyboard macro defined from the keyboard.
list-all	Describe Epsilon's state in text form.
list-buffers	Show a list of the buffers.
list-changes	Find differences between two list-all files.
load-buffer	Interpret a buffer as a command file.
load-bytes	Load compiled EEL commands and variables.
load-changes	Load the changes from list-changes into Epsilon.
load-file	Read in a command file.
lowercase-word	Make the current word lowercase.
make	Run a program and parse its errors.
mark-paragraph	Make the current paragraph the region.
maybe-break-line	Make a new line if past the fill column.
name-kbd-macro	Name last keyboard macro defined.
named-command	Invoke the given command by name.
narrow-to-region	Temporarily restrict editing within the point and mark.
next-error	Find file and line for next error message in process buffer.
next-page	Display the next window full of text.
next-video	Change the number of lines or columns.
next-window	Move to the next window.
normal-character	Put the invoking key into the buffer.
one-window	Display only one window.

12

continues

Table 12.2. Continued

Command/Variable Name	Meaning
open-line	Open up some vertical space.
overwrite-mode	Enter/Exit overwrite mode.
pluck-tag	Go to the definition of the command at point.
previous-page	Display the previous window full of text.
previous-window	Move to the previous window.
profile	Collect timing information on EEL commands.
program-keys	Change low-level key mapping.
push	Invoke an inferior command processor.
query-replace	Interactively replace strings.
quoted-inscrt	Take the next character literally.
rectangle-mode	Modify killing keys to use rectangles.
redisplay	Rewrite the entire screen.
redo	Redo the last buffer change or movement.
redo-changes	Redo, skipping over movement redos.
regex-replace	Substitute for replace expressions.
regex-search	Search for a string after point.
replace-string	Replace one string with another.
reverse-incremental-search	Incremental search backward.
reverse-regex-search	Find a string before point.
reverse-string-search	Reverse search in nonincremental mode.
save-all-buffers	Save every buffer that has a file.
save-file	Save the buffer into its file.
scroll-down	Scroll the buffer contents down.
scroll-left	Scroll the buffer contents to the left.
scroll-right	Scroll the buffer contents to the right.
scroll-up	Scroll the buffer contents up.
select-buffer	Put a buffer in the current window.
select-tag-file	Change to a different tag file.
set-bell	Toggle ringing the bell on errors and aborting.
set-case-fold	Toggle case folding in searches.

Command/Variable Name	Meaning
set-color	Select new screen colors.
set-debug	Enable or disable single-stepping for a command or subroutine.
set-display-characters	Select new screen characters.
set-fill-column	Set the column where filling occurs.
set-kill-buffers	Specify how many kill buffers to use.
set-line-translate	Select whether reading or writing should change line endings.
set-mark	Set the mark to the current position.
set-mention-delay	Set length of the pause before prompting for a key.
set-show-graphic	Enable or disable use of IBM graphics for characters.
set-tab-size	Set number of spaces between tab settings.
set-variable	Set any user-defined variable.
set-video	Change to a particular number of lines or columns.
show-matching-delimiter	Insert character and show match.
show-point	Show information about point.
show-variable	Display the current value of a variable.
shrink-window	Shrink the current window by one line.
shrink-window-horizontally	Shrink the current window by one column.
sort-buffer	Put a sorted copy of the current buffer in another buffer.
split-window	Split the current window in two.
split-window-vertically	Split the current window in two.
start-kbd-macro	Start defining a keyboard macro.
start-process	Invoke a command processor concurrently.
stop-process	Abort the concurrently executing process.
string-search	Start a search in nonincremental mode.
tabify-region	Convert white space to tabs.
tag-files	Locate all tags in the given files.
to-indentation	Move point to the end of the indentation.

12

continues

Table 12.2. Continued

Command/Variable Name	Meaning
transpose-characters	Swap the characters around point.
transpose-lines	Swap the current and previous lines.
transpose-words	Swap the current and previous words.
unbind-key	Remove the binding from a key.
undo	Undo the last buffer change or movement.
undo-changes	Undo, skipping over movement redos.
untabify-region	Convert tabs to spaces between point and mark.
up-line	Move point to the previous line.
uppercase-word	Make the current word uppercase.
visit-file	Read a file into the current buffer.
wall-chart	Makc a chart of the current key bindings.
what-is	Find a command bound to a key.
where-is	Find a key bound to a command.
widen-buffer	Restore normal access to the current buffer.
write-file	Write buffer to a file.
write-region	Write region to the specified file.
write-state	Save all commands and variables for later automatic loading.
yank	Insert the contents of the kill buffer.
yank-pop	Cycle through previous kill buffers.

12

13

Freemacs Reference

F reemacs, written by Russell Nelson, is an excellent subset of GNU Emacs that runs on MS-DOS computers. Freemacs can be obtained on the Internet by FTP from grape.ecs.clarkson.edu. Or you can call the WFM BBS: 315-265-8207, 1200/2400 baud, 8-N-1, open 24 hours. Freemacs is in File Area 4; no registration is required to download it.

Keys

All versions of Emacs can be infinitely customized. We can't just give you a list of key combinations and say they are always true, because many people could have modified your version of Emacs. You probably will want to rearrange the keys to better suit your own needs and preferences. Use Table 13.1, however, as a starting point. This table lists the initial bindings of keys in the current version of Freemacs. You can get a similar listing by typing F1 b (the function key F1, then the letter *b*).

**Table 13.1. Freemacs Emacs Global Commands
and Their Key Bindings**

Key Binding	Command
SPACEBAR	split-space
BACKSPACE	backward-delete
C-SPACEBAR	set-mark
C-@	set-mark
C-END	goto-end
C-HOME	goto-beginning
C-LEFT ARROW	backward-word
C-LEFT DOWN	is Pup
C-M-y	un-kill-pop
C-PGDN	next-buffer
C-PGUP	previous-buffer
C-RIGHT ARROW	forward-word
C-RIGHT DOWN	is Pappend
C-[	prefix-M-
C-a	beginning-of-line
C-b	backward-character
C-c	prefix-C-c
C-c C-c	done-editing
C-d	delete-character
C-e	end-of-line
C-f	forward-character
C-g	ring-the-bell
C-h	backward-delete
C-i	indent
C-j	newline-and-indent
C-k	kill-to-end-of-line
C-l	new-window
C-m	newline
C-n	next-line
C-o	newline-and-backup
C-p	previous-line

Key Binding	Command
C-q	quoted-insert
C-r	isearch-reverse
C-s	isearch-forward
C-t	transpose-characters
C-u	universal-argument
C-v	down-page
C-w	kill-region
C-x	prefix-C-x
C-x !	shell-command
C-x .	set-fill-prefix
C-x 0	one-window
C-x 1	one-window
C-x 2	two-windows
C-x 3	view-two-windows
C-x 4	prefix-C-x 4
C-x 4 C-g	ring-the-bell
C-x 4 b	switch-to-buffer-other-window
C-x 4 d	dired-other-window
C-x 4 f	find-file-other-window
C-x ;	set-comment-column
C-x <	mark-beginning
C-x >	mark-end
C-x C-b	list-buffers
C-x C-c	save-buffers-kill-emacs
C-x C-e	make
C-x C-f	find-file
C-x C-g	ring-the-bell
C-x C-i	indent-rigidly
C-x C-l	lowercase-region
C-x C-n	parse-error
C-x C-p	parse-error-previous
C-x C-r	visit-file

13

continues

Table 13.1. Continued

Key Binding	Command
C-x C-s	write-current-file
C-x C-t	transpose-lines
C-x C-u	uppercase-region
C-x C-v	visit-file
C-x C-w	write-named-file
C-x C-x	swap-point-and-mark
C-x C-z	suspend-emacs
C-x LPar	start-kbd-macro
C-x RPar	stop-kbd-macro
C-x TAB	indent-rigidly
C-x ^	enlarge-window
C-x `	next-error
C-x b	select-buffer
C-x e	execute-kbd-macro
C-x f	set-fill-column
C-x h	mark-whole-buffer
C-x i	insert-file
C-x k	kill-buffer
C-x o	other-window
C-x s	write-modified-files
C-y	un-kill
C-z	suspend-emacs
Comma	Insert-Comma
D Chr	delete-character
DEL	dclctc-character
DEL LINE	kill-to-end-of-line
DELETE	backward-delete
DOWN ARROW	next-line
END	end-of-line
ESCAPE	prefix-M-
F0	goto-end

13

Key Binding	Command
F1	help
F10	spc2tab
F12	auto-fill-mode
F2	try-it
F3	bind-to-key
F5	backward-kill-word
F6	delete-character
F7	kill-word
F8	kill-to-end-of-line
F9	transpose-characters
Help	help
HOME	beginning-of-line
I Chr	overwrite-mode
INS	insert-line
INS LINE	insert-line
C-x C-c	bye
C-x C-f	find-file
C-x C-s	write-named-file
LPar	Insert-LPar
LEFT ARROW	backward-character
LEFT DOWN	staydown
M-	set-mark
M-!	shell-command-to-buffer
M-$	spell-word
M-%	query-replace
M-–	negative-argument
M-0	digit-argument,0
M-1	digit-argument,1
M-2	digit-argument,2
M-3	digit-argument,3
M-4	digit-argument,4

13

continues

Table 13.1. Continued

Key Binding	Command
M-5	digit-argument,5
M-6	digit-argument,6
M-7	digit-argument,7
M-8	digit-argument,8
M-9	digit-argument,9
M-;	indent-for-comment
M-<	goto-beginning
M->	goto-end
M-?	apropos
M-@	mark-word
M-BACKSPACE	backward-kill-word
M-C-J	indent-new-comment-line
M-C-[	execute-buffer
M-C-\	kill-trail-white
M-C-b	backward-list
M-C-f	forward-list
M-C-g	ring-the-bell
M-C-h	backward-kill-word
M-C-n	forward-list
M-C-p	backward-list
M-C-s	isearch-forward-regexp
M-C-v	down-page-other-window
M-C-w	append-next-kill
M-C-y	un-kill-pop
M-DELETE	backward-kill-word
M-ESCAPE	execute-buffer
M-LEFT DOWN	is Pmarkpop
M-RIGHT DOWN	is Pmarkcopy
M-[	backward-paragraph
M-\	kill-whitespace
M-a	backward-sentence
M-b	backward-word

13

Key Binding	Command
M-c	capitalize-word
M-d	kill-word
M-e	forward-sentence
M-f	forward-word
M-g	goto-line
M-l	downcase-word
M-q	fill-paragraph
M-t	transpose-words
M-u	upcase-word
M-v	up-page
M-w	copy-region
M-x	extended-command
M-y	un-kill-pop
M-~	buffer-not-modified
PGDN	down-page
PGUP	up-page
RPar	flash-rpar
ENTER	newline
RIGHT ARROW	forward-character
RIGHT DOWN	mouse-pick
S-DOWN ARROW	down-page
S-F0	goto-beginning
S-LEFT ARROW	beginning-of-line
S-LEFT DOWN	is Pdown
S-RIGHT ARROW	end-of-line
S-UP ARROW	up-page
TAB	Mint-indent
UP ARROW	previous-line
]	flash-rbracket
}	flash-rbrace

13

Commands

Table 13.2 lists the command names generated from the current distribution version of Freemacs using `ESC x apropos`.

Table 13.2. Freemacs Emacs Commands

Command Name	Meaning
ASM-mode	Set the local mode to Fundamental.
Buffer Menu-mode	Set the local mode to Buffer Menu. The code is contained in the D library.
C-mode	Turn C mode on, loading the Lib if necessary.
Dired-mode	Set the local mode to Dired. The code is contained in the D library.
Fun-mode	Set the local mode to Fundamental.
Insert-Comma	Insert a comma.
Insert-LPar	Insert a left parenthesis.
Mint-mode	Set the local mode to Mint. The code is contained in the M library.
Tab	Insert the same white space as on the previous line.
Text-mode	Set the local mode to Text.
append-next-kill	Next kill is appended to the previous kill string.
apropos	Search the names of commands for a substring.
auto-fill-mode	Toggle auto-fill-mode. In fill-mode, space breaks up long lines.
auto-indent-mode	Toggle auto-indent-mode. In indent-mode, ENTER acts like CONTROL-j.
auto-spell-mode	Toggle auto-spell-mode. In spell-mode, SPACEBAR and ENTER spell-check the word before the point.
backward-character	Move the point back by one character.
backward-delete	Delete the character before the point.
backward-kill-word	Delete the word before the point.
backward-paragraph	Move to the beginning of the previous paragraph.

Command Name	*Meaning*
backward-search	Search backward for a string.
backward-sentence	Move backward to the beginning of the previous sentence.
backward-word	Move backward to the beginning of the previous word.
beginning-of-line	Move to the beginning of the current line.
bind-to-key	Bind a key to a command. Prompts for a command name and key.
buffer-menu	List the buffers and enable them to be edited.
buffer-not-modified	Act as if the current buffer hasn't been modified.
capitalize-word	Capitalize the word after point.
center-text-line	Center text based on F-fill column.
compare-windows	Compare the two windows on a line-by-line basis.
copy-region	Copy the contents of the region to the kill ring.
delete-character	Delete the character to the right of the point.
delete-file	Delete an MS-DOS file.
digit-argument	Start parsing meta digits as a numeric argument.
dir	Give a directory. Use the default extension if none is given.
dired	Edit a subdirectory.
dired-other-window	Open a file in another window, creating a window if necessary.
down-page	Move down a page.
down-page-other-window	GNU Emacs' META-CONTROL-v.
downcase-word	Lowercase the next word.
edit-options	Edit the user options.
ef	Edit a command.
ek	Edit a key.
end-of-line	Move to the end of the current line.
enlarge-window	Make the current window larger.
execute-kbd-macro	Execute a previously defined keyboard macro.
extended-command	Read an extended command from the keyboard.

continues

Table 13.2. Continued

Command Name	Meaning
fill-paragraph	Fill out the current paragraph so that no line is longer.
filter-region	Execute a filter with the region as input. Input by the filter deletes characters. Output from the filter inserts characters.
find-file	Make a buffer current if already loaded, or else load it.
find-file-other-window	Open a file in another window, creating a window if necessary.
flash-rbrace	Move the cursor back to the matching }.
flash-rbracket	Move the cursor back to the matching].
flash-rpar	Move the cursor back to the matching).
forward-character	Move forward one character.
forward-search	Search forward for a string.
forward-sentence	Move to the beginning of the next sentence.
forward-word	Move to the beginning of the next word.
goto-beginning	Move to the beginning of the buffer.
goto-end	Move to the end of the buffer.
goto-line	Go to an absolute line in the current buffer.
grep	Search through every string for a specified substring.
help	Give the user some assistance.
indent	Indent to the next tab stop.
indent-for-comment	Insert the indentation for a comment. If given an argument, realign the comments on that many lines.
indent-newline	Insert a newline followed by the same white space as the previous line.
indent-rigidly	Change the indentation on a line.
insert-file	Insert a file into the current buffer.
insert-line	Insert a line at the beginning of this line.
isearch-forward	Incrementally search forward. Use CONTROL-s to search forward again and CONTROL-r to search backward again.

13

Command Name	Meaning
isearch-forward-regexp	Incrementally search forward using a regexp. Use CONTROL-s to search forward again and CONTROL-r to search backward again.
isearch-reverse	Incrementally search backward. Use CONTROL-s to search forward again and CONTROL-r to search backward again.
keys-edit	Edit all the keys.
kill-buffer	Delete a buffer.
kill-comment	Delete the comment on this line.
kill-line	Kill up to the next newline.
kill-rectangle	Call rectangle with point, mark set to the other corner.
kill-region	Kill the text between point and mark.
kill-spaces	Kill space on either side of point.
kill-to-end-of-line	Kill to end of line. If there is nothing to kill, then kill the newline.
kill-trail-white	Remove trailing white space.
kill-whitespace	Kill newlines only if there's an argument.
kill-word	Kill up to the beginning of the next word.
list-buffers	Display a list of the buffers.
lowercase-region	Change the entire region to lowercase.
make	Run MAKE on makefile.
mark-beginning	Set a mark at the beginning of the buffer.
mark-end	Set a mark at the end of the buffer.
mark-whole-buffer	Set the region to the entire buffer.
mark-word	Set a mark at the end of the next word.
masm	Shell to DOS masm.
name-kbd-macro	Give a name to a previously defined keyboard macro.
negative-argument	Give argument a negative value.
new-window	Reposition the line containing the cursor at the middle of the window. If an argument is given, place the cursor at that line.

13

continues

Table 13.2. Continued

Command Name	Meaning
newline	Insert a newline.
newline-and-backup	Insert a newline and return cursor to the previous line.
newline-and-indent	Insert a newline followed by the same white space as on the previous line.
next-buffer	Step forward in buffer list.
next-error	Parse error messages from Turbo-C, MS-Masm, and MS-C.
next-line	Move down a line, remembering previous column location.
one-window	Make the current window fill the screen. If an argument is given, use the other window.
other-window	Switch to the buffer shown in the other window.
overwrite-mode	Toggle Overwrite mode. In Overwrite mode, typed characters replace existing characters.
pop-mark	Modified by Ashok P. Nadkarni. Pop a mark from the mark ring. Direction of ring movement depends on the sign of the arg1. The point is set to the current mark and then the ring is rotated in the appropriate direction.
prefix-C-c	Parse CONTROL-c prefix characters.
prefix-C-x	Parse CONTROL-x prefix characters.
prefix-C-x 4	Parse CONTROL-x 4 prefix characters.
prefix-M-	Parse META- prefix characters; that is, ESCAPE.
previous-buffer	Step backward in buffer list.
previous-error	Search backward for the previous error.
previous-line	Move up a line, remembering previous column location.
query-replace	Search for a string and enable user to replace it.
query-replace-regexp	Search and replace using regular expressions.
quoted-insert	Insert a control character.

Command Name	Meaning
rename-file	Rename a file to another name.
replace-regexp	Replace all strings matching a given regexp with another string.
replace-string	Replace all strings matching a given string with another string.
ring-the-bell	Ring the bell.
save-all-libs	Save all modified libraries.
save-buffers-kill-emacs	User can save buffers before killing Emacs.
select-buffer	Change the current buffer.
set-comment-column	Set the comment column or delete a comment.
set-fill-column	Set the fill-column to the argument if one is given, or else use the current cursor position.
set-fill-prefix	Set the fill prefix to everything at the beginning of the line.
set-mark	Modified by Ashok P. Nadkarni. Set a mark at point if argument is null. If a non-negative argument is given, pop the mark ring. If negative argument, go to next mark.
set-visited-filename	Set the name of the current buffer.
shell-command	Execute a shell command.
shell-command-to-buffer	Execute a shell command and insert its output into a buffer. If given a non-null argument, insert the output into the current buffer.
spell-word	Spell-check the word to the left of point.
split-space	Insert a space. In Spell mode, spell-check the word. In Fill mode, keep line lengths less than #(F-fill-column).
start-kbd-macro	Start storing keys into a keyboard macro.
staydown	Keep repositioning the cursor to match the mouse position.
stop-kbd-macro	Stop storing a keyboard macro. The key can be executed with CONTROL-x e.
suspend-emacs	Execute the program given in EMACS_SHELL if it exists; otherwise, command.com.

13

continues

Table 13.2. Continued

Command Name	Meaning
swap-point-and-mark	Set the mark to where the point is, and set the point to where the mark was.
switch-to-buffer-other-window	Make other window the active buffer.
transpose-characters	Transpose the character before point with the character after point.
transpose-lines	Transpose the current line with the previous line.
transpose-words	Transpose two words.
try-it	Bring the current line of text in and execute it.
two-windows	Split the screen into two windows, moving point to the bottom window.
un-kill	Bring something back from the kill ring.
un-kill-pop	Replace the previously un-killed text with the previous kill ring entry.
unbind-key	Remove a key binding.
universal-argument	Prompt for a numeric argument. Default to four. If pressed again, multiply the count by four.
up-page	Move the cursor up one page.
upcase-word	Uppercase the next word.
uppercase-region	Uppercase the region.
visit-file	Load the current buffer with a file.
word-count	Return a count of words in the buffer.
write-current-file	Write out the current buffer without asking for a file name.
write-modified-files	Write all files that have been modified.
write-named-file	Write out the current buffer, asking for a file name.
yank-rectangle	Insert the previously killed rectangle.

Chapter 14

MicroEmacs Reference

This book has covered five different Emacs: GNU Emacs, Freemacs, Unipress Emacs, Epsilon, and MicroEmacs. There are three different groups among these five versions: GNU Emacs and Freemacs (the "GNUish" Emacs group), Unipress and Epsilon (the "Goslingish" Emacs group), and MicroEmacs. The real differences in user interfaces between the first two groups are minor; they deal mostly with key bindings. However, there is a much bigger difference between MicroEmacs and the other Emacs.

The design philosophy of MicroEmacs is distinctly different from GNU Emacs and Gosling Emacs. The big Emacs (GNU and Unipress) both represent an attempt to provide a complete user environment. MicroEmacs just wants to be an effective, highly portable text editor with many of the features, if not the feel, of a bigger Emacs. Epsilon and FreeEmacs are smaller Emacs implementations that strive to retain the feel of the big Emacs without using as many computer resources. You could say that they are "lite" versions; they offer the same feel but with less filling. MicroEmacs is MicroEmacs. It has many features that are uniquely its own, and many areas where it doesn't act quite like the others. Like GNU Emacs, MicroEmacs has many users who help it evolve by finding and fixing bugs and contributing macros.

MicroEmacs currently is maintained by Daniel Lawrence, who has added many improvements to it. Both the UNIX and the MS-DOS versions are available widely on various computers.

MicroEmacs Help

In Chapter 3 you learned about the help system in Emacs. By typing CONTROL-h (or F1 or CONTROL-_) as a command prefix, you can get help on many different topics: apropos, bindings, commands, keys, variables. This help system is common to all the Emacs discussed except MicroEmacs; MicroEmacs has a different way of handling help. Note that all of the Emacs are constantly evolving, and the next version of MicroEmacs, version 3.11, is supposed to have an improved help system. To get help in MicroEmacs, you type ESC x help.

There are several commands in MicroEmacs that provide some of the functionality known in other Emacs. Only one of these, **apropos**, is bound to a key. **Apropos** is bound to ESC a in MicroEmacs. It works much the same as CONTROL-h a in GNU Emacs. When you enter ESC a (or ESC x apropos), MicroEmacs prompts you to enter a string. A simple string search is performed, and all commands with names including the string you enter are displayed.

Describe-bindings is another useful MicroEmacs help command. If you enter ESC x describe-bindings, MicroEmacs displays a list of all its commands and the keys that each command is bound to, if any. Note an important difference here: MicroEmacs **describe-bindings** actually lists all the MicroEmacs commands, whether they are bound or not. A useful command, even if it doesn't do what its name implies!

Describe-variables is a similar command that lists the MicroEmacs variables and their current values. You also can use **describe-functions** to get a list of the mathematical functions; for example, **$add** and **available**. Functions in MicroEmacs just aren't the same as functions in GNU Emacs! None of the **describe-*** commands actually describes anything. These commands simply generate useful lists. If you need help with understanding what a command, variable, or function does, you need to turn to other methods of help.

You could use the **help** command (ESC ?). This command opens a window and displays a file (emacs.hlp) that describes key bindings and command names by functional group. It is a useful file, but it never will take the place of the info system. To learn how to use MicroEmacs, you need to read the documentation file supplied as part of the MicroEmacs distribution. You can, of course, use MicroEmacs to read it. For people who haven't used an Emacs before, the documentation file includes a good tutorial.

Help is just one area, albeit a major one, where MicroEmacs differs from the other versions of Emacs. Another important area where MicroEmacs is deficient is in programming aids. MicroEmacs has a useful, but limited, C mode. Unfortunately, it has few other features designed to aid in programming. It does not have any other language modes, although you could create them using a macro. It does not have tags or a **compile** command. It has a limited set of shell commands. Another MicroEmacs deficiency is the lack of special modes for editing files other than text. MicroEmacs has no dired or info mode, and no real provision for extending the editor into this realm.

What MicroEmacs Can Do

Now that you know some of the MicroEmacs limitations, you also should know its advantages. The greatest advantage of MicroEmacs is that it is available on so many different kinds of computers. If you need the same editor on DOS, UNIX, VMS, Atari, Amiga, or just about any computer system you can think of, MicroEmacs is the way to go. Many differences between MicroEmacs and Emacs in general can be remedied by a few changes of key bindings.

Having the same text editor on many different systems for text editing is the purpose of MicroEmacs. It is not the start-it-up-when-you-log-in and kill-it-before-you-log-out sort of program that GNU Emacs is. With MicroEmacs, you can't read your mail, compile your code, and ftp to Timbuktu all at once without leaving the comforts of Emacs, but it does do a good job of text editing. It even has a few features that other Emacs don't. For example, MicroEmacs has a crypt mode you can use to encode and decode your files automatically based on a key that you enter. It also supports the use of a mouse on IBM-compatibles with mouse drivers.

Key Bindings and Commands

Tables 14.1 and 14.2 present helpful information on key bindings and commands partially generated by MicroEmacs itself using `ESC x describe-bindings`. You can use this same command to get a current listing for your version of MicroEmacs. As throughout the book, in these tables a capital C indicates the CONTROL key, and a capital M indicates the META key.

Key Bindings

Table 14.1 is a complete list of the key bindings used in MicroEmacs 3.10. Use this table as a wall-chart reference for MicroEmacs commands.

14

Table 14.1. MicroEmacs Global Commands and Their Key Bindings

Key Binding	Description
C-a	Move to start of line
C-b	Move backward by characters
C-c	Insert space
C-d	Forward delete
C-e	Goto end of line
C-f	Move forward by characters
C-g	Abort
C-h	Backward delete
C-i	Insert tab/set tab stops
C-j	Insert newline, then indent
C-k	Kill forward
C-l	Refresh the screen
C-m	Insert newline
C-n	Move forward by lines
C-o	Open up a blank line
C-p	Move backward by lines
C-q	Insert literal
C-r	Search backward
C-s	Search forward
C-t	Transpose characters
C-u	Repeat command four times
C-v	Move forward by pages
C-w	Kill region
C-x !	Run one command in a shell
C-x #	Filter buffer through shell filter
C-x (	Begin macro
C-x)	End macro
C-x =	Show the cursor position
C-x <	Hide some text
C-x >	Restore hidden text
C-x ?	Describe a key

Key Binding	Description
C-x @	Pipe shell command to buffer
C-x ^	Enlarge display window
C-x $	Execute an external program
C-x 0	Delete current window
C-x 1	Delete other windows
C-x 2	Split current window
C-x a	Set variable value
C-x b	Switch a window to a buffer
C-x C-b	Display buffer list
C-x C-c	Exit MicroEmacs
C-x C-d	Detab line
C-x C-e	Entab line
C-x C-f	Find file
C-x C-i	Insert file
C-x C-l	Lowercase region
C-x C-m	Delete mode
C-x C-n	Move window down
C-x C-o	Delete blank lines
C-x C-p	Move window up
C-x C-r	Get a file from disk
C-x C-s	Save current file
C-x C-t	Trim line
C-x C-u	Uppercase region
C-x C-v	View file
C-x C-w	Write a file to disk
C-x C-x	Swap "." and mark
C-x C-z	Shrink window
C-x c	Start a new command processor
C-x d	Suspend MicroEmacs (BSD4.2 only)
C-x e	Execute macro
C-x f	Set fill column
C-x k	Delete buffer

continues

Table 14.1. Continued

Key Binding	Description
C-x m	Add a mode
C-x n	Rename current file name
C-x o	Move to the next window
C-x p	Move to the previous window
C-x r	Incremental reverse search
C-x s	Incremental forward search
C-x w	Resize window
C-x x	Use next buffer
C-x z	Enlarge display window
C-y	Yank back from killbuffer
C-z	Move backward by pages
ESC !	Reposition window
ESC .	Set mark
ESC <	Move to start of buffer
ESC >	Move to end of buffer
ESC ~	Unmark current buffer
ESC a	List some commands
ESC b	Back up by words
ESC C-c	Count words in region
ESC C-e	Execute named procedure
ESC C-f	Goto matching fence
ESC C-h	Delete backward word
ESC C-k	Unbind key from command
ESC C-l	Reposition window
ESC C-m	Delete global mode
ESC C-n	Rename current buffer
ESC C-r	Search and replace with query
ESC C-s	Source command file
ESC C-v	Scroll next window down
ESC C-w	Delete paragraph
ESC C-x	Execute command line
ESC C-z	Scroll next window up

14

Key Binding	Description
ESC c	Initial capitalize word
ESC d	Delete forward word
ESC e	Reset encryption key
ESC f	Advance by words
ESC g	Go to a line
ESC k	Bind key to command
ESC l	Lowercase word
ESC m	Add global mode
ESC n	Goto end of paragraph
ESC p	Goto beginning of paragraph
ESC q	Fill current paragraph
ESC r	Search and replace
ESC RUBOUT	Delete backward word
ESC s	Suspend (BSD only)
ESC SPACEBAR	Set mark
ESC u	Uppercase word
ESC v	Move backward by pages
ESC w	Copy region to kill buffer
ESC x	Execute named command
ESC z	Save all buffers and exit
RUBOUT	Backward delete

14

Commands

Table 14.2 lists the commands included in the current distribution of MicroEmacs. The commands' key bindings, when bound by default, are included as well.

T able 14.2. MicroEmacs Commands

Command Name	Key	Meaning
abort-command	C-g	This enables the user to abort from any command that is waiting for input.
add-mode	C-x m	Add a mode to the current buffer.
add-global-mode	M-m	Add a global mode for all new buffers.
apropos	M-a	List commands whose names contain the string specified.
backward-character	C-b	Move one character to the left.
begin-macro	C-x (	Begin recording a keyboard macro.
beginning-of-file	M-<	Move to the beginning of the file in the current buffer.
beginning-of-line	C-a	Move to the beginning of the current line.
bind-to-key	M-k	Bind a key to a command.
buffer-position	C-x =	List the position of the cursor in the current window on the command line.
case-region-lower	C-x C-l	Lowercase a marked region.
case-region-upper	C-x C-u	Uppercase a marked region.
case-word-capitalize	M-c	Capitalize the following word.
case-word-lower	M-l	Lowercase the following word.
case-word-upper	M-u	Uppercase the following word.
change-file-name	C-x n	Change the name of the file in the current buffer.
change-screen-size		Change the number of lines of the screen currently being used.
change-screen-width		Change the number of columns of the screen currently being used.
clear-and-redraw	C-l	Clear the physical screen and redraw it.
clear-message-line		Clear the command line.
copy-region	M-w	Copy the currently marked region into the killbuffer.

Command Name	Key	Meaning
count-words	M-C-c	Count words, lines, and characters in the currently marked region.
ctlx-prefix	C-x	Change the key used as the C-x prefix.
delete-blank-lines	C-x C-o	Delete all blank lines around the cursor.
delete-buffer	C-x k	Delete a buffer that is not currently being displayed in a window.
delete-mode	C-x C-m	Turn off a mode in the current buffer.
delete-global-mode	M-C-m	Turn off a global mode.
delete-next-character	C-d	Delete the character following the cursor.
delete-next-word	M-d	Delete the word following the cursor.
delete-other-window	C-x 1	Cover entire screen with the current window.
delete-previous-character	C-h	Delete the character to the left of the cursor.
delete-previous-word	M-C-h	Delete the word to the left of the cursor.
delete-window	C-x 0	Remove the current window from the screen.
describe-bindings		List all legal commands.
describe-key	C-x ?	Describe the command bound to a particular keystroke sequence.
detab-region	C-x C-d	Change all tabs in a region to the equivalent spaces.
display	C-x g	Prompt the user for a variable and display its current value.
dump-variables		Place into a buffer the current values of all environment and user variables.
end-macro	C-x)	Stop recording a keyboard macro.
end-of-file	M->	Move cursor to the end of the current buffer.

14

continues

Table 14.2. Continued

Command Name	Key	Meaning
end-of-line	C-e	Move to the end of the current line.
entab-region	C-x C-e	Change multiple spaces to tabs where possible.
exchange-point-and-mark	C-x C-x	Move cursor to the previous marked spot, and make the original position be marked.
execute-buffer		Execute a buffer as a macro.
execute-command-line		Execute a line typed on the command line as a macro command.
execute-file		Execute a file as a macro.
execute-macro	C-x e	Execute the keyboard macro (play back the recorded keystrokes).
execute-macro-<n>		Execute numbered macro <N> in which <N> is an integer from 1 to 40.
execute-named-command	M-x	Execute a command by name.
execute-procedure	M-C-e	Execute a procedure by name.
execute-program	C-x $	Execute a program directly (not through an intervening shell).
exit-emacs	C-x C-c	Exit Emacs. If there are unwritten, changed buffers, Emacs will ask to confirm.
fill-paragraph	M-q	Fill the current paragraph.
filter-buffer	C-x #	Filter the current buffer through an external filter.
find-file	C-x C-f	Find a file to edit in the current window.
forward-character	C-f	Move cursor one character to the right.
goto-line	M-g	Go to a numbered line.
goto-matching-fence	M-C-f	Go to the matching fence.
grow-window	C-x ^	Enlarge the current window.
handle-tab	C-i	Insert a tab or set tab stops.
hunt-forward	ALT-s	Hunt for the next match of the previous search string.

Command Name	Key	Meaning
hunt-backward	ALT-r	Hunt for the previous match of the last search string.
help	M-?	Read emacs.hlp into a buffer and display it.
i-shell	C-x c	Shell to a new command processor.
incremental-search	C-x s	Search for a string, incrementally.
insert-file	C-x C-i	Insert a file at the cursor in the current file.
insert-space	C-c	Insert a space to the right of the cursor.
insert-string		Insert a string at the cursor.
kill-paragraph	M-C-w	Delete the current paragraph.
kill-region	C-w	Delete the current marked region; move it to the killbuffer.
kill-to-end-of-line	C-k	Delete the rest of the current line.
list-buffers	C-x C-b	List all existing buffers.
meta-prefix	ESC	Key used to precede all meta commands.
mouse-move-down	M-SHIFT-a	
mouse-move-up	M-SHIFT-b	
mouse-resize-screen	M-SHIFT-1	
mouse-region-down	M-SHIFT-e	
mouse-region-up	M-SHIFT-f	
move-window-down	C-x C-n	Move all the lines in the current window down.
move-window-up	C-x C-p	Move all the lines in the current window up.
name-buffer	M-C-n	Change the name of the current buffer.
narrow-to-region	C-x <	Hide all text not in the current region.
newline	C-m	Insert a newline at the cursor.
newline-and-indent	C-j	Insert a newline at the cursor and indent it the same as the preceding line.

14

continues

Table 14.2. Continued

Command Name	Key	Meaning
next-buffer	C-x x	Bring the next buffer in the list into the current window.
next-line	C-n	Move the cursor down one line.
next-page	C-v	Move the cursor down one page.
next-paragraph	M-n	Move cursor to the next paragraph.
next-window	C-x o	Move cursor to the next window.
next-word	M-f	Move cursor to the beginning of the next word.
nop		Does nothing.
open-line	C-o	Open a line at the cursor.
overwrite-string		Overwrite a string at the cursor.
pipe-command	C-x @	Execute an external command and place its output in a buffer.
previous-line	C-p	Move cursor up one line.
previous-page	C-z	Move cursor up one page.
previous-paragraph	M-p	Move back one paragraph.
previous-window	C-x p	Move the cursor to the previous window.
previous-word	M-b	Move the cursor to the beginning of the word preceding the cursor.
print		Display a string on the command line (a synonym to write-message).
query-replace-string	M-C-r	Replace one string with another string, interactively querying the user.
quick-exit	M-z	Exit Emacs, writing out all changed buffers.
quote-character	C-q	Insert the next character literally.
read-file	C-x C-r	Read a file into the current buffer.
redraw-display	M-C-l	Redraw the display, centering the current line.
resize-window	C-x w	Change the number of lines in the current window.
restore-window		Move cursor to the previous saved window.

Command Name	Key	Meaning
replace-string	M-r	Replace all occurrences of one string with another string from the cursor to the end of the buffer.
reverse-incremental-search	C-x r	Search backward, incrementally.
run	M-C-e	Execute a named procedure.
save-file	C-x s	Save the current buffer if it is changed.
save-window		Remember current window (to restore later).
scroll-next-up	M-C-z	Scroll the next window up.
scroll-next-down	M-C-v	Scroll the next window down.
search-forward	C-s	Search for a string.
search-reverse	C-r	Search backward for a string.
select-buffer	C-x b	Select a buffer to display in the current window.
set	C-x a	Set a variable to a value.
set-encryption-key	M-e	Set the encryption key of the current buffer.
set-fill-column	C-x f	Set the current fill column.
set-mark	M-.	Set the mark.
shell-command	C-x !	External shell to execute a command.
shrink-window	C-x C-z	Shrink the current window.
source		Execute a file as a macro.
split-current-window	C-x 2	Split the current window in two.
store-macro		Store the following macro lines to a numbered macro.
store-procedure		Store the following macro lines to a named procedure.
transpose-characters	C-t	Transpose the character at the cursor with the character to the left.
trim-region	C-x C-t	Trim any trailing white space from a region.

14

continues

Table 14.2. Continued

Command Name	Key	Meaning
unbind-key	M-C-k	Unbind a key from a command.
universal-argument	C-u	Execute the following command four times.
unmark-buffer	M-~	Unmark the current buffer (so it is no longer changed).
update-screen		Force a screen update during macro execution.
view-file	C-x C-v	Find a file and put it in view mode.
widen-from-region	C-x >	Restore hidden text (see narrow-to-region).
wrap-word		Wrap the current word; this is an internal function.
write-file	C-x C-w	Write the current buffer under a new file name.
write-message		Display a string on the command line.
yank	C-y	Yank the killbuffer into the current buffer at the cursor.

The variables listed in Table 14.3 change different aspects of the way MicroEmacs works, and they also return the current settings if used as part of an expression. This table is reproduced from the documentation accompanying MicroEmacs 3.10, and again, thanks to Daniel Lawrence for doing such an excellent job with MicroEmacs. In MicroEmacs, environmental variable names begin with a dollar sign ($) and are lowercase.

Table 14.3. MicroEmacs Environmental Variables

Variable	Meaning
$account	The countdown of inserted characters until the next savefile.
$asave	The number of inserted characters between automatic file-saves in ASAVE mode.
$bufhook	The function named in this variable is run when a buffer is entered. It can be used to implement modes specific to a paricular file or file type.

Variable	Meaning
$cbflags	Current buffer attribute flags.
$cbufname	Name of the current buffer.
$cfname	File name of the current buffer.
$cmdhook	Name of function to run before accepting a command. This is by default set to nop.
$cmode	Integer containing the mode of the current buffer.
$curchar	ASCII value of the character currently at the point.
$curcol	Current column of point in current buffer.
$curline	Current line of point in current buffer.
$curwidth	Number of columns used currently.
$cwline	Current display line in current window.
$debug	Flag to trigger macro debugging.
$diagflag	If set to TRUE, diagonal dragging of text and mode lines is enabled. If FALSE, text and modelines can only be dragged horizontally or vertically at one time.
$discmd	Flag to disable the echoing of messages on the command line.
$disinp	Flag to disable the echoing of characters during command line input.
$exbhook	This variable holds the name of a function or macro that is run whenever you are switching out of a buffer.
$fcol	The current line position being displayed in the first column of the current window.
$fillcol	Current fill column.
$flicker	Flicker Flag set to TRUE if IBM CGA set to FALSE for most others.
$gflags	Global flags controlling some Emacs internal functions.
$gmode	Global mode flags.
$hardtab	Number of spaces between hard tab stops. Normally 8, this can be used to change indentation only within the editor.
$hjump	The number in here tells Emacs how many columns to scroll the screen horizontally when a horizontal scroll is required.

14

continues

Table 14.3. Continued

Variable	*Meaning*
$hscroll	This flag determines if Emacs will scroll the entire current window horizontally, or just the current line. The default value, TRUE, results in the entire current window being shifted left and right when the cursor goes off the edge of the screen.
$kill	This contains the first 127 characters currently in the kill buffer and can be used to set the contents of the kill buffer.
$language	[READ ONLY]Contains the name of the language that the current Emacs' message will display. (Currently Emacs is available in English, French, Spanish, Pig Latin, Portuguese, Dutch, German, and Esperanto.)
$lastkey	[READ ONLY]Last keyboard character typed.
$lastmesg	[READ ONLY]Contains the text of the last message Emacs wrote on the command line.
$line	The current line in the current buffer can be retrieved and set with this environment variable.
$lwidth	[READ ONLY]Returns the number of characters in the current line.
$match	[READ ONLY]Last string matched in a magic mode search.
$modeflag	Determines if mode lines are currently displayed.
$msflag	If TRUE, the mouse (if present) is active. If FALSE, no mouse cursor is displayed, and no mouse actions are taken.
$pagelen	Number of screen lines used currently.
$palette	String used to control the palette register settings on graphics versions. The usual form consists of groups of three octal digits setting the red, green, and blue levels.
$pending	[READ ONLY]Flag to determine if there are user keystrokes waiting to be processed.
$progname	[READ ONLY]Always contains the string "MicroEmacs" for standard MicroEmacs. Could be something else if Emacs is incorporated as part of someone else's program.
$readhook	This variable holds the name of a function to execute whenever a file is read into Emacs. Normally, using the standard emacs.rc file, this is bound to a function that places Emacs into CMODE if the extension of the file read is .c or .h.

Variable	Meaning
$replace	Current default replace string.
$rval	This contains the return value from the last subprocess invoked from Emacs.
$search	Current default search string.
$seed	Integer seed of the random number generator.
$softtab	Number of spaces inserted by Emacs when the handle-tab command (which is normally bound to the TAB key) is invoked..
$sres	Current screen resolution (CGA, MONO, EGA, or VGA on the IBM-PC driver. LOW, MEDIUM, HIGH, or DENSE on the Atari ST1040, NORMAL on all others).
$ssave	If TRUE, when Emacs is asked to save the current file, it writes all files out to a temporary file, deletes the original, and then renames the temporary to the old file name. The default value of this is TRUE.
$sscroll	Changes Emacs, when set to TRUE, to smoothly scroll windows (one line at a time) when cursoring off the ends of the current window.
$status	[READ ONLY]Status of the success of the last command (TRUE or FALSE). This is usually used with !force to check on the success of a search, or a file operation.
$sterm	This is the character used to terminate search string inputs. The default for this is the last key bound to meta-prefix.
$target	Current target for line moves (setting this fools Emacs into believing the last command was a line move).
$time	[READ ONLY]Contains a string corresponding to the current date and time. Usually this is in a form similar to "Mon May 09 10:10:58 1988". Not all operating systems will support this.
$tpause	Controls the length of the pause to display a matched fence when the current buffer is in CMODE and a close fence has been typed.
$version	[READ ONLY]Contains the current MicroEmacs version number.
$wline	Number of display lines in current window.

14

continues

Table 14.3. Continued

Variable	Meaning
$wraphook	This variable contains the name of an Emacs function executed when a buffer is in WRAP mode and it is time to wrap. By default this is bound to wrap-word.
$writehook	This variable contains the name of an Emacs function or macro invoked whenever Emacs attempts to write a file out to disk. This is executed before the file is written, allowing you to process a file on the way out.
$xpos	The column the mouse was at the last mouse button press

Usable Modes

MicroEmacs provides several modes called Usable modes to make your editing easy. Some, like WRAP (which breaks text lines to keep the whole line on the screen) you will use often. Table 14.4 lists these Usable modes.

Table 14.4. MicroEmacs Usable Modes

Command	Meaning
WRAP	Lines going past right margin wrap to a new line.
VIEW	Read-only mode, in which no modifications are allowed.
CMODE	Change behavior of some commands to work better with C.
EXACT	Exact case matching on search strings.
OVER	Overwrite typed characters rather than insert them.
CRYPT	Current buffer is encrypted on write, decrypted on read.
MAGIC	Use regular expression matching in searches.
ASAVE	Save the file every 256 inserted characters.
WHITE/CYAN/ MAGENTA/YELLOW/ BLUE/RED/GREEN/ BLACK	Set foreground color to white/cyan/magenta/ yellow/blue/red/green/black. Set background color @end(verbatim).

Supported Machines

Table 14.5 lists all the hardware and compilers on which Daniel Lawrence currently supports running MicroEmacs. This list does not include all machines that MicroEmacs runs on, but includes only those Daniel Lawrence has either run or has had a firsthand report of.

Table 14.5. MicroEmacs-Supported Hardware and Compilers

Hardware	OS	Compiler	Comments
VAX 780	UNIX V5	native	
VAX 780	UNIX V7	native	
	BSD 4.2	native	Job control supported
	*VMS	native	
NCR Tower	UNIX V5	native	
IBM-RT PC	BSD 4.3	native	
HP9000	UNIX V5	native	
Fortune 32:16	UNIX V7	native	
IBM-PC	MS-DOS 2.0 & 3.2	LATTICE 2.15	Large CODE/Large DATA
		AZTEC 3.4e	Large CODE/Large DATA
		TURBO C v1.5	LARGE memory model
		MSC 4.0	
		*MWC 86	
	SCO XENIX	native	
HP150	MS-DOS	Lattice 2.15	Function key labels for the touch screen
HP110	MS-DOS	Lattice 2.15	
		Aztec 3.4e	
*Data General 10	MS-DOS	Lattice 2.1	Texas Instruments Professional
	MS-DOS	Lattice 2.15	
Amiga	Intuition	Lattice 3.03	
		Aztec 3.6	
ST520	TOS	Lattice 3.10	Mark Williams C; spawns under MSH (no shell commands)

Systems to Be Supported (Some Code Already Written)

Macintosh	Finder 5.0	Aztec

* means Daniel Lawrence does not own or have access to the listed compiler or machine and must rely on others to help support it.

Function Keys

On the IBM PC, the Atari ST, and the Commodore Amiga, UNIX now supports a set of machine-independent bindings for MicroEmacs function keys. Table 14.6 lists these key names (not all of these are supported on all systems). For example, to exit MicroEmacs, you would type exit-emacs. If you wanted to use the F10 key for this purpose, you would bind the **exit-emacs** command to the key name FN0. If you wanted to use the CONTROL-HOME key combination instead, you would bind the command to the key name FN ^ <. See Chapter 7 for more information about key bindings.

Table 14.6. Key Names in MicroEmacs

Key	*Function*	*SHIFT-Function*	*CTRL-Function*	*ALT-Function*
F1	FN1	S-FN1	FN ^ 1	A-FN1
F2	FN2	S-FN2	FN ^ 2	A-FN2
F3	FN3	S-FN3	FN ^ 3	A-FN3
F4	FN4	S-FN4	FN ^ 4	A-FN4
F5	FN5	S-FN5	FN ^ 5	A-FN5
F6	FN6	S-FN6	FN ^ 6	A-FN6
F7	FN7	S-FN7	FN ^ 7	A-FN7
F8	FN8	S-FN8	FN ^ 8	A-FN8
F9	FN9	S-FN9	FN ^ 9	A-FN9
F10	FN0	S-FN0	FN ^ 0	A-FN0
HOME	FN<		FN ^ <	
UP	FNP		FN ^ P	
PGUP	FNZ		FN ^ Z	
LEFT	FNB		FN ^ B	
RIGHT	FNF		FN ^ F	
END	FN>		FN ^ >	
DOWN	FNN		FN ^ N	
PGDN	FNV		FN ^ V	
INS	FNC		FN ^ C	
DEL	FND		FN ^ D	

IBM and Clones

The IBM-PC family of computers is supported with a variety of display adapters. Emacs attempts to discover what adapter is connected and use the proper driver for it. Table 14.7 lists the current MicroEmacs-supported video adapters.

Table 14.7. MicroEmacs-Supported Adapters

Adapter	Resolution	Original Mode Used
Monochrome Graphics Adapter	MONO	MONO
Color Graphics Adapter	CGA	CGA
Enhanced Graphics Adapter	EGA	CGA
Video Graphics Adapter	VGA	CGA

If a driver for a Microsoft-compatible mouse is installed on the system, Emacs uses the mouse in text mode and allows for the standard mouse functions. The mouse cursor appears to be a block of color in the color opposite the screen's background.

MicroEmacs also takes advantage of various function keys and the keys on the keypad on an IBM-PC. The function keys initially are not bound to any particular commands (except by the emacs.rc start-up file), but in Table 14.8 you find the defaults for the keypad keys. These special keys are indicated in Emacs macros by use of the FN prefix.

Table 14.8. MicroEmacs Default Keypad Keys

Keypad Key	Meaning
HOME	beginning-of-file
UP	previous-line
PGUP	previous-page
LEFT	backward-character
RIGHT	forward-character
END	end-of-file
DOWN	next-line
PGDN	next-page

14

Part

Appendixes

Appendix

The GNU Manifesto

A good part of what makes Emacs so great is the philosophy of its creator, Richard Stallman. Whether or not you agree with Richard, you must admit that he has made Emacs undeniably the most powerful text editing program available.

Following is the *GNU Manifesto*, which is included with GNU Emacs and also is widely available through various other sources.

What's GNU? Gnu's Not UNIX!

GNU, which stands for Gnu's Not UNIX, is the name for the complete UNIX-compatible software system which I am writing so that I can give it away free to everyone who can use it. Several other volunteers are helping me. Contributions of time, money, programs, and equipment are greatly needed.

So far we have an Emacs text editor with Lisp for writing editor commands, a source-level debugger, a yacc-compatible parser generator, a linker, and around 35 utilities. A shell (command interpreter) is nearly completed. A new portable optimizing C compiler has compiled itself and may be released this year. An initial kernel exists, but many more features are needed to emulate UNIX. When the kernel and compiler are finished, it will be possible to distribute a GNU system suitable for program development. We will use @TeX{} as our text formatter, but an nroff is being worked on. We will use the free, portable X window system as well. After this we will add a portable Common Lisp, an Empire game, a spreadsheet, and hundreds of other things, plus on-line documentation. We hope to supply, eventually, everything useful that normally comes with a UNIX system, and more.

GNU will be able to run UNIX programs but will not be identical to UNIX. We will make all improvements that are convenient, based on our experience with other operating systems. In particular, we plan to have longer file names, file version numbers, a crash-proof file system, file name completion perhaps, terminal-independent display support, and perhaps eventually a Lisp-based window system through which several Lisp programs and ordinary UNIX programs can share a screen. Both C and Lisp will be available as system programming languages. We will try to support UUCP, MIT Chaosnet, and Internet protocols for communication.

GNU is aimed initially at machines in the 68000/16000 class with virtual memory, because they are the easiest machines to make it run on. The extra effort to make it run on smaller machines will be left to someone who wants to use it on them.

To avoid horrible confusion, please pronounce the "G" in the word "GNU" when it is the name of this project.

Who Am I?

I am Richard Stallman, inventor of the original much-imitated Emacs editor, formerly at the Artificial Intelligence Lab at MIT. I have worked extensively on compilers, editors, debuggers, command interpreters, the Incompatible Timesharing System, and the Lisp Machine operating system. I pioneered terminal-independent display support in ITS. Since then I have implemented one crash-proof file system and two window systems for Lisp machines and designed a third window system now being implemented; this one will be ported to many systems including use in GNU. (Historical note: The window system project was not completed; GNU now plans to use the X window system.)

Why I Must Write GNU

I consider that the golden rule requires that if I like a program I must share it with other people who like it. Software sellers want to divide the users and conquer them, making each user agree not to share with others. I refuse to break solidarity with other users in this way. I cannot in good conscience sign a nondisclosure agreement or a software license agreement. For years I worked within the Artificial Intelligence Lab to resist such tendencies and other inhospitalities, but eventually they had gone too far: I could not remain in an institution where such things are done for me against my will.

So that I can continue to use computers without dishonor, I have decided to put together a sufficient body of free software so that I will be able to get along without any software that is not free. I have resigned from the AI lab to deny MIT any legal excuse to prevent me from giving GNU away.

Why GNU Will Be Compatible with UNIX

UNIX is not my ideal system, but it is not too bad. The essential features of UNIX seem to be good ones, and I think I can fill in what UNIX lacks without spoiling them. And a system compatible with UNIX would be convenient for many other people to adopt.

How GNU Will Be Available

GNU is not in the public domain. Everyone will be permitted to modify and redistribute GNU, but no distributor will be allowed to restrict its further redistribution. That is to say, proprietary modifications will not be allowed. I want to make sure that all versions of GNU remain free.

A

Why Many Other Programmers Want to Help

I have found many other programmers who are excited about GNU and want to help.

Many programmers are unhappy about the commercialization of system software. It may enable them to make more money, but it requires them to feel in conflict with other programmers in general rather than feel as comrades. The fundamental act of friendship among programmers is the sharing of programs; marketing arrangements now typically used essentially forbid programmers to treat others as friends. The purchaser of software must choose between friendship and obeying the law. Naturally, many decide that friendship is more important. But those who believe in law often do not feel at ease with either choice. They become cynical and think that programming is just a way of making money.

By working on and using GNU rather than proprietary programs, we can be hospitable to everyone and obey the law. In addition, GNU serves as an example to inspire and a banner to rally others to join us in sharing. This can give us a feeling of harmony which is impossible if we use software that is not free. For about half the programmers I talk to, this is an important happiness that money cannot replace.

How You Can Contribute

I am asking computer manufacturers for donations of machines and money. I'm asking individuals for donations of programs and work.

One consequence you can expect if you donate machines is that GNU will run on them at an early date. The machines should be complete, ready-to-use systems, approved for use in a residential area, and not in need of sophisticated cooling or power.

I have found very many programmers eager to contribute part-time work for GNU. For most projects, such part-time distributed work would be very hard to coordinate; the independently written parts would not work together. But for the particular task of replacing UNIX, this problem is absent. A complete UNIX system contains hundreds of utility programs, each of which is documented separately. Most interface specifications are fixed by UNIX compatibility. If each contributor can write a compatible replacement for a single UNIX utility, and make it work properly in place of the original on a UNIX system, then these utilities will work right when put together. Even allowing for Murphy to create a few unexpected problems, assembling these components will be a feasible task. (The kernel will require closer communication and will be worked on by a small, tight group.)

If I get donations of money, I may be able to hire a few people full or part time. The salary won't be high by programmers' standards, but I'm looking for people for whom building community spirit is as important as making money. I view this as a way of enabling dedicated people to devote their full energies to working on GNU by sparing them the need to make a living in another way.

Why All Computer Users Will Benefit

Once GNU is written, everyone will be able to obtain good system software free, just like air.

This means much more than just saving everyone the price of a UNIX license. It means that much wasteful duplication of system programming effort will be avoided. This effort can go instead into advancing the state of the art.

Complete system sources will be available to everyone. As a result, a user who needs changes in the system will always be free to make them himself, or hire any available programmer or company to make them for him. Users will no longer be at the mercy of one programmer or company which owns the sources and is in sole position to make changes.

Schools will be able to provide a much more educational environment by encouraging all students to study and improve the system code. Harvard's computer lab used to have the policy that no program could be installed on the system if its sources were not on public display, and upheld it by actually refusing to install certain programs. I was very much inspired by this.

Finally, the overhead of considering who owns the system software and what one is or is not entitled to do with it will be lifted.

Arrangements to make people pay for using a program, including licensing of copies, always incur a tremendous cost to society through the cumbersome mechanisms necessary to figure out how much (that is, which programs) a person must pay for. And only a police state can force everyone to obey them. Consider a space station where air must be manufactured at great cost: charging each breather per liter of air may be fair, but wearing the metered gas mask all day and all night is intolerable even if everyone can afford to pay the air bill. And the TV cameras everywhere to see if you ever take the mask off are outrageous. It's better to support the air plant with a head tax and chuck the masks.

Copying all or parts of a program is as natural to a programmer as breathing, and as productive. It ought to be as free.

Some Easily Rebutted Objections to GNU's Goals

"Nobody will use it if it is free, because that means they can't rely on any support."

"You have to charge for the program to pay for providing the support."

If people would rather pay for GNU plus service than get GNU free without service, a company to provide just service to people who have obtained GNU free ought to be profitable.

We must distinguish between support in the form of real programming work and mere hand holding. The former is something one cannot rely on from a software vendor. If your problem is not shared by enough people, the vendor will tell you to get lost.

If your business needs to be able to rely on support, the only way is to have all the necessary sources and tools. Then you can hire any available person to fix your problem; you are not at the mercy of any individual. With UNIX, the price of sources puts this out of consideration for most businesses. With GNU this will be easy. It is still possible for there to be no available competent person, but this problem cannot be blamed on distribution arrangements. GNU does not eliminate all the world's problems, only some of them.

Meanwhile, the users who know nothing about computers need hand holding: doing things for them which they could easily do themselves but don't know how.

Such services could be provided by companies that sell just hand-holding and repair service. If it is true that users would rather spend money and get a product with service, they will also be willing to buy the service having got the product free. The service companies will compete in quality and price; users will not be tied to any particular one. Meanwhile, those of us who don't need the service should be able to use the program without paying for the service.

"You cannot reach many people without advertising, and you must charge for the program to support that."

"It's no use advertising a program people can get free."

There are various forms of free or very cheap publicity that can be used to inform numbers of computer users about something like GNU. But it may be true that one can reach more microcomputer users with advertising. If this is really so, a business which advertises the service of copying and mailing GNU for a fee ought to be successful enough to pay for its advertising and more. This way, only the users who benefit from the advertising pay for it.

On the other hand, if many people get GNU from their friends, and such companies don't succeed, this will show that advertising was not really necessary to spread GNU. Why is it that free market advocates don't want to let the free market decide this?

"My company needs a proprietary operating system to get a competitive edge."

GNU will remove operating system software from the realm of competition. You will not be able to get an edge in this area, but neither will your competitors be able to get an edge over you. You and they will compete in other areas, while benefitting mutually in this one. If your business is selling an operating system, you will not like GNU, but that's tough on you. If your business is something else, GNU can save you from being pushed into the expensive business of selling operating systems.

I would like to see GNU development supported by gifts from many manufacturers and users, reducing the cost to each.

"Don't programmers deserve a reward for their creativity?"

If anything deserves a reward, it is social contribution. Creativity can be a social contribution, but only insofar as society is free to use the results. If programmers deserve to be rewarded for creating innovative programs, by the same token they deserve to be punished if they restrict the use of these programs.

"Shouldn't a programmer be able to ask for a reward for his creativity?"

There is nothing wrong with wanting pay for work, or seeking to maximize one's income, as long as one does not use means that are destructive. But the means customary in the field of software today are based on destruction.

Extracting money from users of a program by restricting their use of it is destructive because the restrictions reduce the amount and the ways that the program can be used. This reduces the amount of wealth that humanity derives from the program. When there is a deliberate choice to restrict, the harmful consequences are deliberate destruction.

The reason a good citizen does not use such destructive means to become wealthier is that, if everyone did so, we would all become poorer from the mutual destructiveness. This is Kantian ethics; or, the Golden Rule. Since I do not like the consequences that result if everyone hoards information, I am required to consider it wrong for one to do so. Specifically, the desire to be rewarded for one's creativity does not justify depriving the world in general of all or part of that creativity.

"Won't programmers starve?"

I could answer that nobody is forced to be a programmer. Most of us cannot manage to get any money for standing on the street and making faces. But we are not, as a result, condemned to spend our lives standing on the street making faces, and starving. We do something else.

But that is the wrong answer because it accepts the questioner's implicit assumption: that without ownership of software, programmers cannot possibly be paid a cent. Supposedly it is all or nothing.

The real reason programmers will not starve is that it will still be possible for them to get paid for programming, just not paid as much as now.

Restricting copying is not the only basis for business in software. It is the most common basis because it brings in the most money. If it were prohibited, or rejected by the customer, software business would move to other bases of organization which are now used less often. There are always numerous ways to organize any kind of business.

Probably programming will not be as lucrative on the new basis as it is now. But that is not an argument against the change. It is not considered an injustice that sales clerks make the salaries that they now do. If programmers made the same, that would not be an injustice either. (In practice they would still make considerably more than that.)

"Don't people have a right to control how their creativity is used?"

"Control over the use of one's ideas" really constitutes control over other people's lives, and it is usually used to make their lives more difficult.

People who have studied the issue of intellectual property rights carefully (such as lawyers) say that there is no intrinsic right to intellectual property. The kinds of supposed intellectual property rights that the government recognizes were created by specific acts of legislation for specific purposes.

For example, the patent system was established to encourage inventors to disclose the details of their inventions. Its purpose was to help society rather than to help inventors. At the time, the life span of 17 years for a patent was short compared with the rate of advance of the state of the art. Since patents are an issue only among manufacturers, for whom the cost and effort of a license agreement are small compared with setting up production, the patents often do not do much harm. They do not obstruct most individuals who use patented products.

The idea of copyright did not exist in ancient times, when authors frequently copied other authors at length in works of nonfiction. This practice was useful, and is the only way many authors' works have survived even in part. The copyright system was created expressly for the purpose of encouraging authorship. In the domain for which it was invented—books, which could be copied economically only on a printing press—it did little harm, and did not obstruct most of the individuals who read the books.

All intellectual property rights are just licenses granted by society because it was thought, rightly or wrongly, that society as a whole would benefit by granting them. But in any particular situation, we have to ask: are we really better off granting such license? What kind of act are we licensing a person to do?

The case of programs today is very different from that of books a hundred years ago. The fact that the easiest way to copy a program is from one neighbor to another, the fact that a program has both source code and object code which are distinct, and the fact that a program is used rather than read and enjoyed combine to create a situation in which a person who enforces a copyright is harming society as a whole both materially and spiritually; in which a person should not do so regardless of whether the law enables him to.

"Competition makes things get done better."

The paradigm of competition is a race: by rewarding the winner, we encourage everyone to run faster. When capitalism really works this way, it does a good job, but its defenders are wrong in assuming it always works this way. If the runners forget why the reward is offered and become intent on winning, no matter how, they may find other strategies—such as attacking other runners. If the runners get into a fist fight, they will all finish late.

Proprietary and secret software is the moral equivalent of runners in a fist fight. Sad to say, the only referee we've got does not seem to object to fights; he just regulates them ("For every ten yards you run, you are allowed one kick"). He really ought to break them up, and penalize runners for even trying to fight.

"Won't everyone stop programming without a monetary incentive?"

Actually, many people will program with absolutely no monetary incentive. Programming has an irresistible fascination for some people, usually the people who are best at it. There is no shortage of professional musicians who keep at it even though they have no hope of making a living that way.

But really this question, though commonly asked, is not appropriate to the situation. Pay for programmers will not disappear, only become less. So the right question is will anyone program with a reduced monetary incentive? My experience shows that they will.

For more than ten years, many of the world's best programmers worked at the Artificial Intelligence Lab for far less money than they could have had anywhere else. They got many kinds of nonmonetary rewards: fame and appreciation, for example. And creativity is also fun, a reward in itself.

Then most of them left when offered a chance to do the same interesting work for a lot of money.

What the facts show is that people will program for reasons other than riches, but if given a chance to make a lot of money as well, they will come to expect and demand it. Low-paying organizations do poorly in competition with high-paying ones, but they do not have to do badly if the high-paying ones are banned.

"We need the programmers desperately. If they demand that we stop helping our neighbors, we have to obey."

A

You're never so desperate that you have to obey this sort of demand. Remember: millions for defense, but not a cent for tribute!

"Programmers need to make a living somehow."

In the short run, this is true. However, there are plenty of ways that programmers could make a living without selling the right to use a program. This way is customary now because it brings programmers and businessmen the most money, not because it is the only way to make a living. It is easy to find other ways if you want to find them. Here are a number of examples.

A manufacturer introducing a new computer will pay for the porting of operating systems onto the new hardware.

The sale of teaching, hand-holding, and maintenance services could also employ programmers.

People with new ideas could distribute programs as freeware, asking for donations from satisfied users, or selling hand-holding services. I have met people who are already working this way successfully.

Users with related needs can form users' groups, and pay dues. A group would contract with programming companies to write programs that the group's members would like to use.

All sorts of development can be funded with a Software Tax:

Suppose everyone who buys a computer has to pay x percent of the price as a software tax. The government gives this to an agency like the NSF to spend on software development. But if the computer buyer makes a donation to software development himself, he can take a credit against the tax. He can donate to the project of his own choosing—often, chosen because he hopes to use the results when it is done. He can take a credit for any amount of donation up to the total tax he had to pay.

The total tax rate could be decided by a vote of the payers of the tax, weighted according to the amount they will be taxed on.

The consequences:

- The computer-using community supports software development.

- This community decides what level of support is needed.

- Users who care which projects their share is spent on can choose this for themselves.

In the long run, making programs free is a step toward the post-scarcity world, where nobody will have to work very hard just to make a living. People will be free to devote themselves to activities that are fun, such as programming, after spending the necessary ten hours a week on required tasks such as legislation, family counseling, robot repair, and asteroid prospecting. There will be no need to be able to make a living from programming.

We have already greatly reduced the amount of work that the whole society must do for its actual productivity, but only a little of this has translated itself into leisure for workers because much nonproductive activity is required to accompany productive activity. The main causes of this are bureaucracy and isometric struggles against competition. Free software will greatly reduce these drains in the area of software production. We must do this, in order for technical gains in productivity to translate into less work for us.

Copyright © 1985 Richard M. Stallman

A

Support

he following is a partial list of people willing to provide support services for GNU software, including GNU Emacs. Some charge a fee and others are free. The SERVICE file in the GNU Emacs distribution contains the complete current list at the time of distribution. For an updated copy, or to have yourself listed, contact: gnu@prep.ai.mit.edu.

Giuseppe Attardi
<attardi%dipisa.uucp@uunet.uu.net>
Dipartimento di Informatica
Corso Italia 40
I-56100 Pisa, Italy
+39 (50) 510111

Emacs Services: Installation aid, question answering.

Ian G. Batten
<igb%fulcrum.bt.co.uk@uunet.uu.net>
<...!uunet!mcvax!ukc!fulcrum!igb>
One, Ditton Grove
Birmingham B31 4RY
England
Home: +44 21 476 3782
Work: +44 21 771 2001 x5759

Emacs Services: I assist in porting, customizing, extending, teaching, and troubleshooting Emacs. I've recently been teaching it at new-user level and am happy to do so for other people.

Rates: £200/day, or less for nonprofits.

Experience: I had a large hand in the Sun "Emacstool" facility and have been involved in maintaining Emacs on UNIX and VMS for three years now. Prior to that I wrote a lot of extensions for Multics' Emacs.

Bard Bloom
<bard@theory.lcs.mit.edu>
NE43-301, 545 Technology Sq.
Cambridge, MA 02139
(617) 253-6097

Emacs Services: Installation, customization, answering questions, troubleshooting, writing large programs and major modes.

X11R3 Services: Quick questions.

Experience: I have maintained GNU Emacs on the Theory Group computers at MIT for several years and have done a good deal of GNU Emacs Lisp programming, including several major modes, and two database interfaces. (I have written some 15,000 lines of GNU Emacs code.) I am currently a Ph.D. student in Computer Science at MIT.

Rates: $50/hr., less for nonprofits.

C2V
38, rue Mauconseil
75001 Paris, France
Renaud Dumeur <red@litp.unip6-7.fr>
Jean-Daniel Fekete <jdf@litp.unip6-7.fr>
Jean-Michel Casaubon
(1) 42 47 19 28
Fax: (1) 40 22 06 10

Emacs Services: Questions answered, installation, teaching (all levels), E-Lisp and C extensions and customization, porting, troubleshooting.

gcc Services: Installation, extensions, porting.

gdb Services: Installation, debugging, porting.

X11R3 Services: Installation, debugging, internationalization.

Experience: Yes (ask for details).

Rates: 500ff/hr., negotiable.

Mr. David J. Camp
<david@wubios.wustl.edu>
6103 Charlotte Ave.
Saint Louis, MO 63120-1201

Background: Bachelor of Science in Computer Science, Washington University. Master of Science in Computer Science, Washington University. Over 12 years' experience in the computer industry. Author of the future GNU uu/xxen/decoder program. Skilled in many languages, including C and UNIX scripts.

Services: I can do on-site service in the St. Louis area. I prefer short-term projects. I can handle long projects given time. I reserve the right to refuse work.

Rates: $50 per hour, including travel time.

Rajeev Chandrasekhar
<rajeevc@mipos2.intel.com>
2625 Walsh Ave. MSC SC4-59
Santa Clara, CA 95052
Home: (408) 733-1535
Work: (408) 765-4632

gcc Services: Anything concerning i386 ports. Ports, installation, teaching and extensions. Expert on Intel processors.

Rates: $75/hr.; free for nonprofit organizations.

Stuart Cracraft
<cracraft@venera.isi.edu>
UUCP: <ucbvax!venera.isi.edu!cracraft>
3021-B Harbor Blvd.
Costa Mesa, CA 92626
(714) 751-8744

Emacs Services: Questions answered, teaching, customization, troubleshooting, but not porting.

GNU Chess (developer) Services: Questions answered, porting, and so on.

Rates: $40/hr. short-term, $30/hr. long-term.

Experience: Software researcher, systems programmer, UNIX analyst formerly with Stanford Research Institute, now with Computer Consoles, Inc.

Degree: B.A. Behavioral Sciences, National University.

Cygnus Support
814 University Ave.
Palo Alto, CA 94301
(415) 322-3811
Fax: (415) 322-3270
info@cygnus.com <or> ...uunet!hoptoad!cygint!info

B

Services: Cygnus Support offers warranty protection (service contracts) for a number of free software tools. For a fixed annual fee, our customers receive binary and source distributions, mail and phone support, documentation, and customization assistance on a variety of platforms. At the time of this writing we offer support for a development package including (among other things) gcc, g++, gdb, and, of course, GNU Emacs. However, the set of supported tools and platforms increases frequently, so contact us for the latest catalog.

Rates: $150/hour.

Annual Support: $25,000/year and up.

Dario Dariol
<mcvax!delphi!dariol@uunet.uu.net>
DELPHI SpA via della Vetraia 11
I-55049 Viareggio, Italy
+39 (584) 395161

Bradley N. Davis
<b-davis@cs.utah.edu> <b-davis@cai.utah.edu>
3242 South 540 West
Bountiful, UT 84010
(801) 581-6076, (801) 292-4362

Services: Installation, porting, customizing, troubleshooting. I work on most GNU software. Especially GNU Emacs, gcc, and a little X11 and g++. Experienced with PCs and 386s.

Rates: $20 to $50 per hour, depending on job.

Dynamyx Corporation
<service@creation.UUCP>
P.O. Box 1481
King of Prussia, PA 19406
(215) 265-6833

Services: Porting of all GNU software, installation, customization, and troubleshooting (UNIX, VMS, etc.).

Rates: $50-$100/hr.

Experience: Five years' UNIX application and systems programming. Five years' compiler front-ends, interpreters, and compiler-construction tools. Three years' VMS applications. X, C, and Ada experience.

Mike Haertel
<mike@wheaties.ai.mit.edu>
St. Olaf College
Northfield, MN 55057

Experience: UNIX Systems programmer at St. Olaf for several years. Spent summer of 1988 at FSF writing and modifying various programs.

Rates: $35/hr.

Sanjay Hiranandani
<consp10@bingvaxu.cc.binghamton.edu>
263 Conklin Ave.
Binghamton, NY 13903
(607) 773-1430

Services: Can help with installation, customization, and porting of most GNU software. General UNIX/VMS hacking. If you've got a PC with a hardware problem, I can probably fix that too.

Rates: $30/hour or less, depending on the problem. Will probably work free or at a low cost for nonprofit organizations, and poor students who are committed users of GNU software. Phone consultations free.

Paul Hudson
<..!mcvax!ukc!acorn!moncam!paul> <paul@moncam.co.uk>
40 Dovehouse Close
Ely, Cambs CB7 4BY
England
(0353) 663381
+44 (353) 663381

Services: Installation of all GNU software. Support and changes to gcc, g++. Emacs extensions.

Degree: Mathematics, Cambridge (UK!).

Experience: I've written complete compilers and code generators, a PostScript interpreter, and various graphics programs.

Rates: £25/hour, less for installation or nonprofits.

Jim Kingdon
East Wind
Route 3, Box 6B2
Tecumseh, MO 65760
(417) 679-4682

B

Services: Willing to take on any GNU software; particularly knowledgeable about the debugger (gdb) although I also have (varying amounts of) experience with Emacs, gcc, binutils, and others. I am familiar with both VMS and UNIX. I am particularly interested in porting gdb or gcc to new machines, but am also interested in other programming tasks: installation, user support, etc.

Qualifications: Minor in computer science from Oberlin College, two years experience in programming, helping users, system management. Maintained gdb for the Free Software Foundation for a year.

Rates: Negotiable, but as a ballpark figure: $30/hr. Free or cheap to good causes.

Scott J. Kramer
<sjk@sun.com>
2995 Woodside Rd., Suite 400
Woodside, CA 94062
(415) 961-0684

Emacs Services: Tutoring, installations/upgrades, Lisp customizations, general troubleshooting/support. Prefer that work I do becomes part of the official Free Software Foundation distribution.

Rates: Task- and time-dependent; nonmonetary offers considered.

Fen Labalme
<hoptoad!fen@sun.com>
Metaview Corporation
40 Carl St., #4
San Francisco, CA 94117
(415) 731-1174

Emacs Services: Anything from teaching beginners to advanced users.

UNIX Services: BSD 4.2 is what I have used most and best understand. IGROK: Mailers, network stuff, acronyms like RPC, NFS, and IPC X11.3. By the time you see this, I may understand X Windows.

Rates: Free phone consultation; $100/hour plus; "Talk to me!" nonprofits get lower rates or free; Barter considered.

Ethics: I require that all (most) software I create be available for redistribution as per the guidelines set by the Free Software Foundation's General Public License.

Daniel LaLiberte
<uiucdcs!liberte> <liberte@cs.uiuc.edu>
<liberte%a.cs.uiuc.edu@uiucvmd.bitnet>
University of Illinois, Urbana-Champaign
Department of Computer Science
1304 W. Springfield
Urbana, IL 61801
(217) 333-2518

Emacs Services: Installation, some porting, troubleshooting. Do E-Lisp extensions.

Experience: I have extensive E-Lisp programming experience. I edited the GNU Emacs Lisp Reference Manual. I've maintained Emacs for the UIUC C.S. Department for three years.

Rates: $30/hr.

Jacob Levy
<jaakov%wisdom.bitnet@cunyvm.cuny.edu>
Dept. of Computer Science
Weizmann Institute
Rehovot 76100 Israel
(+972)-8-482856

Services: Electronic, snail-mail, and phone help with installation of GNU Emacs. I hand out, on request, source and local mods for GNU Emacs, as they become available. Willing to help maintain compatibility with other/previous versions of Emacs, such as Gosling, CCA, and MicroEmacs. Preferable contact through electronic mail via BITNET.

Rates: Free. Help as much as possible, not conflicting with my main occupation in life, that of obtaining a Ph.D.

Roland McGrath
<roland@ai.mit.edu>
(617) 253-8568
545 Tech Sq., Room 426
Cambridge, MA 02139

Experience: Coauthor of GNU Make (with Richard Stallman). Author of the GNU C Library. Present maintainer of GNU Make and the GNU C Library. GNU volunteer May 1987 to the present. FSF employee summer 1989, fall 1990 to the present.

B

Services: Installation, maintenance, porting, enhancement of all GNU software.

Rates: Fees negotiable. I can work anywhere in the Boston or SF Bay Area, or anywhere on the Internet.

Lee McLoughlin

<lmjm@doc.ic.ac.uk> <uunet!mcvax!doc.ic.ac.uk!lmjm>
Department of Computing, Imperial College
180 Queens Gate, London SW7 2BZ
England
01-589-5111 X 5028

Experience: I am responsible for putting GNU Emacs up under 4.1 BSD and for the ports to the HLH Orion (and Orion 1/05) and the WhiteChapel MG-1. I also developed and support the UK-UUCP and UK news distribution. Ported X 10 to both the WhiteChapel MG-1 and HLH Orion. Ported X 11 to the HLH Orion 1/05. I have been an invited speaker at several recent UKUUG meetings. Helped, on the software side, in the setting up of UKnet. Run a large Public Domain software archive.

I am also an experienced UNIX systems programmer. I've ported UNIX to a new machine (including porting PCC). Considerable compilers, communications, mail, and graphics experience. Hope to have enough time in 1989 to get all the UK-UUCP goodies into a GNU uucp and to work on porting gcc to the Clipper.

Services: Porting GNU Emacs and X. Installation and troubleshooting of any GNU and X software.

Rates: £200-300 a day, negotiable. General hand-holding is free.

Note: Software archive contains all the current GNU and X software. This is available via Janet (the UK academic network), via uucp, and I can be talked into writing a tape, sun cartridge, or exabyte.

Eric P. Meyer

<emeyer@oracle.com> <oracle!emeyer@uunet.uu.net>
UUCP: {apple,uunet}!oracle!emeyer
Oracle Corp.
20 Davis Dr.
Belmont, CA 94002
Work: (415) 598-0000
Home: (415) 324-0944

Experience/Services: I am familiar with installing GNU Emacs, GNU gcc, GNU g++, libG++, flex, bison, gawk, GNU grep, bin_utils, and so on, on UNIX and VMS systems. Also, I can deal with GNU X-related problems, such as Purdue-Speedups for X servers on SUNs.

Rates: Free for nonprofit associations. $70/hr. for companies.

T. S. Mohan
UUNET: mohan%vidya@shakti.uu.net
KBCS (shakti!turing!vidya!mohan)
Supercomputer Education and Research Centre
Indian Institute of Science
Bangalore 560 012, India

Offer: Willing to share my experience in installing and running GNU software (more specifically Emacs and gcc) on VAXstations (running Ultrix) and other UNIX machines free of cost to all academic brethren; more so in India. All such efforts will be more forthcoming when I have time to spare off other projects.

Optimal Solutions, Inc.
P.O. Box 45818
Seattle, WA 98145
(206) 682-1773
Dennis Gentry <dennis@cpac.washington.edu> <dennis@cpac.bitnet>
Tom May <tom@cpac.washington.edu>
Todd Cromwell <todd@cpac.washington.edu>

Emacs Services: Questions answered, teaching, customization, troubleshooting, porting. Can install, port, and support VMS GNU Emacs, VMS gcc, UNIX gcc and g++, and X Windows.

Rates: $40-60/hr., 20-minute free initial consultation. Nonprofit/educational discounts.

Experience: Compiler, editor, and OS hacking, bit-twiddling, and consulting at: the University of Washington, the Fred Hutchinson Cancer Research Center, the National Science Foundation's Center for Process Analytical Chemistry, Global Technology International, others.

Degrees: Honors B.S. C.S., University of Washington; Summa Cum Laude B.S. E.E., University of Washington.

The Pharos Group, Inc.
Box 3546
Las Cruces, NM 88003-3546
(505) 525-2600

Services: The Pharos Group offers consulting on the installation and customization of GNU software, including GNU Emacs, GNU cc and c++, and the UNIX replacement utilities, on machines running UNIX. We have members who are experienced in system administration, graphics, image processing, and networking. All modifications and extensions that we make to GNU software are freely available.

The best contacts for the Pharos Group are Ted Dunning(ted@pharos.com) or Jeff Harris (jeff@pharos.com).

B

Hedley K.J. Rainnie
<hedley@alaya.nyu.edu>
UUCP: {uunet|ihnp4|allegra|harvard}!cmcl2!alaya!hedley
545 West End Ave., Apt. 11E
New York, NY 10024
Work: (212) 947-5711

Emacs Services: I am able to help in all aspects of GNU Emacs, even porting.

Rates: $12/hr.

Credentials: M.S. in Computer Science from NYU. B.S. same. I have used many versions of Emacs since 1980.

Adam J. Richter
<adamj@monet.berkeley.edu> <...!ucbvax!monet!adamj>
2600 Ridge Rd.
Berkeley, CA 94709
(415) 549-6356

Services: Difficult X-windows ports. Freeware preferred. Also looking for someone to sponsor server improvements, including reorganization and optimizations for the GNU C Compiler's extensions. Experienced.

Bruce Robertson
<bruce@pooh.com> <uunet!heather!bruce>
Hundred Acre Software
1280 Terminal Way, #26
Reno, NV 89502
(702) 329-9333

Rates: $70/hr. long-term, $50/hr. short-term. Nonprofits are lower still, and negotiable.

Services: Anything to do with GNU software. My specialties include porting Emacs, gcc, and gdb to new environments. I also provide general consulting services, in such areas as embedded systems, UNIX kernel porting, and MS-DOS applications.

Experience: Many different areas. UNIX internals (all flavors), SCSI (target and initiator), embedded systems, X11, TCP/IP, compilers, device driver tuning, hardware debugging.

Mike Rowan
<mtr@ai.mit.edu>
mit-eddie!prep.ai.mit.edu!mtr
545 Technology Sq., Room 426

Cambridge, MA 02139
(617) 253-8568
Home: (508) 745-7554

Experience: FSF programmer since 1/90; UNIX Systems programmer and all X11 work from porting to admin. and installation, Purdue University Computing Center, 9/87-12/89.

Rates: $50/hr. as a base, depending on job, time, project length, etc.

Services: Extensive X11 work. GNU libc, Emacs, login, most anything. Extensions, new projects, porting, fixes, installation, system administration; just about anything. Systems programming experience with all major flavors of UNIX including 4.3, Dynix, SunOS, and Ultrix.

Wolfgang S. Rupprecht
<nancy!wsrcc!wolfgang@uunet.uu.net>
P.O. Box 6524
Alexandria, VA 22306
(703) 768-2640

Emacs Services: Anything (Lisp, C, customization, porting, installing).

Rates: $75/hr.

Experience: I have written thousands of lines of GNU Emacs C and Lisp code. Original author of the floating point additions to appear in Emacs 19.

Douglas C. Schmidt
Department of Information and Computer Science
University of California, Irvine
Irvine, CA 92717
Office: (714) 856-4043
email: schmidt@ics.uci.edu

Services: gcc and g++ installation and porting, question answering, customizing, etc.

Experience: Wrote the GNU GPERF perfect hashing program, available from the libg++ distribution, wrote the perfect hash functions that recognize reserved words for g++ and gcc, contributed mRates and range of services not received. Any bug reports for gcc and g++ and also contributed bug fixes for g++. In addition, I am actively building and maintaining a g++ and gcc regression test suite (available on request).

Rates: Negotiable.

B

Randal L. Schwartz
Stonehenge Consulting Services
(503) 777-0095
Beaverton, OR (The Silicon Rain Forest)
Electronic address variable (for now); call for the current one. (I read and post to comp.emacs and GNU.emacs on USENET.)

GNU Emacs Services: Questions about general use, teaching, customization, documentation, troubleshooting, porting, cute hacks.

Other GNU Software: Cross-trained on UN*X...proceed with caution.

Experience: 17 years' software development (one year with GNU Emacs), 11 years' technical communication (concurrent). Also a C hacker and UNIX guru.

Rates: Free for short projects. Long projects may require money if the project consumes significant billable time.

John Sechrest
<sechrest@oregon-state>(hplabs!hp pcd!orstcs!sechrest)
30606 Petersen Rd.
Corvallis, OR 97333
Home: (503) 929-6278
Work: (503) 754-3273

Emacs Services: User support, tutorials/training, system consulting.

Other Services: I am willing to help people install and use both GNU and Emacs. I am particularly interested in installing GNU on the National ICM 3216.

Rates: $50/hr., negotiable. As a consultant my normal fees are $50/hour. This is mostly a guideline that varies on a case-by-case basis.

Experience: I worked at Hewlett-Packard for four years: two years working on the HP 41C extended I/O Rom and two years working on systems support. For the past year and a half I have worked as the Lab Coordinator for Oregon State University Computer Science coordinating the use and maintenance of several machines. I am most familiar with 4.2BSD on the VAX 11/750 and HP-UX on the HP series 200.

Steven C. Simmons
9353 Hidden Lake Circle
Dexter, MI 48130
Home: (313) 426-8981
Office: (313) 769-4086
Internet: scs@lokkur.dexter.mi.us
UUCP: ...!sharkey!lokkur!scs

B

GNU Software Service: bison, flex, gcc, etc. Experience porting to BSD4.3VAXes, Suns, Gould, some System V hosts. No MS-DOS.

Rates: If all you need is a piece of source, I gladly supply it. Rates and range of services not received. Gratis if local call, at cost for long distance or tape (bring me a blank). Can make std tar [standard tape archive] magtape or Sun cartridges. Advice is free to a point. Compiling, porting, customizing: $65/hr. plus phone charges for off-site work; on-site rates negotiable.

Professional Data: Currently administrator of a large UNIX shop in Ann Arbor, Michigan. Maintain and support a variety of PD and freely redistributable software on a variety of hosts.

Lynn R. Slater
<lrs@esl.com>
4433 Inyo Ct.
Fremont, CA 94528
(415) 796-4149

Emacs Services: Ada, X11, Lisp, interfaces to subordinate shell processes. Prefer that work I do becomes part of the official Free Software Foundation distribution.

Rate: Free for good cause, otherwise task- and time-dependent.

Small Business Systems, Inc.
Box 17220, Route 104
Smithfield, RI 02917
(401) 273-4669

Principal Contact: mpd@anomaly.sbs.com (Michael P. Deignan, President). Secondary Contact: ccc@anomaly.sbs.com (Cole C. Calistra, UNIX Systems Manager).

Services: All GNU packages. Training (singular or classroom environments). User support (varied levels, including on-site and 24-hour "on call"), customization, installation, troubleshooting, you name it.

Rates: Up to $75/hr.

Notes: Services limited to Southeastern New England area (Route 128/93 in MA and points south and east). Provide support into CT, only as far west as Groton/ New London area. (Anything beyond these boundaries strains the acceptable level of user support we attempt to maintain.)

B

Richard M. Stallman
<rms@prep.ai.mit.edu>
UUCP: {mit-eddie,ucbvax,uunet,harvard,uw-beaver}!ai.mit.edu!rms 545
Tech Sq., Room 430
Cambridge, MA 02139

Emacs Services: Anything whatsoever.

Rates: $6/min. or $250/hr.

Note: Is anyone interested in courses in using or extending GNU Emacs?

Experience: Original inventor of Emacs and main author of GNU Emacs and gcc.

Bob Sutterfield
<bob@cis.ohio-state.edu> <osu-cis!bob>
Work: (614) 292-7348
2036 Neil Ave.
Ohio State University CIS Dept.
Columbus, OH 43210-1277
Home: (614) 267-7611
3542 Norwood St.
Columbus, OH 43224-3424

Rates: $50/hr. (negotiable), plus travel expenses.

Services: Installation, troubleshooting, and mild customization of most GNU production and beta-test products; tutorials, training, and hand-holding; general UNIX system and network consulting.

James W. Thompson
jthomp@sun.com
uunet!sun.com!jthomp
17601 Preson Rd., #274
Dallas, TX 75252
(214) 788-1951

Emacs/gdb Services: Installation, porting, troubleshooting, hand-holding Emacs E-Lisp and C extensions and customization.

gcc Services: Porting, debugging, installation.

MIT X11R3 Services: Installation, porting.

Specialties: Convex, Vaxes and Suns. Can do VMS, not locally. Network setup and troubleshooting.

Experience: Have hacked many (10+) different architectures in C, Lisp, and FORTRAN. Thorough understanding of BSD networking/NFS/RPC.

Responsible for Convex port of GNU Emacs, gdb, gcc. Eight years' system "mothering" experience. Resume available on request.

Rates: $30/hour, plus travel expenses. Free for nonprofits.

Leonard H. Tower Jr.
<tower@wheaties.ai.mit.edu>
36 Porter St.
Somerville, MA 02143
(617) 623-7739

Services: Work on most GNU software. Installation, hand-holding, troubleshooting, extensions, teaching.

Rates: $50/hour, plus travel expenses. Negotiable for nonprofits.

Experience: Have hacked on over a dozen architectures in many languages. Have system-mothered several varieties of UNIXes. Assisted RMS with the front end of gcc and its back-end support. Resume available on request.

Scott Weikart
<cdp!scott@parcvax.xerox.com> (hplabs!cdp!scott)
East Palo Alto, CA 94303
(415) 322-9069

Emacs Services: User hand-holding, E-Lisp programming and troubleshooting, porting 1944c University. I used ITS Emacs for five years and Gosling Emacs for two years. I've written thousands of lines of TECO and thousands of lines of mlisp. I've ported many programs to SysIII/SysV UNIX.

Rates: Sliding scale rates, barter possible, lower rates for nonprofits.

Pace Willisson
<pace@blitz.com> uunet!blitz!pace
Blitz Product Development Corporation
6 Hudson St.
Somerville, MA 02143
(617) 625-3452

Services: Work on any GNU software.

Rates: $80/hour.

Experience: B.S. in Computer Science from MIT. 11 years' working with C, UNIX, and Lisp machines including compilation systems, networks, device drivers, demand paging systems, boot programs, and window systems. Ported gdb to 80386. Designed COFF encapsulation scheme to run GNU linker output on System 5 kernels. Author of UNIX "ispell."

Updated: 10/27/90

B

Patrick Wood
Pipeline Associates, Inc.
{sun,motown,amdcad}!pipeline!phw

Services: Installing gcc, using gcc as cross-compiler and embedded system development, ditto for GNU binutils, help with 680x0 systems, UNIX security, UNIX internals, graphics, embedded systems programming.

Rates: Free for email (one- to two-day turnaround); too busy for phone or direct consultation.

Qualifications: B.S. C.S. Purdue, M.S. CICE Michigan, six years' Bell Labs (security, performance measurement/tuning, graphics, device drivers, embedded OS development), five years VP R&D Pipeline Associates, Inc. (graphics, PostScript, training, security auditing software, embedded systems programming, color print drivers, color separation, writing, editing). Used gcc and binutils for about two years now (starting with gcc 1.31) on VAX/Ultrix, Sony News, 386/ix, and embedded systems (Intel 960 and 68000). Modified gcc and binutils for cross-development on 386 to 68000 embedded system. Wrote general-purpose peephole optimizer for assembly output of gcc.

B

Regular Expressions

Regular Expressions (REs) are a simple kind of grammar. A grammar is a way of specifying a set of strings. An RE is a simple string expression matched by any string in a set of strings. Emacs uses the RE and attempts to find strings that belong to that set. Each string that belongs must be on a single line, but many matches are possible within a single line. If there are many matches on a line, Emacs always chooses the longest possible match on the line.

There are several different kinds of characters used in REs, each one of which has its own purpose. The simplest kind is the characters that match themselves. The set of characters that match themselves consists of all the characters that do not have a special meaning as well as special characters when they are preceded by the quote (\) special character. The quote character causes the character that follows it to get special treatment, and it is also used as a prefix character to create two-character sequences called \ constructs.

The five classes of special characters are the special characters that match any character, the special characters that specify a position rather than a character, the special characters that are used to create REs that match one of a group of characters, the special characters that repeat an RE, and the special characters that group REs. Note that some of these special characters are actually two-character sequences starting with the \ character.

There is one very special RE: . (the period), the wild card RE. This RE matches any single character. As an example of its use, the RE r.d will match "red" or "rod" or "r d" or any other string starting with *r*, having one other character, and ending in *d*. We show more examples using this RE later, because it usually is used with special characters that control repetition.

Another class of special characters has two members: [and]. These characters are used to delimit a set of characters to be matched by any one character from the set.

Note that special characters are not special when they are inside a character set, but there is one character that is special if it comes right after the opening square brace. If ^ follows the [, then the RE selects all the characters that aren't listed. There is also one character that isn't special if it comes right after the [or [^ but is special anywhere else. If - comes right after the [, it is a character in the set, but if it comes between two other characters, it indicates a range.

Here are some examples of the use of sets in REs:

[a-z]   Matches any one lowercase letter

[^0-9]   Matches any character that is not a digit

[-+*]   Matches any of the arithmetic operators

[[a^b-d]   Matches "[", "a", " ^ ", "b", "c", and "d"

The next class of special characters used in REs are REs that match the empty string in a special position. The simplest of these are $ and ^ .

The ^ and $ characters are used in REs to select strings starting and ending lines. If ^ is the first character of an RE, that RE will match only strings starting at the beginning of a line. The $ character does not have a special meaning unless it occurs at the end of the RE. If an RE ends with $, the RE can match only strings that extend to the end of a line. These *empty string* REs can be thought of as a way to require regular expressions to match strings only at special locations. There are a number of two-character REs that also are used for this function. They are called \ constructs because they start with \.

These \ constructs are used for matching empty strings at special positions.

At the beginning of the buffer	\`
At the end of the buffer	\'
At the beginning or end of a word	\b
Not at the beginning or end of a word	\B

C

At the beginning of a word	\<
At the end of a word	\>
Matches any word-constituent character	\w
Matches any non-word-constituent character	\W

Here are some example REs that use these special characters:

`\<red\>`	Matches only the word "red", but not the string "red" as part of another word.
`\Bred`	Matches only the suffix "red" or the string "red" as part of another word, but not the word "red".
`\Bred\B`	Matches only the string "red" as part of another word, but not the word "red" or the suffix "red".
`red\B`	Matches only the prefix "red", or the string "red" as part of another word, but not the word "red".

A fourth type of special characters is used to indicate repetition. Like the set delimiter characters, these characters are not REs themselves but are used with REs to build more complicated REs. *, +, and ? are the characters that can cause the preceding RE to be repeated.

*	Used to indicate that the single-character RE it follows can be repeated zero or more times.
+	Used to indicate that the single-character RE preceding it can be repeated one or more times.
?	Used to indicate that the single-character RE preceding it can be repeated zero or one time.

Repetition operators, when used with the wild-card RE, ., enable creation of REs that can match many different strings. For example:

`.*`	The total wild card. Matches any string including the empty string.
`a+`	Matches "a", "aa", "aaa", "aaaa", and so on.
`[a-z]?`	Matches the empty string or any single lowercase letter.
`\<reds?\>`	Matches the words "red" and "reds".

The final type of special characters are used to group REs.

`|`	An OR operator for REs. As an example, `ta?¦b?` will match a string consisting of "t" followed by at least one "a" or at least one "b". This operator is much more useful because there also are the \(and \) operators.

C

\(and \)   Used to group REs so that you can control which REs are
used in the OR grouping. The RE `\(hello\)¦\(goodbye\)`
matches the string "hello" or the string "goodbye". The RE
`hello¦goodbye` matches only the strings "hellooodbye" and
the string "hellgoodbye". These operators enable us to
group REs built up from single-character REs.

This grouping also is used with the \Digit special character.

\Digit   Selects the string matched by the nth RE in parenthesis in
the current RE. Note that this matches a string matched
earlier in the RE. This lets you construct REs that match
only strings with repeated parts.

For example, the RE `\<\(.+\).\1\>` will match only words composed of
two identical strings separated by a single character. The first (and only)
grouped RE matches any string of one or more characters. The . means that can
be followed by any character. Finally, the \1 recalls whatever string was matched
by the first parenthesized RE. This means that if the .+ matched the string "hi"
and . matched the string "d", \1 would become "hi". This would match "hidhi".

More complicated REs are formed by juxtaposition of simple REs, and
possibly with the \¦, \(...\), and \Digit constructs.

C

Appendix

Emacs Implementations

This appendix provides a partial list of implementations of Emacs-type editors. Remember that it is not comprehensive. You can help update it by sending any additional information to the address listed at the end of this appendix. The revised version will be posted every two months.

To be included in this list, an implementation must either be "advertised" as an Emacs-type editor or be extensible and come with an Emacs command set "mode" already written. Editors that are extensible but do not come with such a mode (meaning you have to write it yourself) are not listed.

The following information is included for each Emacs implementation:

- The **Name** line contains the name of the implementation. Implementations are listed alphabetically by name.

- The **Version** is the latest known version. It might be out-of-date.

- The **Implementation language** is the language that the bulk of the implementation is written in. A compiler or interpreter for this language would be needed to use the editor (unless it is an executable file).

- The **Extension language** is the language, often custom or modified, used when altering or writing extensions to the implementation. It is "none" if there is no extension language.

- The **Scope of implementation** is either "command set" or "extensible." In the first case, the implementation offers a basic Emacs command set; however, the user cannot readily change what the commands do. In the second case, the user can control fully what all the commands do.

- The **Requirements** are a brief characterization of what hardware or software is required. The purpose of this item is to offer a broad selection key, not to be a comprehensive list. Consult the implementation for free software, or consult the vendor to find out whether a specific implementation works in your environment. For example, "IBM PC" is used to cover MS/DOS, OS/2, and Windows implementations. "UNIX" refers to any version of UNIX from any vendor.

- The **Organization** is the name of and contact information for the implementor.

- The **Status** is one of the following:

  Free: The implementation is available to most people at no charge. Even such "free" implementations may have restrictions; consult information about the particular implementation. When available, information on how to obtain a copy is listed.

  Commercial: The implementation is for sale. Contact the vendor for specific information.

  No longer available: Self-explanatory.

  Full source code is available for all the free implementations. Source availability varies among the commercial implementations; check with the vendor before you buy.

Acronyms

Part of the history of Emacs-type editors can be studied by tracing the evolution of the acronyms used for implementations. The acronyms and their expansions that follow are listed in (more or less) chronological order:

TECO	TAPE Editor and COrrector (later: Text Editor and COrrector)
EMACS	Editor MACroS
EINE	EINE Is Not Emacs (the first known recursive acronym)
SINE	SINE Is Not EINE (the first known doubly recursive acronym)

ZWEI	Zwei Was Eine, Initially (the author knew German)
FINE	Fine Is Not Emacs
VINE	Vine Is Not Emacs
TORES	Text ORiented Editing System
MINCE	Mince Is Not Complete Emacs
JOVE	Jonathan's Own Version of Emacs

GNU Emacs

Name: GNU Emacs
Version: 18.57
Implementation language: C
Extension language: Lisp
Scope of implementation: extensible
Hardware/software requirements: UNIX, VMS
Organization:
    Free Software Foundation
    675 Massachusetts Ave.
    Cambridge, MA 02139
    USA
    +1 617 876 3296
    gnu@prep.ai.mit.edu
Status: free; anonymous FTP from:
    prep.ai.mit.edu
    scam.berkeley.edu
    itstd.sri.com
    wuarchive.wustl.edu
    wsmr-simtel20.army.mil (under "PD:<UNIX.GNU>")
    bu.edu
    louie.udel.edu
    nic.nyser.net
    ftp.cs.titech.ac.jp
    funic.hut.fi
    sunic.sunet.se
    freja.diku.dk
    gatekeeper.dec.com
    mango.miami.edu (VMS G++)
    cc.utah.edu (VMS GNU Emacs)
    uunet.uu.net
    tut.cis.ohio-state.edu

D

On the SPAN network, contact rdss::corbet.

On UUCP, contact one of the following:

> hao!scicom!qetzal!upba!ugn!nepa!denny
> acornrc!bob
> hqda-ai!merlin
> uunet!hutch!barber
> sun!nosun!illian!darylm
> oli-stl!root
> bigtex!james
> postmaster@uunet.uu.net
> uucp@cis.ohio-state.edu (or osu-cis!uucp)

Ohio State also posts its UUCP instructions regularly to the newsgroup comp.sources.d.

Free Implementations

Name: AMIS
Version:
Implementation language: Pascal
Extension language: none
Scope of implementation: command set
Hardware/software requirements: VMS, Norsk Data, Tops10, RSTS
Organization/author:

> Stacken Computer Club
> c/o NADA
> S-100 44 Stockholm
> Sweden
> stacken@stacken.kth.se

Note: The name is an acronym of "Anti-MISaer" ("AE" is the "ae" glyph). "Misaer" is Swedish (svenska) for "piece of junk." Tops10, RSTS, and Norsk Data versions are free if you send a ½-inch, 2,400-foot magnetic tape and return postage. The VMS version is $1,000 US (the money supports a DEC10 museum).

Name: Edwin
Version:
Implementation language: CScheme
Extension language: CScheme
Scope of implementation: extensible

Hardware/software requirements: UNIX, VMS
Organization/author:
Scheme Distribution
c/o Prof. Hal Abelson
545 Technology Sq., Room 410
Cambridge, MA 02139
USA

info-cscheme-request@zurich.ai.mit.edu
Status: free; anonymous FTP from
zurich.ai.mit.edu in pub/scheme/README
Also, check out other Scheme implementations.

Name: Elle
Version: 4.1g
Implementation language: C
Extension language: none
Scope of implementation: command set
Hardware/software requirements: UNIX, MINIX, TOPS-20, TOPS-10 (!)
Organization/author:
Ken Harrenstein
c/o SRI International
333 Ravenswood Ave.
Menlo Park, CA 94025
USA
klh@nisc.sri.com
Status: free; anonymous FTP from
nisc.sri.com in pub/klh/elle.tar (or elle.tar.Z)

Name: Emacs
Version:
Implementation language: MIDAS (PDP10/DEC-20 assembly language)
Extension language: TECO
Scope of implementation: extensible
Hardware/software requirements: PDP10/ITS or DEC-20/TOPS-20
Organization/author:
MIT AI Lab/MIT Laboratory for Computer Science
545 Technology Sq.
Cambridge, MA 02139
USA
Note: This is the original.
Status: free; anonymous FTP from
mc.lcs.mit.edu in its/ai/emacs/*, its/ai/emacs1/*
osu-20.ircc.ohio-state.edu (executable)

D

Name: Epoch
Version: 3.2
Implementation language: C
Extension language: Lisp
Scope of implementation: extensible
Hardware/software requirements: UNIX, VMS, others
Organization/author:
    University of Illinois at Urbana-Champaign
    Urbana-Champaign, IL
    USA
    epoch-request@cs.uiuc.edu
    uunet!uiucdcs!epoch-request
    epoch-request%cs.uiuc.edu@uiucvmd.bitnet
Note: This is a modified GNU Emacs.
Status: free; anonymous FTP from
    cs.uiuc.edu in pub/epoch-files/epoch/*

Name: Freemacs
Version: 1.6a
Implementation language: 8086 assembler
Extension language: MINT, a string-oriented interpreter inspired by TRAC
    (MINT means "Mint is not TRAC").
Scope of implementation: extensible
Hardware/software requirements: IBM PC
Organization/author:
    Russell Nelson
    11 Grant Street
    Potsdam, NY 13676
    USA
Status: free
Internet: anonymous FTP from:
    simtel20.army.mil from PD:<MSDOS.FREEMACS>
    grape.ecs.clarkson.edu [128.153.28.129] in /pub/msdos/freemacs
BBS:
    +1 315 268 6667—1200/2400 bps, 8N1, 24 hrs., pub/msdos/freemacs
    No registration required to download Freemacs.
BITNET and UUCP:
    Send mail to archive-server@sun.soe.clarkson.edu. You may use archive-server%sun.soe@omnigate if you are on BITNET, or {smart-host}!sun.soe.clarkson.edu! archive-server if you are using UUCP. The mail message should consist of "help." If you do not get a reply within a day,

D

your return path is broken. You need to use the path command to give a mail address that our mailer can grok. Our mailer can send mail to any address with an "@" in it, with the exception of ".UUCP" pseudoaddresses.

Mail:

$15 check or $17 P.O. copying fee to the author. This assures you of the latest version. Please specify floppy format: 5¼-inch, 1.2M; 5¼-inch, 360K; 3½-inch, 720K.

Name: Hemlock
Version:
Implementation language: Lisp
Extension language: Lisp
Scope of implementation: extensible
Hardware/software requirements: ?
Organization/author:

Scott Fahlman
Spice Lisp project
Carnegie Melon University
USA
fahlman@cmuc (fahlman@cmuc.bitnet?)

Status: free; anonymous FTP from

gatekeeper.dec.com in pub/editors/hemlock.tar.Z
Commercial as part of Lucid Common Lisp.

Name: JOVE
Version: 4.14
Implementation language: C
Extension language: none
Scope of implementation: command set
Hardware/software requirements: UNIX, IBM PC, Macintosh
Organization/author:

Jonathan Payne
Sun Microsystems, Inc.
2550 Garcia Ave.
Mountain View, CA 94043
USA

Status: free; anonymous FTP from

cayuga.cs.rochester.edu in pub/jove.*
cs.toronto.edu in pub/moraes/jove.*.*
comp.sources.[misc,unix] archives
Also in the Berkeley UNIX distribution.

D

Name: KEmacs (Kanji Emacs)

Version:

Implementation language: C

Extension language: custom

Scope of implementation: extensible

Hardware/software requirements: UNIX, VMS, IBM PC, Amiga, Atari ST, Macintosh, Wicat, Data General

Organization/author:

SANETO (sanewo) Takanori

Corporate Research Laboratories Atsugi

SONY

Japan

Note: Japanese (Kanji) adaptation of MicroEmacs version 3.8i.

Status: free; anonymous FTP from

uhccux.uhcc.hawaii.edu in editors/=TAR.Z=FILES=/kemacs.tar.Z

Name: Leif

Version:

Implementation language: C

Extension language: Lisp

Scope of implementation: extensible

Hardware/software requirements: UNIX, VMS

Organization/author:

The Saga Group

Department of Computer Science

University of Illinois at Urbana-Champaign

1304 W. Springfield

Urbana-Champaign, IL 61801

USA

leif@a.cs.uiuc.edu

{pur-ee|ihnp4}!uiucdcs!leif

Note: Leif is equivalent to GNU Emacs with a small modification, an elisp extension, and an external parser.

Status: free; anonymous FTP from

cs.uiuc.edu

Name: MG (MicroGNU Emacs)

Version: 2a

Implementation language: C

Extension language: none

Scope of implementation: command set

Hardware/software requirements: UNIX, VMS, AmigaDOS, Atari ST, OS/9-68K, Primos

Organization/author:
    University of Texas
    USA
Status: free; anonymous FTP from
    utadnx.cc.utexas.edu in MG2A.BCK_LZW

Name: MicroEmacs
Version: 3.10m
Implementation language: C
Extension language: custom
Scope of implementation: extensible
Hardware/software requirements: UNIX, VMS, IBM PC (DOS & OS/2), HP 110
    and 150, Amiga, Atari ST, Macintosh, Wicat, Data General AOS/VS
    kanji: Fujitsu FMR-70, NEC PC-9891
Organization/author:
    Daniel M. Lawrence
    617 New York St.
    Lafayette, IN 47901
    USA
    +1 317 742 5153
    dan@mdbs.uucp
FIDO: The Programmer's Room 201/10
    +1 317 742 5533
    24 hours 300/1200/2400 baud
Status: free; anonymous FTP from
    midas.mgmt.purdue.edu in dist/uemacs3.10m/ue310m.arc.
    midas.mgmt.purdue.edu in dist/uemacs310/*
    between the hours of 5 p.m. and 8 a.m.
    Ask author about commercial use and distribution through a disk.

Name: Nemacs (Nihongo Emacs)
Version: 3.3.2
Implementation language: C
Extension language: Lisp
Scope of implementation: extensible
Hardware/software requirements: UNIX, VMS
Maintainer:
    nemacs@ctl.go.jp
Organization/author:
    Ken'ichi HANDA
    Electrotechnical Lab
    Machine Inference Section
    ElectroTechnical Laboratory
    Umezono 1-1-4

D

Tsukuba City
Japan 305
+81 298 58 5916
fax +81 298 58 5918
handa@etl.go.jp
handa%etl.go.jp@relay.cs.net
Note: Japanese (Nihongo) adaptation of GNU Emacs.
Status: free; anonymous FTP from
    uhccux.uhcc.hawaii.edu in editors/NEmacs/*

Name: Origami
Version: 1.5
Implementation language: C
Extension language: OCL (custom)
Scope of implementation: extensible
Hardware/software requirements: UNIX
Organization:
    Michael Haardt
    Auf der Hoern 40
    5100 Aachen 1
    Germany
    +49 (0241) 85848
    mhaardt@ftp.thp.uni-koeln.de
Status: free; anonymous FTP from
    ftp.thp.uni-koeln.de [134.95.64.1] (Germany) in minix/commands/
        editors/origami.tar.Z
    plains.nodak.edu [134.129.111.64] (USA) in pub/Minix/all.contrib/Origami/*

Name: Scame
Version:
Implementation language: C
Extension language: none
Scope of implementation: command set
Hardware/software requirements: UNIX, VMS, IBM PC
Organization/author:
    Multihouse Automatisering bv
    c/o Johan Vromans
    Doesburgweg 7
    2803 PL Gouda
    The Netherlands
    +31 1820 62911
    fax +31 1820 62500
    jv@mh.nl

D

Note: Loosely based on an editor called Scame by Leif Samuelsson.
Status: free; ask the author for information on how to get a copy.

Name: treemacs
Version:
Implementation language: C
Extension language: Lisp
Scope of implementation: extensible
Hardware/software requirements: UNIX, VMS, others
Organization/author:
    Vipin Swarup
    Dept. of Computer Science
    University of Illinois at Urbana-Champaign
    USA
    swarup@a.cs.uiuc.eduo
    USENET ...!{cmcl2,seismo,uunet}!uiucdcs!swarup
Note: This is a modified GNU Emacs.
Status: free; anonymous FTP from
    cs.uiuc.edu in pub/treemacs/*

Commercial Implementations

Name: amacs
Version: 3.0 Release 2.8
Implementation language: 6502 assembler
Extension language: macros/loadable libraries (assembled)
Scope of implementation: extensible
Hardware/software requirements: Apple II with ProDOS
Organization/author:
      Creative Thinking, Included
      Brian Fox
      bfox@ai.mit.edu
Status: commercial; contact vendor for price information

Name: Brief
Version: 3.0
Implementation language: C
Extension language: Lisp/C combination
Scope of implementation: extensible
Hardware/software requirements: MS-DOS

D

Organization/author:
    Solution Systems
    Suite 410
    541 Main St.
    South Weymouth, MA 02190
    USA
    +1 800 821 2492
    +1 617 337 6963
    fax +1 617 337 7719
Status: commercial; contact vendor for price information

Name: CCA Emacs
Version:
Implementation language: C
Extension language: ELisp
Scope of implementation: extensible
Hardware/software requirements: UNIX, VMS
Organization/author:
    Uniworks Inc.
    P.O. Box K
    Suite 323
    Maynard, MA 01754
    USA
    +1 508 897 6650
    emacs!mau
Status: commercial; contact vendor for price information

Name: E3
Version: internal?
Implementation language: ?
Extension language: REXX
Scope of implementation: extensible
Hardware/software requirements: ?
Organization/author:
    IBM Corp.
    ?
Status: commercial; contact vendor for price information

Name: Emacs
Version:
Implementation language: SPL, a variant of PL/1
Extension language: Lisp

D

Scope of implementation: extensible
Hardware/software requirements: Prime
Organization/author:
    Prime Computer, Inc.
    24 Prime Park Way
    Natick, MA 07160
    USA
    +1 508 651 3342
    telex 174519
    telex +1 612 508 651 2769
Status: commercial; contact vendor for price information

Name: EMACS-TC
Version:
Implementation language: C
Extension language: Lisp-like
Scope of implementation: extensible
Hardware/software requirements: UNIX
Organization/author:
    AT&T Toolchest
    +1 201 522 6900, then log in "guest"
    USA
    Warren A. Montgomery
    +1 708 713 5090
    att!iexist!warren
Status: commercial; contact vendor for price information

Name: Epsilon
Version:
Implementation language: C
Extension language: EEL, a dialect of C.
Scope of implementation: extensible
Hardware/software requirements: UNIX, IBM PC
Organization/author:
    Lugaru Software Ltd.
    5843 Forbes Ave.
    Pittsburgh, PA 15217
    USA
    +1 412 421 5911
    fax +1 412 421 6371
Status: commercial; contact vendor for price information

D

Name: EVE (Extensible VAX Editor)
Implementation language: C ?, TPU ?
Extension language: TPU (Text Processing Utility)
Scope of implementation: extensible
Hardware/software requirements: VMS
Organization/author:
    Digital Equipment Corp.
    ?
    USA
    +1 ?
    ?
Notes: (Courtesy of Juergen Nickelsen) It is not Emacs-like, but it is fully
    extensible. Source (TPU) is included. TPU is a programming language for
    text processing that is also bundled with VMS. EVE is the next best thing
    to GNU Emacs on a VAX.
Status: unofficial project; not released

Name: FrameMaker
Version: 2.1
Implementation language: ?
Extension language: custom
Scope of implementation: extensible
Hardware/software requirements: UNIX, Macintosh
Organization/author:
    ?
Status: commercial; contact vendor for price information

Name: Infinitor
Version:
Implementation language: C?
Extension language: TPL
Scope of implementation: extensible
Hardware/software requirements: IBM PC
Organization/author:
    Agranat Systems
    P.O. Box 191
    Weston, MA 02193
    USA
    +1 617 893 7868
Status: commercial; contact vendor for price information

D

Name: Interleaf
Version: 4.0
Implementation language: ?
Extension language: Interlisp
Scope of implementation: extensible
Hardware/software requirements: UNIX
Organization/author:
    Interleaf
    ?
Status: commercial; contact vendor for price information

Name: ME2 (Mutt Editor II)
Version: ?
Implementation language: C
Extension language: Mutt ("A bizarre mix of Lisp and Algol-like languages,
    compiled external to the editor.")
Scope of implementation: extensible
Hardware/software requirements: UNIX, MS-DOS
Organization/author:
    Craig Durland
    Hewlett-Packard
    1000 NE Circle Blvd.
    Corvallis, OR 97330
    USA
    craig@cv.hp.com
Experimental; not released.

Name: Mince/PerfectWriter/The FinalWord/FinalWordII
Version:
Implementation language: C
Extension language: none/key rebinding only/key rebinding only/custom
Scope of implementation: command/command/command/extensible
Hardware/software requirements: IBM PC, CP/M
Organization/author:
    Mark of the Unicorn, Inc.
    222 Third Street
    Cambridge, MA 02139
    USA
    +1 617 576 2760
Status: commercial; contact vendor for price information
(Only Mince for CP/M is still available.)

D

Name: Multics Emacs
Version:
Implementation language: PL/1
Extension language: Lisp
Scope of implementation: extensible
Hardware/software requirements: Honeywell Multics
Organization:
      Bernard Greenberg
      Honeywell Bull
Status: commercial; contact vendor for price information

Name: PMATE, ZMATE
Version: PMATE (DOS) 4.0, PMATE (CP/M) 3.21, ZMATE (CP/M, Z System) 1.0
Implementation language: assembly language (not needed to use Editors)
Extension language: MATE macro language (TECO-like)
Scope of implementation: extensible
Hardware/software requirements: IBM PC, CP/M, Z-System
Organization/author:
      original by Michael Aronson (MATE = Michael Aronson's Text Editor)
ZMATE version by Bridger Mitchell and Jay Sage
ZMATE available from
      Sage Microsystems East
      1435 Centre St.
      Newton, MA 02159-2469
      USA
      +1 617 965 3552
(Availability of PMATE for the PC is not certain at this time.) Sage Microsystems
may be able to offer it.
Status: commercial; contact vendor for price information

Name: Sage Professional Editor
Version:
Implementation language: C?
Extension language: custom, C- and Awk-like
Scope of implementation: extensible
Hardware/software requirements: IBM PC
Organization/author:
      Sage Software, Inc.
      1700 NW 167th Pl.
      Beaverton, OR 97006
      USA
      +1 503 645 1150
      fax +1 503 645 4576
Status: commercial; contact vendor for price information

D

Name: Slick
Version:
Implementation language: C
Extension language: Slick extension language, REXX-like
Scope of implementation: extensible
Hardware/software requirements: IBM PC
Organization/author:
> MicroEdge Inc.
> P.O. Box 2367
> Fairfax, VA 22031
> USA
> +1 703 670 4575

Status: commercial; contact vendor for price information

Name: SPE Editor
Version:
Implementation language: Lisp
Extension language: Lisp
Scope of implementation: extensible
Hardware/software requirements: UNIX
Organization/author:
> Sun Microsystems, Inc.
> 2550 Garcia Ave.
> Mountain View, CA 94043
> USA
> +1 415 960 1300
> telex 37 29639

Status: commercial; contact vendor for price information

Name: Sprint
Version:
Implementation language: C
Extension language: custom
Scope of implementation: extensible
Hardware/software requirements: IBM PC
Organization/author:
> Borland International
> 1800 Green Hills Rd.
> Scotts Valley, CA 95067
> USA

Status: commercial; contact vendor for price information

D

Name: Sys-IX Editor
Version:
Implementation language: C?
Extension language: macro
Scope of implementation: command set
Hardware/software requirements: UNIX, IBM PC
Organization/author:
    System-IX (Networks) Ltd.
    55 Bedford Court Mansions
    Bedford Ave.
    London WC1B 3AD
    UK
    +44 71 636 8210
    fax +44 71 255 1038
    G.W. Computers Inc.
    4 Eagle Square
    East Boston, MA 02128
    USA
    +1 617 569 5990
    fax +1 617 567 2981
Note: May not be Emacs.
Status: commercial; contact vendor for price information

Name: TI Explorer Emacs
Version:
Implementation language: Lisp
Extension language: Lisp
Scope of implementation: extensible
Hardware/software requirements: Explorer
Organization/author:
    Texas Instruments
    12501 Research Blvd.
    Austin, TX 78759
    USA
    +1 512 250 7111
    +1 800 232 3200
    fax +1 512 250 6522
Status: commercial; contact vendor for price information

D

Name: Unipress Emacs
Version:
Implementation language: C
Extension language: MLisp
Scope of implementation: extensible

Hardware/software requirements: UNIX, VMS, IBM PC
Organization/author:
    Unipress Software Inc.
    2025 Lincoln Hwy.
    Edison, NJ 08817
    USA
    +1 201 287 2100
    fax +1 201 287 4929
    telex 709418
Note: Was Gosling's Emacs.
Status: commercial; contact vendor for price information

Name: ZMACS
Version:
Implementation language: Lisp
Extension language: Lisp
Scope of implementation: extensible
Hardware/software requirements: Symbolics
Organization/author:
    Symbolics, Inc.
    8 New England Executive Park
    Burlington, MA 01803
    USA
    +1 617 221 1000
    +1 800 533 7629
Status: commercial; contact vendor for price information

Implementations That Are No Longer Available

Name: EINE, ZWEI
Version:
Implementation language: Lisp
Extension language: Lisp
Scope of implementation: extensible
Hardware/software requirements: Lisp Machine
Organization/author:
    MIT
    USA
Status: no longer available

D

Name: FINE
Version:
Implementation language: BLISS
Extension language: none
Scope of implementation: command set
Hardware/software requirements: PDP-10
Organization/author:
    Mike Kazar
    Carnegie Melon University
    USA
Status: no longer available

Name: TORES
Version:
Implementation language: C
Extension language: none
Scope of implementation: command set
Hardware/software requirements: UNIX
Organization/author:
    Jeffrey Schiller
    MIT
    USA
Status: no longer available

Name: tv (aka otv, SINE)
Version:
Implementation language: PL/1
Extension language: SINE (Lisp-like)
Scope of implementation: extensible
Hardware/software requirements: MagicSix on Perkin-Elmer 3200series
Organization/author:
    Owen "Ted" Anderson
    MIT Architecture Machine Group
    USA
Status: no longer available

D

Name: VINE
Version:
Implementation language: FORTRAN (!)
Extension language: none
Scope of implementation: command set
Hardware/software requirements: VMS
Organization/author:
    Craig Finseth
    Texas Instruments
    Dallas, TX
    USA
Status: no longer available

The information in this appendix is courtesy of Craig A. Finseth and is current as of June 6, 1991. Send any changes and additions to:

Craig A. Finseth
fin@unet.umn.edu
+1 612 624 3375
University Networking Services
University of Minnesota
130 Lind Hall, 207 Church St. SE
Minneapolis, MN 55455-0134
USA

D

Index

Symbols

A

B